THE HUNDRED YEARS' WAR

MODERN WAR POEMS

EDITED BY

NEIL ASTLEY

BLOODAXE BOOKS

ISBN: 978 1 78037 100 9

First published 2014 by
Bloodaxe Books Ltd,
Eastburn,
South Park,
Hexham,
Northumberland NE46 1BS.

www.bloodaxebooks.com
For further information about Bloodaxe titles
please visit our website or write to
the above address for a catalogue.

Supported by
**ARTS COUNCIL
ENGLAND**

Cover design: Neil Astley & Pamela Robertson-Pearce.

Printed in Great Britain by Bell & Bain Limited, Glasgow, Scotland, on acid-free paper sourced from mills with FSC chain of custody certification.

CONTENTS

EDITORIAL NOTE

An ellipsis in square brackets [...] in this anthology denotes an editorial cut to the text. An ellipsis without square brackets is part of the original text. American spellings are retained in work by American authors, except for *-ize* suffixes, which are modernised to *-ise*. Punctuation follows Bloodaxe house style (single inverted commas for quotation, double for qualified expressions).

Dates in roman type in square brackets are dates of writing, those in italic type of first publication.

Each poet has a contextualising biographical note, which usually appears just once in the anthology, with page reference links to other poems by that writer; and where those other poems appear some pages later these have page references linking back to the author's note. Page number links within notes or commentaries refer to related poems in other sections of the book, sometimes by the same writer.

INTRODUCTION

War never ends. There have been two world wars since 1914 lasting for ten years, but wars have continued for a hundred years since then in many parts of the world: wars between nations, tribes and factions, wars over religion and beliefs, wars fought for land or oil or history or power, civil wars, political wars, and the Cold War when the West remained on a war-footing while supposedly at peace.

This anthology presents poems from a hundred years of war by poets writing as combatants on opposite sides, or as victims or anguished witnesses. It chronicles times of war and conflict from the trenches of the Somme through the Spanish Civil War to the horrors of the Second World War, Hiroshima and the Holocaust; and in Korea, the Middle East, Vietnam, Ireland, the Balkans, Iraq and Afghanistan and other theatres of war. There are poems from years when the world was threatened by all-out nuclear war and more recent poems written in response to international terrorism.

Where possible, the poems from each conflict are presented chronologically in terms of when they were written or set, building up a picture of what individual poets from different nations were experiencing at the same time, either on the same battlegrounds or in other parts of the world (including the home front), with, for example, British, French and German poets all writing of shared experiences in opposite trenches during the five-month Battle of the Somme.

Some of the poets felt they had more in common with enemy soldiers facing them across No-Man's-Land or across a jungle clearing than they did with their own commanding officers, with the politicians who sent them to war, or the people back home who had little idea of what they were going through in the war. The Cain and Abel theme of brother killing brother (or neighbour killing neighbour) occurs again and again in these poems. Many write out of shared cultural histories, for example with David Jones (First World War), Tony Conran (Falklands) and Owen Sheers (Afghanistan) all using the medieval Welsh war elegy, *Y Gododdin*, as a touchstone in poems relating to very different wars.

At different stages of each war there are poets responding to particular events in their own countries. For example, in just one three-month period, from August to November 1944, Polish poets join the Warsaw Uprising, Miklós Radnóti is herded on a forced march from Serbia to Hungary (where he is killed), other Hungarian poets witness deportations to camps, Dylan Thomas voices the anguish of Londoners under V-bomb attack, and Louis Simpson is a foot soldier caught up in the chaotic Battle of the Bulge.

I have included very few "anti-war poems" on the grounds that their effectiveness tends to be confined to the time when they were written in response to a particular conflict, and where there are other poems by actual participants or witnesses, I wanted to include those poems in preference to those by observers, protesters or proselytisers. Also, apart from some of the poems written during the First World War and those by Taliban fighters in Afghanistan, most poems about war are against war in any case, even if that war is felt to be "necessary" or when there is no choice but to fight.

But there are exceptions, such as poets whose engagement with the language of war, drawing on newspaper and media reports, produces challenging work which adds significantly to the poetry of experience. For example, Robert Lowell's 'Women, Children, Banies, Cows, Cats' [➤ 381], about the My Lai Massacre in Vietnam in 1968, is voiced using phrases from the testimonies of Lt William Calley and one of the men at his court-martial.

Other poets have responded to the unprecedented direct and round-the-clock media coverage of more recent conflicts, involving videos uploaded from war zones, live footage of missile strikes, running commentaries by reporters "embedded" with frontline troops, drawing upon the language and imagery of modern televised warfare in provocative ways. Tony Harrison's 'A Cold Coming' [➤ 504] is one of many poems written in response to graphic pictures of war and destruction published in the press.

Some poets of note have been involved in wars as combatants in more recent conflicts, including American conscripts in Vietnam, Israeli writers compelled to do national service, and Bosnians and Croats caught up in their wars of survival; among a handful of poets to have done so out of choice are Brian Turner and Kevin Powers, who served with US forces in Iraq. Other writers have been journalists in war zones, reporting on conflicts in their working capacity as well as responding to what they have seen or experienced in their poetry, notably James Fenton and – even more so – Eliza Griswold.

Now that poets with direct war experience are so few in number, personal and public initiatives in which poets have worked with people who've lived through wars (or drawn on their writings) have helped create a new kind of war poetry in which first hand experience is translated into powerful poetry of personal testimony. Poets such as Simon Armitage, Ruth Awad, Andrew Motion, Dan O'Brien, Mario Petrucci and Owen Sheers have drawn on discussions with family members, soldiers, veterans, medics and war reporters, or on with their recollections or writings – or written collaboratively with them – to produce poetry which offers new perspectives on areas such as personal survival in war zones and post-traumatic stress disorder.

In compiling an anthology covering many different wars fought over the past hundred years, I had difficult decisions to make as regards which international conflicts could be adequately covered in a book of this scope, given the restrictions of space (and so had to omit those less relevant to readers in Britain and Ireland), as well as which well-known poets to include or exclude when the emphasis has to be on the poem itself, not the reputation of the poet.

For example, Wilfred Gibson's poems written from newspaper reports about soldiers in the trenches had a certain authenticity at the start of the First World War, when he was viewed as one of the war's foremost poets, but once poets such as Siegfried Sassoon began writing from the front line – albeit influenced by Gibson's plain, unheroic style – I don't see that Gibson's work quite holds its place alongside their poetry, and indeed he later chose to stop writing about the war.

Moreover, as my commentary [➤ 23] makes clear, agreement as to who were the most significant poets of the First World War (Wilfred Owen, Siegfried Sassoon, Isaac Rosenberg, Edward Thomas, David Jones, Ivor Gurney) took many years, and yet even that consensus only holds in relation to the British poets, omitting as it does French poets such as François Porché [➤ 56], whose work stands comparison with that of David Jones, and Henry-Jacques [➤ 96], whose poetry conveys the harsh reality of the war's terrible carnage and suffering more vividly than that of any other poet of that time, as well as the phantasmagorical war poetry of Guillaume Apollinaire [➤ 41]. And the French canon itself has had to be revised in the light of the recent rediscovery of the poetry of Albert-Paul Granier [➤ 35]. His single collection of war poetry, *Les Coqs et les Vautours* (1917), unknown for the past 90 years, was republished in French only in 2008 and published in English translation for the first time in 2014.

The First World War section of this anthology interweaves poems by the key poets writing in English, French and German with others relating to particular events, phases or aspects of the war, in a more or less chronological sequence. By the time Sassoon makes an appearance on the Somme with 'the first of [his] "outspoken" war poems' [➤ 59], written in February 1916, we've already heard from Alfred Lichtenstein, Wilhelm Klemm, Albert-Paul Granier, Peter Baum, Apollinaire, Anton Schnack, Jean Cocteau and François Porché, writing then of – or recalling later – their own experiences of brutal warfare on the Western Front, over a period of eighteen months when the British public back home still thought of Rupert Brooke, Julian Grenfell and Charles Sorley – all dead by then – as the significant poets of the war, along with Wilfred Gibson, who hadn't even been allowed to enlist. Robert Graves would have been included in this section, but his estate demanded fees so high that his two poems had to be dropped.

Parts or all of some anthology sections are concurrent with others, so that the overall chronology backtracks in places. Some poems could belong in more than one section, especially with the Cold War narrative ghosting later sections – appropriately given that the US, Soviet Union or China supported or fuelled several proxy wars.

Just as the original Hundred Years' War in the 14th and 15th centuries was actually a series of nationalistic conflicts rooted in disputes over territory, so it has been in the wars fought over the past century, but with even worse suffering inflicted on countries and people subjected to warfare and mass killing on a scale unimaginable in any earlier time. And yet amidst all that horror, there are individual voices bearing witness to our shared humanity, somehow surviving the folly with defiance and hope, yet often aware that the lessons of history are rarely passed on from one generation to the next. As Germany's Günter Kunert writes in his poem 'On Certain Survivors' [➤ 311] in which a man is dragged out from the debris of his shelled house: 'He shook himself | And said | Never again. | | At least, not right away.'

NEIL ASTLEY

Special thanks are due to Jonathan Davidson, for asking for my list of modern war poems for a Midland Creative Projects live literature production, which grew into this anthology; and to Ian Higgins, Michael Copp, Damir Šodan, Chris Agee, Noel Russell and Sarah Maguire for their invaluable assistance.

20

Grass

Pile the bodies high at Austerlitz and Waterloo.
Shovel them under and let me work –
    I am the grass; I cover all.

And pile them high at Gettysburg
And pile them high at Ypres and Verdun.
Shovel them under and let me work.
Two years, ten years, and passengers ask the conductor:
    What place is this?
    Where are we now?

    I am the grass.
    Let me work.

CARL SANDBURG

Inscription for a War

> *Stranger, go tell the Spartans*
> *we died here obedient to their commands.*
> Inscription at Thermopylae

Linger not, stranger; shed no tear;
Go back to those who sent us here.

We are the young they drafted out
To wars their folly brought about.

Go tell those old men, safe in bed,
We took their orders and are dead.

A.D. HOPE

Carl Sandburg (1878-1967) was an American writer who won three Pulitzer prizes, two of these for his poetry. A.D. Hope (1907-2000) was one of the major Australian poets of the 20th century known especially for his satirical verse.

The Horses

For all of the horses butchered on the battlefield,
Shell-shocked, tripping up over their own intestines,
Drowning in the mud, the best war memorial
Is in Homer: two horses that refuse to budge
Despite threats and sweet-talk and the whistling whip,
Immovable as a tombstone, their heads drooping
In front of the streamlined motionless chariot,
Hot tears spilling from their eyelids onto the ground
Because they are still in mourning for Patroclus
Their charioteer, their shiny manes bedraggled
Under the yoke pads on either side of the yoke.

MICHAEL LONGLEY
➣ 430

The Visitor

In Spanish he whispers there is no time left.
It is the sound of scythes arcing in wheat,
the ache of some field song in Salvador.
The wind along the prison, cautious
as Francisco's hands on the inside, touching
the walls as he walks, it is his wife's breath
slipping into his cell each night while he
imagines his hand to be hers. It is a small country.

There is nothing one man will not do to another.

CAROLYN FORCHÉ
➣ 366

22

FIRST WORLD WAR | 1914–1918

TOTAL DEATHS: OVER 37 MILLION

This selection of poems written during or about the First World War bears little relation to what was popular or even known at the time, which included, in the early part of the war, idealistic scribblings by ordinary soldiers and patriotic calls to arms by civilian versifiers, published in anthologies selling thousands of copies to a public largely unaware of the horrors of trench warfare. Traumatised returning soldiers found it difficult to speak about mechanised slaughter on the Western Front when government censorship ensured that newspaper reports omitted anything that might discourage young men from enlisting. By late 1917, the best-known soldier poets were Rupert Brooke, Julian Grenfell and Charles Sorley (who had all died in 1915), along with Robert Nichols, while Edward Thomas was known only as a critic and Siegfried Sassoon more for his declaration refusing to fight [➤ 93] than for his poetry. Wilfred Owen and Isaac Rosenberg were unread until the 1920s. Ivor Gurney, Edmund Blunden and David Jones wrote their best work after the war.

Frederick Brereton's *Anthology of War Poems* (1930) was the first book to present anything like the canon of First World War poetry familiar to readers today, with Blunden's introduction arguing that Owen and Sassoon were the greatest poets of the war, and three poems included by Rosenberg, his first in any anthology. Yet W.B. Yeats so misjudged Owen's work ('unworthy of the poets' corner of a country newspaper') that he omitted him and other significant war poets from his influential *Oxford Book of Modern Verse* (1936), having 'a distaste for certain poems written in the midst of the great war [...] passive suffering is not a theme for poetry. In all the great tragedies, tragedy is a joy to the man who dies [...] If the war is necessary, or necessary in our time and place, it is best to forget its suffering as we do the discomfort of fever...'

First World War poetry was still largely ignored by critics until the 1960s, when Brian Gardner's anthology *Up the Line to Death* (1964) and Ian Parsons' *Men Who March Away* (1965) established the core syllabus of British war poetry studied since in schools and universities. That reappraisal and desire to focus attention on these poets had much to do with anti-war sentiment during the Vietnam War. Taking its cue from the phrase 'lions led by donkeys', Alan Clark's scathing study of the generals, *The Donkeys* (1961), influenced works such as Theatre Workshop's satirical musical *Oh! What a Lovely War* (1963), later made into a film (1969), which in turn helped foster the public view that obstinate politicians, incompetent generals and profiteering industrialists were as much responsible for the earlier war as for the current one.

Editors and critics have also ignored or sidelined the central contribution made by both Modernist and European poets to First World War poetry, with Tim Kendall, in *Poetry of the First World War* (2013), even asserting that David Jones was 'the only Modernist soldier-poet of any note'. Evidence to the contrary is clear from the work of poets such as Apollinaire, Cocteau, Porché and Ungaretti from the First World War, and numerous others from the Second World War represented in this book.

23

War

He's risen now, who slept so long,
He's risen from deep vaults, among
The day's remains. Huge and unknown
He stands. His black hands crush the moon.

Into the cities' evening crack
A shadow-frost falls, alien dark.
It makes the downtown bustle freeze.
Go quiet. Glance round. No one sees.

In side-streets, something grasps an arm.
A question. Answerless. Stay calm.
Far off, the bells are trembling thin
And stubble stirs on each sharp chin.

He's started. There, up on the fells
He's dancing, shouting: *Men! To kill!*
And when he shakes his dark head, chains
Of skulls go rattling round his brain.

A moving tower, he tramples out
The last of light. The river clots
As countless bodies staunch and dam
Its reedy flow. The white birds swarm.

He steeplechases through the night
This red wild-shrieking hound, and out
Of darkness spring night's secret shows,
Footlit as if by lava flows.

The fields are scattered with the pointed
Caps of a thousand flames; the hunted
Refugees below are thrust
Into the forest fires to roast.

From tree to tree, like yellow bats
The flames spread as inferno eats
Each forest. Rattling at the bars,
The stoker prods it till it roars.

24

A city sank into the reeking
Yellow, hurled itself, unspeaking.
But he stands vast above the glow
And shakes his torch three times to show

The storm-zagged clouds, the frigid wastes
Of darkness, he has seared this place
To ash; then brings to his dry lips
His brimstone spit: apocalypse.

[1911]

GEORG HEYM
translated from the German by John Greening

Georg Heym (1887-1912) was a German Expressionist poet. Much of his work
was only published after his early death. He was skating on the frozen Havel
river and drowned when trying to rescue a friend who'd fallen through the ice.

MCMXIV

Those long uneven lines
Standing as patiently
As if they were stretched outside
The Oval or Villa Park,
The crowns of hats, the sun
On moustached archaic faces
Grinning as if it were all
An August Bank Holiday lark;

And the shut shops, the bleached
Established names on the sunblinds,
The farthings and sovereigns,
And dark-clothed children at play
Called after kings and queens,
The tin advertisements
For cocoa and twist, and the pubs
Wide open all day;

And the countryside not caring:
The place-names all hazed over
With flowering grasses, and fields
Shadowing Domesday lines
Under wheat's restless silence;
The differently-dressed servants
With tiny rooms in huge houses,
The dust behind limousines;

Never such innocence,
Never before or since,
As changed itself to past
Without a word – the men
Leaving the gardens tidy,
The thousands of marriages
Lasting a little while longer:
Never such innocence again.

PHILIP LARKIN

Philip Larkin (1922-85) was the leading figure in the Movement group of poets whose plain-speaking, descriptive poetry using traditional forms was the dominant poetic mode in British poetry of the 1950s and early 60s. This poem is one single fatalistic sentence, the lines all leading to war, loss and the passing of the old order.

All the hills and vales along

All the hills and vales along
Earth is bursting into song,
And the singers are the chaps
Who are going to die perhaps.
    O sing, marching men,
    Till the valleys ring again.
    Give your gladness to earth's keeping,
    So be glad, when you are sleeping.

Cast away regret and rue,
Think what you are marching to.
Little live, great pass.
Jesus Christ and Barabbas
Were found the same day.
This died, that went his way.
    So sing with joyful breath.
    For why, you are going to death.
    Teeming earth will surely store
    All the gladness that you pour.

Earth that never doubts nor fears,
Earth that knows of death, not tears,
Earth that bore with joyful ease
Hemlock for Socrates,
Earth that blossomed and was glad
'Neath the cross that Christ had,
Shall rejoice and blossom too
When the bullet reaches you.
    Wherefore, men marching
    On the road to death, sing!
    Pour your gladness on earth's head,
    So be merry, so be dead.

From the hills and valleys earth
Shouts back the sound of mirth,
Tramp of feet and lilt of song
Ringing all the road along.
All the music of their going,
Ringing swinging glad song-throwing,
Earth will echo still, when foot
Lies numb and voice mute.
    On marching men, on
    To the gates of death with song.
    Sow your gladness for earth's reaping,
    So you may be glad, though sleeping.
    Strew your gladness on earth's bed,
    So be merry, so be dead.

[*c.* August 1914]

CHARLES SORLEY

27

Charles Hamilton Sorley (1895-1915) was an English poet of great promise whose work only became known after his death at the age of 20. Some of his poems anticipate the later protest poetry of Siegfried Sassoon and Wilfred Owen, notably 'All the hills and vales along' [➤ 26] which 'ironically slurs the notes of patriotic recruitment-calls' and his last poem, 'When you see millions of the mouthless dead' [➤ 39], which 'undermines the language of all commemoration' (Edna Longley). Found in his kit sent home from France after his death, his final sonnet is critical of the pro-war sonnets of Rupert Brooke, of whom he wrote elsewhere: 'He has clothed his attitude in fine words: but he has taken the sentimental attitude.'

Sorley was studying in Germany when war broke out. Returning to England to volunteer, he joined the Suffolk Regiment, arriving in France as a lieutenant on 30 May 1915, and was soon promoted to captain. He was killed in action at the Battle of Loos, shot in the head by a sniper on 13 October 1915 near Hulluch. His only book, *Marlborough and Other Poems*, was published in January 1916, and reprinted several times that year.

Leaving for the Front

(to Peter Scher)

Before dying I must just make my poem.
Quiet, comrades, don't disturb me.

We are going off to war. Death is our bond.
Oh, if only my girlfriend would stop howling.

What do I matter? I'm happy to go.
My mother's crying. You need to be made of iron.

The sun is falling down on to the horizon.
Soon they'll be throwing me into a nice mass grave.

In the sky the good old sunset is glowing red.
In thirteen days maybe I'll be dead.

[7 August 1914]

ALFRED LICHTENSTEIN
translated from the German by Patrick Bridgwater

28

Prayer Before Battle

The men are singing fervently, every man thinking of himself:
God, protect me from accidents,
Father, Son and Holy Ghost,
Don't let shells hit me,
Don't let those bastards, our enemies,
Catch me or shoot me,
Don't let me snuff it like a dog
For my dear Fatherland.

Look, I'd like to go on living,
Milking cows, stuffing girls
And beating up that blighter Joe,
Getting tight many more times
Before I die like a Christian.
Look, I'll pray well and willingly,
I'll say seven rosaries a day,
If you, God, in your mercy
Will kill my friend Huber, or
Meier, and spare me.

But if I get my lot,
Don't let me be too badly wounded.
Send me a slight leg wound,
A small arm injury,
So that I may return home as a hero
Who has a tale to tell.

ALFRED LICHTENSTEIN
translated from the German by Patrick Bridgwater

Alfred Lichtenstein (1889-1914) was the son of a Prussian Jewish factory owner, a promising young writer whose poetry depicted the industralised world with realistic gloom and grim wit. The war began before he had completed his year of compulsory military service, and his 2nd Bavarian Infantry Regiment was sent to the Western Front immediately. Wounded in the attack on Vermandovillers on the Somme on 24 September 1914, he died soon afterwards. Wilfred Owen's regiment would retake Vermandovillers exactly four years later.

The Soldier

If I should die, think only this of me:
    That there's some corner of a foreign field
That is for ever England. There shall be
    In that rich earth a richer dust concealed;
A dust whom England bore, shaped, made aware,
    Gave, once, her flowers to love, her ways to roam,
A body of England's, breathing English air,
    Washed by the rivers, blest by suns of home.

And think, this heart, all evil shed away,
    A pulse in the eternal mind, no less
        Gives somewhere back the thoughts by England given;
Her sights and sounds; dreams happy as her day;
    And laughter, learnt of friends; and gentleness,
        In hearts at peace, under an English heaven.

[October 1914]

RUPERT BROOKE

Rupert Brooke (1887-1915) was already a much-fêted poet when war broke out, the leading figure in the circle of Georgian poets, publishing his first collection in 1911. His patriotic, lyrical verse, coupled with his dashing good looks, had made him a national hero by the time of his death, when the full horrors of the war were not yet widely known. Yet Brooke's belief in the justness of the war was fuelled by his experience of 'incessant mechanical slaughter' during the German bombardment of Antwerp in October 1914, which he called 'one of the greatest crimes in history'. His poem 'The Soldier' was the fifth and final sonnet in the sequence '1914', written on his return from Belgium, and published in *The Times Literary Supplement* on 11 March 1915. By that time he was on his way to Gallipoli with the British Mediterranean Expeditionary Force, but suffering from sepsis from an infected mosquito bite. The poem was read from the pulpit of St Paul's Cathedral on Easter Sunday, 4 April 1915. He died on 23 April on a hospital ship moored off the Greek island of Skyros, and was buried there. His second collection, *1914 and Other Poems*, was published in May 1915 and reprinted eleven times that year; and was so popular that by June 1918 it had reached its 24th impression.

Clearing-Station

Straw rustling everywhere.
The candle-stumps stand there staring solemnly.
Across the nocturnal vault of the church
Moans go drifting and choking words.

There's a stench of blood, pus, shit and sweat.
Bandages ooze away underneath torn uniforms.
Clammy trembling hands and wasted faces.
Bodies stay propped up as their dying heads slump down.

In the distance the battle thunders grimly on,
Day and night, groaning and grumbling non-stop,
And to the dying men patiently waiting for their graves
It sounds for all the world like the words of God.

[November 1914]

WILHELM KLEMM
translated from the German by Patrick Bridgwater

Wilhelm Klemm (1881-1968) was a German avant-garde poet and physician called up to serve as an army field-surgeon in General von Hausen's Third Army in Flanders. Leaving for the Front on 10 August 1914, he looked after soldiers wounded in the French counter-attack during the First Battle of the Marne in September 1914, and continued to serve throughout the war. Detailed and explicit, with many striking images, his war poems were published in several collections from 1915. After a final book dealing with themes of violence and cruelty, *Die Satanspuppe* (1922, as Felix Brazil), he fell silent and devoted himself to the business of publishing. His publishing houses were destroyed by Allied bombing in 1943, and his two sons were killed in the same year.

Wildfire

Down into the barn
a shell came crashing,
like the hopes of all the years collapsing,

and from the shell, jack
from tiny box, sprang the devil fire.

Through the great slatted door
I see fire rise and sneak
among the season's gathered straw and hay,
then, chattering in glee,
dance in sparks across the floor
a light fantastic reel...

Fire knows it has the run of the place,
and prospecting, paces out its new demesne,
climbs the beams and eaves,
then slides back down on the heaps of straw
like a haymaking child left to play.

Fire skips and whistles with glee,
ripples, flows, unfolds and spreads,
and punches window-panes
to take a peep outside:
Fire mellows wormy timbers
with velvet crimson,
splits open sacks of grain
and spills cascades of gold and ruby,
then bushes up between the tiles
and red-heads the roof;

Fire nuzzles through the slats to look,
and strokes the wood, illuminating every fret
with gaudy scarlet.

Fire's cutting loose in glee;
there's no one now to spoil its sport
and torment it with the hose
it used to seethe to,
big cat to the tamer's whip.
Fire dances whooping through the blazing barn.

Then, when it's had enough
rumbustious ladder-tumbling,
it swarms unruffled-burglar-like
up over the roof, breaks the tiles and

like a child in a tantrum
who suddenly takes against his game,
twists off the breaking door,
punches in the roof and brings it down,
and jumps onto the house behind:

Inquisitively, through the skylights,
it looks inside, snake-necks about inside,
and suddenly it's itching
to poke and pry and play again,
and dance itself breathless,
like a drunk in a pub...

Fire, monster of beauty,
beautiful, unstrokeable,
pacing the village
like a tiger in its cage...

[Kœur-la-Grande, 1914]

ALBERT-PAUL GRANIER
translated from the French by Ian Higgins

Squall

A steel squall of gluttonous thrusting shells smashed
thunderclaps through clear sky
straight at the village, ferocious
as a swoop of eagles on a flock of grazing sheep.

And when the bloated eddies of smoke had rolled away
across the quiet pastureland,
the peaceful village by its river
was gone, and in its place was only ruin, desolation.

The church, amidst the dead of years past, is doomed,
but just still standing, like a dying horse, its very soul
bleeding from the riven stones,

weeping from every dead louvre in the lurching belfry
that it cannot sound this night a pious death-knell
for the peaceful village by the river.

[1914]

ALBERT-PAUL GRANIER
translated from the French by Ian Higgins

Nocturne

The guns have fallen silent, gagged with fog,
in the winter's night that cancels space,
and a calm, full of menace
as the screech of owls over castle walls,
hangs in the many-hearted silence.

Sentries, peering out,
tense every muscle, edgily
awaiting the unexpected.

A thwack like wet cloth
sounds from the valley –
sudden muffled rifle-shots
unsure of guessed-at shadows
and the rustling emptiness.

Tonight
is like the nights in Breton legend
when hell-hag washerwomen
kneel invisible at riverside stones,
beating shrouds in the thick water.

[Observation post, Meuse, 1915]

ALBERT-PAUL GRANIER
translated from the French by Ian Higgins

Albert-Paul Granier (1888-1917) was a talented sportsman, musician and poet from Le Croisic on the Atlantic coast of Brittany. He qualified as a solicitor but compulsory national service in France required him to serve in the army from 1911 to 1913, where he trained as an artillery officer. Recalled to the army in August 1914, he served on the Western Front and became an airborne artillery observer. Granier's aeroplane was obliterated over the battlefields of Verdun on 17 August 1917. No trace of his body was found. His collection of war poetry, *Les Coqs et les Vautours*, had just been published in Paris, and was singled out for praise by the Académie Française in 1918 before falling, unaccountably, into obscurity. For almost 90 years this outstanding French poet of the First World War was unknown in his own country. The chance finding of a slim and musty little volume of his poetry at a jumble sale in France in 2008 was a revelation to the finder, and Granier was republished to the astonishment of French readers. Ian Higgins' English translation, *Cockerels and Vultures*, was published in 2014.

Rouen

(26 April–25 May 1915)

Early morning over Rouen, hopeful, high, courageous morning,
And the laughter of adventure and the steepness of the stair,
And the dawn across the river, and the wind across the bridges,
And the empty littered station, and the tired people there.

Can you recall those mornings and the hurry of awakening,
And the long-forgotten wonder if we should miss the way,
And the unfamiliar faces, and the coming of provisions,
And the freshness and the glory of the labour of the day?

Hot noontide over Rouen, and the sun upon the city,
Sun and dust unceasing, and the glare of cloudless skies,
And the voices of the Indians and the endless stream of soldiers,
And the clicking of the tatties,[1] and the buzzing of the flies.

Can you recall those noontides and the reek of steam and coffee,
Heavy-laden noontides with the evening's peace to win,
And the little piles of Woodbines, and the sticky soda bottles,
And the crushes in the 'Parlour', and the letters coming in?

1. *tatties:* dampened screens placed over windows or doors to freshen the air.

Quiet night-time over Rouen, and the station full of soldiers,
All the youth and pride of England from the ends of all the earth;
And the rifles piled together, and the creaking of the sword-belts,
And the faces bent above them, and the gay, heart-breaking mirth.

Can I forget the passage from the cool white-bedded Aid Post
Past the long sun-blistered coaches of the khaki Red Cross train
To the truck train full of wounded, and the weariness and laughter,
And 'Goodbye, and thank you, Sister', and the empty yards again?

Can you recall the parcels that we made then for the railroad,
Crammed and bulging parcels held together by their string,
And the voices of the sergeants who called the Drafts together,
And the agony and splendour when they stood to save the King?

Can you forget their passing, the cheering and the waving,
The little group of people at the doorway of the shed,
The sudden awful silence when the last train swung to darkness,
And the lonely desolation, and the mocking stars o'erhead?

Can you recall the midnights, and the footsteps of night watchers,
Men who came from darkness and went back to dark again,
And the shadows on the rail-lines and the all-inglorious labour,
And the promise of the daylight firing blue the window-pane?

Can you recall the passing through the kitchen door to morning,
Morning very still and solemn breaking slowly on the town,
And the early coastways engines that had met the ships at daybreak,
And the Drafts just out from England, and the day shift coming down?

Can you forget returning slowly, stumbling on the cobbles,
And the white-decked Red Cross barges dropping seawards for the tide,
And the search for English papers, and the blessed cool of water,
And the peace of half-closed shutters that shut out the world outside?

Can I forget the evenings and the sunsets on the island,
And the tall black ships at anchor far below our balcony,
And the distant call of bugles, and the white wine in the glasses,
And the long line of the street lamps, stretching Eastwards to the sea?

...When the world slips slow to darkness, when the office fire burns
        lower,
My heart goes out to Rouen, Rouen all the world away;
When other men remember I remember our Adventure
And the trains that go from Rouen at the ending of the day.

[November 1915; *published 1917*]

MAY WEDDERBURN CANNAN

May Wedderburn Cannan (1893-1973) served as a nurse during the First
World War. She helped run the canteen at the railhead in Rouen for four
weeks during 1915, returning to France in 1918 to work in the espionage
department of the War Office in Paris. She published three books of poetry
during and after the war, and later, a semi-autobiographical novel, *The Lonely
Generation* (1934). Her memoir, *Grey Ghosts and Voices*, was published in 1976.

At the Beginning of the War

At the beginning of the war there was a rainbow.
Birds, black, wheeled against grey clouds.
Pigeons shone silver as on their circular journey
They turned through a narrow strip of sunlight.

Battle takes place hard by battle. They lied like troopers.
Row upon row of stoved-in heads fill one with horror.
Shells often explode
As they tumble on beginning to lose velocity.
The shells' pain-bow grows all the time.

Caught between Death and the bow of peace,
They clutch their rifle barrels more firmly, to defend their homeland,
Spitting at the enemy, leaning on one another as they totter,
Tumbling over hills, like waves of the sea,
Staggering on, attracted magnetically by Death.

[1915]

PETER BAUM
translated from the German by Patrick Bridgwater
➤ 38

37

Wartime April

The north wind whistling round the doors,
Snow, filling the lanes and tracks with white.
Wartime April, April caught
And pinioned with the gale's lash,
April of the stricken light.

The women wear black veils,
The girls a grown-up dignity.
The talk is in murmurs. Night
Closes in... Silence... A splinter
Of hope gleams in the dark, like driftwood.

Here we sit, no one speaking now.
What do you say to a woman crying?
Here we sit, like prisoners.
Never stirring, each in her house,
We sit, and know the men are dying.

[*c.* 1915]

CÉCILE PÉRIN
translated from the French by Ian Higgins

Cécile Périn (1877-1959) was a prolific French poet, the author of over 20 volumes of poetry produced between 1906 and 1959. Her poems relating to the First World War were included in *Les captives: poèmes 1914-1918* (1919).

Peter Baum (1869-1916) was a writer of strange and fantastical stories and poems. His poetry changed dramatically when he found himself, at the age of 45, serving as a stretcher-bearer on the Western Front, tending to wounded and dying soldiers. He was digging graves when hit by stray shrapnel on 5 June 1916 and died the following day. ➢ 37

John McCrae (1872-1918) was a physician who served as a field surgeon with the Canadian artillery during the Second Battle of Ypres. He wrote 'In Flanders Fields' after burying a friend killed in battle. Published in *Punch* in December 1915, his rondeau became the most popular poem of the war, its references to poppies on soldiers' graves leading to the adoption of the poppy as a symbol of remembrance. Also used in propaganda, it has been much criticised for what Paul Fussell called its 'recruiting-poster rhetoric'. McCrae died from pneumonia while commanding No. 3 Canadian General Hospital (McGill) at Boulogne.

In Flanders Fields

In Flanders fields the poppies blow
Between the crosses, row on row,
   That mark our place; and in the sky
   The larks, still bravely singing, fly
Scarce heard amid the guns below.

We are the Dead. Short days ago
We lived, felt dawn, saw sunset glow,
   Loved and were loved, and now we lie
      In Flanders fields.

Take up our quarrel with the foe:
To you from failing hands we throw
   The torch; be yours to hold it high.
   If ye break faith with us who die
We shall not sleep, though poppies grow
      In Flanders fields.

[3 May 1915]

JOHN McCRAE

When you see millions of the mouthless dead

When you see millions of the mouthless dead
Across your dreams in pale battalions go,
Say not soft things as other men have said,
That you'll remember. For you need not so.
Give them not praise. For, deaf, how should they know
It is not curses heaped on each gashed head?
Nor tears. Their blind eyes see not your tears flow.
Nor honour. It is easy to be dead.
Say only this, 'They are dead.' Then add thereto,
'Yet many a better one[1] has died before.'

39

Then, scanning all the o'ercrowded mass, should you
Perceive one face that you loved heretofore,
It is a spook. None wears the face you knew.
Great death has made all his for evermore.

CHARLES SORLEY
➤ 28

1. *many a better one:* from Achilles' 'Thus died Patroclus, a better man than
thou' (*Iliad*, XXI), quoted by Sorley in a November 1914 letter.

This poem was found in Sorley's kit after his death on 13 October 1915.

All Souls' Day

Public mourning, unconsoled,
A landscape hunching drab and bare
Among the plundering flames of autumn,
Bells tolling, guns' thunder rolling,

All Souls' Day, day of graveside prayer,
Bells tolling, guns' thunder rolling,
Our wearying hearts grown dull and numb
To bells, the alarms, and everywhere

Entire tragedies of lives undone.
In the sad, soft wind, we feel
Brush round us as we kneel
Dead leaves and sundered souls.

At last the bells pause for breath;
But not the drumming, willing guns –
While we are celebrating death,
The distance dins with killing, killing.

[*c.* 1915]

LUCIE DELARUE-MARDRUS
translated from the French by Ian Higgins

Execution

Itching all night long, it's never ended.
Stem the evil of the scratch:
In a shirt-seam, where they hatch,
One of the scoundrels is apprehended.

The time has come, let justice be enacted,
In all its rigour, with all speed:
Against such unrepentant greed
Humanity has suddenly reacted.

Louse, your bliss was brief as mayfly's breath –
The verdict's quick, no pity is expressed,
The perpetrator is condemned to death

And fingernail to fingernail is pressed.
– A bit like us, as the war grinds on:
One sharp crack, you're gone.

[*c.* 1915]

ANDRÉ MARTEL
translated from the French by Ian Higgins

André Martel (1893-1976) was a French writer, poet and man of letters known for his experimental writing. Several of his books were written in his own invented language of Paralloïdre. After becoming secretary to the artist Jean Dubuffet, he was made Regent of the College of Pataphysics.

Lucie Delarue-Mardrus (1874-1945) was a prolific French writer and sculptor, the author of more than 70 books, including poetry collections, biographies and novels, many of the latter featuring lesbian characters. ➤ 40

Guillaume Apollinaire [Wilhelm Apollinaris de Kostrowitzky] (1880-1918) was born in Rome of mixed Polish and Italian parentage. France became his adoptive country, but only in the war, by volunteering, could he finally obtain French nationality. In pre-war Paris, apart from writing poetry (*Alcools*, 1912), he championed Picasso and other modernist painters in his *Les Peintres Cubistes: Méditations Esthétiques* (1913).

He enlisted in the artillery and was sent to a wood in Champagne where he came under shellfire. In November 1915, he took up a commission in the infantry, the switch bringing him face to face with the harsher side of the war, but, whatever the context, he found 'in war and in the perpetual balance between life and death an excitement and a constant source of new impressions and joys. [...] For him the war was a prodigious adventure and its slightest detail was the occasion for poetic or epistolary outbursts' (George Steiner).

On 17 March 1916 in the trenches at Bois des Buttes, near Berry-au-Bac, he received a head wound from a shrapnel splinter which penetrated his helmet and his skull, rendering him unfit for combat. He was awarded the Croix de Guerre. Although weakened by his head wound, trepanned, and suffering from exposure to gas, he continued to write back in Paris. However, in November 1918 he fell victim to the virulent influenza pandemic and died on 9 November, two days before the Armistice.

Apollinaire was a leading figure, along with Picasso and Cocteau [➤ 53] of the avant-garde in France. His poems may appear fragmented, and occasionally flippant, and he has also been accused of beautifying war. But this is is to isolate particular lines or words and remove them from their context. In fact, he creates extraordinary syntheses, juxtapositions, simultaneities, of the beautiful and the horrific, of the serious and the jocular. It is this trajectory towards wholeness that is Apollinaire's particular way of arriving at a very special kind of strength and integrity, and of producing a coherent, if idiosyncratically achieved, vision of the experience of war.   [Michael Copp]   ➤ 42, 44, 112

Desire

My desire is the region before me
Behind the Boche lines
My desire is also behind me
Farther away than the armies' zone

My desire is the Butte of Mesnil [1]
My desire is there where I'm firing
Of my desire which is beyond the armies' zone
I don't speak about it today but I think of it

Mesnil Butte I picture you in vain
Barbed wire machine guns over-confident enemy
Sunk too far under ground already buried

Tac a tac of gunfire that fades away and dies

Keeping watch there late at night
The Decauville railway[2] coughing

Corrugated iron in the rain
And in the rain my helmet

Hear the violent earth
See the flashes before hearing the gunfire

And the mad whistling of some shell or other
Or the monotonous brief tac tac tac full of disgust

I long
To hold you in my hand Main de Massiges[3]
So fleshless on the map

Goethe's trench I fired at
I even fired at Nietzsche's guts[4]
Undoubtedly I respect no fame

Night violent and violet and dark and golden now and then
Night of men only
Night of September 24
Tomorrow the attack
Night violent O night whose dreadful deep cry
        became more intense every minute
Night that cried like a woman in labour
Night of men only

[Sent to Madeleine Pagès on 6 October 1915][5]

GUILLAUME APOLLINAIRE
translated from the French by Michael Copp

1. A bitterly contested position. 2. Light, narrow-gauge railway (named after its inventor) used to transport ammunition and supplies to the trenches. 3. Another bitterly contested position. 4. The word *boyau*, used in this and the previous line, can mean both 'trench' and 'guts'. 5. During 1915 Apollinaire was writing to *Madeleine Pagès*, a teacher from Algeria, to whom he was briefly engaged. [Tr.]

The Falling Leaves

Today, as I rode by,
I saw the brown leaves dropping from their tree
In a still afternoon,
When no wind whirled them whistling to the sky,
But thickly, silently,
They fell, like snowflakes wiping out the noon;
And wandered slowly thence
For thinking of a gallant multitude
Which now all withering lay,
Slain by no wind of age or pestilence,
But in their beauty strewed
Like snowflakes falling on the Flemish clay.

[November 1915]

MARGARET POSTGATE COLE

Margaret Postgate Cole (1893-1980) was an English author, social campaigner
and educationalist who worked for the peace movement during the First World
War, helping her brother and others denied the right to refuse military service
as conscientious objectors. ➢ 123, 124

War Marvel

How beautiful these flares that light up the night
They rise to their own peak and lean over to have a look
They are ladies dancing and looking for eyes arms hearts

I recognised your smile and your vivacity [1]

It's also the daily apotheosis of all my Berenices
        whose hair has become comets [2]
These over-gilded dancers belong to all times and all races
They give sudden birth to children who only have time to die

How beautiful all these flares are
But it would be much better if there were even more
If there were millions that would have a complete and relative
                                                      meaning
            like the letters of a book
Yet it's as beautiful as if life itself was emerging from the dying

But it would be much more beautiful if there were even more
However I look at them as at a beauty that presents itself
            and immediately vanishes
I seem to be present at a great daylight [3] festivity
It's a banquet being offered to the earth
Which is hungry and opens long pale mouths [4]
The earth is hungry and here is its cannibal Belshazzar feast
Who would have said that one could be so anthropophagic
And that so much fire was needed to roast the human body
That's why the air has a little empyromatic [5] taste
            That is not well unpleasant
But the festivity would be even more beautiful if the sky was
                                                      eating there
            with the earth
It only swallows souls
Which is a way of not feeding oneself
And is happy to juggle with versicoloured [6] lights

But I have flowed into the softness of this war with all my company
            through long saps
A few shouts of flame incessantly announce my presence
I've dug the bed into which I flow branching out into a thousand
                                                      little rivers
            that go everywhere
I'm in a front line trench and yet I'm everywhere or rather
            I'm beginning to be everywhere
It is I who begins this thing of future centuries
It takes longer to come about than the story of Icarus flying

I bequeath to the future the story of Guillaume Apollinaire
Who was at the war and was able to be everywhere
In the cheerful towns in the rear
In all the rest of the universe

In those who die while making no progress through the barbed wire
In the women in the guns in the horses
At the zenith at the nadir at the 4 cardinal points
And in the unique fervour of this night before battle

And it would no doubt be much more beautiful
If I could suppose that all these things in which I am everywhere
Could occupy me as well
But in that sense there is nothing done
For just now I am everywhere however there's only me who is in me

[December 1915]

GUILLAUME APOLLINAIRE
translated from the French by Michael Copp
➤ 41

1. This line is addressed to Madeleine Pagès [➤ 43 *n*.5]. 2. *Berenice's Hair* is
the name of a constellation. According to legend, a lock of hair of the Egyptian
princess Berenice formed the constellation of stars called the Coma Berenices.
3. A *giorno* (Italian) in the original. 4. Trenches dug out of the chalk of the
Champagne region. 5. The first part of Apollinaire's invented word, *'empyreum-
atique'*, suggests 'empyrean' (the highest heaven), while the second part of the
word suggests 'automatic'. 6. Apollinaire's invented word, *'versicolores'*, suggests
coloured lights pouring down (*verser* = to pour). [Tr.]

Nocturnal Landscape

A constellation like day; the horizon behind it by lights and flares
    fingered and shrouded,
That went and came, fell or stood, restless, phantom-like; and if it
    went, deep night fell,
And if it came, then somewhere a town lay, white, shifting furtive
    a forest was made and a vale
Full of sleep, with torrents and indeterminate things, with graves
    and churchtowers, smashed, with climbing mists, moist, big-
    clouded,

With huts, where sleepers lay, where a dream walked, full of fever,
    full of strangeness, full of animal splendour, where abruptly a
    screen
Of cloud split open; and behind it swelled and ocean of stars, a
    dominion of rockets, a light sprang from the ravine,
Terrible, roaring, rumble of wheels on roads, and a man stepped
    darkly into the dark, by a dreadful nightmare amazed,
Saw the flight of fires migrating, heard butchery below, saw behind
    the darkness the city that ceaselessly blazed,
Heard in earth's belly a rolling, ponderous, gigantic, primeval, heard
    traffic travelling the roads, into the void, into the widening night,
    into a storm, grim in the west. Frantic, the ear
With the front's countless hammers, with the riders who came,
    stamping, hurrying, with the riders who rode away, to turn into
    shadows, melt into the night, there to rot,
Death slaughters them, and they lie under weeds, heavy, fossil,
    with hands full of spiders, mouths scabbed red and brown,
Eyes full of uttermost sleep, the circlet of shadow around their
    brows, blue, waxen, decaying in the smoke of the night
Which sank down, threw shadows far which spread its vault from
    hill to hill, over forest and rottenness, over brains full of dreams,
    over the hundred dead none carried away,
Over the mass of fire, over laughter and madness, over crosses in
    fields, over pain and despair, over rubble and ash, over the river
    and the ruined town...

[written 1920]

ANTON SCHNACK
translated from the German by Christopher Middleton

Anton Schnack (1892-1973) was a German writer whose literary reputation
was damaged by his support for the Nazis during the 1930s and 40s. Called
up in November 1915, he served with the Bavarian infantry on the Western
Front, taking part in the German offensive at Verdun during February 1916,
but was discharged as unfit for service in April 1916 after contracting prostatitis.
He published his war poems in four collections, the most notable being *Tier
rang gewaltig mit Tier* (Beast strove mightily with beast, 1920). He joined the
Wehrmacht in 1944 and was captured by US forces.

Vigil

An entire night
thrown down
beside a
butchered
companion with his
grimacing
mouth turned
to the full moon
with his congested hands
thrust
into my silence
I wrote
letters full of love

I have never held
so hard
to life

[Cima Quattro, 23 December 1915]

GIUSEPPE UNGARETTI
translated from the Italian by Andrew Frisardi

Giuseppe Ungaretti (1888-1970) was one of Italy's great Modernist poets, and a leading figure, with Eugenio Montale and Salvatore Quasimodo, in the Ermetismo (Hermeticism) grouping during the 1930s. He served as an infantry-man on the lower Isonzo front with the 3rd Army from 1915 until early 1918; in the spring, he was transferred to the Western Front. Many of his earliest published poems relate to his wartime experiences, including 'The Rivers' [> 78], one of the most celebrated Italian war poems. However, during the 1920s Ungaretti joined the National Fascist Party, his support for Mussolini resulting in the loss of his professorship at the University of Rome at the end of the war until colleagues insisted on his reinstatement.

He began writing his first book of poems in December 1915, on his first day in the trenches: 'I spent those nights lying in mud, opposite the enemy who was positioned higher than us and who was a hundred times better armed. In the trenches, almost always in those same trenches, because we stayed on San Michele even during breaks – the battles went on for a year. *Il porto sepolto* contains the experience of that year.'

This is no case of petty right or wrong

This is no case of petty right or wrong
That politicians or philosophers
Can judge. I hate not Germans, nor grow hot
With love of Englishmen, to please newspapers.
Beside my hate for one fat patriot
My hatred of the Kaiser is love true: –
A kind of god he is, banging a gong.
But I have not to choose between the two,
Or between justice and injustice. Dinned
With war and argument I read no more
Than in the storm smoking along the wind
Athwart the wood. Two witches' cauldrons roar.
From one the weather shall rise clear and gay;
Out of the other an England beautiful
And like her mother that died yesterday.
Little I know or care if, being dull,
I shall miss something that historians
Can rake out of the ashes when perchance
The phoenix broods serene above their ken.
But with the best and meanest Englishmen
I am one in crying, God save England, lest
We lose what never slaves and cattle blessed.
The ages made her that made us from the dust:
She is all we know and live by, and we trust
She is good and must endure, loving her so:
And as we love ourselves we hate her foe.

[26 December 1915]

EDWARD THOMAS

Edward Thomas (1878-1917) wrote a lifetime's poetry in two years. Already a dedicated prose writer and influential critic, he became a poet only in December 1914, at the age of 36, kick-started into poetry by his conversations with Robert Frost. Often viewed as a "war poet", he wrote nothing directly about the trenches, finishing his last poem in January 1917 before embarking for France. And yet all his poetry was written during the war and is shadowed by its presence. A poem like 'This is no case of petty right or wrong' shows how – as Edna Longley has written – 'Thomas rejected imperialism and defined English nationality in terms of locality or "home". His thinking about England was conditioned by social change, war and his ecological sense of habitats and history. [...] "Rain" (in which "Myriads of broken reeds" alludes to dead soldiers) builds up a complex and chilling symbol of dissolution.'

Thomas was plagued by self-recrimination over whether or not he should follow friends and fellow writers who had enlisted, these doubts surfacing in a number of poems reflecting on the state of England during the war. Over-age, he was under no obligation to do so, but in July 1915 he finally volunteered, joining the Artists' Rifles as a private. The 'bleak hut' in 'Rain' was at Hare Hall Camp in Essex where he acted as a map-reading instructor (and may have taught Wilfred Owen, trained at the same camp at that time). In November 1916 he was commissioned as a 2nd Lieutenant with Artillery, arriving at Arras on the front line in February 1917, where he was killed on 9 April when a shell-blast stopped his heart. His first and only poetry collection, *Poems*, was published posthumously under the name of Edward Eastaway. ➤ 49, 50, 62

Rain

Rain, midnight rain, nothing but the wild rain
On this bleak hut, and solitude, and me
Remembering again that I shall die
And neither hear the rain nor give it thanks
For washing me cleaner than I have been
Since I was born into this solitude.
Blessed are the dead that the rain rains upon:
But here I pray that none whom once I loved
Is dying tonight or lying still awake
Solitary, listening to the rain,
Either in pain or thus in sympathy
Helpless among the living and the dead,
Like a cold water among broken reeds,
Myriads of broken reeds all still and stiff,
Like me who have no love which this wild rain
Has not dissolved except the love of death,
If love it be for what is perfect and
Cannot, the tempest tells me, disappoint.

[7 January 1916]

EDWARD THOMAS

Then my guide in the blue overcoat...

Then my guide in the blue overcoat
got down on all fours.
Like a hunting dog, he went into a hole
and gestured for me to follow him.

Will the burrow fall in,
will it bury me? My shoulders
are in contact with each side.

My head emerges into a sort
of padded bowl,
where two men and my guide are holding out.
I absolutely wouldn't hold out.

I heard a new sort of silence.
For, twelve metres from that spot,
begins the German silence.

Between the two of them, grows
the barbed wire undergrowth where rear up
the *chevaux de frise*.[1]
It's the boulevard of death,
the killing ground
if you walk there,
like on the red metro rail.

The strip jointly used,
the devastating zone.
For on top of the little
periscope towers,
the eye perches, alone on the sandbags,
like a blue bird turning
its head in all directions.

They give it a nickname: *rue de la Paix*.
Across the whole of Europe
the tradesmen of the left pavement

and those of the right pavement
keep watch on each other
through a tiny window.

Then I stretched out my arm in the sap.
And I tugged on Amette's waterproof;
I didn't want to stay there any more.

I couldn't bear this zone
made of deceptive gentleness.
For the Germans often sing
the songs I sang as a child
with my brother and sister:
O Tannenbaum,[2] *Le Roi des Aulnes*.[3]

Amette, how can you want me
to hate the Germans?
On Tuesday the marines at the listening
post at Mamelon-Vert,
called out to two Germans
in order to have a game of cards.
The admiral condemned them to death.

We make our way back by a dreamed of
Venice, empty Algiers,
the Herculaneum of trenches.

We come across blue Arabs,
men of ashes,
blue gondolas.

JEAN COCTEAU
translated from the French by Michael Copp

1. A defensive structure consisting of a movable obstacle of barbed wire
attached to a wooden frame. 2. A German song, originally a folksong, that
became associated with the Christmas tree. 3. The French title of Goethe's
poem, 'Der Erlkönig', which was set to music by Schubert. 4. The original
'Mamelon-Vert' earthwork was part of the Russian defences at Sevastopol in
the Crimean War. 5. The ancient Roman town of Herculaneum was buried
by the eruption of Mount Vesuvius in 79 AD. [Tr.]

Jean Cocteau (1889-1963), poet, dramatist, novelist, and film-maker, was a leading figure, along with Apollinaire and Picasso, of the French avant-garde in the early 20th century. Ruled unfit for military service, he joined the Red Cross in August 1914. In September he was attached to a convoy to evacuate the wounded from Champagne, and witnessed the bombardment of Reims and the battle of the Marne. He volunteered for the army's ambulance section and left for the front in Flanders, spending the entire winter of 1916 at the front in Yser, and was later posted to Amiens. Returning to Paris in 1917, he was transferred to the French Foreign Ministry's Propaganda Department.

Cocteau articulated his war experiences in *Discours du Grand Sommeil* (1916-1918), a sequence of poems which includes 'Then my guide in the blue overcoat...'. This remains a little-known and neglected modernist work. In this collection he employs quirky imagery and dislocated syntax. The poems can be impressionistic, with disconcerting transitions, switching unexpectedly between trivial and inconsequential matters on the one hand, and serious issues and tragic events on the other. [Michael Copp]

from Trench Poem

FROM *The Day Before*

II

It will soon be two years that *they* have been hanging on
To the woods, the abandoned walls and the fields lying fallow.
Oozing into the soil like some sullied spring,
They grope around searching for a narrow fissure
That could open the way for their vast flood.
But we mirror their course of action, expose their plot,
And so long as we are aware of every step they make,
We return their ungodly patience against them.

The space between the two camps is pitted with craters.
Behind a low clump of bristling things,
Our trenches and theirs form thin black lines
   Like screwed up eyelids.

Nothing can distract these long vertical eyes
   From their resolute vigilance:
Each gaze that dies in the darkness of the target
   Gives way to a fresh gaze.

When the grass on one side thinks up a surprise,
    The grass opposite becomes suspicious;
    At times hardly more than a grey cap
    Glimpsed through the bushes.

    Less frequently a sad song wafts up,
        Unknown words floating
        A hostile dream to ours.

Everything is numbered and classified: thicket, open ground,
Everything has its destiny marked on the sights of a weapon,
Each moment prepares for the moment that will follow
        A ghastly awakening.

    The sun is already sinking over the horizon.
    We demand their life, they demand ours.
    This craving is all we have in common.
            Nothing else.

[...]

FROM *The Day*

I

            Four flashes of light over a wood;
            Accompanied by four angry explosions;
The sky is filled with screaming, God goes back up and hides.

            Four more explosions, abrupt, incensed,
            Carry off the morning mists in their wind,
                Then another four
                Follow rapidly.

            Day breaks: all the scourges
        Can be heard flailing down, four at a time,
Far off the ears of corn burst on the threshing floor.
        Each scourge flails in its appointed place.

*

All of them, seventy-fives and nineties,[1]
    The latter ringing like a bell,
    The former with a harder sound,
Grey steel yesterday, before that, black,
Stretching their necks, striking as one,
    Straight ahead:
    The rock trembles
    Like a rickety table.

The fresh shells, hastily taken out of the wagons
    Gleaming like ripe apples
    Under the branches,
Are going to spread their scent in the promised land:
    The same fruit
    Passes continually from hand to hand,
    Their departure shifts the air
        With the same noise.

        Sweating bodies,
        Eager levers
        Like the teeth
        Of a single gear;
        A copper wire
        Twangs in the grass,
        The firing assumes
        A fiercer tone;
        The gun-layer bends
        With half-closed eyes;
        The smoke lies white
        On the scythed fields.

        *

    In the rear, the long one-twenties
        Roar with upraised muzzles:
At the bottom of the valleys the hamlets feign death,
        Windows rattle.

    Squatting down on their runners,
The one-five-fives crush with their arching fire
    Distant railway lines, the station
And the road where axles get bogged down in the mud.

And, for all those who need to be convinced by proof,
The ponderous and slow two-twenties
Manage to think up
A persuasive argument.

*

Fire has rescued a range of metals from
The obscurity of their gloomy constraint:
Their reign has begun, their dreadful progress
Scars the ancient face of the hillsides.

The beautiful pages of the fields can no longer be read:
Following on from God, the ploughman
Had been able to add his marginal note under the Master's eye.
This mistake has been deleted.

The fort loses a corner,
The pine crashes down on the willow,
The lips of the craters
Burn and whine.

Great slanting curtains unroll in the wind,
Stippled with flashes and thick, black swirls.

Pestles crush the forest.

As it did in the times of biblical wrath,
The sun staggers and disappears.

Suddenly, out of the open earth,
A spray fans out,
A hundred feet high, white and deafening:
As it goes up and comes down,
A green pillbox
Disappears.

[January–May 1916]

FRANÇOIS PORCHÉ
translated from the French by Michael Copp

1.   Seventy-fives and nineties: French artillery, the quick-firing 75mm field
gun adopted in 1898 superseding the breech-loading 90mm field artillery piece
dating from 1877, both guns being in use on the Western Front.

François Porché (1877-1944) was born in Cognac, and published four collec-
tions from 1904 to 1912 which established his reputation as a poet of consider-
able psychological subtlety and feeling. In the early months of the war he saw
service on the Yser front, but on 1 December 1914 was discharged as unfit
for military service, suffering from double pneumonia. He was subsequently
bedridden for two years. His first two books of war poetry, *L'Arrêt sur la Marne*
(The Halt on the Marne) and *Le Poème de la Tranchée* (Trench Poem), were
written and published while he was convalescing in Nice in the early months
of 1916. These two, together with the later *Le Poème de la Délivrance* (The
Poem of Deliverance), were published in 1921 as a trilogy entitled *Les Com-
mandements du Destin*, the three parts of which are all quite substantial in
length. *Trench Poem*, written between January and May 1916, is 50 pages
long, and divided into three sections: 'The Day Before', 'The Day' and 'The
Next Day'. They are full of realistic detail, are cumulative in effect, and are
suffused with an understated patriotism. This epic-like, narrative format is
used not only by Porché but by other French poets such as Maurice Bouignol,
Marc Leclerc and Henri Dérieux, and all were published during the war years.
They have no counterparts in English war poetry until Herbert Read's *The
End of a War* (1933) and David Jones's *In Parenthesis* (1937). His other work
includes a verse play, *Les Butors de la Finette* (1917), an attempt to achieve an
allegorical synthesis of the war. [Michael Copp]

The Deserter

There was a man, – don't mind his name,
Whom Fear had dogged by night and day.
He could not face the German guns
And so he turned and ran away.
Just that – he turned and ran away,
But who can judge him, you or I?
God makes a man of flesh and blood
Who yearns to live and not to die.
And this man when he feared to die
Was scared as any frightened child,
His knees were shaking under him,
His breath came fast, his eyes were wild.

I've seen a hare with eyes as wild,
With throbbing heart and sobbing breath.
But oh! it shames one's soul to see
A man in abject fear of death.
But fear had gripped him, so had death;
His number had gone up that day,
They might not heed his frightened eyes,
They shot him when the dawn was grey.
Blindfolded, when the dawn was grey,
He stood there in a place apart,
The shots rang out and down he fell,
An English bullet in his heart.
An English bullet in his heart!
But here's the irony of life, –
His mother thinks he fought and fell
A hero, foremost in the strife.
So she goes proudly; to the strife
Her best, her hero son she gave.
O well for her she does not know
He lies in a deserter's grave.

[1916]

WINIFRED M. LETTS

Winifred M. Letts (1882-1972) was an English-born Irish author known mostly for her plays and novels. She served as a Voluntary Aid Detachment nurse in 1915 at Manchester base hospital, working later at Command Depot Camps in Manchester and Alnwick.

Siegfried Sassoon (1886-1967) was the son of wealthy Anglo-Jewish parents. Before 1914 he lived a leisured life, golfing, hunting, writing derivative poetry. He joined up on the first day of the Great War, and won a Military Cross which he later renounced. Sassoon had become radicalised by the losses at the Battle of the Somme and by meeting leftwing pacifist intellectuals. His famous protest against the politics of the war – 'A Soldier's Declaration' – was printed in the *Times* and quoted in parliament [in 1917 ≻ 93]. To prevent Sassoon from being court-martialled, Robert Graves, a fellow-officer in the Royal Welch Fusiliers, got him admitted to Craiglockhart War Hospital near Edinburgh where the psychological effects of war were treated. There he wrote the poems in *Counter-Attack* (1918), and met and influenced Wilfred Owen. Sassoon returned to action: another expression of solidarity with ordinary soldiers.

58

His most significant postwar writings are memoirs that obsessively revisit his lost generation, partly in an effort to exorcise survivor-guilt. Sassoon's 'Declaration' ends by deploring 'the callous complacence with which the majority of those at home regard the continuance of agonies which they do not share, and which they have not sufficient imagination to realise'. Sassoon's verse-satires attack the ignorance or indifference that sustains both the war and war-rhetoric. [Edna Longley] ➤ 60, 75, 77, 81, 83, 84, 85, 86, 93.

In the Pink

So Davies wrote: 'This leaves me in the pink.'
Then scrawled his name: 'Your loving sweetheart Willie'.
With crosses for a hug. He'd had a drink
Of rum and tea; and, though the barn was chilly,
For once his blood ran warm; he had pay to spend,
Winter was passing; soon the year would mend.

He couldn't sleep that night. Stiff in the dark
He groaned and thought of Sundays at the farm,
When he'd go out as cheerful as a lark
In his best suit, to wander arm-in-arm
With brown-eyed Gwen, and whisper in her ear
The simple, silly things she liked to hear.

And then he thought: tomorrow night we trudge
Up to the trenches, and my boots are rotten.
Five miles of stodgy clay and freezing sludge,
And everything but wretchedness forgotten.
Tonight he's in the pink; but soon he'll die.
And still the war goes on – *he* don't know why.

[10 February 1916]

SIEGFRIED SASSOON

'The first of my "outspoken" war poems. I wrote it one cold morning at Mor-lancourt, sitting by the fire in the Quartermaster's billet, while our Machine-Gun Officer shivered in his blankets on the floor. [...] The *Westminster* refused the poem, as they thought it might prejudice recruiting!!' [SS]

The Kite

Describing circle after circle,
a wheeling kite scans a field
lying desolate. In her hovel
a mother's wailing to her child:
'Come, take my breast, boy, feed on this,
grow, know your place, shoulder the cross.'

Centuries pass, villages flame,
are stunned by war and civil war.
My country, you are still the same,
tragic, beautiful as before.
In beauty ancient and tear-stained.
How long must the mother wail?
How long must the kite wheel?

[22 March 1916]

ALEKSANDR BLOK
translated from the Russian by Peter France

Aleksandr Blok (1880-1921) was one of Russia's greatest poets, a major figure in the Russian Symbolist movement, and the author of a much celebrated poem of the Bolshevik Revolution, 'The Twelve', written in January 1918. 'The Kite' was one of his last short poems, adapted from a rough draft for the first chapter of his panoramic historical poem *Retribution*, where the images of the hawk of disaster and grieving mother-Russia also appear.

A Working Party

Three hours ago he blundered up the trench,
Sliding and poising, groping with his boots;
Sometimes he tripped and lurched against the walls
With hands that pawed the sodden bags of chalk.

He couldn't see the man who walked in front;
Only he heard the drum and rattle of feet
Stepping along barred trench boards, often splashing
Wretchedly where the sludge was ankle-deep.

Voices would grunt 'Keep to your right -- make way!'
When squeezing past some men from the front-line:
White faces peered, puffing a point of red;
Candles and braziers glinted through the chinks
And curtain-flaps of dug-outs; then the gloom
Swallowed his sense of sight; he stooped and swore
Because a sagging wire had caught his neck.

A flare went up; the shining whiteness spread
And flickered upward, showing nimble rats
And mounds of glimmering sand-bags, bleached with rain;
Then the slow silver moment died in dark.
The wind came posting by with chilly gusts
And buffeting at the corners, piping thin.
And dreary through the crannies; rifle-shots
Would split and crack and sing along the night,
And shells came calmly through the drizzling air
To burst with hollow bang below the hill.

Three hours ago, he stumbled up the trench;
Now he will never walk that road again:
He must be carried back, a jolting lump
Beyond all needs of tenderness and care.
He was a young man with a meagre wife
And two small children in a Midland town,
He showed their photographs to all his mates,
And they considered him a decent chap
Who did his work and hadn't much to say,
And always laughed at other people's jokes
Because he hadn't any of his own.

That night when he was busy at his job
Of piling bags along the parapet,
He thought how slow time went, stamping his feet
And blowing on his fingers, pinched with cold.

He thought of getting back by half-past twelve,
And tot of rum to send him warm to sleep
In draughty dug-out frowsty with the fumes
Of coke, and full of snoring weary men.

He pushed another bag along the top,
Craning his body outward; then a flare
Gave one white glimpse of No Man's Land and wire;
And as he dropped his head the instant split
His startled life with lead, and all went out.

[30 March 1916]

SIEGFRIED SASSOON
➤ 58

'Written while in the Front Line during my first tour of the trenches.' [SS]

As the team's head brass

As the team's head brass flashed out on the turn
The lovers disappeared into the wood.
I sat among the boughs of the fallen elm
That strewed an angle of the fallow, and
Watched the plough narrowing a yellow square
Of charlock. Every time the horses turned
Instead of treading me down, the ploughman leaned
Upon the handles to say or ask a word,
About the weather, next about the war.
Scraping the share he faced towards the wood,
And screwed along the furrow till the brass flashed
Once more.
            The blizzard felled the elm whose crest
I sat in, by a woodpecker's round hole,
The ploughman said. 'When will they take it away?'
'When the war's over.' So the talk began –
One minute and an interval of ten,
A minute more and the same interval.

62

'Have you been out?' 'No.' 'And don't want to, perhaps?'
'If I could only come back again, I should.
I could spare an arm. I shouldn't want to lose
A leg. If I should lose my head, why, so,
I should want nothing more.... Have many gone
From here?' 'Yes.' 'Many lost?' 'Yes, a good few.
Only two teams work on the farm this year.
One of my mates is dead. The second day
In France they killed him. It was back in March,
The very night of the blizzard, too. Now if
He had stayed here we should have moved the tree.'
'And I should not have sat here. Everything
Would have been different. For it would have been
Another world.' 'Ay, and a better, though
If we could see all all might seem good.' Then
The lovers came out of the wood again:
The horses started and for the last time
I watched the clods crumble and topple over
After the ploughshare and the stumbling team.

[27 May 1916]

EDWARD THOMAS
➤ 49

The Silent One

Who died on the wires, and hung there, one of two –
Who for his hours of life had chattered through
Infinite lovely chatter of Bucks accent:
Yet faced unbroken wires; stepped over, and went
A noble fool, faithful to his stripes – and ended.
But I weak, hungry, and willing only for the chance
Of line – to fight in the line, lay down under unbroken
Wires, and saw the flashes and kept unshaken,
Till the politest voice – a finicking accent, said:
'Do you think you might crawl through there: there's a hole.'
Darkness, shot at: I smiled, as politely replied –

'I'm afraid not, Sir.' There was no hole no way to be seen,
Nothing but chance of death, after tearing of clothes.
Kept flat, and watched the darkness, hearing bullets whizzing–
And thought of music– and swore deep heart's deep oaths
(Polite to God) and retreated and came on again,
Again retreated– and a second time faced the screen.

IVOR GURNEY

Ivor Gurney (1890-1937) was a musician and composer as well as one of the
English poets who survived the First World War at great personal cost. Born
and Gloucester and raised in his beloved Gloucestershire, he left his studies
at the Royal College of Music to enlist as a private with the Gloucestershire
Regiment in February 1915, and was shipped to Flanders in May 1916. He
started writing poetry seriously while in the trenches. In April 1917 he was
shot in the arm, and treated in a military hospital in Rouen before being
transferred to a machine gun battery at Passchendaele. In September he was
gassed at St Julien and invalided back to Britain. Always prone to depression,
he suffered a progressive mental breakdown and was treated in various hospitals
until his discharge from the Army in October 1918. He then produced some
of his finest music during a period of continuing mental instability until being
certified insane and incarcerated for the last 15 years of his life.

His first book of poems, *Severn and Somme*, was published in 1917, and
the second, *War's Embers*, in 1919. 'The Silent One' was written either while
Gurney was at Barnwood House asylum, Gloucester, from September 1922,
or at Stone House, Dartford, Kent (City of London Mental Hospital) where
he stayed from December 1922 until his death from tuberculosis in 1937. 'His
mind inhabited the past. He continued writing songs until 1926, but their
quality diminished; his poetry, on the other hand, gathered quality and strength.
Gurney's best war poems belong to these asylum years; they have such imm-
ediacy it is as if, in his mind, the war carried on' (Anthony Boden). ➤ 108

Arthur Graeme West (1891-1917) wrote one of the most scathing, vivid and
disenchanted accounts of life in the trenches, published posthumously as *Diary
of a Dead Officer* (1919). Enlisting as a private in the Public Schools Battalion
in February 1915, he was posted to the front line in November. In August
1916 he was commissioned as an infantry 2nd lieutenant with the 'Ox and
Bucks'. He was killed by a chance sniper's bullet as he was leaving his trench
at Bapaume on 3 April 1917. This poem is a rejoinder to the first wave of
piously patriotic, sentimental war poets, and in particular, one H. Rex Freston
(remembered now only for West's attack on his verse): 'His attitude is that
God is good, amused, rather, at us fighting. "Oh happy to have lived in these
epic days," he writes (of us). This (he had been three years at Oxford) is his
address to the Atheists: "*I know that God will never let me die | He is too
passionate and intense for that.*"' Freston's sonnet continues in that vein...

God! How I hate you, you young cheerful men!

On an Oxford University undergraduate moved to verse by the war

God! How I hate you, you young cheerful men,
Whose pious poetry blossoms on your graves
As soon as you are in them, nurtured up
By the salt of your corruption, and the tears
Of mothers, local vicars, college deans,
And flanked by prefaces and photographs
From all your minor poet friends – the fools –
Who paint their sentimental elegies
Where sure, no angel treads; and, living, share
The dead's brief immortality.
                                    Oh Christ!
To think that one could spread the ductile wax
Of his fluid youth to Oxford's glowing fires
And take her seal so ill! Hark how one chants –
'Oh happy to have lived these epic days' –
'These epic days'! And *he'd* been to France,
And seen the trenches, glimpsed the huddled dead
In the periscope, hung in the rusting wire:
Choked by their sickly fœtor, day and night
Blown down his throat: stumbled through ruined hearths,
Proved all that muddy brown monotony,
Where blood's the only coloured thing. Perhaps
Had seen a man killed, a sentry shot at night,
Hunched as he fell, his feet on the firing-step,
His neck against the back slope of the trench,
And the rest doubled up between, his head
Smashed like an egg-shell, and the warm grey brain
Spattered all bloody on the parados:
Had flashed a torch on his face, and known his friend,
Shot, breathing hardly, in ten minutes – gone!
Yet still God's in His heaven, all is right
In the best possible of worlds. The woe,
Even His scaled eyes *must* see, is partial, only
A seeming woe, we cannot understand.
God loves us, God looks down on this out strife
And smiles in pity, blows a pipe at times

And calls some warriors home. We do not die,
God would not let us, He is too 'intense',
Too 'passionate', a whole day sorrows He
Because a grass-blade dies. How rare life is!
On earth, the love and fellowship of men,
Men sternly banded: banded for what end?
Banded to maim and kill their fellow men –
For even Huns are men. In heaven above
A genial umpire, a good judge of sport,
Won't let us hurt each other! Let's rejoice
God keeps us faithful, pens us still in fold.
Ah, what a faith is ours (almost, it seems,
Large as a mustard-seed) – we trust and trust,
Nothing can shake us! Ah, how good God is
To suffer us to be born just now, when youth
That else would rust, can slake his blade in gore,
Where very God Himself does seem to walk
The bloody fields of Flanders He so loves!

[1916 (?)]

ARTHUR GRAEME WEST

Break of Day in the Trenches

The darkness crumbles away.
It is the same old druid Time as ever,
Only a live thing leaps my hand,
A queer sardonic rat,
As I pull the parapet's poppy
To stick behind my ear.
Droll rat, they would shoot you if they knew
Your cosmopolitan sympathies.
Now you have touched this English hand
You will do the same to a German
Soon, no doubt, if it be your pleasure

To cross the sleeping green between.
It seems you inwardly grin as you pass
Strong eyes, fine limbs, haughty athletes,
Less chanced than you for life,
Bonds to the whims of murder,
Sprawled in the bowels of the earth,
The torn fields of France.
What do you see in our eyes
At the shrieking iron and flame
Hurled through still heavens?
What quaver – what heart aghast?
Poppies whose roots are in man's veins
Drop, and are ever dropping;
But mine in my ear is safe –
Just a little white with the dust.

[June 1916]

ISAAC ROSENBERG

Isaac Rosenberg (1890-1918) was the son of Jewish immigrants from Eastern Europe, and grew up in the East End of London. He left school at 14 to become an apprentice engraver. Later, he received financial help to study art at the Slade School but remained undecided between poetry and art. Edward Marsh, editor of the 'Georgian' anthologies, noticed his poetry. Rosenberg wrote to Marsh in 1916: 'The Homer for this war has yet to be found.' He told another friend that he disliked Rupert Brooke's 'begloried sonnets' because war 'should be approached in a colder way, more abstract, with less of the million feelings everybody feels; or all these should be concentrated in one distinguished emotion'. Rosenberg hated war ('Now is the time to go on an exploring expedition to the North Pole') but in 1915 he enlisted in the Suffolk Regiment to help his family out financially. [Edna Longley]

Rosenberg was assigned to a Suffolk "bantam battalion" for undersized recruits, and sent to France with the King's Own Royal Lancaster Regiment in June 1916. All the poems included in this selection were written in France, including his masterpiece 'Dead Man's Dump' [➤ 88], regarded by many critics as 'the greatest poem of the war' (Paul Fussell). He was killed returning from a night patrol at dawn on 1 April 1918 at Fampoux near Arras.

Rosenberg published two collections of poetry, *Night and Day* (1912) and *Youth* (1915), and a verse play, *Moses*, during his pre-embarkation leave, in May 1916. 'Break of Day in the Trenches' appeared in *Poetry* (Chicago) in December 1916, but his great war poems of 1916-17 were not published in a single volume until after the war, in 1922. ➤ 66, 86, 87, 88

from In Parenthesis

But sweet sister death has gone debauched today and stalks on this high ground with strumpet confidence, makes no coy veiling of her appetite but leers from you to me with all her parts discovered.

By one and one the line gaps, where her fancy will – howsoever they may howl for their virginity
she holds them – who impinge less on space
sink simply to a heap
nourish a lesser category of being
like those other who fructify the land
[...]

But how intolerably bright the morning is where we who are alive and remain, walk lifted up, carried forward by an effective word.

But red horses now – blare every trump without economy, burn boat and sever every tie every held thing goes west and tethering snapt, bolts unshot and brass doors flung wide and you go forward, foot goes another step further.

The immediate foreground sheers up, tilts toward,
like an high wall falling.
There she breaches black perpendiculars
where the counter-barrage warms to the seventh power where
the Three Children walk under the fair morning
and the Twin Brother [1]
and the high grass soddens through your puttees
and dew asperges the freshly dead.

There doesn't seem a soul about yet surely we walk already near his preserves; there goes old Dawes as large as life and there is Lazarus Cohen like on field-days, he always would have his entrenching-tool-blade-carrier hung low, jogging on his fat arse.

They pass a quite ordinary message about keeping aligned with No. 8.

You drop apprehensively – the sun gone out,
strange airs smite your body
and muck rains straight from heaven
and everlasting doors lift up for '02 Weavel.
    You cant see anything but sheen on drifting particles and you
move forward in your private bright cloud like
one assumed
who is borne up by an exterior volition.

You stumble on a bunch of six with Sergeant Quilter getting them
out again to the proper interval, and when the chemical thick air
dispels you see briefly and with great clearness what kind of a show
this is.

The gentle slopes are green to remind you
of South English places, only far wider and flatter spread and grooved
and harrowed criss-cross whitely and the disturbed subsoil heaped
up albescent.

Across upon this undulated board of verdure chequered bright
when you look to left and right
small, drab, bundled pawns severally make effort
moved in tenuous line
and if you looked behind – the next wave came slowly, as successive
surfs creep in to dissipate on flat shore;
and to your front, stretched long laterally,
and receded deeply,
the dark wood.

And now the gradient runs more flatly toward the separate scared
saplings, where they make fringe for the interior thicket and you
take notice.
    There between the thinning uprights
at the margin
straggle tangled oak and flayed sheeny beech-bole, and fragile birch
whose silver queenery is draggled and ungraced
and June shoots lopt
and fresh stalks bled
            runs the Jerry trench.
And cork-screw stapled trip-wire

to snare among the briars
and iron warp with bramble weft
with meadow-sweet and lady-smock
for a fair camouflage.

Mr Jenkins half inclined his head to them – he walked just barely in
advance of his platoon and immediately to the left of Private Ball.
    He makes the conventional sign
and there is the deeply inward effort of spent men who would make
response for him,
and take it at the double.
He sinks on one knee
and now on the other,
his upper body tilts in rigid inclination
this way and back;
weighted lanyard runs out to full tether,
                swings like a pendulum
                and the clock run down.
Lurched over, jerked iron saucer over tilted brow,
clampt unkindly over lip and chin
nor no ventaille to this darkening
                and masked face lifts to grope the air
and so disconsolate;
enfeebled fingering at a paltry strap –
buckle holds,
holds him blind against the morning.
    Then stretch still where weeds pattern the chalk predella – where
it rises to his wire[2] – and Sergeant T. Quilter takes over.

Sergeant Quilter is shouting his encouragements, you can almost
hear him, he opens his mouth so wide.
    Sergeant Quilter breaks into double-time
and so do the remainder.
    You stumble in a place of tentacle
you seek a place made straight
you unreasonably blame the artillery
you stand waist-deep
you stand upright
you stretch out hands to pluck at Jerry wire as if it were bramble
mesh.

No. 3 section inclined a little right where a sequence of 9.2's have done well their work of preparation and cratered a plain passage. They bunch, a bewildered half dozen, like sheep where the wall is tumbled – but high-perched Brandenburghers
from their leafy vantage-tops observe
that kind of folly:
nevertheless, you and one other walk alive before his parapets.

Yet a taut prehensile strand gets you at the instep, even so, and sprawls you useless to the First Objective. But Private Watcyn takes it with blameless technique, and even remembers to halloo the official blasphemies.[3]

The inorganic earth where your body presses seems itself to pulse deep down with your heart's acceleration...but you go on living, lying with your face bedded in neatly folded, red-piped, greatcoat and yet no cold cleaving thing drives in between expectant shoulder-blades, so you get to your feet, and the sun-lit chalk is everywhere absorbing fresh stains.

Dark gobbets stiften skewered to revetment-hurdles and dyed garments strung-up for a sign;
                    but the sun shines also
on the living
and on Private Watcyn, who wears a strange look under his iron brim, like a small child caught at some bravado in a garden, and old Dawes comes so queerly from the thing he saw in the next bay but one.

But for all that it is relatively pleasant here under the first trees and lying in good cover.

But Sergeant Quilter is already on the parados. He sorts them out a bit
they are five of No. 1
six of No. 2
two of No. 3 four of No. 4 a lance-jack, and a corporal.

So these nineteen deploy
between the rowan and the hazel,
go forward to the deeper shades.

And now all the wood-ways live with familiar faces and your mate moves like Jack o' the Green: for this season's fertility gone unpruned, & this year's renewing sap shot up fresh tendrils to cumber greenly the heaped decay of last fall, and no forester to tend the paths,

nor strike with axes to the root of selected boles, nor had come
Jacqueline to fill a pinafore with may-thorn.
But keepers who engineer new and powerful devices,
forewarned against this morning
prepared with booby-trap beneath
and platforms in the stronger branches
like main-top for an arbalestier,
precisely and competently advised and all in the know, as to this
hour when
                when unicorns break cover
and come down
and foxes flee, whose warrens know the shock,
and birds complain in flight – for their nests fall like stars
            and all their airy world gone crazed
and the whole woodland rocks where these break their horns.

It was largely his machine guns in Acid Copse that did it, and our
own heavies firing by map reference, with all lines phut and no
reliable liaison.

So you just lay where you were and shielded what you could of
your body.

It slackened a little and they try short rushes and you find your-
self alone in a denseness of hazel-brush and body high bramble
and between the bright interstices and multifarious green-stuff,
grey textile, scarlet-edged goes and comes – and there is another
withdrawing-heel from the thicket.

His light stick-bomb winged above your thorn-bush, and aged
oak-timbers shiver and leaves shower like thrown blossom for a
conqueror.
You tug at rusted pin –
it gives unexpectedly and your fingers pressed to released flange.
You loose the thing into the underbrush.

Dark-faceted iron oval lobs heavily to fungus-cushioned dank,
wobbles under low leaf to lie, near where the heel drew out just
now; and tough root-fibres boomerang to top-most green filigree
and earth clods flung disturb fresh fragile shoots that brush the
sky.

You huddle closer to your mossy bed
you make yourself scarce
you scramble forward and pretend not to see,

but ruby drops from young beech-sprigs –
are bright your hands and face.

And the other one cries from the breaking-buckthorn.

He calls for Elsa, for Manuela
for the parish priest of Burkersdorf in Saxe Altenburg.

You grab his dropt stick-bomb as you go, but somehow you don't fancy it and anyway you forget how it works. You definitely like the coloured label on the handle,[4] you throw it to the tall wood-weeds.

So double detonations, back and fro like well-played-up-to service at a net, mark left and right the forcing of the groves.

But there where a small pathway winds and sun shafts play, a dozen of them walk toward, they come in file, their lifted arms like Jansenist Redeemers, who would save, at least, themselves.[5] Some come furtively who peer sideways, inquisitive of their captors, and one hides a face twisted for intolerable pain and one other casts about him, acutely, as who would take his opportunity, but for the most part they come as sleepwalkers whose bodies go unbidden of the mind, without malevolence, seeking only rest.

[...]

Now you looked about you for what next to do, or you fired blindly among the trees and ventured a little further inward; but already, diagonally to your front, they were coming back in ones and twos.

You wished you could see people you knew better than the 'C' Company man on your right or the bloke from 'A' on your left, there were certainly a few of No. 8, but not a soul of your own – which ever way.

No mess-mates at call in cool interior aisles, where the light came muted, filtered from high up traceries, varied a refracted lozenge-play on pale cheeks turned; on the bowels of Sergeant Quilter,
and across feet that hasted
and awkward for anxiety,
            and behind your hurrying
you could hear his tripod's clank[6] nearer than just now.
But where four spreading beeches stood in line and the ground
shelved away about splayed-out roots to afford them cover
Dawes and Diamond Phelps
and the man from Rotherhithe

with five more from 'D', and two H.Q. details, and two from some other unit altogether.

And next to Diamond, and newly dead the lance-jack from No. 5, and three besides, distinguished only in their variant mutilation.

DAVID JONES

AUTHOR'S NOTES:

1. *seventh power... Three Children... Twin Brother.* Cf. Book of Daniel, ch. III. 'Here I identify 'The Great Twin Brethren' at the battle of Lake Regillus with the Second Person of the Blessed Trinity – who walked with the Three Children in the fiery furnace. 2. *chalk predella...his wire.* The approach to the German trenches here rose slightly, in low chalk ridges. 3. *halloo the official blasphemies.* Refers to instructions given in bayonet-fighting drill. Men were cautioned to look fiercely upon the enemy when engaging him and to shout some violent word – and to not spare his genitals. This attempt to stimulate an artificial hate by parade-ground Staff-Instruction was not popular among men fresh from actual contact with the enemy. 4. *coloured label on the handle.* I cannot recall what it was, either stamped or labelled on the handle of a German stick-bomb, but I know the sight of it gave me some kind of pleasure – just as one likes any foreign manufacture, I suppose. 5. *Jansenist Redeemers... themselves.* There are crucifixes attributed to the Jansenists with our Lord's arms stretched narrowly above the head indicative of their error concerning the exclusiveness of the redemptive act. 6. *tripod's clank.* The movement of a German machine gun was often recognisable by the clank of chain or of some metal on metal.

David Jones (1895-1974) published his book-length epic *In Parenthesis* in 1937, twenty years after the wartime experiences it draws upon. 'This writing has to do with some things I saw, felt, & was part of,' he wrote in a preface. 'The period covered begins early in December 1915 and ends early in July 1916.' [The extracts in this selection are from section VII, relating to the attack on Mametz Wood during the Battle of the Somme on 10-11 July 1916, when Jones was wounded, and his company – unknown to him at the time – was relieving Sassoon's. Sassoon's poem 'A Night Attack' [➤ 75] dates from that time.

'This writing is called "In Parenthesis" because I have written it in a kind of space between – I don't know between quite what – but as you turn aside to do something; and because for us amateur soldiers (and especially for the writer, who was not only amateur, but grotesquely incompetent, a knocker-over of piles [rifle stacks], a parade's despair) the war itself was a parenthesis – how glad we thought we were to step outside its brackets at the end of '18 – and also because our curious existence here is altogether in parenthesis.'

His publisher T.S. Eliot called *In Parenthesis* 'a work of genius', while for W.H. Auden it was 'the greatest book about the First World War' he had read, a work in which Jones did 'for the British and the Germans what Homer did for the Greeks and the Trojans' in 'a masterpiece' comparable in quality to Dante's *Divine Comedy*.

David Jones was both an artist and a poet, an innovative painter, engraver and calligrapher known for his religious art and 'painted inscriptions' as well as a major figure in 20th-century Modernist poetry. Born to a Welsh father in Brockley, Kent, he became fascinated as a child with all things Welsh, his interest in the language, songs, poetry and mythology stimulated by family visits to North Wales. Years later, amid the chaos and horror of the trenches, he recalls lines and images from all he'd read and absorbed – Aneirin's Welsh epic *Y Goddodin* (6th century), Malory's *Morte d'Arthur*, the Bible… – and this synthesis of ancient, medieval and modern registers in the writing of *In Parenthesis* helps him make sense of his own part, as an 'individual rifle-man' caught up in 'the wholesale slaughter'.

Jones enlisted as a private in the Royal Welch Fusiliers in January 1915, embarking for France in December of that year. Wounded on the Somme in July 1916, he returned from convalescence in England that autumn, serving as an observer with the 2nd Field Survey Company at Ploegsteert Wood, and saw action again on the Ypres salient at Bosinghe, Pilkem Ridge, Langemark and Passchendaele. He was evacuated to Ireland in February 1918 suffering from trench fever.

A Night Attack

The rank stench of those bodies haunts me still,
And I remember things I'd best forget.
For now we've marched to a green, trenchless land
Twelve miles from battering guns: along the grass
Brown lines of tents are hives for snoring men;
Wide, radiant water sways the floating sky
Below dark, shivering trees. And living-clean
Comes back with thoughts of home and hours of sleep.

Tonight I smell the battle; miles away
Gun-thunder leaps and thuds along the ridge;
The spouting shells dig pits in fields of death,
And wounded men, are moaning in the woods.
If any friend be there whom I have loved,
God speed him safe to England with a gash.

It's sundown in the camp; some youngster laughs,
Lifting his mug and drinking health to all
Who come unscathed from that unpitying waste.

(Terror and ruin lurk behind his gaze.)
Another sits with tranquil, musing face,
Puffing his pipe and dreaming of the girl
Whose last scrawled letter lies upon his knee.
The sunlight falls, low-ruddy from the west,
Upon their heads; last week they might have died;
And now they stretch their limbs in tired content.

One says 'The bloody Bosche has got the knock;
And soon they'll crumple up and chuck their games.
We've got the beggars on the run at last!'
    Then I remembered someone that I'd seen
Dead in a squalid, miserable ditch,
Heedless of toiling feet that trod him down.
He was a Prussian with a decent face,
Young, fresh, and pleasant, so I dare to say.
No doubt he loathed the war and longed for peace,
And cursed our souls because we'd killed his friends.

One night he yawned along a half-dug trench
Midnight; and then the British guns began
With heavy shrapnel bursting low, and 'hows'
Whistling to cut the wire with blinding din.
    He didn't move; the digging still went on;
Men stooped and shovelled; someone gave a grunt,
And moaned and died with agony in the sludge.
Then the long hiss of shells lifted and stopped.

He stared into the gloom; a rocket curved,
And rifles rattled angrily on the left
Down by the wood, and there was noise of bombs.
    Then the damned English loomed in scrambling haste
Out of the dark and struggled through the wire,
And there were shouts and curses; someone screamed
And men began to blunder down the trench
Without their rifles. It was time to go:
He grabbed his coat; stood up, gulping some bread;
Then clutched his head and fell.
                    I found him there
In the gray morning when the place was held.

His face was in the mud; one arm flung out
As when he crumpled up; his sturdy legs
Were bent beneath his trunk; heels to the sky

[July 1916]

SIEGFRIED SASSOON
➤ 58

Counter-Attack

We'd gained our first objective hours before
While dawn broke like a face with blinking eyes,
Pallid, unshaved and thirsty, blind with smoke.
Things seemed all right at first. We held their line,
With bombers posted, Lewis guns well placed,
And clink of shovels deepening the shallow trench.
The place was rotten with dead; green clumsy legs
High-booted, sprawled and grovelled along the saps
And trunks, face downward, in the sucking mud,
Wallowed like trodden sand-bags loosely filled;
And naked sodden buttocks, mats of hair,
Bulged, clotted heads slept in the plastering slime.
And then the rain began, – the jolly old rain!

A yawning soldier knelt against the bank,
Staring across the morning blear with fog;
He wondered when the Allemands would get busy;
And then, of course, they started with five-nines[1]
Traversing, sure as fate, and never a dud.
Mute in the clamour of shells he watched them burst
Spouting dark earth and wire with gusts from hell,
While posturing giants dissolved in drifts of smoke.
He crouched and flinched, dizzy with galloping fear,
Sick for escape, – loathing the strangled horror
And butchered, frantic gestures of the dead.

An officer came blundering down the trench:
'Stand-to and man the fire-step!' On he went...

Gasping and bawling, 'Fire-step...counter-attack!'
Then the haze lifted. Bombing on the right
Down the old sap: machine-guns on the left;
And stumbling figures looming out in front.
'O Christ, they're coming at us!' Bullets spat,
And he remembered his rifle...rapid fire...
And started blazing wildly...then a bang
Crumpled and spun him sideways, knocked him out
To grunt and wriggle: none heeded him; he choked
And fought the flapping veils of smothering gloom,
Lost in a blurred confusion of yells and groans...
Down, and down, and down, he sank and drowned,
Bleeding to death. The counter-attack had failed.

[Craiglockhart, 1917, from a July 1916 draft]

SIEGFRIED SASSOON
➤ 58

1. *five-nines:* 5.9-inch (150 mm) artillery shells used by the Germans to deliver poison gas. Men who stood up on the fire-step were less affected by the gas than those who lay down or sat at the bottom of a trench where it was denser.

The Rivers

I hang on to this mangled tree
abandoned in this sinkhole
that is listless
as a circus
before or after the show
and watch
the quiet passage
of clouds across the moon

This morning I stretched out
in an urn of water
and rested
like a relic

The flowing Isonzo
smoothed me
like one of its stones

I hoisted up
my sack of bones
and got out of there
like an acrobat
over the water

I crouched
beside my grimy
battle clothes
and like a Bedouin
bent to greet
the sun

This is the Isonzo
and here I recognised myself
more clearly
as a pliant fibre
of the universe

My affliction
is when
I don't believe myself
in harmony

But those hidden
hands
that knead me
freely give
the uncommon
bliss

I went back over
the ages
of my life

These are
my rivers

This is the Serchio[1]
where maybe
two millennia of my farming people
and my father and mother
drew their water

This is the Nile[2]
that saw me
born and raised
and burn with unawareness
on the sweeping flatlands

This is the Seine[3]
within whose roiling waters
I was mixed again
and came to know myself

These are my rivers
reckoned in the Isonzo

This is my longing for home
that in each one
shines through me
now that it's night
that my life seems
a corolla
of darkness

[Cotici, 16 August 1916][4]

GIUSEPPE UNGARETTI

translated from the Italian by Andrew Frisardi
➤ 48

1. Serchio, the Tuscan river which watered the farmland where Ungaretti's
ancestors lived. 2. The Nile, from his birthplace in Egypt. 3. The Seine and
Paris, where he lived before the war and discovered his vocation. 4. 'The date
of this poem is very significant: one day before the end of an important battle,
Italy's first victory against Austria at the Isonzo River.[...] Eventually the
Germans sent reinforcements to help the Austrian army, and on November 7
the Italian army suffered "one of the worst defeats on Italian history".' [Tr.]

The Hero

'Jack fell as he'd have wished,' the Mother said,
And folded up the letter that she'd read.
'The Colonel writes so nicely.' Something broke
In the tired voice that quavered to a choke.
She half looked up. 'We mothers are so proud
Of our dead soldiers.' Then her face was bowed.

Quietly the Brother Officer went out.
He'd told the poor old dear some gallant lies
That she would nourish all her days, no doubt
For while he coughed and mumbled, her weak eyes
Had shone with gentle triumph, brimmed with joy,
Because he'd been so brave, her glorious boy.

He thought how 'Jack', cold-footed, useless swine,
Had panicked down the trench that night the mine
Went up at Wicked Corner; how he'd tried
To get sent home, and how, at last, he died,
Blown to small bits. And no one seemed to care
Except that lonely woman with white hair.

[August 1916]

SIEGFRIED SASSOON
➤ 58

The Sentry

We'd found an old Boche dug-out,[1] and he knew,
And gave us hell; for shell on frantic shell
Lit full on top, but never quite burst through.
Rain, guttering down in waterfalls of slime,
Kept slush waist-high and rising hour by hour,
And choked the steps too thick with clay to climb.

81

What murk of air remained stank old, and sour
With fumes from whizz-bangs,[2] and the smell of men
Who'd lived there years, and left their curse in the den,
If not their corpses...
                There we herded from the blast
Of whizz-bangs; but one found our door at last, –
Buffeting eyes and breath, snuffing the candles.
And thud! flump! thud! down the steep steps came thumping
And sploshing in the flood, deluging muck,
The sentry's body; then his rifle, handles
Of old Boche bombs, and mud in ruck on ruck.
We dredged it up, for dead, until he whined,
'O sir – my eyes – I'm blind, – I'm blind, – I'm blind.'
Coaxing, I held a flame against his lids
And said if he could see the least blurred light
He was not blind; in time they'd get all right.
'I can't,' he sobbed. Eyeballs, huge-bulged like squids',
Watch my dreams still, – yet I forgot him there
In posting Next for duty, and sending a scout
To beg a stretcher somewhere, and flound'ring about
To other posts under the shrieking air.

Those other wretches, how they bled and spewed,
And one who would have drowned himself for good, –
I try not to remember these things now.
Let Dread hark back for one word only: how
Half-listening to that sentry's moans and jumps,
And the wild chattering of his shivered teeth,
Renewed most horribly whenever crumps
Pummelled the roof and slogged the air beneath, –
Through the dense din, I say, we heard him shout
'I see your lights!' – But ours had long gone out.

[Based on an incident in January 1917; begun at Craiglockhart,
August–October 1917; finished in France, September 1918]

WILFRED OWEN

1. *dug-out:* a covered excavation dug to provide shelter. 2. *whizz-bangs:* high
velocity shells.

Wilfred Owen (1893-1918) was the foremost British poet of the First World War, but only five of his poems were published in his lifetime. Working as a tutor in France when war was declared, he returned to England during the summer of 1915, enlisted with the Artists' Rifles in October, and was later commissioned as a 2nd Lieutenant.

Arriving in France on 1 January 1917, he joined the 2nd Manchester Regiment as an officer reinforcement in charge of 'A' Company in the front line at Serre. 'The Sentry' was based on an incident on 12 January when his platoon occupied a former German bunker in No Man's Land, as he told his mother: 'In the Platoon on my left the sentries over the dug-out were blown to nothing. One of these poor fellows was my first servant whom I rejected. If I had kept him he would have lived, for servants don't do Sentry Duty. I kept my own sentries half way down the stairs during the more terrific bombardment. In spite of this one lad was blown down and, I am afraid, blinded.' [Letter to Mrs Susan Owen, 16 January 1917]

Edna Longley writes: 'His trench poems are based on four months in France from January 1917. In June he was sent to Craiglockhart War Hospital near Edinburgh suffering from shellshock. In August 1917 he met Siegfried Sassoon there. [> 58] Owen returned to France, and was killed a week before the Armistice. [...] Owen's mature poems date from meeting Sassoon, whose example and criticism, Owen said, '*fixed* my Life'. Yet, as Louis MacNeice observes, the war "could only make [Owen] a poet thanks to the lesser poet whom it broke in him". His powerfully immediate images reinvent Keats's doctrine of 'Negative Capability', of receptivity to experience. It becomes an art of empathy: Owen termed himself "a conscientious objector with a very seared conscience". Like Rosenberg, he turns the trench landscape into an elemental and cosmic space.'

In his preface to the book of poems he never saw published, he wrote of his work: 'Above all I am not concerned with Poetry. My subject is War, and the pity of War. The Poetry is in the pity. Yet these elegies are to this generation in no sense consolatory. They may be to the next. All a poet can do today is warn. That is why the true Poets must be truthful.'

Owen was shot while helping his men to cross the Sambre-Oise Canal on 4 November 1918, aged 25, a week before the Armistice was signed. This selection includes eight poems by Owen: > 81, 97, 99, 103, 104, 106, 109, 111

Base Details

If I were fierce, and bald, and short of breath,
    I'd live with scarlet Majors at the Base,
And speed glum heroes up the line to death.
    You'd see me with my puffy petulant face,
Guzzling and gulping in the best hotel,

Reading the Roll of Honour. 'Poor young chap,'
I'd say – 'I used to know his father well;
    Yes, we've lost heavily in this last scrap.'
And when the war is done and youth stone dead,
I'd toddle safely home and die – in bed.

[Rouen, 4 March 1917]

SIEGFRIED SASSOON
➤ 58

The Rear-Guard

(Hindenburg Line, April 1917)

Groping along the tunnel, step by step,
He winked his prying torch with patching glare
From side to side, and sniffed the unwholesome air.

Tins, boxes, bottles, shapes too vague to know;
A mirror smashed, the mattress from a bed;
And he, exploring fifty feet below
The rosy gloom of battle overhead.

Tripping, he grabbed the wall; saw some one lie
Humped at his feet, half-hidden by a rug,
And stooped to give the sleeper's arm a tug.
'I'm looking for headquarters.' No reply.
'God blast your neck!' (For days he'd had no sleep,)
'Get up and guide me through this stinking place.'

Savage, he kicked a soft, unanswering heap,
And flashed his beam across the livid face
Terribly glaring up, whose eyes yet wore
Agony dying hard ten days before;
And fists of fingers clutched a blackening wound.

Alone he staggered on until he found
Dawn's ghost that filtered down a shafted stair

To the dazed, muttering creatures underground
Who hear the boom of shells in muffled sound.
At last, with sweat of horror in his hair,
He climbed through darkness to the twilight air,
Unloading hell behind him step by step.

[22 April 1917]

SIEGFRIED SASSOON

'Written at Denmark Hill Hospital about ten days after I was wounded. Gosse, after seeing me there, wrote to Uncle Hamo that he thought I was suffering from severe shock. But if so, could I have written such a strong poem?' [SS]

Attack

At dawn the ridge emerges massed and dun
In the wild purple of the glow'ring sun,
Smouldering through spouts of drifting smoke that shroud
The menacing scarred slope; and, one by one,
Tanks creep and topple forward to the wire.
The barrage roars and lifts. Then, clumsily bowed
With bombs and guns and shovels and battle-gear,
Men jostle and climb to, meet the bristling fire.
Lines of grey, muttering faces, masked with fear,
They leave their trenches, going over the top,
While time ticks blank and busy on their wrists,
And hope, with furtive eyes and grappling fists,
Flounders in mud. O Jesus, make it stop!

[Craiglockart, 1917]

SIEGFRIED SASSOON

'From a note in my diary while observing the Hindenburg Line attack.' [SS]
Published in the liberal *Cambridge Magazine*, 20 October 1917.

The General

'Good-morning; good-morning!' the General said
When we met him last week on our way to the line.
Now the soldiers he smiled at are most of 'em dead,
And we're cursing his staff for incompetent swine.
'He's a cheery old card,' grunted Harry to Jack
As they slogged up to Arras with rifle and pack.

                    .   .   .   .

But he did for them both by his plan of attack.

[Denmark Hill Hospital, April 1917]

SIEGFRIED SASSOON
➤ 58

Louse Hunting

Nudes – stark and glistening,
Yelling in lurid glee. Grinning faces
And raging limbs
Whirl over the floor one fire.
For a shirt verminously busy
Yon soldier tore from his throat, with oaths
Godhead might shrink at, but not the lice.
And soon the shirt was aflare
Over the candle he'd lit while we lay.

Then we all sprang up and stript
To hunt the verminous brood.
Soon like a demons' pantomime
The place was raging.
See the silhouettes agape,
See the gibbering shadows
Mixed with the battled arms on the wall.

See gargantuan hooked fingers
Pluck in supreme flesh
To smutch supreme littleness.
See the merry limbs in hot Highland fling
Because some wizard vermin
Charmed from the quiet this revel
When our ears were half lulled
By the dark music
Blown from Sleep's trumpet.

[1917]

ISAAC ROSENBERG
➤ 67

Returning, we hear the Larks

Sombre the night is.
And though we have our lives, we know
What sinister threat lurks there.

Dragging these anguished limbs, we only know
This poison-blasted track opens on our camp –
On a little safe sleep.

But hark! joy – joy – strange joy.
Lo! heights of night ringing with unseen larks.
Music showering our upturned list'ning faces.

Death could drop from the dark
As easily as song –
But song only dropped,
Like a blind man's dreams on the sand
By dangerous tides,
Like a girl's dark hair for she dreams no ruin lies there,
Or her kisses where a serpent hides.

[1917]

ISAAC ROSENBERG

Dead Man's Dump

The plunging limbers over the shattered track
Racketed with their rusty freight,
Stuck out like many crowns of thorns,
And the rusty stakes like sceptres old
To stay the flood of brutish men
Upon our brothers dear.

The wheels lurched over sprawled dead
But pained them not, though their bones crunched,
Their shut mouths made no moan,
They lie there huddled, friend and foeman,
Man born of man, and born of woman,
And shells go crying over them
From night till night and now.

Earth has waited for them
All the time of their growth
Fretting for their decay:
Now she has them at last!
In the strength of their strength
Suspended – stopped and held.

What fierce imaginings their dark souls lit
Earth! have they gone into you?
Somewhere they must have gone,
And flung on your hard back
Is their souls' sack,
Emptied of God-ancestralled essences.
Who hurled them out? Who hurled?

None saw their spirits' shadow shake the grass,
Or stood aside for the half used life to pass
Out of those doomed nostrils and the doomed mouth,
When the swift iron burning bee
Drained the wild honey of their youth.

What of us, who flung on the shrieking pyre,
Walk, our usual thoughts untouched,
Our lucky limbs as on ichor fed,
Immortal seeming ever?
Perhaps when the flames beat loud on us,
A fear may choke in our veins
And the startled blood may stop.

The air is loud with death,
The dark air spurts with fire
The explosions ceaseless are.
Timelessly now, some minutes past,
These dead strode time with vigorous life,
Till the shrapnel called 'an end!'
But not to all. In bleeding pangs
Some borne on stretchers dreamed of home,
Dear things, war-blotted from their hearts.

A man's brains splattered on
A stretcher-bearer's face;
His shook shoulders slipped their load,
But when they bent to look again
The drowning soul was sunk too deep
For human tenderness.

They left this dead with the older dead,
Stretched at the cross roads.

Burnt black by strange decay,
Their sinister faces lie
The lid over each eye,
The grass and coloured clay
More motion have than they,
Joined to the great sunk silences.

Here is one not long dead;
His dark hearing caught our far wheels,
And the choked soul stretched weak hands
To reach the living word the far wheels said,
The blood-dazed intelligence beating for light,

Crying through the suspense of the far torturing wheels
Swift for the end to break,
Or the wheels to break,
Cried as the tide of the world broke over his sight.

Will they come? Will they ever come?
Even as the mixed hoofs of the mules,
The quivering-bellied mules,
And the rushing wheels all mixed
With his tortured upturned sight,
So we crashed round the bend,
We heard his weak scream,
We heard his very last sound,
And our wheels grazed his dead face.

[14 May 1917]

ISAAC ROSENBERG
➤ 67

French Soldiers Mutiny – 1917

For years the troops have gone
like lambs to the slaughter

but these are bleating
They are marching through the town

They are marching
and they are bleating like sheep

By bleating they cease to be
a herd of sheep

ERICH FRIED
translated from the German by Stuart Hood
➤ 309

Mutinying French soldiers did actually bleat as a protest. [EF]

The women say...

The women say: Yes, of course,
It's sad. All those young men!
And they don't always receive the best of care. One can't do
    everything, can one?

A friend of ours who did some hospital work
(The one with the military cross)
Told us. Oh, it is sad.

But even so.
If we were to pay attention to that Barbusse [1]
– That Latzko,[2] said the other one opposite –
Oh, no, no, dear. That would be too awful.
No, no.

If it was as they say, don't you agree,
So horrible,
We couldn't bear it,
We are not so hard-hearted,
It's just not possible.

Besides, my brother, the captain,
Writes to say that it's being exaggerated...
That there are actually good times,
Times of enthusiasm, like when they attack, eh?
Another cup of tea, dear?
(We've been able to save a bit of sugar.)

MARCEL MARTINET
translated from the French by Michael Copp
➤ 92

---

1. Henri Barbusse (1873-1935). His realistic novel *Le Feu* (Under Fire), one of
the first war novels to be published (1916), was based on his experiences in
the trenches. 2. Andreas Latzko (1876-1943). His anti-war novel, *Menschen im
Krieg*, was published in Zurich in 1917, and was soon translated into French
as *Hommes dans la Guerre* (Men in War). [Tr.]

Medals

Disabled men,
With ribbons and crosses on your chests,
You are heroes, today.

Disabled men,
With ribbons and crosses on your chests,
Tomorrow, at your bosses' workplace,
You will be clumsier workers,
Worse paid,
Your children will go hungry.

And if tomorrow, tomorrow even,
We say to you
That you have spilled your blood
For your masters to become harsher masters,
You will raise your stumps against us,
Your crutches of glory and pain,
Disabled men, with your ribbons and crosses,
Who won't accept that you suffered for nothing.

MARCEL MARTINET
translated from the French by Michael Copp

Marcel Martinet (1887-1944) was a poet, novelist, playwright and political writer. Exempt from military service for health reasons, he spent the war in Paris. His political activity and various writings bear witness to the intensity of his desire to end war and to push for the development of an international syndicalist movement. The two poems here are both from *Les Temps Maudits* (1917), which includes many of his typically ferocious anti-war poems. To avoid the censor's wrath or possible imprisonment, he had the poems published in Switzerland, and distributed in *samizdat* form. [Michael Copp] ➤ 91

Siegfried Sassoon [➤ 58] wrote his famous protest after convalescing at Lady Ottoline Morrell's house where he'd met prominent pacifists including Bertrand Russell. Read out in Parliament on 30 July, his statement was published in *The Times* the following day. To save him from being court-martialled and executed, Robert Graves used his influence to have Sassoon declared medically unfit, supported by the War Office which didn't want a high profile martyr to the pacifist cause. Sassoon was admitted to Craiglockhart War Hospital near Edinburgh, to be treated neurasthenia (shellshock), where he was later joined by Wilfred Owen.

A Soldier's Declaration

I am making this statement as an act of wilful defiance of military authority, because I believe that the War is being deliberately prolonged by those who have the power to end it. I am a soldier, convinced that I am acting on behalf of soldiers. I believe that this War, on which I entered as a war of defence and liberation, has now become a war of aggression and conquest. I believe that the purpose for which I and my fellow soldiers entered upon this war should have been so clearly stated as to have made it impossible to change them, and that, had this been done, the objects which actuated us would now be attainable by negotiation. I have seen and endured the sufferings of the troops, and I can no longer be a party to prolong these sufferings for ends which I believe to be evil and unjust. I am not protesting against the conduct of the War, but against the political errors and insincerities for which the fighting men are being sacrificed. On behalf of those who are suffering now, I make this protest against the deception which is being practised on them; also I believe that I may help to destroy the callous complacence with which the majority of those at home regard the continuance of agonies which they do not share, and which they have not sufficient imagination to realise.

[15 June 1917]

SIEGFRIED SASSOON

Still Life

1

An expanse of punctured fields
Where the mouths of craters gape
In the billowing earth.

Death has passed its shearing knife
A hundred times, over man
And object – everything.

And, scattered in all directions,
Logs of wood float
Like spars on the motionless mud.

II

The sky above is hollowed out
Like a split-open barrel,
A bottomless gulf.

The sun's dead eye moves over
The colourless water in the trench,
Mud-coloured, sulphur-coloured.

And beneath the crust of embankments,
Where the pus-like slime streams,
The pock-marked plain suffers.

III

Square-shaped pieces of rubble
Carefully lined up along
A deeply furrowed track.

A lunar soil studded
With holes that stick together
Like globules in a bowl of soup.

Here and there a few bodies stick up
Among the stones: here lies
Some village or other.

IV

That's a forgotten corpse.
It's hard work to get round it
On the saturated khaki soil.

The mud which has given it back twenty times
Doesn't want to lose it, and so
It tucks it away in its turbulent belly.

It's neither French nor Prussian,
Just a bit of man, rather less than nothing.
It emerges from nothingness...and goes back again..

[Verdun, 1917]

HENRY-JACQUES
translated from the French by Michael Copp

The Mass Grave

Lads, struck down as they climbed out on to the plain,
All of them thrown on to the edge of a sap.
Their faces preserve their last human expression
And their nullified movements still seem warm.

Flattened corpses wearing their miserable uniforms,
Here in the open air they have lost the harmonious contours
They possessed as beings when life encircled their flesh.
It is as though death misrepresents their shapes.

Their feet hang down as stiff as bits of wood,
As you go past you bump against heavy boots.
Staring wide-eyed through his glassy pupils
A corpse continues to point at some distant object.

They are piled up, in tragic overlapping postures
Or side by side, friends in affliction and sleep.
Beneath them blood spreads and blackens in the sun;
Their wounds are already covered with flies.

Several stare at the sky they can no longer see.
Please God, see to it they neither remember or hate.
Without respite, they keep on bringing them on stretchers
To the monstrous charnel pit manured by the slaughterhouse.

We would like to close our eyes, but we keep on looking
Just the same, racked by a feeling of gloomy despair.
O hide these martyrs or else tonight we will have
The hideous nightmare of their haggard faces.

Just thinking about this terrible word: death,
And seeing so many livid, crucified corpses,
We end up doubting everything, including ourselves...
But the suffering is here and says to us: you are still alive!

[Champagne, May 1917]

HENRY-JACQUES
translated from the French by Michael Copp

Henry-Jacques [Henri Edmond Jacques] (1886-1973) wrote a number of novels of seafaring life, based on his experiences as a sailor on a three-masted merchant vessel, including two voyages round Cape Horn, in the early years of the 20th century. In 1904 he volunteered for army service with the 89th Infantry regiment. This lasted until 1907 when he passed into the Active Reserve of the Army. From 1909 until the outbreak of war he worked as a journalist. He was recalled to active service with the 25th Infantry Regiment on 3 August 1914. At his own request he remained a Private, 2nd class. In September 1915 he was wounded in the right shoulder by a shell splinter and evacuated. In August 1916, at Chailly on the Somme, he was again wounded by a shell splinter, was again evacuated, and resumed active service in December 1916. In August 1917 illness caused him to be evacuated for the third time. He rejoined his Depot in December 1917, by which time his war was over. He received the Croix de Guerre, and also held the rank of Officier de la Légion d'Honneur. His military dossier includes the information: 'On 1 March 1917 he was awarded the Military Medal by His Majesty the King of England.'

    Many of his war poems are dedicated to specific individuals, either to fellow soldiers who served with him in the 25th Infantry Regiment, or to other soldier-writers such as Maurice Genevoix, author of the outstanding tetralogy, *Ceux de 14* (1922). Rupert Brooke and Wilfred Owen are joint dedicatees of another poem. No poet has surpassed Henry-Jacques in so vividly and so vigorously conveying the harsh reality of the terrible carnage of the war, and of the muddy, blood-drenched suffering it entailed. He compels the reader to confront the ghastly aspects of war with clinical remorselessness.   [Michael Copp] ➢ 93, 95, 117, 118, 119

The Dead-Beat

He dropped, – more sullenly than wearily,
Lay stupid like a cod, heavy like meat,
And none of us could kick him to his feet;
– Just blinked at my revolver, blearily;
– Didn't appear to know a war was on,
Or see the blasted trench at which he stared.
'I'll do 'em in,' he whined. 'If this hand's spared,
I'll murder them, I will.'

      A low voice said,
'It's Blighty,¹ p'raps, he sees; his pluck's all gone,
Dreaming of all the valiant, that *aren't* dead:
Bold uncles, smiling ministerially;
Maybe his brave young wife, getting her fun
In some new home, improved materially.
It's not these stiffs have crazed him; nor the Hun.'

We sent him down at last, out of the way.
Unwounded; – stout lad, too, before that strafe.
Malingering? Stretcher-bearers winked, 'Not half!'

Next day I heard the Doc's well-whiskied laugh:
'That scum you sent last night soon died. Hooray!'

[Begun at Craiglockhart, 22 August 1917; revised March–May 1918]

WILFRED OWEN
➤ 83

1. *Blighty:* Britain (sentimental slang). A 'Blighty wound' was one serious enough to need recuperation away from the trenches, but not serious enough to kill or maim; was hoped for by many soldiers, and might be self-inflicted.

Pluck

Crippled for life at seventeen,
  His great eyes seems to question why:
With both legs smashed it might have been
    Better in that grim trench to die
    Than drag maimed years out helplessly.

A child – so wasted and so white,
  He told a lie to get his way,
To march, a man with men, and fight
    While other boys are still at play.
    A gallant lie your heart will say.

So broke with pain, he shrinks in dread
  To see the 'dresser' drawing near;
And winds the clothes about his head
    That none may see his heart-sick fear.
    His shaking, strangled sobs you hear.

But when the dreaded moment's there
  He'll face us all, a soldier yet,
Watch his bared wounds with unmoved air,
    (Though tell-tale lashes still are wet),
    And smoke his Woodbine cigarette.

EVA DOBELL

Eva Dobell (1876-1963) was a Gloucestershire writer who volunteered as a nurse during the First World War, writing a number of poems about wounded soldiers. She also took part in the morale-boosting work of writing to prisoners of war.

Yvan Goll (1891-1950) was a bilingual French-German poet, novelist and dramatist whose work synthesised German Expressionism and French Surrealism. He grew up in Lorraine, then a predominantly French-speaking part of Germany, escaping to Switzerland at the outbreak of the First World War to avoid conscription. Later persecuted as a Jew, he spent the Second World War in exile in the US. ➤ 99

Anthem for Doomed Youth

What passing-bells for these who die as cattle?
   – Only the monstrous anger of the guns.
   Only the stuttering rifles' rapid rattle
Can patter out their hasty orisons.
No mockeries now for them; no prayers nor bells;
   Nor any voice of mourning save the choirs, –
The shrill, demented choirs of wailing shells;
   And bugles calling for them from sad shires.

What candles may be held to speed them all?
   Not in the hands of boys but in their eyes
Shall shine the holy glimmers of goodbyes.
   The pallor of girls' brows shall be their pall;
Their flowers the tenderness of patient minds,
And each slow dusk a drawing-down of blinds.

[Craiglockhart, September–October 1917]

WILFRED OWEN
➤ 83

from Requiem for the Dead of Europe

Recitative (VIII)

Like a grey wall around Europe
The long battle ran.
The never-ending battle, the bogged-down battle, the softening-up
    battle,
The battle that was never the final battle.
Oh, the monotony of trench-warfare! Oh, trench-grave!
Oh, sleep of starvation!
The bridges built of corpses!
The roads surfaced with corpses!
The walls cemented with corpses!

For months on end the horizon stared mysteriously and glassily like
    a dead man's eye.
For years on end the distance rang like the same old passing-bell.
The days were as alike as a pair of graves.
Oh, you heroes!
Crawling out on wet nights, mewling in the bitter cold, you from
    your all-electric cities!
The sentry swapped ten nights' sleep for one cigarette; whole
    regiments gambled away eternity for ten yards of wasteland.
Full-blooded curses spat into the starlit mire. Damp cellars littered
    with tinny booty captured from the enemy.
Oh, you Greek dancers, dwarfed in lousy caverns! Popping up like
    Indians in fancy-dress when the drums sounded the attack:
Before sticking your bayonet into his groin, did not one of you see
    the Christ-like look of his opponent, did not one of you notice
    that the man over there had a kingly heart full of love?
Did not one of you still believe in his own and mankind's conscience?
You brothers, fellow-men! Oh, you heroes!

[1917]

YVAN GOLL
translated from the German by Patrick Bridgwater

from Kneeshaw Goes to War

4

There are a few left who will find it hard to forget
Polygonveld.
The earth was scarr'd and broken
By torrents of plunging shells;
Then wash'd and sodden with autumnal rains.
And Polygonbeke
(Perhaps a rippling stream
In the days of Kneeshaw's gloom)
Spread itself like a fatal quicksand, –
A sucking, clutching death.

They had to be across the beke
And in their line before dawn.
A man who was marching by Kneeshaw's side
Hesitated in the middle of the mud,
And slowly sank, weighted down by equipment and arms.
He cried for help;
Rifles were stretched to him;
He clutched and they tugged,
But slowly he sank.
His terror grew –
Grew visibly when the viscous ooze
Reached his neck.

And there he seemed to stick,
Sinking no more.
They could not dig him out –
The oozing mud would flow back again.

The dawn was very near.

An officer shot him through the head:
Not a neat job – the revolver
Was too close.

[20 September 1917]

HERBERT READ

Sir Herbert Read (1893-1968) was an English modernist poet and art critic.
His first two collections *Songs of Chaos* (1915) and *Naked Warriors* (1919) and
his major work *The End of a War* (1933) drew on his experiences of fighting
in the trenches during the First World War. He was a highly influential critic,
championing the work of modern British artists such as Barbara Hepworth,
Henry Moore, Paul Nash and Ben Nicholson as well as the French and English
surrealists. His own influences included William Morris, Max Stirner, Carl
Jung, anarchism, French existentialism and American modernist poetry. ➤ 101,
166.

Pillbox

Just see what's happening, Worley! – Worley rose
And round the angled doorway thrust his nose,
And Sergeant Hoad went too to snuff the air.
Then war brought down his fist, and missed the pair!
Yet Hoad was scratched by a splinter, the blood came,
And out burst terrors that he'd striven to tame.
A good man, Hoad, for weeks. *I'm blown to bits*,
He groans, he screams. *Come, Bluffer, where's your wits?*
Says Worley. *Bluffer, you've a blighty, man!*
All in the pillbox urged him, here began
His freedom: *Think of Eastbourne and your dad.*
The poor man lay at length and brief and mad
Flung out his cry of doom; soon ebbed and dumb
He yielded. Worley with a tot of rum
And shouting in his face could not restore him.
The ship of Charon over channel bore him.
All marvelled even on that most deathly day
To see this life so spirited away.

['Tower Hamlets', Menin Road, 29 September 1917]

EDMUND BLUNDEN

Edmund Blunden (1896-1974) is said to have been the longest serving British First World War poet, seeing continuous action in the front line between 1916 and 1918. Commissioned as a 2nd Lieutenant in the 11th Royal Sussex Regiment, he saw active service in 1916 at Festubert, Cuinchy and Givenchy, and later that year at the Somme, the Ancre valley and Thiepval. He won the Military Cross after he and a runner carried out an almost suicidal reconnaissance mission under constant shelling. In November 1916 his battalion was transferred to the Ypres salient, where he was gassed twice and remained through the battle of Passchendaele until January 1918 when they returned to the Somme. His many books include his memoir *Undertones of War* (1928). A distinguished scholar and editor, he also helped bring about the publication of the work of Wilfred Owen and Ivor Gurney after the war.

Dulce et Decorum Est

Bent double, like old beggars under sacks,
Knock-kneed, coughing like hags, we cursed through sludge,
Till on the haunting flares we turned our backs
And towards our distant rest began to trudge.
Men marched asleep. Many had lost their boots
But limped on, blood-shod. All went lame; all blind;
Drunk with fatigue; deaf even to the hoots
Of tired, outstripped Five-Nines[1] that dropped behind.

Gas! GAS! Quick, boys! – An ecstasy of fumbling,
Fitting the clumsy helmets just in time;
But someone still was yelling out and stumbling,
And flound'ring like a man in fire or lime...
Dim, through the misty panes and thick green light,
As under a green sea, I saw him drowning.

In all my dreams, before my helpless sight,
He plunges at me, guttering, choking, drowning.

If in some smothering dreams you too could pace
Behind the wagon that we flung him in,
And watch the white eyes writhing in his face,
His hanging face, like a devil's sick of sin;
If you could hear, at every jolt, the blood
Come gargling from the froth-corrupted lungs,
Obscene as cancer, bitter as the cud
Of vile, incurable sores on innocent tongues, –
My friend, you would not tell with such high zest
To children ardent for some desperate glory,
The old Lie: Dulce et decorum est
Pro patria mori.[2]

[Craiglockhart, September–October 1917]

WILFRED OWEN

1. *Five-Nines:* 5.9-inch (150 mm) artillery shells used by the Germans to deliver poison gas. 2. Writing to his mother, Owen translated the Latin tag from Horace (*Odes*, III. ii. 13) as 'It is sweet and meet to die for one's country! Sweet! and decorous!'

Insensibility

1

Happy are men who yet before they are killed
Can let their veins run cold.
Whom no compassion fleers
Or makes their feet
Sore on the alleys cobbled with their brothers.
The front line withers.
But they are troops who fade, not flowers,
For poets' tearful fooling:
Men, gaps for filling:
Losses, who might have fought
Longer; but no one bothers.

2

And some cease feeling
Even themselves or for themselves.
Dullness best solves
The tease and doubt of shelling,
And Chance's strange arithmetic
Comes simpler than the reckoning of their shilling.
They keep no check on armies' decimation.

3

Happy are these who lose imagination:
They have enough to carry with ammunition.
Their spirit drags no pack.
Their old wounds, save with cold, can not more ache.
Having seen all things red,
Their eyes are rid
Of the hurt of the colour of blood for ever.
And terror's first constriction over,
Their hearts remain small-drawn.
Their senses in some scorching cautery of battle
Now long since ironed,
Can laugh among the dying, unconcerned.

4

Happy the soldier home, with not a notion
How somewhere, every dawn, some men attack,
And many sighs are drained.
Happy the lad whose mind was never trained:
His days are worth forgetting more than not.
He sings along the march
Which we march taciturn, because of dusk,
The long, forlorn, relentless trend
From larger day to huger night.

5

We wise, who with a thought besmirch
Blood over all our soul,
How should we see our task
But through his blunt and lashless eyes?
Alive, he is not vital overmuch;
Dying, not mortal overmuch;
Nor sad, nor proud,
Nor curious at all.
He cannot tell
Old men's placidity from his.

6

But cursed are dullards whom no cannon stuns,
That they should be as stones.
Wretched are they, and mean
With paucity that never was simplicity.
By choice they made themselves immune
To pity and whatever moans in man
Before the last sea and the hapless stars;
Whatever mourns when many leave these shores;
Whatever shares
The eternal reciprocity of tears.

[Drafted either at Craiglockhart, October–November 1917, or at
Scarborough, November 1917–January 1918. Pindaric ode modelled on
Wordsworth's 'Intimations of Immortality'.]

WILFRED OWEN

Exposure

Our brains ache, in the merciless iced east winds that knive us...
Wearied we keep awake because the night is silent...
Low, drooping flares confuse our memory of the salient...
Worried by silence, sentries whisper, curious, nervous,
        But nothing happens.

Watching, we hear the mad gusts tugging on the wire,
Like twitching agonies of men among its brambles.
Northward, incessantly, the flickering gunnery rumbles,
Far off, like a dull rumour of some other war.
        What are we doing here?

The poignant misery of dawn begins to grow...
We only know war lasts, rain soaks, and clouds sag stormy.
Dawn massing in the east her melancholy army
Attacks once more in ranks on shivering ranks of grey,
        But nothing happens.

Sudden successive flights of bullets streak the silence.
Less deathly than the air that shudders black with snow,
With sidelong flowing flakes that flock, pause, and renew;
We watch them wandering up and down the wind's nonchalance,
        But nothing happens.

Pale flakes with fingering stealth come feeling for our faces –
We cringe in holes, back on forgotten dreams, and stare, snow-dazed,
Deep into grassier ditches. So we drowse, sun-dozed,
Littered with blossoms trickling where the blackbird fusses,
        – Is it that we are dying?

Slowly our ghosts drag home: glimpsing the sunk fires, glozed
With crusted dark-red jewels; crickets jingle there;
For hours the innocent mice rejoice: the house is theirs;
Shutters and doors, all closed: on us the doors are closed, –
        We turn back to our dying.

Since we believe not otherwise can kind fires burn;
Nor ever suns smile true on child, or field, or fruit.
For God's invincible spring our love is made afraid;

Therefore, not loath, we lie out here; therefore were born,
　　For love of God seems dying.

Tonight, this frost will fasten on this mud and us,
Shrivelling many hands, puckering foreheads crisp.
The burying-party, picks and shovels in shaking grasp,
Pause over half-known faces. All their eyes are ice,
　　But nothing happens.

[Begun at Scarborough, 1917; finished in France, September 1918]

WILFRED OWEN
➤ 83

The Deserter

'I'm sorry I done it, Major.'
We bandaged the livid face;
And led him out, ere the wan sun rose,
To die his death of disgrace.

The bolt-heads locked to the cartridge;
The rifles stead to rest,
As cold stock nestled at colder cheek
And foresight lined on the breast.

'Fire!' called the Sergeant-Major.
The muzzles flamed as he spoke:
And the shameless soul of a nameless man
Went up in cordite-smoke.

[The Barn, 6 December 1917]

GILBERT FRANKAU

Born into a Jewish family in London, **Gilbert Frankau** (1884-1952) was a popular English novelist who failed to achieve his right-wing political ambitions during the 1930s. He was commissioned in the 9th Battalion of the East Surrey Regiment in October 1914 and later made a Staff Captain. He saw action at Loos, Ypres and the Somme and was invalided out of the army in February 1918 suffering from delayed shellshock.

To His Love

He's gone, and all our plans
  Are useless indeed.
We'll walk no more on Cotswold
  Where the sheep feed
  Quietly and take no heed.

His body that was so quick
  Is not as you
Knew it, on Severn river
  Under the blue
  Driving our small boat through.

You would not know him now...
  But still he died
Nobly, so cover him over
  With violets of pride
  Purple from Severn side.

Cover him, cover him soon!
  And with thick-set
Masses of memoried flowers –
  Hide that red wet
  Thing I must somehow forget.

[Seaton Delaval, Northumberland, January 1918]

IVOR GURNEY
➤ 64

W.B. Yeats [➤ 133] wrote his poem 'An Irish Airman Foresees His Death'
(opposite) in the "voice" of Major Robert Gregory (1881-1918), son of Lady
Gregory, who lived at Coole Park, near Kiltartan, Gort, Co. Galway. Gregory
was killed at the age of 36 flying over Italy in January 1918 when an Italian
pilot mistakenly shot him down. Yeats's later poem 'Reprisals' [➤ 139] (1921)
is addressed to Robert Gregory's ghost.

An Irish Airman Foresees His Death

I know that I shall meet my fate
Somewhere among the clouds above;
Those that I fight I do not hate,
Those that I guard I do not love;
My country is Kiltartan Cross,
My countrymen Kiltartan's poor,
No likely end could bring them loss
Or leave them happier than before.
Nor law, nor duty bade me fight,
Nor public men, nor cheering crowds,
A lonely impulse of delight
Drove to this tumult in the clouds;
I balanced all, brought all to mind,
The years to come seemed waste of breath,
A waste of breath the years behind
In balance with this life, this death.

[1918]

W.B. YEATS

Strange Meeting

It seemed that out of battle I escaped
Down some profound dull tunnel, long since scooped
Through granites which titanic wars had groined.

Yet also there encumbered sleepers groaned,
Too fast in thought or death to be bestirred.
Then, as I probed them, one sprang up, and stared
With piteous recognition in fixed eyes,
Lifting distressful hands, as if to bless.
And by his smile, I knew that sullen hall, –
By his dead smile I knew we stood in Hell.

With a thousand pains that vision's face was grained;
Yet no blood reached there from the upper ground,
And no guns thumped, or down the flues made moan.
'Strange friend,' I said, 'here is no cause to mourn.'
'None,' said that other, 'save the undone years,
The hopelessness. Whatever hope is yours,
Was my life also; I went hunting wild
After the wildest beauty in the world,
Which lies not calm in eyes, or braided hair,
But mocks the steady running of the hour,
And if it grieves, grieves richlier than here.
For by my glee might many men have laughed,
And of my weeping something had been left,
Which must die now. I mean the truth untold,
The pity of war, the pity war distilled.
Now men will go content with what we spoiled,
Or, discontent, boil bloody, and be spilled.
They will be swift with swiftness of the tigress.
None will break ranks, though nations trek from progress.
Courage was mine, and I had mystery,
Wisdom was mine, and I had mastery:
To miss the march of this retreating world
Into vain citadels that are not walled.
Then, when much blood had clogged their chariot-wheels,
I would go up and wash them from sweet wells,
Even with truths that lie too deep for taint.
I would have poured my spirit without stint
But not through wounds; not on the cess of war.
Foreheads of men have bled where no wounds were.

'I am the enemy you killed, my friend.
I knew you in this dark: for so you frowned
Yesterday through me as you jabbed and killed.
I parried; but my hands were loath and cold.
Let us sleep now....'

[Scarborough (?), January–March 1918]

WILFRED OWEN
➤ 83

110

The Send-Off

Down the close darkening lanes they sang their way
To the siding-shed,
And lined the train with faces grimly gay.

Their breasts were stuck all white with wreath and spray
As men's are, dead.

Dull porters watched them, and a casual tramp
Stood staring hard,
Sorry to miss them from the upland camp.

Then, unmoved, signals nodded, and a lamp
Winked to the guard.

So secretly, like wrongs hushed-up, they went.
They were not ours:
We never heard to which front these were sent;

Nor there if they yet mock what women meant
Who gave them flowers.

Shall they return to beating of great bells
In wild train-loads?
A few, a few, too few for drums and yells,

May creep back, silent, to village wells;
Up half-known roads.

[Ripon, April–May 1918]

WILFRED OWEN

The Bleeding-Heart Dove and the Fountain

Gentle faces stabbed and bleeding **S**weetheart lips in bloom

MIA MAREYE

YETTE LOREYE

ANNIE and you MARIE

where are

you O

sweet girls

BUT

above

a praying

weeping fountain

hovers this ecstatic dove

These memories are all so recent Where are Dalize Billy Raynal

O you my friends marched off to war Their names diffusing into sorrow

Welling and hurling heavenwards Like sombre footfalls in a church

Your eyes' light drowsing in the water Cremnitz volunteered where is he

Sorrowfully fading dying All already dead perhaps

Where are Braque and Max Jacob Memories brimming in my heart

Derain with those dawn-grey eyes The fountain weeping to my pain

?

THOSE STATIONED IN THE NORTH ARE IN THE FRONT LINE FIGHTING NOW

Evening falls **O** sea of blood

Warrior oleander blossom bleeding wreathes the garden walls

GUILLAUME APOLLINAIRE

translated from the French by Ian Higgins

➤ 41

Gamecocks

I come crawling out of my hole,
my black trench, where the mud
sucks us back.
Neck stretched out I crawl,
not daring raise my head,
temples hot with thudding blood.
I crawl,
and after me my men
come crawling
through the mud,
till they catch in the wire
and it screeches, and skins them
with hatchet fangs,
and clashes on their bayonets.

Rat-tat-tat... Zing! Zing!
Lie flat... Rat-tat-tat... Zing!
If only we could flatten further.
'They've seen us... They've heard us!'
Bayonet-sharp,
a shudder chills our spines...
My clenched fist clutches my revolver.
And I do just raise my head,
brow and body sweat-soaked.

But they've stopped firing.
We struggle further forward,
crawling... Shh!!
For God's sake make less noise!
Careful with your bayonets.
You over there, come on!
Crack!... Shhwhizzz...
A flare comes climbing to its zenith
and opens out, a blinding flower
over our cringing heads.

Rat-tat-tat!... We can't be seen,
but: Rat-tat-tat-tat-tat!... and: Zing! Zing! Zing!
Boche bastards!
Then blacker night returns,
and we can find a shell-hole
and breathe again.

Ker-rack!... Ker-rack!...
This is horrible!
Zing!... Rat-tat-tat!
For God's sake, Boche bastard,
how long's it going on for,
this machine gun?
Yes, I know: you can see us crawling
towards you.
So, behind your parapet,
you're pumping your mechanical pig.
Wouldn't you just love to smash us...
If you heard us scream, you savage,
wouldn't you just roar: *'Komm, Fritz!*
Hör' die Franzosen singen!'
Rat-tat-tat!... Rat-tat-tat!...
But what have we done to you?
We're in the middle of our wire,
our wire;
we're going to cut a way right through!
Tomorrow, when we've reached you,
and the raid's on, hell, defend yourself then,
fire then – but not tonight!
just leave us be, we've work to do.

Rat-tat!... Zing!...
All right, you brute,
go on, fire!
That's what you're there for. Fire away!
You're doing your job, like us.
Ker-rack!
We don't give a damn,
fire all you like –
you can't see us, you're firing blind

at the night we're hidden in.
Your pig's spitting in the wind.

I don't really mind, you know.
That's four years now you've been on this job
behind your parapet...
And *we've* been at work for four years, too,
knitting great meshes of entanglement,
then cutting fresh tracks through them, ready
to attack next day and flush you
from your trenches.

Look – your works gates
are next to mine, we're almost mates.
We've been flogging ourselves for rival firms,
each as bad as the other, perhaps –
we can't be sure!
My boss has told me yours
is a villainous, treacherous, murderous,
good-for-nothing swine!
But yours, perhaps,
has said the same of mine.

Anyhow, we're scrapping like dogs,
like gamecocks
with masters relentlessly
and furiously betting one another
and themselves into frenzy;
when it's over, one'll be ruined,
and the other no better off.
And their birds'll have slashed each other
to shreds, feathers and flesh,
and bled to death...

Rat-tat! Rat-tat!
That'll do, old son!
You're stupider than those cocks.
Zing!... Zing!...
You idiot! Don't be stupid!
Rat-tat!... Right, I've had enough!

My master's right,
you're just a brute.
Perhaps you'll kill me.
I've got children and a wife...
Rat-tat! Old son, you're going to pay for this.
I'll skewer you tomorrow, right by your Spandau!
And if you've got a wife,
that's just too bad,
and too bad for your children!
I'm a brute as well,
when I'm pushed too far.

And we'll do as brave gamecocks do, when
they're thrown into the pit at one another,
and unflinchingly, heroically
and ruthlessly fight,
till they drop and die at nightfall of their wounds,
roared on and clapped by an ecstatic crowd,
for the glory, but the ruin too,
alas,
of their unpardonable masters.

[14 May 1918]

EDMOND ADAM
translated from the French by Ian Higgins

Edmond Adam (1889-1918) was an engineer who volunteered for the front and saw active service with the French Army from December 1914. He died on 24 August 1918 at La Veuve, from shrapnel wounds sustained on a reconnaissance mission three days earlier between Courmelois and Thuisy. While unconscious in hospital, he was awarded the Légion d'honneur. Very little is known of him. 'Gamecocks' ('Coqs de combat') was apparently written in two nights, on the Somme, and captures exactly the true mood of the French infantryman or '*poilu*', a mixture of 'chirpy good humour, grandeur, anger and resignation' (Roland Dorgelès, *Bleu horizon*, 1949). It was published in *Les Humbles*, a literary magazine fiercely opposed what it saw as the senseless and immoral butchery of the war, in June 1918, but with lines 83-102 and 109-28 cut out by order of the censor. [Ian Higgins]

Absolution

He stayed in the shell-hole,
Dead in his shelter, minced meat.
His face has already turned black,
His hands still clutch the earth...
...What were you fighting for,
What master were you defending?
Towards what unknown mirages
Were you walking in total ignorance?
What sort of offer did your country's
Shady dealers make for your blood?
They gave you nothing, but took
Your sole possession: life.
And now you lie on our land, alone,
Spurned, your belly open,
A piece of dead and captive flesh,
Wearing your gloomy green uniform.
If I had found you still alive
Just now in the furnace,
I would have killed you without remorse,
With no regrets or malice.
But now that you no longer exist
I think I no longer hate you.
I am free of anger as I look at you.
Dead man from far away,
I forgive you the agony and torment
Of my great family of humankind.
I forgive you our calamities.
I also forgive you my hatred,
For I hate with all my might
Those brought here by war
And thrown against me.
But you are no longer an enemy,
Your soul has been set free
Now and floats above the fray.
Death has made you like my own dead.
How can I still hate you, Prussian?
Rest in peace, you have conquered
This France in which your body is caught.

Rest in peace, it's your turn now,
Next to the dead that lie around,
Whoever they are, martyrs whom the earth,
Contemptuous of our angers,
Cradles and receives lime brothers.

[1918]

HENRY-JACQUES
translated from the French by Michael Copp
➢ 96

Dead Men with Masks

The plain where men kill, die and suffer,
Is as yellow as a vat of sulphur;
The wind still stirs a poisonous smell
And green clouds float on the horizon.
Gas roams around in the trenches,
Spreading spasms and suffocation,
As it searches for human agony.
On reddish grass and under dead thistles, bodies,
Lying motionless on their backs or bellies.
No one could name them, not even their mothers.
Beneath the glass plate their eyes are all the same.
Their faces are screwed up in the same way,
Masks frozen in silent and prolonged laughter.
Impossible to say how handsome or plain they were.
Under the weird hood, sometimes stained with red blood,
They look like puppets exhausted from their exertions,
With their big round eyes and their bird-like profile,
Spectres of the monstrous Carnival of war.
With a crude piece of rag fate has moulded
A hundred times the same head above a hundred bodies,
As if all these lads were but a single corpse.

HENRY-JACQUES
translated from the French by Michael Copp

By the Side of the Road

(for Jacques Vincent)

A ten-minute break and the column sinks down.
The road forms a shadowy corridor in the darkness.
The men, exhausted by pulling their feet
Out of unseen, thick, implacable mud,
Rest their stiffened limbs a moment
On the cold grass of embankments.
Collapsed on the earth, one of the youngsters
Has suddenly rolled over in the depths of sleep,
His face livid and his limbs inert.
His breathing has stopped on his parted lips
And fatigue appears to be arranging his body
Into the shape that death will give it tomorrow.

HENRY-JACQUES
translated from the French by Michael Copp

from THE T.E. LAWRENCE POEMS

Apologies

I did not choose Arabia; it chose me. The shabby money
That the desert offered us bought lies, bought victory.
　　　　What was I, that soiled Outsider, doing
Among them? I was not becoming one of them, no matter
What you think. They found it easier to learn my kind
　　　　of Arabic, than to teach me theirs.
And they were all mad; they mounted their horses and camels
　　　　from the right.

But my mind's twin kingdoms waged an everlasting war;
The reckless Bedouin and the civilised Englishman
　　　　fought for control, so that I, whatever I was,
Fell into a dumb void that even a false god could not fill,
　　　　could not inhabit.

The Arabs are children of the idea; dangle an idea
In front of them, and you can swing them wherever.
        I was also a child of the idea; I wanted
        no liberty for myself, but to bestow it
Upon them. I wanted to present them with a gift so fine
        it would outshine all other gifts in their eyes;
        it would be *worthy*. Then I at last could be
Empty.

You can't imagine how beautiful it is to be empty.
Out of this grand emptiness wonderful things must surely
        come into being.
When we set out, it was morning. We hardly knew
That when we moved we would not be an army, but a world.

Damascus

The dream was dead in me before we reached Damascus;
        it died with your death, and dead love
Was all I carried around with me in the clumsy luggage
        of the desert. But I remember
Entering the city, and the air silk with locusts;
        there was the smell of eternal cookies baking,
And someone ran up to me with a bunch of yellow grapes.

In the crowds, the Arabs smelled of dried sweat,
        and the English had a hot aura of piss
And naptha. For some reason I noticed a sword
        lying unused in a garden, a still garden
Behind a palm tree. And the worthless Turkish money
        was flying crazily through the air.
Later, in the evening, the satiny white sand cooled
        my feet; nowhere else was there such sand.

That night the Turks and Germans burned what was left
        of their ammunition dumps.
They're burning Damascus, I said. And then I fell asleep.

The Peace Conference

After prostituting myself in the service of an alien race,
       I was too mangled for politics; the world
       swirled around me and I was its still center.
Old men crawled out from the woodwork and seized upon
       our victory, to re-shape it at their will.
We stammered that we had worked for a new heaven and
       a new earth. They thanked us kindly, and
       made their peace.

France carved up Syria as Feisal questioned their rights
       to do so, inquiring gently which one of them
       had won the Crusades;
                     everyone was carving up
     the kingdoms of each other's minds.
I quietly arranged everyone's destiny to my satisfaction,
       without revealing it out loud, as an inner voice
       informed me I had not done well at all –
I had freed the Arabs from everyone but ourselves.

My ideas were simple, always have been; I wanted only:
       an association of free, separate Arab states,
       the beginning of the United States of Arabia,
       the first brown dominion within the Empire,
And no mad talk of Arab unity; no one can unite
       the facets of a jewel.

Everything sickened me; I had been betrayed from the moment
       I was born. I betrayed the Arabs;
       Everything betrays everything.
It was an Arab war, waged and led by Arabs, for an Arab aim
In Arabia, I said, as the bedlam grew louder,
       and France and Britain played chess
       with the world.
                   Feisal caught my eye, saying
Without words: *I've given you my dreams, and now*
       you have to dream them.

Tall Tales

It has been said that I sometimes lie, or bend the truth
       to suit me. Did I make that four hundred mile
       trip alone in Turkish territory or not?
       I wonder if it is anybody's business
       to know. Syria is still there,
       and the long lie that the war was.

Was there a poster of me offering money for my capture,
       and did I stand there staring at myself,
       daring anyone to know me? Consider
       truth and untruth, consider why they call them
       the *theatres* of war. All of us
       played our roles to the hilt.

Poets only play with words, you know; they too
       are masters of the Lie, the Grand Fiction.
       Poets and men like me who fight for something
       contained in words, but not words.

What if the whole show was a lie, and it bloody well was –
       would I still lie to you? Of course I would.

GWENDOLYN MACEWEN

Gwendolyn MacEwen (1941-87) was a leading Canadian poet and novelist whose many books included *The T.E. Lawrence Poems* (1982), a whole collection of poems written in the voice of Lawrence of Arabia:

'In 1962 I was staying in a hotel in Tiberias, Israel; the tall, white-haired proprietor invited me downstairs one evening and served me syrupy tea and a plate of fruit. He showed me a series of old sepiatone photographs which lined the walls – photographs of blurred riders on camels riding to the left into some uncharted desert just beyond the door. Some of them were signed.

"It's Lawrence, isn't it?" I asked, walking up to one.

"Yes," said my host, offering me a huge section of an orange. "I rode with him once a long time ago. I see you always carry a pen and paper to write things down. I thought you'd be interested; I thought you'd like to know."

These poems were written some twenty years later.'

[Foreword to *The T.E. Lawrence Poems*]

The Lament of the Demobilised

'Four years,' some say consolingly. 'Oh well,
What's that? You're young. And then it must have been
A very fine experience for you!'
And they forget
How others stayed behind and just got on –
Got on the better since we were away.
And we came home and found
They had achieved, and men revered their names,
But never mentioned ours;
And no one talked heroics now, and we
Must just go back and start again once more.
'You threw four years into the melting-pot –
Did you indeed!' these others cry. 'Oh well,
The more fool you!'
And we're beginning to agree with them.

VERA BRITTAIN

Vera Brittain (1893-1970) was a writer and pacifist best-known for *Testament of Youth* (1933), the first instalment of her memoir including her experiences during the First World War, when she volunteered as a nurse, tending to the wounded in London, Malta and Étaples, France. Her fiancé, the poet Roland Leighton, her brother Edward and other close friends were all killed during the war.

Præmaturi

When men are old, and their friends die,
They are not so sad,
Because their love is running slow,
And cannot spring from the wound with so sharp a pain;
And they are happy with many memories,
And only a little while to be alone.

But we are young, and our friends are dead
Suddenly, and our quick love is torn in two;
So our memories are only hopes that came to nothing.
We are left alone like old men; we should be dead
– But there are years and years in which we shall still be young.

MARGARET POSTGATE COLE

➤ 44

Afterwards

Oh, my beloved, shall you and I
Ever be young again, be young again?
The people that were resigned said to me
– Peace will come and you will lie
Under the larches up in Sheer,
Sleeping,
And eating strawberries and cream and cakes –
          O cakes, O cakes, O cakes from Fuller's!
And quite forgetting there's a train to town,
Plotting in an afternoon the new curves for the world.

And peace came. And lying in Sheer
I look round at the corpses of the larches
Whom they slew to make pit-props
For mining the coal for the great armies.
And think, a pit prop cannot move in the wind,
Nor have red manes hanging in spring from its branches,
And sap making the warm air sweet.
Though you planted it out on the hill again it would be dead.
And if these years have made you into a pit-prop,
To carry the twisting galleries of the world's reconstruction
(Where you may thank God I suppose
That they set you the sole stay of a nasty corner)
What use is it to you? What use
To have your body lying here
In Sheer, underneath the larches?

MARGARET POSTGATE COLE

An Equal Voice

We hear more from doctors than patients. However hard he tries,
the historian cannot even the account, cannot give the patients an equal
voice, because most of them chose not to recount their experiences.

BEN SHEPHARD: A War of Nerves

War from behind the lines is a dizzy jumble.
Revolving chairs, stuffy offices, dry as dust
reports, blueprints one day and the next –
with the help of a broken-down motor car
and a few gallons of petrol – marching men
with sweat-stained faces and shining eyes,
horses straining and plunging at the guns,
white sweat clouds drifting beneath them,
and piles of bloody clothes and leggings
outside the canvas door of a field hospital.
At the end of the week there is no telling
whether you spent Tuesday going over
the specifications of a possible laundry
or skirting the edge of hell in an automobile.

*

There were some cases of nervous collapse
as the whistle blew on the first day of battle.
In general however it is perfectly astonishing
and terrifying how bravely the men fight.
From my position on rising ground I watched
one entire brigade advancing in line after line,
dressed as smartly as if they were on parade,
and not a single man shirked going through
the barrage, or facing the rapid machine gun
and rifle fire that finally wiped them out.
I saw with my own eyes the lines advancing
in such admirable order quickly melt away.
Yet not a man wavered, or broke the ranks,
or made any attempt to turn back again.

*

A soft siffle, high in the air like a distant lark,
or the note of a penny whistle, faint and falling.
But then, with a spiral, pulsing flutter, it grew
to a hissing whirr, landing with ferocious blasts,
with tremendous thumps and then their echoes,
followed by the whine of fragments that cut
into the trees, driving white scars into their trunks
and filling the air with torn shreds of foliage.
The detonation, the flash, the heat of explosion.
And all the while fear, crawling into my heart.
I felt it. Crawling into me. I had to set my teeth
and steadied myself, but with no avail. I clutched
the earth, pressing against it. There was no one
to help me then. O how one loves mother earth.

*

One or two friends stood like granite rocks
round which the seas raged, but very many
other men broke in pieces. Everyone called it
shell-shock, meaning concussion. But shell-
shock is rare. What 90% get is justifiable funk
due to the collapse of the helm of self-control.
You understand what you see but cannot think.
Your head is in agony and you want relief for that.
The more you struggle, the more madness creeps
over you. The brain cannot think of anything at all.
I don't ask you what you feel like but I tell you,
because I have been like you. I have been ill as you
and got better. I will teach you, you will get better.
Try and keep on trying what I tell you and you will.

*

The place was full of men whose slumbers were morbid,
titubating shell-shockers with their bizarre paralyses
and stares, their stammers and tremors, their nightmares
and hallucinations, their unstoppable fits and shakings.
Each was back in his doomed shelter, when the panic
and stampede was re-enacted among long-dead faces,
or still caught in the open and under fire. This officer
was quietly feasting with imaginary knives and forks;

that group roamed around clutching Teddy Bears;
one man stripped to his underclothes and proclaimed
himself to be Mahatma Gandhi; another sat cramped
in a corner clutching a champagne cork; one chanted,
with his hands over an imaginary basket of eggs, Lord
have mercy on us, Christ have mercy, Lord have mercy.

*

I could feel the bullets hit my body. I could feel
myself being hit by gunfire and this is what made me
sit up and scream. What I saw round me were others
walking with the bent and contorted spines of old age,
or moving without their lifting their legs but vibrating them
on the ground. All equally unfortunate, filled with sadness.
Dead friends gazed at them. Rats emerged from the cavities
of bodies. Then trembling began, and losing control of legs:
you never dreamt of such gaits. One fellow cannot hold
his head still or even stand except with incessant jerking.
Instantly the man across the aisle follows suit. In this way
the infection spreads in widening circles until the whole
ward is jerking and twitching, all in their hospital blues,
their limbs shaking and flapping like the tails of dogs.

*

Naturally it can save a good deal of time if men,
before battle, have pictures from the Hate Room hung
in their minds of things the enemy has already done,
waiting to be remembered. Starving people for instance
and sick people, and dead people in ones and in heaps,
with bodies all bearing witness to hideous cruelties.
Compulsory mourning is no longer recommended
whereby the hospital confines a man for three days
alone in a darkened room and orders him to grieve
for dead comrades. But other cures must be attempted,
and in some cases men wish to return to do their duty.
See, your eyes are already heavier. Heavier and heavier.
You are going into a deep, deep sleep. A deep, far sleep.
You are far asleep. You are fast sleep. You have no fear.

*

I am quiet and healthy but cannot bear being away
from England. I have been away too long and seen
too many things. My best friend was killed beside me,
I have a wife and two children and I have done enough.
I thought my nerves were better but they are worse.
The first fight, the fight with my own self, has ended.
I may be ready to fight again but I am not willing.
I am in urgent need of outdoor work and would be glad
to accept a position as a gardener at a nominal salary.
My best friend walked back into my room this morning,
shimmering white and transparent. I saw him clearly.
He stood at the foot of my bed and looked right at me.
I asked him, What do you want? What do you want?
Eventually I woke up and of course I was by myself.

ANDREW MOTION

Sir Andrew Motion (*b.* 1952) is a poet, novelist and biographer who was the
UK's Poet Laureate from 1999 to 2009. Many of his poems relate to the human
cost of war. Several are based on memories of his father, who took part in
the D-day landings and fought in France and Germany, while others take the
words of other soldiers (from accounts in books, interviews and meetings) to
create 'found poems' which he hopes can be read as collaborations between
the author and his source. The title and most of the content of 'An Equal
Voice' are taken from the historian Ben Shephard's book *A War of Nerves.
Soldiers and Psychiatrists, 1914-1944* (Pimlico, 2002).

Andrew Motion: 'Doctors, historians and other experts have documented
the effects of shellshock – thanks to them, we know that the term covers a
multitude of ailments, and is the result of far more than just shells going off.
But, as Ben Shephard wrote in his history of medical psychiatry, the people
who have suffered from it have often been too ill to speak. They have been
left out of the record. I wanted to hear from them. This is a "found" poem,
a stitching together of the voices of shellshocked people. Their words have
been taken from a variety of sources, from the first world war to the present,
and are presented in the poem in roughly chronological order. There's a
fragment of Siegfried Sassoon in there, but most are from unknown soldiers.
Together, they give a sense of moving through time to establish what is
horribly recurrent about this affliction. It is a poem by them, orchestrated by
me.' [*Guardian*, 7 November 2009]

Motion's most recent war poems were published in *Laurels and Donkeys*
(2010) and *The Customs House* (2012). He also edited the Faber anthology *First
World War Poems* (2003). ➤ 248, 558.

Soldiering On

We need another monument. Everywhere
Has Tommy Atkins with his head bowed down
For all his pals, the alphabetical dead,
And that is sweet and right and every year
We freshen the whited cenotaph with red

But no one seems to have thought of standing her
In all the parishes in bronze or stone
With bags, with heavy bags, with bags of spuds
And flour and tins of peas and clinging kids
Lending the bags their bit of extra weight –

Flat-chested little woman in a hat,
Thin as a rake, tough as old boots, with feet
That ache, ache, ache. I've read
He staggered into battle carrying sixty pounds
Of things for killing with. She looked after the pence,

She made ends meet, she had her ports of call
For things that keep body and soul together
Like sugar, tea, a loaf, spare ribs and lard,
And things the big ship brings that light the ends
Of years, like oranges. On maps of France

I've trailed him down the chalky roads to where
They end and her on the oldest A to Z
Down streets, thin as a wraith, year in, year out
Bidding the youngest put her best foot forward,
Lugging the rations past the war memorial.

DAVID CONSTANTINE

David Constantine (*b.* 1944) is a leading English poet known also for his translations of poets such as Brecht, Goethe, Hölderlin and Jaccottet. Like the work of the European poets who have nourished him, his poetry is informed by a profoundly humane vision of the world. The last stanza of this poem alludes to the death of his grandfather on the Somme in 1916.

IRELAND | 1916–1923

TOTAL DEATHS: 4,000 to 6,000

Irish nationalists have been opposed to rule from England or Britain for many centuries. A rebellion by the United Irishmen led by Wolfe Tone with French support was quashed in 1798, as was Robert Emmet's abortive rebellion in 1803. During the early 19th century Daniel O'Connell led moderate Irish nationalists calling for Irish self-government under the Crown, a cause later revived under Charles Stewart Parnell's leadership of the Irish Parliamentary Party (IPP) and the Home Rule movement, supported by the Liberal Party Prime Minister William Gladstone, whose two attempts to have Home Rule bills passed by Parliament were blocked by the Conservative Party's pro-unionists. Home Rule was eventually secured in 1914 by the IPP's John Redmond with Irish self-government limited by a proposed partitition of the north and south, but the Home Rule Act was suspended for the duration of the First World War.

The Irish Republican Brotherhood, successors to the United Irishmen as the main body of nationalist resistance, opposed the war, and it was a dissident faction from this group (notably Pádraic Pearse, Thomas MacDonagh and Tom Clarke), along with labour leader James Connolly, who planned insurrections against British rule in Ireland while the war was going on. These came together to stage the Easter Rising on 24–29 April 1916, put down by the British Army at a cost of around 500 lives, many of these uninvolved civilians, with the main rebel leaders executed (memorialised by W.B. Yeats in 'Easter 1916' ➢ 131). Although the Rising failed, it galvanised nationalist support, resulting in Sinn Féin winning most of Ireland's seats in the 1918 general election, proclaiming an Irish Republic and forming a breakaway government in January 1919.

Over 2,000 people were killed in the Irish War of Independence (21 January 1919 – 11 July 1921). This began with Irish Republican Army (IRA) attacks on British Army patrols and members of the armed police force, the Royal Irish Constabulary (RIC), soon bolstered by the Black and Tans, a militia brought over from Britain drawn mostly from war veterans who became infamous for their attacks on civilians [➢ 138, *n.* 1], for the indiscriminate shooting of Gaelic football supporters at Croke Park on 21 November 1920 (Bloody Sunday), and for their part in the burning and looting of Cork on 11–12 December 1920.

A ceasefire on 11 July 1921 was followed by negotiations led by Michael Collins and the signing of the Anglo-Irish Treaty on 6 December, establishing the Irish Free State as an autonomous dominion of the British Empire but with Northern Ireland opting to remain part of the United Kingdom. However, nationalists opposed to the treaty, led by Sinn Féin's Éamon de Valera, wanted full independence, and the Irish Civil War which followed (28 June 1922 – 24 May 1923) cost even more lives (2,000 to 4,000) than the War of Independence, with former allies taking up arms against one other, families divided, and many of the old Anglo-Irish landowners' "big houses" burned to the ground. With Dublin and all major towns secured by Free State forces by August 1922, the Anti-Treaty IRA resorted to guerrilla tactics in rural areas, but were eventually defeated after nine further months of intermittent conflict.

Easter 1916 [1]

I have met them at close of day
Coming with vivid faces
From counter or desk among grey
Eighteenth-century houses.
I have passed with a nod of the head
Or polite meaningless words,
Or have lingered awhile and said
Polite meaningless words,
And thought before I had done
Of a mocking tale or a gibe
To please a companion
Around the fire at the club,
Being certain that they and I
But lived where motley is worn:
All changed, changed utterly:
A terrible beauty is born.

That woman's [2] days were spent
In ignorant good-will,
Her nights in argument
Until her voice grew shrill.
What voice more sweet than hers
When, young and beautiful,
She rode to harriers?
This man [3] had kept a school
And rode our wingèd horse;
This other [4] his helper and friend
Was coming into his force;
He might have won fame in the end,
So sensitive his nature seemed,
So daring and sweet his thought.
This other man [5] I had dreamed
A drunken, vainglorious lout.
He had done most bitter wrong
To some who are near my heart, [6]
Yet I number him in the song;
He, too, has resigned his part

In the casual comedy;
He, too, has been changed in his turn,
Transformed utterly:
A terrible beauty is born.

Hearts with one purpose alone
Through summer and winter seem
Enchanted to a stone
To trouble the living stream.
The horse that comes from the road,
The rider, the birds that range
From cloud to tumbling cloud,
Minute by minute they change;
A shadow of cloud on the stream
Changes minute by minute;
A horse-hoof slides on the brim,
And a horse plashes within it;
The long-legged moor-hens dive,
And hens to moor-cocks call;
Minute by minute they live:
The stone's in the midst of all.

Too long a sacrifice
Can make a stone of the heart.
O when may it suffice?
That is Heaven's part, our part
To murmur name upon name,
As a mother names her child
When sleep at last has come
On limbs that had run wild.
What is it but nightfall?
No, no, not night but death;
Was it needless death after all?
For England may keep faith
For all that is done and said.
We know their dream; enough
To know they dreamed and are dead;
And what if excess of love
Bewildered them till they died?
I write it out in a verse –

MacDonagh and MacBride
And Connolly[7] and Pearse
Now and in time to be,
Wherever green is worn,
Are changed, changed utterly:
A terrible beauty is born.

[25 September 1916]

W.B. YEATS

William Butler Yeats (1865-1939) was Ireland's greatest modern poet and one of the foremost figures in 20th century literature. During the 1890s he became one of the driving forces behind the Irish Literary Revival, co-founding the Abbey Theatre in Dublin with Lady Gregory and others. He was a senator of the new Irish Free State from 1922 to 1928. Yet Yeats was fearful of how his poetry and plays stirred up Irish nationalist feelings, distancing himself from political activism and its consequences at the time of the Easter Rising ('Easter 1916' [➤ 131] is his ambiguous response) and during the Irish Civil War. While accepting the Anglo-Irish Treaty, he was ambivalent about a tragic conflict that split communities and even families, creating 'a whirlpool of hate' for which he felt 'both sides were responsible', refusing to 'take any position in life where I have to speak but half my mind' (1923 letter to Lady Gregory), as is clear from 'Meditations in Time of Civil War' [➤ 143], and 'Nineteen Hundred and Nineteen' [➤ 137], which he called 'a lamentation over lost peace and lost hope'. Awarded the Nobel Prize in Literature in 1923, a year after Ireland gained its independence, he asserted its symbolic value in the world's eyes, claiming that the honour came to him 'less as an individual than as a representative of Irish literature, it is part of Europe's welcome to the Free State'.

1. Yeats's poem alludes to or names several of the leaders of the Easter Rising, as follows... 2. *That woman:* Constance Markewicz, *née* Gore-Booth (1867-1927), revolutionary nationalist, subject of Yeats's poem 'In Memory of Eva Gore-Booth and Con Markewicz'; sentenced to death but eventually released; later a minister in the Irish government. 3. *This man:* Pádraic H. Pearse (1879-1916), teacher, barrister, writer and commander-in-chief; executed. 4. *This other:* Thomas MacDonagh (1878-1916), lecturer, poet and commander of the garrison at Jacob's biscuit factory; executed. 5. *This other man:* John MacBride (1868-1916), nationalist who fought against British rule in South Africa and was made a Major in the Boer army; executed. 6. *He had done most bitter wrong / to some who are near my heart*: MacBride was briefly married to Yeats's great love Maud Gonne in 1903, whom he is said to have ill-treated (and may also have abused her daughter Iseult). 7. *Connolly:* James Connolly (1898-1916), socialist leader, founder of the Citizen Army, who first came to Ireland as a British soldier, deserting in 1891; executed.

Sixteen Dead Men

O but we talked at large before
The sixteen men [1] were shot,
But who can talk of give and take,
What should be and what not
While those dead men are loitering there
To stir the boiling pot?

You say that we should still the land
Till Germany's overcome;
But who is there to argue that
Now Pearse is deaf and dumb?
And is their logic to outweigh
MacDonagh's bony thumb? [2]

How could you dream they'd listen
That have an ear alone
For those new comrades they have found,
Lord Edward and Wolfe Tone, [3]
Or meddle with our give and take
That converse bone to bone?

[December 1916]

W.B. YEATS

1. *Sixteen men:* The fifteen rebel leaders executed after the Easter Rising [see 'Easter 1916' ➤ 131] and Sir Roger Casement, the British diplomat who joined Sinn Féin in 1914 and tried to raise an Irish Brigade in Germany from Irish prisoners of war. Returned to Ireland by German U-boat, Casement was arrested, tried for high treason and hanged (not shot) in August 1916. 2. *Pearse / MacDonagh:* See 'Easter 1916' [➤ 133, *n.* 3 & 4]. 3. *Lord Edward and Wolfe Tone:* Irish revolutionaries Lord Edward FitzGerald (1763-98) and Theobald Wolfe Tone (1763-98) who both died during or following the 1798 Rebellion.

Imperial Measure

We have plenty of the best food, all the meals being as good as if
served in a hotel. The dining-room here is very comfortable.

P.H. Pearse, the GPO, Easter 1916, in a letter to his mother

The kitchens of the Metropole and Imperial hotels yielded up to the
       Irish Republic
their armoury of fillet, brisket, flank. Though destined for more
       palatable tongues,
it was pressed to service in an Irish stew and served on fine bone china
with bread that turned to powder in their mouths. Brioche, artichokes,
       tomatoes
tasted for the first time: staunch and sweet on Monday, but by
       Thursday,
they had overstretched to spill their livid plenitude on the fires of
       Sackville Street.

A cow and her two calves were commandeered. One calf was killed,
its harnessed blood clotting the morning like news that wasn't welcome
when, eventually, it came. The women managed the blood into black
       puddings
washed down with milk from the cow in the yard who smelt smoke on
       the wind
and fire on the skin of her calf. Whose fear they took for loss and
       fretted with her
until daylight crept between crossfire and the sights of Marrowbone
       Lane.

Brownies, Simnel cake, biscuits slumped under royal icing. Éclairs with
       their cream
already turned. Crackers, tonnes of them: the floor of Jacobs' studded
       with crumbs,
so every footfall was a recoil from a gunshot across town, and the flakes
a constant needling in mouths already seared by the one drink – a gross
or two of cooking chocolate, stewed and taken without sweetener or
       milk.
Its skin was riven every time the ladle dipped but, just as quickly, it
       seized up again.

Nellie Gifford magicked oatmeal and a half-crowned loaf to make
   porridge
in a grate in the College of Surgeons where drawings of field surgery
had spilled from Ypres to drench in wounds the whitewashed walls
of the lecture hall. When the porridge gave out, there was rice:
a biscuit-tin of it for fourteen men, a ladleful each that scarcely
   knocked
the corners off their undiminished appetites; their vast, undaunted
   thirst.

The sacks of flour ballasting the garrison gave up their downy protest
   under fire.
It might have been a fall of Easter snow sent to muffle the rifles or to
   deaden the aim.
Every blow was a flurry that thickened the air of Boland's Mill, so
   breath
was ghosted by its own white consequence. The men's clothes were
   talced with it,
as though they were newborns, palmed and swathed, their foreheads
   kissed,
their grip unclenched, their fists and arms first blessed and, then,
   made much of.

The cellars of the Four Courts were intact at the surrender, but the
   hock
had been agitated, the Riesling set astir. For years, the wines were
   sullied
with a leaden aftertaste, although the champagne had as full a throat
   as ever,
and the spirits kept their heady confidence, for all the stockpiled
   bottles
had chimed with every hit, and the calculating scales above it all
had had the measure of nothing, or nothing if not smoke, and then
   wildfire.

VONA GROARKE

Vona Groarke (*b.* 1964) is a contemporary Irish poet. This poem is from her collection *Flight* (2002).

Nineteen sixteen, or The terrible beauty

Once, as a boy of nine, he heard his teacher
back from his interrupted holiday,
a red-faced, white-haired man, repeating wildly
all he had seen of Dublin's rash affray:

'The abandoned motor cars, the carcasses
of army horses littering the street...'
No more remains of all he must have told them
of that remote, ambiguous defeat.

It took those decades crammed with guns and ballads
to sanctify the names which star that myth;
and, to this day, the fierce infection pulses
in the hot blood of half our ghetto-youth.

Yet, sitting there, that long-remembered morning,
he caught no hint he'd cast an ageing eye
on angled rifles, parcels left in doorways,
or unattended cars, he'd sidle by.

[14-15 March 1973]

JOHN HEWITT
➢ 141

from Nineteen Hundred and Nineteen

All teeth were drawn, all ancient tricks unlearned,
And a great army but a showy thing;
What matter that no cannon had been turned
Into a ploughshare? Parliament and king
Thought that unless a little powder burned
The trumpeters might burst with trumpeting
And yet it lack all glory; and perchance
The guardsmen's drowsy chargers would not prance.

Now days are dragon-ridden, the nightmare
Rides upon sleep: a drunken soldiery
Can leave the mother, murdered at her door,[1]
To crawl in her own blood, and go scot-free;
The night can sweat with terror as before
We pieced our thoughts into philosophy,
And planned to bring the world under a rule,
Who are but weasels fighting in a hole.

He who can read the signs nor sink unmanned
Into the half-deceit of some intoxicant
From shallow wits; who knows no work can stand,
Whether health, wealth or peace of mind were spent
On master-work of intellect or hand,
No honour leave its mighty monument,
Has but one comfort left: all triumph would
But break upon his ghostly solitude.

But is there any comfort to be found?
Man is in love and loves what vanishes,
What more is there to say? That country round
None dared admit, if such a thought were his,
Incendiary or bigot could be found
To burn that stump on the Acropolis,
Or break in bits the famous ivories
Or traffic in the grasshoppers or bees.[3]

[April 1921]

W.B. YEATS

1. The Black and Tans [➤ 130] were responsible for atrocities against local people in the Gort area of Co. Galway where Lady Gregory and Yeats both lived. Yeats wrote in a letter that two brothers from Loughnane had been 'tied alive to a lorry by their heels, till their bodies were rent in pieces' in December 1920. Similar references to a murder by 'drunken soldiery' in two of Yeats's poems relate to the killing of Mrs Ellen Quinn, a pregnant wife shot dead by Black and Tans while sitting outside her cottage door as they drove through Gort in their Crossley tender in November 1920. 2. *burn that stump:* Herodotus tells how a sacred olive tree on the Acropolis burned by the Persians grew 'two cubits' the following day. 3. *grasshoppers and bees:* image of lost brooches and hair ornaments from a past age repeated from earlier in the poem.

Reprisals [1]

Some nineteen German planes, they say,
You had brought down before you died. [2]
We called it a good death. Today
Can ghost or man be satisfied?
Although your last exciting year
Outweighed all other years, you said,
Though battle joy may be so dear
A memory, even to the dead,
It chases other thought away,
Yet rise from your Italian tomb,
Flit to Kiltartan cross and stay
Till certain second thoughts have come
Upon the cause you served, that we
Imagined such a fine affair:
Half-drunk or whole-mad soldiery
Are murdering your tenants there. [3]
Men that revere your father yet
Are shot at on the open plain.
Where may new-married women sit
And suckle children now? Armed men
May murder them in passing by
Nor law nor parliament take heed. [4]
Then close your ears with dust and lie
Among the other cheated dead.

W.B. YEATS

[1921]

1. *Reprisals:* Atrocities committed by British armed forces, notably the Black
and Tans, in response to IRA attacks during the Irish War of Independence
in 1920-21. 2. The poem is addressed to the ghost of Major Robert Gregory
(1881-1918), subject of Yeats's poem 'An Irish Airman Foresees His Death'
[➤ 109], son of Lady Gregory, who lived at Coole Park, near Kiltartan, Gort,
Co. Galway. Gregory was killed at the age of 36 flying over Italy when an
Italian pilot mistakenly shot him down. 3 & 4. See 'Nineteen Hundred and
Nineteen' ➤ 138, *n.* 1.

The Troubles, 1922

The Troubles came; by nineteen twenty-two
we knew of and accepted violence
in the small streets at hand. With Curfew tense,
each evening when that quiet hour was due,
I never ventured far from where I knew
I could reach home in safety. At the door
I'd sometimes stand, till with oncoming roar,
the wire-cage Crossley tenders swept in view.

Once, from front bedroom window, I could mark
black shapes, flat-capped, across the shadowed street,
two policemen on patrol. With crack and spark
fierce bullets struck the kerb beneath their feet;
below the shattered streetlamp in the dark
blurred shadow crouched, then pattered quick retreat.

[27 January 1979]

JOHN HEWITT

An Ulsterman in England remembers

Here at a distance, rocked by hopes and fears
with each convulsion of that fevered state,
the chafing thoughts attract, in sudden spate,
neglected shadows from my boyhood years:
the Crossley tenders caged and roofed with wire,
the crouching Black and Tans, the Lewis gun,
the dead lad in the entry; one by one
the Catholic public houses set on fire;
the anxious curfew of the summer night,
the thoroughfares deserted, at a door
three figures standing, till the tender's roar,
approaching closer, drives them out of sight;
and on the broad roof of the County Gaol
the singing prisoners brief freedom take

to keep an angry neighbourhood awake
with rattled plate and pot and metal pail;
below my bedroom window, bullet-spark
along the kerb, the beat of rapid feet
of the lone sniper, clipping up the street,
soon lost, the gas lamps shattered, in the dark;
and on the paved edge of our cinder-field,
intent till dusk upon the game, I ran
against a briskly striding, tall young man,
and glimpsed the rifle he thought well concealed.
At Auschwitz, Dallas, I felt no surprise
when violence, across the world's wide screen,
declared the age imperilled: I had seen
the future in that frightened gunman's eyes.

[28-31 August 1969]

JOHN HEWITT

John Hewitt (1907-87) was a poet, art historian and political activist, born in Belfast, who became the father-figure of 'Northern Irish poetry'. Apart from 15 years spent in Coventry as an art gallery director, when 'An Ulsterman Remembers' was written, at the start of the Troubles, he lived in Belfast all his life. The 'boyhood years' described in the poem included the Irish War of Independence, when the Black and Tans were attacking civilians and burning houses in Belfast as well as in the south of Ireland, before the country was partitioned. Drawn to the Ulster dissenting tradition, he was an early advocate of the concept of regional identity within the island of Ireland and famously described his identity as 'Ulster, Irish, British and European'.

Gravel

The soldiers had strong ropes and electric cord.
Each prisoner's hands were tied
Behind his back. His arms were tied above the elbows
To those of the man on either side.
Their feet were bound together above the ankles,
Their legs were bound together above the knees.
A rope was passed around the nine.

The soldiers moved away.

The prisoners' backs were to the mine.
When it exploded, the sudden hole in the road
Said nothing of our loss
And instead of singing in the dawn
Birds pecked the flesh off the trees
At Ballyseedy Cross.
Yet one prisoner escaped. He said 'Goodbye, lads' as the mine
Exploded, then he was on his hands and knees
In the road. Finding he was a whole man,
Free though burnt, he ran for the ditch, through trees,
Across the side of a hill, over a river, ran
Till he came to a sheltering house.
There was a girl. While he lay, she picked gravel
Out of his body.
              He has gravel in him to this day.

For months then he stole from house to house,
Sleeping in dugouts, hearing the midnight rain,
Waiting for bullets in the back and head.
They never came. He kept moving though,
Stayed clear of his own place for a long time.
He went home in the end. They took him in.

BRENDAN KENNELLY

One of Ireland's leading poets, **Brendan Kennelly** (*b.* 1936) grew up in the village of Ballylongford in Co. Kerry, and taught at Trinity College Dublin for over 30 years. Most of his work is concerned with the people, landscapes, wildlife and history of Ireland, and with language, religion and politics. 'Gravel' is from *Cromwell* (1983), his controversial book-length poem exploring 'the nightmare of Irish history' through the anachronistic figure of Oliver Cromwell. It describes an atrocity committed by Irish Free State soldiers at Ballyseedy crossroads near Tralee, Co. Kerry, towards the end of the Civil War, on 7 March 1923. Nine republican prisoners were tied to a landmine which was then detonated, after which the survivors were machine-gunned, but one man, Stephen Fuller (later a Fianna Fáil TD), was blown into a ditch by the blast and managed to escape. The Free State government claimed at the time that the prisoners had been a work-party clearing mines, but Fuller's re-appearance after the ceasefire exposed the lie. Nine more men were killed in two other landmine executions in Kerry that month. A total of 23 prisoners died in un-official executions and five others were judicially executed in just four weeks.

from Meditations in Time of Civil War

V *The Road at My Door*

An affable Irregular,[1]
A heavily-built Falstaffian man,
Comes cracking jokes of civil war
As though to die by gunshot were
The finest play under the sun.

A brown Lieutenant[2] and his men,
Half dressed in national uniform,
Stand at my door, and I complain
Of the foul weather, hail and rain,
A pear tree broken by the storm.

I count those feathered balls of soot
The moor-hen guides upon the stream,
To silence the envy in my thought;
And turn towards my chamber, caught
In the cold snows of a dream.

VI *The Stare's Nest by My Window*

The bees build in the crevices
Of loosening masonry, and there
The mother birds bring grubs and flies.
My wall is loosening; honey-bees
Come build in the empty house of the stare.[2]

We are closed in, and the key is turned
On our uncertainty; somewhere
A man is killed, or a house burned,
Yet no clear fact to be discerned;
Come build in the empty house of the stare.

A barricade of stone or of wood;
Some fourteen days of civil war;
Last night they trundled down the road
That dead young soldier in his blood;
Come build in the empty house of the stare.

We had fed the heart on fantasies,
The heart's grown brutal from the fare;
More substance in our enmities
Than in our love; O honey-bees,
Come build in the empty house of the stare.

[Thoor Ballylee, 1922] [4]

W.B. YEATS

1. *Irregular:* name used by supporters of the 1921 Anglo-Irish Treaty for its opponents, the Anti-Treatyites, or combatants in their forces. 2. *brown Lieutenant:* officer in the Free State's National Army (with improvised brown uniforms). 3. *stare:* starling. 4. *Thoor Ballylee:* This poem, like many in his 1928 collection *The Tower*, was written at his fortified Anglo-Norman tower house near Gort, Co. Galway, bought from Lady Gregory in 1917, where Yeats lived from 1921 to 1929.

Yeats described the background to this poem in a paragraph added to the text of his Nobel Prize acceptance lecture, published in *The Bounty of Sweden* (1925): 'I was in my Galway house during the first months of civil war, the railway bridges blown up and the roads blocked with stones and trees. For the first week there were no newspapers, no reliable news, we did not know who had won nor who had lost, and even after newspapers came, one never knew what was happening on the other side of the hill or of the line of trees. Ford cars passed the house from time to time with coffins standing upon end between the seats, and sometimes at night we heard an explosion, and once by day saw the smoke made by the burning of a great neighbouring house. [...] A stare (our West of Ireland name for a starling) had built in a hole beside my window and I made these verses [the first two stanzas] out of the feeling of the moment [...] Presently a strange thing happened; I began to smell honey in places where honey could not be, at the end of a stone passage or at some windy turn of the road and it came always with certain thoughts. When I got back to Dublin I was with angry people, who argued over everything or were eager to know the exact facts.'

Yeats in Civil War

Presently a strange thing happened:
I began to smell honey in places
where honey could not be.

In middle age you exchanged the sandals
Of a pilgrim for a Norman keep
In Galway. Civil war started, vandals
Sacked your country, made off with your sleep;

Somehow you arranged your escape
Aboard a spirit-ship which every day
Hoisted sail out of fire and rape,
And on that ship your mind was stowaway.

The sun mounted on a wasted place,
But the wind at every door and turn
Blew the smell of honey in your face
Where there was none. Whatever we may learn

You are its sum, struggling to survive –
A fantasy of honey in your reprieve.

EAVAN BOLAND

Eavan Boland (*b.* 1944) is one of Ireland's leading poets. This poem is from her 1967 collection *New Territory*. The three italicised lines quote from Yeats's comment on 'The Stare's Nest by My Window': ➤ 130 *n*. Author note ➤ 435.

from The Man and the Echo

In a cleft that's christened Alt[1]
Under broken stone I halt
At the bottom of a pit
That broad noon has never lit,
And shout a secret to the stone.
All that I have said and done,
Now that I am old and ill,
Turns into a question till
I lie awake night after night
And never get the answers right.
Did that play of mine[2] send out

Certain men the English shot?[3]
Did words of mine put too great strain
On that woman's reeling brain?
Could my spoken words have checked
That whereby a house lay wrecked?[4]
And all seems evil until I
Sleepless would lie down and die.

[1938]

W.B. YEATS

1. A fissure on Knocknarea, a hill near Sligo with Neolithic remains, possibly the source of the limestone used to build Medb's Cairn on the summit. 2. Yeats's play *Cathleen ni Houlihan*, written with Lady Gregory, staged at the Abbey Theatre in 1902 with his muse, the firebrand Maud Gonne, in the lead role, stirred up nationalist feeling in Dublin, as did his Cuchulain plays. 3. Men inspired by his play's patriotic, even propagandistic, glorifying of blood sacrifice for Mother Ireland, died in the Easter Rising or Irish War of Independence. In another late poem, 'The Statues', also from 1938, Yeats seems 'at once proud and disturbed that Pádraic Pearse and some of the other leaders of the Easter Rising had made a cult of the ancient Irish hero Yeats had revived, in the process unleashing an uncanny power: "When Pearse summoned Cuchulain to his side, | What stalked through the Post Office?"' [Patrick J. Keane] 4. Many of the big houses of the Anglo-Irish and Free State sympathisers were torched by 'incendiary and bigot' (see 'Nineteen Hundred and Nineteen', ➤ 142, *n.* 1) between 1919 and 1923. Yeats's beloved Coole Park may have been damaged at that time, and was sold by Lady Gregory in 1927, later falling into ruin before finally being demolished in 1941.

from **Wall**

I surround the Big House
hundreds of years old.
Craggy, cracked, indigenous,

I'm close to the Shannon tides,
aware of what it means to be
the line between warring sides.

I saw the Civil War, I was there
the day Eddie Carmody was shot.
A quiet man, Eddie. He whispered a prayer.

Others shouted curses. They swore
they were doing a favour to those
they chose to murder.

One said it was the Civil War
made the Irish grow up, made
men of them. I stood there, undismayed.

Killers will justify whatever they do.
A man must face himself, know the world.
Killing one neighbour can be hard. It's easier to kill two.

BRENDAN KENNELLY
➤ 142

A Disused Shed in Co. Wexford

Let them not forget us, the weak souls among the asphodels.
                SEFERIS, Mythistorema

(for J.G. Farrell)

Even now there are places where a thought might grow –
Peruvian mines, worked out and abandoned
To a slow clock of condensation,
An echo trapped for ever, and a flutter
Of wild flowers in the lift-shaft,
Indian compounds where the wind dances
And a door bangs with diminished confidence,
Lime crevices behind rippling rain-barrels,
Dog corners for bone burials;
And in a disused shed in Co. Wexford,

Deep in the grounds of a burnt-out hotel,
Among the bathtubs and the washbasins
A thousand mushrooms crowd to a keyhole.
This is the one star in their firmament
Or frames a star within a star.
What should they do there but desire?
So many days beyond the rhododendrons
With the world waltzing in its bowl of cloud,
They have learnt patience and silence
Listening to the rooks querulous in the high wood.

They have been waiting for us in a foetor
Of vegetable sweat since civil war days,
Since the gravel-crunching, interminable departure
Of the expropriated mycologist.
He never came back, and light since then
Is a keyhole rusting gently after rain.
Spiders have spun, flies dusted to mildew
And once a day, perhaps, they have heard something –
A trickle of masonry, a shout from the blue
Or a lorry changing gear at the end of the lane.

There have been deaths, the pale flesh flaking
Into the earth that nourished it;
And nightmares, born of these and the grim
Dominion of stale air and rank moisture.
Those nearest the door grow strong –
'Elbow room! Elbow room!'
The rest, dim in a twilight of crumbling
Utensils and broken pitchers, groaning
For their deliverance, have been so long
Expectant that there is left only the posture.

A half century, without visitors, in the dark –
Poor preparation for the cracking lock
And creak of hinges; magi, moonmen,
Powdery prisoners of the old regime,
Web-throated, stalked like triffids, racked by drought
And insomnia, only the ghost of a scream
At the flash-bulb firing-squad we wake them with

Shows there is life yet in their feverish forms.
Grown beyond nature now, soft food for worms,
They lift frail heads in gravity and good faith.

They are begging us, you see, in their wordless way,
To do something, to speak on their behalf
Or at least not to close the door again.
Lost people of Treblinka and Pompeii!
'Save us, save us,' they seem to say,
'Let the god not abandon us
Who have come so far in darkness and in pain.
We too had our lives to live.
You with your light meter and relaxed itinerary,
Let not our naive labours have been in vain!'

DEREK MAHON

Derek Mahon (*b.* 1941) is one of Ireland's leading contemporary poets, and a distinguished translator of French poetry as well as a journalist. Born and raised in Belfast, he now lives in Co. Cork.

The mushrooms in Mahon's 'Disused Shed' have been waiting in the dark 'since civil war days'. Their presence is symbolic, standing for all the marginalised people and mute victims of history. Charged with meaning and remembrance by the poem, this forgotten shed behind the rhododendrons is an imagined lost world ('one of those places where a thought might grow') remembered from *Troubles* (1970), a novel set in 1919 during the Irish War of Independence in the decaying Majestic Hotel in rural Ireland by J.G. Farrell, to whom the poem is dedicated (Mahon's friend was a polio victim, and died in Ireland in a drowning accident not long after the poem was written).

Written during the Irish 'Troubles' [➤ 427] in the 1970s, the poem is both timeless and timely, as Seamus Deane points out: 'It is a poem that heart-breakingly dwells on and gives voice to all those peoples and civilisations that have been lost and/or destroyed. Since it is set in Ireland, with all the characteristics of an Irish "Big House" ruin, it speaks with a special sharpness to the present moment and the fear, rampant in Northern Ireland, of communities that fear they too might perish and be lost, with none to speak for them.'

SPANISH CIVIL WAR | 1936–1939

TOTAL DEATHS: 500,000

The Spanish Civil War began when a group of rebel generals staged a coup in July 1936 to overthrow the democratically elected Republican government. Led in the war by General Francisco Franco, various conservative, monarchist or fascist groups were unified under the Nationalist banner, supported with arms and soldiers from Hitler's Germany and Mussolini's Italy, and opposed by the Republicans, an uneasy alliance of political groups and military loyal to the Second Spanish Republic which included socialist and communists of various persuasions, supported by the Soviet Union and Mexico. The Nationalists initially controlled the north and the south-east around Seville. With Madrid besieged for much of the war, the Republican government moved to Valencia.

Britain had a non-intervention policy, much to the frustration of left-wing writers and intellectuals during the 1930s, for whom Spain became the central political and humanitarian cause, especially after German planes bombed the Basque town of Guernica on 26 April 1937 at a cost of around 400 lives, one of the first air raids on a defenceless civilian population. W.H. Auden spoke for many in voicing support for the Republican government 'because its defeat by the forces of International Fascism would be a major disaster for Europe. It would make a European war more probable; and the spread of Fascist ideology and practice to countries as yet comparatively free from them, which would inevitably follow a Fascist victory in Spain, would create an atmosphere in which the creative artist and all who care for justice, liberty and culture would find it impossible to work or even exist.' The eventual defeat of the Republican government did make the Second World War inevitable. For Spain it was a disaster, with Franco's dictatorship lasting for 40 years until 1975.

Those writers prepared to lay down their lives in the cause of liberty went to Spain, many fighting as volunteers with the communist International Brigades or with the anti-Stalinist POUM militias (Orwell described their murderous falling out in *Homage to Catalonia* in 1938.) Others gave their support as journalists, broadcasters or drivers, but this was never a poets' war, as the myth has it: 80% of the recruits were working-class volunteers.

Auden's 'Spain', probably the best-known poem to come out of the war, is omitted from this selection because it says very little about the conflict itself and more about Auden's own disengaged standoffishness. Arriving in Spain in January 1937 ('Famous Poet to Drive Ambulance in Spain' announced the *Daily Worker*), Auden found his services not required, spent just seven weeks in the country, and returned home disillusioned, deeply affected by the discovery that political realities were much more ambiguous and complex than he had imagined. Orwell objected to the phrase 'the necessary murder' used in 'Spain', which Auden later amended to 'the fact of murder' before disowning the poem as 'dishonest', excluding it from editions of his *Collected Poems*.

For a full selection of poetry and prose by British and Irish poets, prefaced by a comprehensive introductory essay, Valentine Cunningham's *Penguin Book of Spanish Civil War Verse* (1978/1996) is unsurpassed.

from Mediterranean

1

At the end of July, exile. We watched the gangplank go
cutting the boat away, indicating: sea.
Barcelona, the sun, the fire-bright harbor, war.
Five days.
        Here at the rail, foreign and refugee,
we saw the city, remembered that zero of attack,
alarm in the groves, snares through the olive hills,
rebel defeat: leaders, two regiments,
broadcasts of victory, tango, surrender.
The truckride to the city, barricades,
bricks pried at corners, rifle-shot in street,
car-burning, bombs, blank warnings, fists up, guns
busy sniping, the town walls, towers of smoke.
And order making, committees taking charge, foreigners
commanded out by boat.

I saw the city, sunwhite flew on glass,
trucewhite from window, the personal lighting found
eyes on the dock, sunset-lit faces of singers,
eyes, goodbye into exile. Saw where Columbus rides
black-pillared: discovery, turn back, explore
a new found Spain, coast-province, city-harbor.
Saw our parades ended, the last marchers on board
listed by nation.

I saw first of the faces going home into war
the brave man Otto Boch, the German exile, knowing
he quieted tourists during machine-gun battle,
he kept his life straight as a single issue –
left at that dock we left, his gazing Brueghel face,
square forehead and eyes, strong square breast fading,
the narrow runner's hips diminishing dark.
I see this man, dock, war, a latent image.

The boat *Ciudad di Ibiza*, built for 200,
loaded with 500, manned by loyal sailors,

chartered by Belgians when consulates were helpless,
through a garden of gunboats, margin of the port,
entered: Mediterranean.

MURIEL RUKEYSER

On the evening of July 25, 1936, five days after the outbreak of the Spanish
Civil War, Americans with the Anti-Fascist Olympic Games were evacuated
from Barcelona at the order of the Catalonian Government. In a small Spanish
boat, the *Ciudad di Ibiza*, which the Belgians had chartered, they and a group
of five hundred, including the Hungarian and Belgian teams as well as the
American, sailed overnight to Sète, the first port in France. The only men
who remained were those who had volunteered in the Loyalist forces: the core
of the future International Column. [MR]

One of America's foremost political poets, **Muriel Rukeyser** (1913-80) worked
as a journalist in her 20s, witnessing events which were to make a serious
impact on her life and poetry: 'In July 1936, Rukeyser was sent to Spain on
assignment for *Life* and *Letters Today* to cover the People's Olympiad in
Barcelona, a protest and alternative to Hitler's Berlin Games. Instead, she
witnessed the first days of the Spanish Civil War. Rukeyser was on the last
train to cross the Spanish border as the military coup began and a general
strike was called in defence of the Spanish Republic. While stranded on the
train in Moncada, she met and fell in love with the Rotfrontkämpfer Otto
Boch [...] who had been exiled from Germany and was travelling to the
Barcelona games as a long-distance runner.' [Rowena Kennedy-Epstein]
　　Rukeyser's autobiographical novel *Savage Coast* draws on her experiences in
Spain and her love affair with Otto Boch, dedicatee of her war-related *Elegies*
(1949). Written in 1936 and rejected by publishers at the time, *Savage Coast* was
finally published in 2013 by the Feminist Press in New York. Otto Boch joined
the first International Brigade and was killed in battle at the Ebro River on
11 April 1938, the news of his death not reaching her until Christmas 1943.

from Fable of Three Friends to be Sung in Rounds

When the pure shapes sank
under the chirping daisies,[1]
I knew I'd been murdered.
They searched the cafés, cemeteries and churches.
They broke open wine-casks and cupboards.

They defiled three skeletons to pull out their gold teeth.
But they couldn't find me now.
They couldn't find me?
No. They couldn't find me.
And so it was that the sixth moon fled with the torrent,
and the sea suddenly recalled
the names of all its drowned.

FEDERICO GARCÍA LORCA
translated from the Spanish by Neil Astley

1. *bajo el cri cri de las margaritas*: literally, under the *cri cri* (chirping sound made by *grillos*, crickets, rubbing their wings together) of the daisies, possibly playing on the idiom, common to Spanish and English, *criar las margaritas*, to be pushing up the daisies.

Federico García Lorca (1898-1936), Spain's greatest modern poet and dramatist, was executed by Fascist partisans near Granada on 19 August 1936, shortly after the outbreak of the Spanish Civil War. He was by then an immensely popular figure, celebrated throughout the Spanish-speaking world, and at the height of his creative powers. After his death, with his work suppressed, he became a potent symbol of the martyrdom of Spain. The prophetic poem from which the above extract is taken was written in 1930, and published posthumously in *The Poet in New York* in 1940. Although likely sites of his grave have been excavated over the years, his remains have never been found.

The Crime Was in Granada
(to Federico García Lorca)

1 *The Crime*

He was seen, walking between rifles
down a long street
and going out to the cold countryside
still with stars of early dawn.
They killed Federico
when light came.
The squad of executioners
didn't dare look him in the face.

153

They all closed their eyes.
They prayed, 'Not God can save you!'
Dead fell Federico,
– blood on his forehead and lead in his stomach –.
That the crime was in Granada –
know it – poor Granada! – in his Granada.

2 *The Poet and Death*

He was seen walking alone with her,
not afraid of her scythe.
– The sun already on tower and tower; the hammers
on the anvil – anvil and anvil of the forges.
Federico was speaking,
flirting with death. She listened.
'Companion, because yesterday in my verse,
the clapping of your dry palms resounded
and you gave ice to my song, and edge
of your sickle of silver to my tragedy,
I will sing you your missing flesh,
the eyes you lack,
your hair the wind was ruffling,
the red lips where they kissed you...
Today as yesterday, gypsy, my death,
how good alone with you
in these breezes of Granada, my Granada!

3

He was seen walking...
                        Friends, carve
a tomb of stone and dream in the Alhambra,
for the poet,
over a fountain where the water weeps
and forever says,
The crime was in Granada, in his Granada!

ANTONIO MACHADO
translated from the Spanish by Willis Barnstone

154

Antonio Machado (1875-1939) was one of the leading figures in Spanish literature's 'Generation of '98'. Forced to flee Spain as Franco's forces closed in on the last Republican strongholds, he died in France the following year. He wrote his elegy a few days after hearing of García Lorca's murder, which Machado believed was politically motivated, writing in a letter (of 1936 or 1937): 'The death of García Lorca has greatly saddened me [...] A stupid crime has silenced his voice forever [...] Could Granada have defended its poet? I think so. It would have been easy for it to prove to the Fascist assassins that Lorca was politically innocuous and that the common people whom Federico loved and whose songs he collected were not precisely those who sing "the Internationale".' [tr. from *Obras. Poesía y Prosa* (1964), 671-72]

I'm Explaining a Few Things

You are going to ask: and where are the lilacs?
and the poppy-petalled metaphysics?
and the rain repeatedly spattering
its words and drilling them full
of apertures and birds?

I'll tell you all the news.

I lived in a suburb,
a suburb of Madrid, with bells,
and clocks, and trees.

From there you could look out
over Castille's dry face:
a leather ocean.
                My house was called
the house of flowers, because in every cranny
geraniums burst: it was
a good-looking house
with its dogs and children.
                        Remember, Raúl?
Eh, Rafael?
            Federico, do you remember
from under the ground
my balconies on which
the light of June drowned flowers in your mouth?

155

                                             Brother, my brother!
Everything
loud with big voices, the salt of merchandises,
pile-ups of palpitating bread,
the stalls of my suburb of Argüelles with its statue
like a drained inkwell in a swirl of hake:
oil flowed into spoons,
a deep baying
of feet and hands swelled in the streets,
metres, litres, the sharp
measure of life,
                    stacked-up fish,
the texture of roofs with a cold sun in which
the weather vane falters,
the fine, frenzied ivory of potatoes,
wave on wave of tomatoes rolling down the sea.

And one morning all that was burning,
one morning the bonfires
leapt out of the earth
devouring human beings –
and from then on fire,
gunpowder from then on,
and from then on blood.
Bandits with planes and Moors,
bandits with finger-rings and duchesses,
bandits with black friars spattering blessings
came through the sky to kill children
and the blood of children ran through the streets
without fuss, like children's blood.

Jackals that the jackals would despise,
stones that the dry thistle would bite on and spit out,
vipers that the vipers would abominate!

Face to face with you I have seen the blood
of Spain tower like a tide
to drown you in one wave
of pride and knives!

Treacherous
generals:

see my dead house,
look at broken Spain:
from every house burning metal flows
instead of flowers,
from every socket of Spain
Spain emerges
and from every dead child a rifle with eyes,
and from every crime bullets are born
which will one day find
the bull's eye of your hearts.

And you'll ask: why doesn't his poetry
speak of dreams and leaves
and the great volcanoes of his native land?

Come and see the blood in the streets.
Come and see
the blood in the streets.
Come and see the blood
in the streets!

PABLO NERUDA
translated from the Spanish by Nathaniel Tarn

Pablo Neruda (*b.* 1904-73), known in Chile as 'the people's poet', was one of the greatest and most influential poets of the 20th century, receiving the Nobel Prize in Literature in 1971. He served his country as a diplomat for many years, and was a consul in Madrid when the Spanish Civil War started. His early poetry was fiercely surreal, reflecting ancient terrors, modern anxieties and his near-religious desolation. The Spanish Civil War and the murder of his friend García Lorca changed Neruda's life and work as he moved to a more personal voice and to more politically involved and ideological positions.

Tom Wintringham (1898-1949) was a man of action, a revolutionary, a soldier and a poet. During the First World War he served as a motorcycle despatch rider on the Western Front; in the Spanish Civil War he commanded the British battalion of the International Brigade; in the Second World War he was the driving force and inspiration behind the establishment of the Home Guard. He helped found the Communist Party, was one of twelve Communist leaders jailed for 'sedition' in 1925, and was expelled from the party in 1938. Wounded twice, at the Battle of Jarama in February 1937 and again on the Aragon front in August 1937, he was repatriated at the end of that year. ➤ 158

We're Going On!

Neither fools nor children any longer;
Those ways, traits, gone and away.
That once made life a luck-game, death a stranger
We're going on.

Dynamo-driven city waiting bombers
Roadways barricade-unpaved, fear
In the torn minds: the mind remembers
What it's all for.

Death means the corpses warm alive when buried:
Death means the retching brothels where on black
Death's tide, death fear, an army of boys is carried
To a pox wreck.

And life's a matter of beating this, of breaking
By our hardness, and a held hand, out
Of fury, frustration, fear, the waiting, the shouting,
The hate of the fate.

Neither fools nor children, we who are joining
(twenty years ago I knew war's face)
We make what can wreck others into our gaining,
Into our choice.

[Barcelona, 19 September 1936]

TOM WINTRINGHAM

A Letter from Aragon

This is a quiet sector of a quiet front.

We buried Ruiz in a new pine coffin,
But the shroud was too small and his washed feet stuck out.
The stink of his corpse came through the clean pine boards

And some of the bearers wrapped handkerchiefs round their faces.
Death was not dignified.
We hacked a ragged grave in the unfriendly earth
And fired a ragged volley over the grave.

You could tell from our listlessness, no one much missed him.

This is a quiet sector of a quiet front.
There is no poison gas and no H.E.[1]

But when they shelled the other end of the village
And the streets were choked with dust
Women came screaming out of the crumbling houses,
Clutched under one arm the naked rump of an infant.
I thought: how ugly fear is.

This is a quiet sector of a quiet front.
Our nerves are steady; we all sleep soundly.

In the clean hospital bed my eyes were so heavy
Sleep easily blotted out one ugly picture,
A wounded militiaman moaning on a stretcher,
Now out of danger, but still crying for water,
Strong against death, but unprepared for such pain.

This on a quiet front.

But when I shook hands to leave, an Anarchist worker
Said: 'Tell the workers of England
This was a war not of our own making,
We did not seek it.
But if ever the Fascists again rule Barcelona
It will be as a heap of ruins with us workers beneath it.'

JOHN CORNFORD

1. *H.E.:* High explosives.

John Cornford (1915-36) was an English poet who joined the Communist Party
while at Cambridge. After a brief spell with the POUM militia in Barcelona,
he served with a machine-gun unit of the International Brigade, fighting in the
defence of Madrid through November and December 1936, and was killed on
or shortly after his 21st birthday at Lopera, near Córdoba.

The wounded man

(for the wall of a hospital in all the gore)

I

The wounded stretch across the battlefields.
And from the long length of these fighters' bodies
a wheatfield of warm fountains springs up,
spreading into raucous jets.

Blood always rains upside down, toward the sky.
And wounds make sounds, just like conch shells
when the rapidity of flight is in them,
the essence of waves.

Blood smells like the sea, tastes like the sea, and the wine cellar.
The wine cellar of the sea, of hardy wine, breaks open
where the wounded man, shivering, goes under,
blossoms, and finds himself.

I am wounded. Look at me: I need more lives.
The one I have is too small for the consignment
of blood that I want to give up through my wounds.
Tell me who has not been wounded.

My life is a wound with a happy childhood.
Ay, the poor man who is not wounded, who never feels
wounded by life, never rests in life,
happily wounded!

If a man goes cheerfully to hospitals,
they change into gardens of half-opened wounds,
of flowering oleanders in front of the operating room
with its bloodstained doors.

II

I bleed for freedom, I fight, I survive.
For freedom I give my eyes and hands,
like a generous and captive tree of flesh,
to the surgeons.

For freedom I feel more hearts
in me than grains of sand: my veins give up foam,
and I enter the hospitals, I enter the bandages
as if they were lilies.

For freedom I sever myself, with bullets,
from those who dumped her statue into the mud.
And I sever myself from my feet, my arms,
my house – from everything.

Because where these empty eye-sockets dawn
she will put two stones that see the future,
and make new arms and new legs grow
from the pruned flesh.

The body's relics that I give up in each wound
will bud again in autumnless flutterings of sap.
Because I am like the cropped tree, and I bud again:
because I still have life.

MIGUEL HERNÁNDEZ
translated from the Spanish by Don Share

Miguel Hernández (1910-42) was a self-educated goatherd from the tiny
Spanish town of Orihuela who became a hugely popular poet. Campaigning
for the Republic, he addressed troops deployed to the front, volunteered
himself and took part in the defence of Madrid. When the city finally fell to
Franco in 1939, he tried to cross into Portugal but was turned back, arrested
and sentenced to death (commuted to a prison term of 30 years). Over three
years in various prisons, enduring extremely harsh conditions and contracting
tuberculosis, Hernández wrote numerous poems and songs, but died aged 31,
his TB untreated, still in jail three years after the war had ended. ➢ 168, 172.

The Tolerance of Crows

Death comes in quantity from solved
Problems on maps, well-ordered dispositions,
Angles of elevation and direction;

Comes innocent from tools children might
Love, retaining under pillows,
Innocently impales on any flesh.

And with flesh falls apart the mind
That trails thought from the mind that cuts
Thought clearly for a waiting purpose.

Progress of poison in the nerves and
Discipline's collapse is halted.
Body awaits the tolerance of crows.

CHARLES DONNELLY

Charles Donnelly (1914-37) was an Irish poet and political activist who was killed at the Battle of Jarama on 27 February 1937, aged 22, a month after arriving in Spain. Pinned down by machine-gun fire in an olive grove, he was heard to say 'Even the olives are bleeding' a few minutes before being caught in a burst of gunfire as his unit retreated.

In Memory of Charles Donnelly

I
Minutes before a bullet hits you in the forehead
There is a lull in the machine-gun fire, time to pick
From the dust a bunch of olives, time to squeeze them,
To understand the groans and screams and big abstractions
By saying quietly 'Even the olives are bleeding'.

II
Buried among the roots of that olive tree, you are
Wood and fruit and the skylight its branches make
Through which to read as they accumulate for ever
The poems you go on not writing in the tree's shadow
As it circles the fallen olives and the olive-stones.

MICHAEL LONGLEY

➤ 430

Ultima Ratio Regum

The guns spell money's ultimate reason
In letters of lead on the spring hillside.
But the boy lying dead under the olive trees
Was too young and too silly
To have been notable to their important eye.
He was a better target for a kiss.

When he lived, tall factory hooters never summoned him
Nor did restaurant plate-glass doors revolve to wave him in.
His name never appeared in the papers.
The world maintained its traditional wall
Round the dead with their gold sunk deep as a well,
Whilst his life, intangible as a Stock Exchange rumour, drifted outside.

O too lightly he threw down his cap
One day when the breeze threw petals from the trees.
The unflowering wall sprouted with guns,
Machine-gun anger quickly scythed the grasses;
Flags and leaves fell from hands and branches;
The tweed cap rotted in the nettles.

Consider his life which was valueless
In terms of employment, hotel ledgers, news files.
Consider. One bullet in ten thousand kills a man.
Ask. Was so much expenditure justified
On the death of one so young and so silly
Lying under the olive tree, O world, O death?

STEPHEN SPENDER

Sir Stephen Spender (1909-95) was one of the 30s generation of socially com-
mitted English poets, along with Auden, MacNeice and Day Lewis. In February
1937 he arrived in Valencia to work as an English radio broadcaster for the
Socialist Party, only to find Auden had just left for home and the radio station
didn't want him. Much of his time in Spain was spent trying to help his
former lover Tony Hyndman, who'd survived the Battle of Jarama but become
disillusioned with the war and was charged with desertion from the International
Brigade. Spender also hitchhiked to the corpse-strewn front line near Madrid
where he was told to fire some shots at the enemy trenches.

David Guest

Well O.K., he was wrong
Getting killed in Spain
Like that. Wal Hannington
Sat and tried to argue him out of going.
He was wrong, he was wrong,
The angel has not descended, the state
Hasn't the faintest chance of withering away,
And nobody is sure which way Hegel is up any more.
He was the greatest hero I've met because he was brave,
And would argue with anybody,
And could interest people because he was interested –
If he was so bloody interested he should have gone on talking,
        gone on talking,
Something might have been talked out.
Near to a saint, he should not have got himself killed,
Thereby making himself an ineffectual angel, a moth.
The Professor of economics was right:
He just couldn't keep still at a public meeting,
He would keep turning round and standing up to see what was
        happening and who was talking,
And this was probably how the bullet got him in the trenches at
        Jarama.

MARTIN BELL

Martin Bell (1918-78) was an influential English poet and translator of French
poetry known for his belligerent, often fantastical poetry. His friend David
Guest was a mathematician and philosopher who joined the International
Brigade and was shot by a sniper while reading a newspaper (not at Jarama,
as Bell has it, but in July 1938 at Gandesa during the later Battle of the Ebro).

Wings Overhead

Over Brunete came the sound
Of black wings crawling up the sky;
The soldier crouched against the ground
With straining limbs till they went by.
He heard the bombs sing down the air,
He felt them land, and everywhere
The earth in an advancing line
Rose up. The soldier said 'This time'.
This time he laughed at what he said,
And stretched his body to the heat;
The sun alone was overhead
And warmed the terror out of it.

Now, when the thin December gleam
Is driven off the sky by snow
And breath hangs in the air like steam,
The soldier on the plain below
Hears the familiar song of hate
And stoops behind the parapet.
When the black wings have passed beyond
He pulls his blanket closer round,
Grins at the younger man, who tries
To catch his courage from his eyes.
'We'll bring them all down bye and bye,
And then,' he says, 'they'll never come.'
The young man, looking at the sky,
Sees only white wings of the storm.

MILES TOMALIN

Miles Tomalin (1904-83) was an English poet, writer and virtuoso recorder player. A photograph from December 1937 shows him posed with a group of comrades, his foot resting on their 37mm anti-tank gun before the Battle of Teruel, playing the Dolmetsch recorder on which he inscribed the names of all the battles in which he fought. He later became a documentary scriptwriter specialising in the Industrial Revolution. His wife was textile designer Elisabeth Tomalin, whom he married in 1940 after she'd fled Dresden to escape Nazi persecution. Their son, journalist Nicholas Tomalin, was killed in Israel by a Syrian missile while reporting the Yom Kippur War in 1973.

Bombing Casualties in Spain

Dolls' faces are rosier but these were children
their eyes not glass but gleaming gristle
dark lenses in whose quick silvery glances
the sunlight quivered. These blenched lips
were warm once and bright with blood
but blood
held in a moist blob of flesh
not spilt and spatter'd in tousled hair.

In these shadowy tresses
red petals did not always
thus clot and blacken to a scar.
These are dead faces:
wasps' nests are not more wanly waxen
wood embers not so greyly ashen.

They are laid out in ranks
like paper lanterns that have fallen
after a night of riot
extinct in the dry morning air.

HERBERT READ
➤ 101

Bombers

Through the vague morning, the heart preoccupied,
A deep in air buried grain of sound
Starts and grows, as yet unwarning –
The tremor of baited deepsea line.

Swells the seed, and now tight sound-buds
Vibrate, upholding their paean flowers
To the sun. There are bees in sky-bells droning,
Flares of crimson at the heart unfold.

Children look up, and the elms spring-garlanded
Tossing their heads and marked for the axe.
Gallant or woebegone, alike unlucky –
Earth shakes beneath us: we imagine loss.

Black as vermin, crawling in echelon
Beneath the cloud-floor, the bombers come:
The heavy angels, carrying harm in
Their wombs that ache to be rid of death.

This is the seed that grows for ruin,
The iron embryo conceived in fear.
Soon or late its need must be answered
In fear delivered and screeching fire.

Choose between your child and this fatal embryo.
Shall your guilt bear arms, and the children you want
Be condemned to die by the powers you paid for
And haunt the houses you never built?

C. DAY LEWIS

C. Day Lewis (1904-72) was one of the 30s generation of socially committed
English poets, along with Auden, MacNeice and Spender. Born in Ireland,
he was Britain's Poet Laureate from 1968 to 1972 and wrote mystery stories
as Nicholas Blake.

Death Sentence Commuted to Thirty Years

When this sunrise put the question 'why
should birds sing?' Even the machine-gun
kills in rhythm. For the ordinary eye
enjoys the redness in blood, the purple of wine,
Death's proud carnation
a murdered man twists at the corner of his mouth.

While we sat down by the river barbed wire
was stretched between us and a circling cloud
to emphasise our horizon, perpetual window,
wall's edge, the beat of a guard on duty.
Caged in, to see a star, to think the world,
to live life's compass in a flat gravel yard,

The homeward rail imagination ran
outdistanced time with modern mockery.
Slow passed each day, compiled a week,
our patient waiting streamed by the prison bars
till we grew tired of counting; only knew
Death is no sudden, but reiterated speed.

CLIVE BRANSON

➤ 173

Sunset

Like a new cut on a young girl's shoulder
the sun left a crimson scar.
Through barbed wire
we can feel the day's passing
and evening
warns us of night, the complete end.

[Palencia, 1938]

CLIVE BRANSON

18 July 1936 – 18 July 1938

Blood, not hail, pounds at my temples.
Two years of blood: two floods.
Blood, circulating like the sun, swallowing everything
until the balconies are left drowned and empty.

Blood, the finest of all treasures.
Blood, which stored up its gifts for love.
See it churning up oceans, surprising trains,
breaking down bulls as it heartens lions.

Time is blood. Time pumps through my veins.
And here with the clock and dawn, I am more than wounded,
and I hear blood collisions of every kind.

Blood, where death itself could scarcely bathe:
Excited brilliance that has not grown pale
because my eyes, for a thousand years, have sheltered it.

MIGUEL HERNÁNDEZ
translated from the Spanish by Don Share
➤ 161

from Autumn Journal

VI

And I remember Spain
    At Easter ripe as an egg for revolt and ruin
Though for a tripper the rain
    Was worse than the surly or the worried or the haunted faces
With writings on the walls –
    Hammer and sickle, Boicot, Viva, Muerra;
With café-au-lait brimming the waterfalls,
    With sherry, shellfish, omelettes.
With fretted stone the Moor
    Had chiselled for effects of sun and shadow;
With shadows of the poor,
    The begging cripples and the children begging.
The churches full of saints
    Tortured on racks of marble –
The old complaints
    Covered with gilt and dimly lit with candles.
With powerful or banal
    Monuments of riches or repression

And the Escorial
     Cold for ever within like the heart of Philip.
With ranks of dominoes
     Deployed on café tables the whole of Sunday;
With cabarets that call the tourist, shows
     Of thighs and eyes and nipples.
With slovenly soldiers, nuns,
     And peeling posters from the last elections
Promising bread or guns
     Or an amnesty or another
Order or else the old
     Glory veneered and varnished
As if veneer could hold
     The rotten guts and crumbled bones together.
And a vulture hung in air
     Below the cliffs of Ronda and below him
His hook-winged shadow wavered like despair
     Across the chequered vineyards.
And the boot-blacks in Madrid
     Kept us half an hour with polish and pincers
And all we did
     In that city was drink and think and loiter.
And in the Prado half-
     wit princes looked from the canvas they had paid for
(Goya had the laugh –
     But can what is corrupt be cured by laughter?)
And the day at Aranjuez
     When the sun came out for once on the yellow river
With Valdepeñas burdening the breath
     We slept a royal sleep in the royal gardens;
And at Toledo walked
     Around the ramparts where they throw the garbage
And glibly talked
     Of how the Spaniards lack all sense of business.
And Avila was cold
     And Segovia was picturesque and smelly
And a goat on the road seemed old
     As the rocks or the Roman arches.
And Easter was wet and full
     In Seville and in the ring on Easter Sunday

A clumsy bull and then a clumsy bull
  Nodding his banderillas died of boredom.
And the standard of living was low
  But that, we thought to ourselves, was not our business;
All that the tripper wants is the *status quo*
  Cut and dried for trippers.
And we thought the papers a lark
  With their party politics and blank invective;
And we thought the dark
  Women who dyed their hair should have it dyed more often.
And we sat in trains all night
  With the windows shut among civil guards and peasants
And tried to play piquet by a tiny light
  And tried to sleep bolt upright;
And cursed the Spanish rain
  And cursed their cigarettes which came to pieces
And caught heavy colds in Cordova and in vain
  Waited for the right light for taking photos.
And we met a Cambridge don who said with an air
  'There's going to be trouble shortly in this country,'
And ordered anis, pudgy and debonair,
  Glad to show off his mastery of the language.
But only an inch behind
  This map of olive and ilex, this painted hoarding,
Careless of visitors the people's mind
  Was tunnelling like a mole to day and danger.
And the day before we left
  We saw the mob in flower at Algeciras
Outside a toothless door, a church bereft
  Of its images and its aura.
And at La Linea while
  The night put miles between us and Gibraltar
We heard the blood-lust of a drunkard pile
  His heaven high with curses;
And next day took the boat
  For home, forgetting Spain, not realising
That Spain would soon denote
  Our grief, our aspirations;
Not knowing that our blunt
  Ideals would find their whetstone, that our spirit

Would find its frontier on the Spanish front,
Its body in a rag-tag army.

[August–December 1938]

LOUIS MACNEICE

Louis MacNeice (1907-63) was born in Belfast, joining Auden's group of left-wing poets at Oxford, where Stephen Spender and C. Day Lewis were already part of his circle. In a note to his long poem *Autumn Journal* (1939), he says that this *zeitgeist* work was written from August to December 1938: 'Not strictly a journal but giving the tenor of my emotional experiences during the period. It is about everything which from first-hand experience I consider important. [...] It contains rapportage [sic], metaphysics, ethics, lyrical emotion, autobiography, nightmare. [...] Places visited include Hampshire, Spain, Birmingham, Ireland, & – especially – London.' The poem includes reflections on the Munich crisis and on his visit to Barcelona just before the city fell to Franco's forces. A second extract appears in the Second World War section [➤ 186] of this anthology.

War

Old age in the villages.
The heart with no master.
Love with no object.
Grass, dust, crow.
And children?
In the coffin.

The tree alone and dry.
Woman like a log
of widowhood lying on the bed.
Incurable hatred.
And children?
In the coffin.

MIGUEL HERNÁNDEZ
translated from the Spanish by Don Share
➤ 161

Spain. December 1936

You, English!
Can't you hear the barrage creeping
that levels the Pyrenees?

Is time tangible
that bears so audible
and visible a thing?

Can't you hear the men scream
where the fascist bomb
makes the people's home
a tomb for you and me?

Can't you see the gashes in the street
where our people stumble
when the city trembles?
Can't you smell the rose held in their teeth
tighter than death?

They who lie so still
with no Cross,
only this, their courage, their faith
manures the barren earth
for new trees
to spring up the hillside to the very sky.

That we should be insensible at such a time
makes deafness kill and peace the bloodier crime.

[London, 1939]

CLIVE BRANSON

Clive Branson (1907-44) was an English artist, poet, Communist activist and recruiter for the International Brigade. He fought in the Spanish Civil War from January 1938, was captured at Calaceite on 31 March and sentenced to death but held as a prisoner of war for eight months before being repatriated. He was killed in Burma in February 1944 while serving as a tank commander in the British Army when his vehicle was hit by an enemy shell. ➢ 168

SECOND WORLD WAR | 1939–1945

TOTAL DEATHS: 78 MILLION

Whereas the First World War was mainly fought on the ground along frontlines dividing rival armies, the Second World War was a global conflict involving 100 million people from more than 30 different countries. The total number of people killed is estimated at 78 million: 2.5% of the world's population. Only 5% of casualties in the First World War were civilians, whereas the proportion of civilian deaths in the Second World War was massively higher: 68%, including six million Jews who died in the concentration camps and 14-16 million others (including Poles, Romanies, the disabled and mentally ill, homosexuals, political opponents and prisoners of war) deliberately murdered by the Nazis and their collaborators. The home front became the front line as whole countries were subjected to sustained bombing campaigns. Over 40,000 civilians died in the eight-month Blitz against Britain in 1940-41, around half of those in London. The death toll from the Allied bombing of Dresden was 35,000; and in a single raid on Tokyo, over 83,000 people were killed, 20,000 more than all the British deaths from air attack throughout the war. The atom bombs dropped on Hiroshima and Nagasaki in 1945 resulted in the ➢ 186deaths of over 200,000 people, mostly civilians.

The poetry of the Second World War was in consequence more varied and more challenged than that of any previous or subsequent conflict, drawn from the experiences of combatants, victims and witnesses in many different "theatres of war", including most of Europe, Russia, the North African desert, the Middle East, the Far East, Japan and the Pacific, and encompassing invasions, tank battles, deportations, death marches, displaced refugees, the war at sea, the war in the air, devastated cities, genocide, the Holocaust, and the total destruction of two Japanese cities using nuclear weapons, the first and only such attacks in world history.

While there have been several excellent anthologies of Second World War poetry, no one book can possibly accommodate the range of work written during and since the six years of the war, let alone a section in a book covering the past hundred years of war. My aim with this compilation was to present the strongest poems by a wide range of writers, including key poets (Auden, Brecht, Keith Douglas, Hamish Henderson, Randall Jarrell, Miklós Radnóti), in a narrative taking in major phases of the war as well as significant episodes or events, along with the lead-up to the war and its immediate aftermath.

Where possible, the poems are presented chronologically in terms of when they were written or set, building up a picture of what individual poets from different nations were experiencing at the same time. For example, in one three-month period, from August to November 1944, Polish poets join the Warsaw Uprising, Miklós Radnóti is herded on a forced march from Serbia to Hungary (where he is killed), other Hungarian poets witness deportations to camps, Dylan Thomas voices the anguish of Londoners under V-bomb attack, and Louis Simpson is a foot soldier caught up in the chaotic Battle of the Bulge.

A Thousand Killed

I read of a thousand killed.
And am glad because the scrounging imperial paw
Was there so bitten:
As a man at elections is thrilled
When the results pour in, and the North goes with him
And the West breaks in the thaw.

(That fighting was a long way off.)

Forgetting therefore an election
Being fought with votes and lies and catch-cries
And orator's frowns and flowers and posters' noise,
Is paid for with cheques and toys:
Wars the most glorious
Victory-winged and steeple-uproarious
...With the lives, burned-off,
Of young men and boys.

[*c.* January 1936]

BERNARD SPENCER

Bernard Spencer (1909-63) was a distinctive voice in 20th-century English poetry, and a central figure in the *Personal Landscape* group of wartime Cairo writers. He spent much of his life working for the British Council, in Greece, Egypt, Italy, Spain, Turkey and Austria, the settings for many of his poems. This poem was inspired by reading about the First Battle of Tembien (20-24 January 1936) in the Second Italo-Ethiopian War of 1935-36, an inconclusive encounter in which the Italians had just over 'a thousand killed' (while the Ethiopians casualties were 8,000...). First published in the April–May 1936 issue of *New Verse*, before the outbreak of the Spanish Civil War, it has been wrongly linked with that conflict by editors of several war poetry anthologies. Here 'the scrounging imperial paw' is Mussolini's, not Franco's, but as in Auden's non-specific 'Epitaph on a Tyrant' [> 186], one dictator stands for all.

Our Town Is Burning

Our town is burning, brothers, burning,
Our poor little town is burning.
Angry winds are fanning higher
The leaping tongues of flame and fire,
The evil winds are roaring!
Our whole town burns!

And you stand looking on with folded arms,
And shake your heads.
You stand looking on, with folded arms
While the fire spreads!

Our town is burning, brothers, burning,
Our poor little town is burning.
Tongues of flame are leaping,
The fire through our town goes sweeping,
Through roofs and windows pouring.
All around us burns.

And you stand looking on with folded arms,
And shake your heads.
You stand looking on with folded arms
While the fire spreads!

Our town is burning, brothers, burning.
Any moment the fire may
Sweep the whole of our town away,
And leave only ashes, black and grey,
Like after a battle, where dead walls stand,
Broken and ruined in a desolate land.

And you stand looking on with folded arms,
And shake your heads.
You stand looking on with folded arms
While the fire spreads!

Our town is burning, brothers, burning.
All now depends on you.
Our only help is what you do.

You can still put out the fire
With your blood, if you desire.

Don't look on with folded arms.
And shake your heads.
Don't look on with folded arms
While the fire spreads!

[1938]

MORDECAI GEBIRTIG
translated from the Yiddish by Joseph Leftwich

Mordecai Gebirtig (1877-1942) was a Yiddish poet and songwriter from
Kraków, Poland. His best-known song, 'Our Town Is Burning', written in
response to the pogrom in Przytyk in March 1936, was later adopted by the
Jewish youth of Kraków and others as a battle song against the Nazis. He was
shot in the Kraków Ghetto on the infamous 'Bloody Thursday', 4 June 1942.

The Hitler Spring

> *Né quella ch'a veder lo sol si gira ...*[1]
> — DANTE (?) TO GIOVANNI QUIRINI

The thick white cloud of mad moths whirls
around the pale lights and the parapets,
spreading a blanket on the earth that snaps
like sugar underfoot; the coming summer
frees the night frost locked in the dead season's
secret cellars and the gardens
that scale down from Maiano to these sands.

An infernal messenger flew just now along the avenue,
to a chant of thugs; an orchestra pit,
firelit and arrayed with swastikas,
seized and devoured him, the windows,
shabby and inoffensive, though adorned
with cannons and war toys, are shuttered up,
the butcher who laid berries on the snouts

177

of his slaughtered goats has closed; the feast
of the mild murderers still innocent of blood
has turned into a foul Virginia reel of shattered wings,
larvae on the sandbars, and the water rushes in
to eat the shore and no one's blameless anymore.

All for nothing then? – and the Roman
candles at San Giovanni, slowly whitening
the horizon, and the vows and long farewells
definitive as baptism in the dismal
vigil of the horde (but a jewel scored the air,
sowing the icy edges of your beaches
with the angels of Tobias, the seven,
seed of the future) and the sunflowers born
of your hands – all burned, sucked dry
by pollen that hisses like fire
and stings like hail...
                                     Oh the wounded spring
is still a festival if it will chill
this death to death!
Clizia, it's your fate: look up again,
changed one harboring your changeless love,
until the sightless sun you bear within you
is blinded in the Other and consumed
in Him, for all. Perhaps the sirens and the tolling
that hail the monsters on the eve
of their pandemonium already blend
with the sound released from the sky that descends victorious –
with the breath of a dawn that may break tomorrow for all,
white, but without wings of terror,
over the scorched rockbeds of the south...

EUGENIO MONTALE
translated from the Italian by Jonathan Galassi

1. 'Nor did she who turns to see the sun...' (sonnet attributed to Dante).

Eugenio Montale (1896-1981) was Italy's greatest modern poet, winner of the
Nobel Prize in 1975. He was drafted during the First World War, serving as
an infantry officer on the Austrian front. In 1938 he was dismissed as director
of the Gabinetto Vieusseux Library in Florence for refusing to join the Fascist
party.

from A German War Primer

THE BRASS SAY: PEACE AND WAR
Are made of different stuff.
But their peace and their war
Are like wind and storm.

War grows from their peace
Like son from his mother
It bears
Her terrible features.

Their war kills only
Whatever their peace
Has left over.

          * * *

WHEN THE TOP BRASS SPEAK OF PEACE
The common folk know
There'll be war.

When the leaders inveigh against war
The draft papers have already been printed.

          * * *

ON THE WALL IN CHALK WERE THE WORDS:
They want war.
He who wrote it
Has already fallen.

          * * *

IT IS NIGHT
The married couples
Take themselves off to their beds. The young women
Will bear orphans.

          * * *

179

WHEN IT COMES TO MARCHING MANY DO NOT KNOW
That their enemy marches at their head.
The voice that commands them
Is the voice of their enemy.
He who speaks of the enemy
Is himself the enemy.

*   *   *

GENERAL, YOUR TANK IS A POWERFUL THING.
It can break down a forest and crush a hundred men.
But it has one defect:
It needs a driver.

General, your bomber is powerful.
It flies faster than the wind and carries more than an elephant.
But it has one defect:
It needs a mechanic.

General, a man can be turned to many uses.
He can fly and he can kill.
But he has one defect:
He can think.

[1937]

BERTOLT BRECHT
translated from the German by Tom Kuhn

Bertolt Brecht (1898-1965), one of the most influential dramatists of the 20th century, was one of Germany's foremost modern poets. He only published one single collection in his lifetime but his collected poems in German comes to 1300 pages. His poetry addresses private or public concerns, confronting whatever life throws at him, with a matter-of-fact, disaffected or bitterly ironic tone.

His plays were banned in Germany during the 1930s. When Hitler seized power in 1933, Brecht went into exile in Denmark, living there for six years until he had to move on to Sweden and then Finland before he was able to leave for the US in 1941. He returned to Europe in 1947, living first in Switzerland and from 1949 in East Berlin where he ran the Berliner Ensemble. Written in Denmark, his sequence *A German War Primer* was first published in the exile periodical *Das Wort* (The Word) in Moscow in 1937. ➤ 190, 191, 306

from In Time of War

XIV

Yes, we are going to suffer, now; the sky
Throbs like a feverish forehead; pain is real;
The groping searchlights suddenly reveal
The little natures that will make us cry,

Who never quite believed they could exist,
Not where we were. They take us by surprise
Like ugly long-forgotten memories,
And like a conscience all the guns resist.

Behind each sociable home-loving eye
The private massacres are taking place;
All Women, Jews, the Rich, the Human Race.

The mountains cannot judge us when we lie:
We dwell upon the earth; the earth obeys
The intelligent and evil till they die.

XV

Engines bear them through the sky: they're free
And isolated like the very rich;
Remote like savants, they can only see
The breathing city as a target which

Requires their skill; will never see how flying
Is the creation of ideas they hate,
Nor how their own machines are always trying
To push through into life. They chose a fate

The islands where they live did not compel.
Though earth may teach our proper discipline,
At any time it will be possible

To turn away from freedom and become
Bound like the heiress in her mother's womb,
And helpless as the poor have always been.

XVI

Here war is simple like a monument:
A telephone is speaking to a man;
Flags on a map assert that troops were sent;
A boy brings milk in bowls. There is a plan

For living men in terror of their lives,
Who thirst at nine who were to thirst at noon,
And can be lost and are, and miss their wives,
And, unlike an idea, can die too soon.

But ideas can be true although men die,
And we can watch a thousand faces
Made active by one lie:

And maps can really point to places
Where life is evil now:
Nanking; Dachau.

[1938]

W.H. AUDEN
➤ 189

from Autumn Journal

VII

Conferences, adjournments, ultimatums,
    Flights in the air, castles in the air,
The autopsy of treaties, dynamite under the bridges,
    The end of *laissez faire*.
After the warm days the rain comes pimpling
    The paving stones with white
And with the rain the national conscience, creeping,
    Seeping through the night.
And in the sodden park on Sunday protest
    Meetings assemble not, as so often, now
Merely to advertise some patent panacea

But simply to avow
The need to hold the ditch; a bare avowal
   That may perhaps imply
Death at the doors in a week but perhaps in the long run
   Exposure of the lie.
Think of a number, double it, treble it, square it,
   And sponge it out
And repeat *ad lib.* and mark the slate with crosses;
   There is no time to doubt
If the puzzle really has an answer. Hitler yells on the wireless,
   The night is damp and still
And I hear dull blows on wood outside my window;
   They are cutting down the trees on Primrose Hill.
The wood is white like the roast flesh of chicken,
   Each tree falling like a closing fan;
No more looking at the view from seats beneath the branches,
   Everything is going to plan;
They want the crest of this hill for anti-aircraft,
   The guns will take the view
And searchlights probe the heavens for bacilli
   With narrow wands of blue.
And the rain came on as I watched the territorials
   Sawing and chopping and pulling on ropes like a team
In a village tug-of-war; and I found my dog had vanished
   And thought 'This is the end of the old régime,'
But found the police had got her at St John's Wood station
   And fetched her in the rain and went for a cup
Of coffee to an all-night shelter and heard a taxi-driver
   Say 'It turns me up
When I see these soldiers in lorries' – rumble of tumbrils
   Drums in the trees
Breaking the eardrums of the ravished dryads –
   It turns me up; a coffee, please.
And as I go out I see a windscreen-wiper
   In an empty car
Wiping away like mad and I feel astounded
   That things have gone so far.
And I come back here to my flat and wonder whether
   From now on I need take
The trouble to go out choosing stuff for curtains
   As I don't know anyone to make

Curtains quickly. Rather one should quickly
Stop the cracks for gas or dig a trench
And take one's paltry measures against the coming
Of the unknown Uebermensch.
But one – meaning I – is bored, am bored, the issue
Involving principle but bound in fact
To squander principle in panic and self-deception –
Accessories after the act,
So that all we foresee is rivers in spate sprouting
With drowning hands
And men like dead frogs floating till the rivers
Lose themselves in the sands.
And we who have been brought up to think of 'Gallant Belgium'
As so much blague
Are now preparing again to essay good through evil
For the sake of Prague;
And must, we suppose, become uncritical, vindictive,
And must, in order to beat
The enemy, model ourselves upon the enemy,
A howling radio for our paraclete.
The night continues wet, the axe keeps falling,
The hill grows bald and bleak
No longer one of the sights of London but maybe
We shall have fireworks here by this day week.

from VIII

And the next day begins
Again with alarm and anxious
Listening to bulletins
From distant, measured voices
Arguing for peace
While the zero hour approaches,
While the eagles gather and the petrol and oil and grease
Have all been applied and the vultures back the eagles.
But once again
The crisis is put off and things look better
And we feel negotiation is not vain –
Save my skin and damn my conscience.
And negotiation wins,
If you can call it winning,

And here we are – just as before – safe in our skins;
    Glory to God for Munich.
And stocks go up and wrecks
    Are salved and politicians' reputations
Go up like Jack-on-the-Beanstalk; only the Czechs
    Go down and without fighting.

from **XVIII**

It is December now, the trees are naked
    As the three crosses on the hill;
Through the white fog the face of the orange sun is cryptic
    Like a lawyer making the year's will.
The year has little to show, will leave a heavy
    Overdraft to its heir;
Shall we try to meet the deficit or passing
    By on the other side continue *laissez-faire*?
International betrayals, public murder,
    The devil quoting scripture, the traitor, the coward, the thug
Eating dinner in the name of peace and progress,
    The doped public sucking a dry dug;
Official recognition of rape, revival of the ghetto
    And free speech gagged and free
Energy scrapped and dropped like surplus herring
    Back into the barren sea;
Brains and beauty festering in exile,
    The shadow of bars
Falling across each page, each field, each raddled sunset,
    The alien lawn and the pool of nenuphars;
And hordes of homeless poor running the gauntlet
    In hostile city streets of white and violet lamps
Whose flight is without a terminus but better
    Than the repose of concentration camps.
Come over, they said, into Macedonia and help us
    But the chance is gone;
Now we must help ourselves, we can leave the vulture
    To pick the corpses clean in Macedon.
No wonder many would renounce their birthright,
    The responsibility of moral choice,
And sit with a mess of pottage taking orders
    Out of a square box from a mad voice –

Lies on the air endlessly repeated
    Turning the air to fog,
Blanket on blanket of lie, no room to breathe or fidget
    And nobody to jog
Your elbow and say 'Up there the sun is rising;
    Take it on trust, the sun will always shine.'
The sun may shine no doubt but how many people
    Will see it with their eyes in Nineteen-Thirty-Nine?
Yes, the earlier days had their music,
    We have some still today,
But the orchestra is due for the bonfire
    If things go on this way.
Still there are still the seeds of energy and choice
    Still alive even if forbidden, hidden,
And while a man has voice
    He may recover music.

[August–December 1938]

LOUIS MACNEICE
➤ 172

Epitaph on a Tyrant

Perfection, of a kind, was what he was after,
And the poetry he invented was easy to understand;
He knew human folly like the back of his hand,
And was greatly interested in armies and fleets;
When he laughed, respectable senators burst with laughter,
And when he cried the little children died in the streets.

[January 1939]

W.H. AUDEN
➤ 189

September 1, 1939

I sit in one of the dives
On Fifty-Second Street
Uncertain and afraid
As the clever hopes expire
Of a low dishonest decade:
Waves of anger and fear
Circulate over the bright
And darkened lands of the earth,
Obsessing our private lives;
The unmentionable odour of death
Offends the September night.

Accurate scholarship can
Unearth the whole offence
From Luther until now
That has driven a culture mad,
Find what occurred at Linz,[2]
What huge imago made
A psychopathic god:
I and the public know
What all schoolchildren learn,
Those to whom evil is done
Do evil in return.

Exiled Thucydides knew
All that a speech can say
About Democracy,
And what dictators do,
The elderly rubbish they talk
To an apathetic grave;
Analysed all in his book,
The enlightenment driven away,
The habit-forming pain,
Mismanagement and grief:
We must suffer them all again.

1. Germany invaded Poland on 1 September 1939. 2. Hitler's speech in his
hometown of Linz on 12 March 1938 heralded the annexation of Austria.

Into this neutral air
Where blind skyscrapers use
The full height to proclaim
The strength of Collective Man,
Each language pours its vain
Competitive excuse:
But who can live for long
In an euphoric dream;
Out of the mirror they stare,
Imperialism's face
And the international wrong.

Faces along the bar
Cling to their average day:
The lights must never go out,
The music must always play,
All the conventions conspire
To make this fort assume
The furniture of home;
Lest we should see where we are,
Lost in a haunted wood,
Children afraid of the night
Who have never been happy or good.

The windiest militant trash
Important Persons shout
Is not so crude as our wish:
What mad Nijinsky wrote
About Diaghilev
Is true of the normal heart;
For the error bred in the bone
Of each woman and each man
Craves what it cannot have,
Not universal love
But to be loved alone.

From the conservative dark
Into the ethical life
The dense commuters come,
Repeating their morning vow,
'I *will* be true to the wife,

I'll concentrate more on my work',
And helpless governors wake
To resume their compulsory game:
Who can release them now,
Who can reach the deaf,
Who can speak for the dumb?

All I have is a voice
To undo the folded lie,
The romantic lie in the brain
Of the sensual man-in-the-street
And the lie of Authority
Whose buildings grope the sky:
There is no such thing as the State
And no one exists alone;
Hunger allows no choice
To the citizen or the police;
We must love one another or die.

Defenceless under the night
Our world in stupor lies;
Yet, dotted everywhere,
Ironic points of light
Flash out wherever the Just
Exchange their messages:
May I, composed like them
Of Eros and of dust,
Beleaguered by the same
Negation and despair,
Show an affirming flame.

W.H. AUDEN

W.H. Auden (1907-73) was the foremost English poet of the 20th century,
influencing a whole generation of politically engaged writers in the 1930s.
His poetry's central themes are love, politics, religion, morals, the individual
human being and the impersonality of nature. According to Philip Larkin,
Auden 'lost his key subject and emotion – Europe and the fear of war' when
he moved to America in January 1939. Much criticised for 'dodging the war',
he had earlier spent seven weeks in Spain in 1937 during the Spanish Civil
War [> 150] and six months with Christopher Isherwood in 1938 visiting the
Sino-Japanese War, the subject of their book *Journey to a War* (1939).

from **1940**

I

Spring is coming. The mild breezes
Free the skerries from their winter ice.
Trembling, the peoples of the north await
The house painter's[1] battle fleets.

V

I am living on the small island of Lidingö.[2]
But one night recently
Dreaming heavily I dreamed I was in a city
And discovered that on the streets
The signs were German. Drenched in sweat
I woke and to my relief
I saw the night-black fir at the window and knew:
I was in a foreign country.

VIII

Fleeing my compatriots
I have now reached Finland. Friends
Who yesterday were unknown to me have placed a couple of beds
In clean rooms. On the radio
I hear the scum of the earth announcing their victories. With
interest
I study the map of this part of the world. High up, in Lappland
Towards the northern sea of ice
I see there is still a small door.

[1939–1940]

BERTOLT BRECHT
translated from the German by David Constantine
➤ 180

---

1. 'The house painter' was Brecht's contemptuous name for Hitler.
2. Lidingö, one of Stockholm's islands.

from Finland 1940

Now we are refugees in Finland...

Now we are refugees in Finland.

My little daughter
Comes home in the evening and complains
No child will play with her. She is German and born of
A tribe of brigands!

If I converse loudly in the tram
I am told to be quiet. Here they don't like
Loud words from a man
Who is born of a tribe of brigands.

When I remind my little daughter
That the Germans are a tribe of brigands
She is glad with me that they are not liked
And we laugh together.

This is the year...

This is the year people will talk about.
This is the year people will keep quiet about.

The old see the young dying.
The foolish see the wise dying.

The earth no longer bears fruit, but it swallows.
Rain does not fall from the sky, only iron.

[*c*. April 1940]

BERTOLT BRECHT
translated from the German by David Constantine

from Ode Written during the Battle of Dunkirk, May 1940

The old guns
barked into my ear. Day and night
they shook the earth in which I cowered
or rained round me
detonations of steel and fire.

One of the dazed and disinherited
I crawled out of that mess
with two medals and a gift of blood-money.
No visible wounds to lick – only a resolve
to tell the truth without rhetoric
the truth about war and about men
involved in the indignities of war.

But the world was tired and would forget
forget the pain and squalor
forget the hunger and dread
forget the cry of those who died in agony
and the unbearable silence of those who suddenly
as we talked
fell sniped
with mouth still open and uncomprehending eyes.

It is right to forget
sights the mind cannot accommodate
terror that cannot be described
experience that cannot be exorcised in thought.

It is natural for others to resent
the parade of wounds
eyes haunted with unrevealed sorrows
the unholy pride of sacrifice.

Human, to relapse
into the old ways, to resume
the normality so patiently acquired
in days of peace.

And so we drifted twenty years
downt the stream of time
feeling that such a storm
could not break again.

Feeling that our little house-boat was safe
until the last lock was reached.
Another twenty years
would see us home.

The day passes
the sun swerves
silently like a cyclist round the bend.
Disembodied voices drift past behind the hedge
the vespers of the blackbird and the thrush
rise and die. A golden frog
leaps out of the grasses.

In the silence of the twilight
I hear in the distance
the new guns.
I listen, no longer apt in war
unable to distinguish between bombs and shells.

As the evening deepens
searchlights begin to waver in the sky
the air-planes throb invisibly above me
There is still a glow in the west
and Venus shines brightly over the wooded hill.

Unreal war! No single friend
links me with its immediacy.
It is a voice out of a cabinet
a printed sheet, and these faint reverberations
selected in the silence
by my attentive ear.

Presently I shall sleep
and sink into a deeper oblivion.

HERBERT READ
➤ 101

193

The Retreat from Dunkirk

(from 'British Expeditionary Force')

That night we blew our guns. We placed a shell
Fuze downwards in each muzzle. Then we put
Another in the breech, secured a wire
Fast to the firing lever, crouched, and pulled.
It sounded like a cry of agony,
The crash and clang of splitting, tempered steel.
Thus did our guns, our treasured colours, pass;
And we were left bewildered, weaponless,
And rose and marched, our faces to the sea.

We formed in line beside the water's edge.
The little waves made oddly home-like sounds,
Breaking in half-seen surf upon the strand.
The night was full of noise; the whistling thud
The shells made in the sand, and pattering stones;
The cries cut short, the shouts of units' names;
The crack of distant shots, and Bren gun fire;
The sudden clattering crash of masonry.
Steadily, all the time, the marching tramp
Of feet passed by along the shell-torn road,
Under the growling thunder of the guns.

The major said 'The boats cannot get in,
There is no depth of water. Follow me.'
And so we followed, wading in our ranks
Into the blackness of the sea. And there,
Lit by the burning oil across the swell,
We stood and waited for the unseen boats.

Oars in the darkness, rowlocks, shadowy shapes
Of boats that searched. We heard a seaman's hail.
Then we swam out, and struggled with our gear,
Clutching the looming gunwales. Strong hands pulled,
And we were in and heaving with the rest,
Until at last they turned. The dark oars dipped,
The laden craft crept slowly out to sea,
To where in silence lay the English ships.

B.G. BONALLACK

Listening to Distant Guns

The roses tremble; oh, the sunflower's eye
Is opened wide in sad expectancy.
Westward and back the circling swallows fly,
The rooks' battalions dwindle near the hill.

That low pulsation in the east is war:
No bell now breaks the evening's silent dream.
The bloodless clarity of the evening's sky
Betrays no whisper of the battle-scream.

[Buckinghamshire, June 1940]

DENISE LEVERTOV

'Listening to Distant Guns' was **Denise Levertov**'s first published poem, 'written during or just before Dunkirk. In Buckinghamshire, where I was "evacuated", one could hear the big guns across the Channel even though Bucks is an inland county' (author's note). ➤ 374

The Dunkirk evacuation (27 May – 4 June 1940) of 338,226 Allied soldiers from the beaches and harbour of the French port by a hastily assembled flotilla of hundreds of boats followed the failure of the British Expeditionary Force to repel the German invasion of Belgium, the Netherlands and France. **B.G. Bonallack** (1907-2003) was commissioned into the 92nd Field Regiment, Royal Artillery, at the outbreak of war, was mentioned in despatches (Dunkirk) and awarded the Military Cross in 1943 (Primasol Bridge, Sicily). After the war he commanded a Territorial Army regiment and managed a family firm of coachbuilders. He also published an historical novel, *The Flame in the Dark: A Chronicle of Alfred the Great* (1976).

All Day It Has Rained...

All day it has rained, and we on the edge of the moors
Have sprawled in our bell-tents, moody and dull as boors,
Groundsheets and blankets spread on the muddy ground
And from the first grey wakening we have found
No refuge from the skirmishing fine rain
And the wind that made the canvas heave and flap

And the taut wet guy-ropes ravel out and snap.
All day the rain has glided, wave and mist and dream,
Drenching the gorse and heather, a gossamer stream
Too light to stir the acorns that suddenly
Snatched from their cups by the wild south-westerly
Pattered against the tent and our upturned dreaming faces.
And we stretched out, unbuttoning our braces,
Smoking a Woodbine, darning dirty socks,
Reading the Sunday papers – I saw a fox
And mentioned it in the note I scribbled home; –
And we talked of girls, and dropping bombs on Rome,
And thought of the quiet dead and the loud celebrities
Exhorting us to slaughter, and the herded refugees;
– Yet thought softly, morosely of them, and as indifferently
As of ourselves or those whom we
For years have loved, and will again
Tomorrow maybe love; but now it is the rain
Possesses us entirely, the twilight and the rain.

And I can remember nothing dearer or more to my heart
Than the children I watched in the woods on Saturday
Shaking down burning chestnuts for the schoolyard's merry play,
Or the shaggy patient dog who followed me
By Sheet and Steep and up the wooded scree
To the Shoulder o' Mutton where Edward Thomas brooded long
On death and beauty – till a bullet stopped his song.

[October 1940]

ALUN LEWIS

Alun Lewis (1915-44) was a Welsh writer from a mining village in Mid-Glamorgan. After much deliberation, he volunteered for the army in March 1940, his horror at what the Nazis were doing in Europe having forced him to modify his pacifist position. In 1942, he published *The Last Inspection*, a book of stories, and *Raiders' Dawn*, a collection of poems, and was sent to India with the South Wales Borderers. 'All Day It Has Rained…', with its echoes of Edward Thomas's 'Rain' [➤ 50], was written following a visit to the Hampshire villages of Sheet and Steep where Thomas lived (the Shoulder o' Mutton was a favourite hill). Thomas was actually killed when the force of a shell-blast stopped his heart [➤ 49]; 'till a bullet stopped his song' in the last line would have better fitted the manner of Lewis's own death, 'accidentally wounded by a pistol shot' in Burma in March 1944.

Survivors

With the ship burning in their eyes
The white faces float like refuse
In the darkness – the water screwing
Oily circles where the hot steel lies.

They clutch with fingers frozen into claws
The lifebelts thrown from a destroyer,
And see, between the future's doors,
The gasping entrance of the sea.

Taken on board as many as lived, who
Had a mind left for living and the ocean,
They open eyes running with surf,
Heavy with the grey ghosts of explosion.

The meaning is not yet clear,
Where daybreak died in the smile –
And the mouth remained stiff
And grinning, stupid for a while.

But soon they joke, easy and warm,
As men will who have died once
Yet somehow were able to find their way –
Muttering about their food and pay.

Later, sleepless at night, the brain spinning
With cracked images, they won't forget
The confusion and the oily dead,
Nor yet the casual knack of living.

ALAN ROSS

Alan Ross (1922-2001) was editor of *London Magazine* for 40 years. Born in Calcutta, he left Oxford to join the Royal Navy in 1941, going straight into journalism after being demobbed. He served on several destroyers escorting supply ships to the Soviet Union, and was almost killed trying to fight an onboard fire during the Battle of the Barents Sea in December 1942. He wrote some of the best poems of the war about the Navy, most notably those collected later in *Open Sea* (1975); and published several books on cricket and travel.

Seaman, 1941

This was not to be expected.

Waves, wind, and tide brought him again
to Barra. Clinging to driftwood many hours
the night before, he had not recognised
the current far off-shore his own nor
known he drifted home. He gave up, anyway,
some time before the smell of land reached out
or dawn outlined the morning gulls.

      They found him
on the white sand southward of the ness,
not long enough in the sea to be
disfigured, cheek sideways as in sleep,
old men who had fished with his father
and grandfather and knew him at once,
before they even turned him on his back, by the set
of the dead shoulders, and were shocked.

This was not to be expected.

His mother, with hot eyes, preparing the parlour
for his corpse, would have preferred, she thought,
to have been told by telegram rather
than so to know that convoy, ship, and son
had only been a hundred miles north-west
of home when the torpedoes struck.
She could have gone on thinking that
he'd had no chance; but to die offshore,
in Hebridean tides, as if he'd stayed
a fisherman for life and never gone to war
was not to be expected.

MOLLY HOLDEN

Molly Holden (1927-81) was an English poet and novelist who published her first collection in 1964, the same year she was diagnosed as suffering from multiple sclerosis. Her collection *To Make Me Grieve* (1967) includes poems that chronicle her struggle with the disease

Requiem

for the seven hundred from the church in Glina

1

I cannot stay silent; the walls stayed silent
And crumbled. One, I carry them all inside me, unspoken,
Overgrown with my adulthood, their faces
Rotted away. I cannot evict them from the
Infinite glassy space of the sleepless nights.
They are not grass. At night, from within,
They cautiously tap at the trembling panes
Of my eyes; all dead, and all their throats
Have blossomed into roses. I cannot stay silent
About this colony in my blood, for I am one,
And they were more than seven hundred then.

2

Within the walls, behind the bolted doors,
Filled with a hideous waiting, as if with sand,
Empty-handed, soft before the blades, aware,
Beneath a vault convulsed with dawning horror...
I, once a boy, imagine the first dull thrust
Which frees the warm, dark blood from the body
Of the first: treacherous blood, quick to flee.
And I hear the first scream, wet with reddish foam
From a throat whose songs are forever slashed,
Whose words are unspoken, split in half
Like green apples in its darkness.
Steel. And the first, waiting for his companions
In a death shamefaced and roomy enough
To receive them. Here are their eyes, here their eyes
Are extinguished two by two, lifeless lights in a morning street,
But the horror is left inside like grit in a cube of ice.
Blood, inquisitive, stripped, flows across
The flagstones. Steel in flesh, steel which trembles still
In the sleeplessness of one who was once a boy.
They fell into blood, their senses crushed,
And could not hear the next, the one with branded eyes,
Or the one pruned with steel like a tree,

Between the walls grown thick with screams
And rich with fear. And the red mouths
Of fresh wounds were mute, filled with blood.
There they lay, abased, stripped of self,
Stripped of all but death, red, sticky,
Slaughtered, slaughtered, slaughtered.

3

I cannot stay silent, the walls stayed silent
And crumbled. But the ones from the church, the ones
Who are dead, have not yet fallen asleep. They lie awake,
Unbidden, in one who was once a boy. I cannot evict them
Into the space of wind where the church once stood,
Where the weeds grow all red with their blood.
So let them stay, awake, unbidden, for they would despise me
If I were to try to sing them to sleep.

IVAN L. LALIĆ
translated from the Serbian by Francis R. Jones

Ivan L. Lalić (1931-96) was born and died in Belgrade. He and Vasko Popa
were the foremost poets of Yugoslavia in the postwar period.

The massacre of Orthodox Serbs in the church at Glina (July 1941) was one
of the most hideous acts of the Ustaše, the paramilitary force of the Croatian
fascists during the Second World War. After the German invasion in 1941,
Hitler carved Yugoslavia up between Germany, Italy, Bulgaria, Hungary and
the Nazi puppet state of Croatia, and proceeded to govern by divide-and-rule
tactics. Tito's partisans represented a welcome force for unity in the face of
vicious inter-ethnic and inter-religious bloodletting, and this played no small
part in their success. It also meant, however, that this bloodletting was best
not talked of publicly in post-war Yugoslavia – and certainly not in 1953,
when this poem was written. [Francis R. Jones]

Lalić lived through harsh times: born in 1931, as a child he experienced the
trauma of seeing many of his school-friends perish in an air-raid, and he died
at a time of violent darkness in his native land. All his work is marked by the
knowledge of sudden, brutal death and the profound sense of responsibility
entailed by survival: a duty to remember, to bear witness and to face the crucial
questions of human existence.' [Celia Hawkesworth]

August 1941

For August, which is under Leo.
It stinks.

Summer came, and carrion was the sign.
The corn stank of undernourished corpse.
The Arctic was haunted, the Northern Cross
Hung with rotten blood; and Poland dying.

Somewhere, in the distance, mediums hanged
For falsely reading the green in the guts
Of blown-open bullocks. Fish fled through nets
In blood-black cities. It was one huge spat

Gob of phlegm. Man is a land-borne squid
That bursts a bag of night the moment
It fights. Life then was lived by secret,
With beatings for daily bread, and buttoned lips.

They never handed bodies back. Twelve
Rifles blew open the heart and guts
Of travellers, who shouted as they shot
That no deal of night ever did outsell

The light. Summertime: grist in mills of silence.
Lovely Summer: thoroughblood hound full of fleas;
The weevil deep in the heart of Greece;
The radio with hackles of iron spikes;

Rising vomit for sap in every tree;
Dynamite fouling the womb of the sea.
Summer, dear God: quicklime for sperm and grain.
Great work. And if it fails, they start again.

PIERRE SEGHERS
translated from the French by Ian Higgins

Pierre Seghers (1906-87) was renowned as both poet and publisher, editing the magazine *Poésie* during the war to promote poetry and publish the *contrebande* writing of French Resistance poets, while himself producing work ranging from the vituperative, through *contrebande* to love poetry. As well as the review, he also published books by some of the best-known poets of the war.

Ascension

Today is execution day for the pacifists.
Escaping from the gunfire as their corpses topple,
Their souls have ascended to heaven.
To proclaim injustice and iniquity.

In grief, their spirits have begun to relent,
Calling from the edge
Of a great four-cornered ice-floe,
Turning to a rainbow flickering in the dark.

Bombs have exploded; fireworks have crackled:
Their souls, sent drifting to one corner of heaven,
Turned into mist, into spume, into cloud-drifts,
To stain the sky with blood that is still hot.

MITSUHARU KANEKO
translated from the Japanese by Geoffrey Bownas & Anthony Thwaite

How Did They Kill My Grandmother?

How did they kill my grandmother?
I'll tell you how they killed her.
One morning a tank rolled up to
a building where
the hundred and fifty Jews of our town who,
weightless
                from a year's starvation,
and white
                with the knowledge of death,
were gathered holding their bundles.

And the German polizei were
herding the old people briskly;
and their tin mugs clanked as
the young men led them away
                                far away.

But my small grandmother
my seventy-year-old grandmother
began to curse and
scream at the Germans;
shouting that I was a soldier.
She yelled at them: My grandson
is off at the front fighting!
Don't you dare
touch me!
Listen, you
   can hear our guns!

Even as she went off, my grandmother
cried abuse,
   starting all over again
with her curses.
From every window then
Ivanovnas and Andreyevnas
Sidorovnas and Petrovnas
sobbed: You tell them, Polina
Matveyevna, keep it up!
They all yelled together:
   'What can we do against
this enemy, the Hun?'
Which was why the Germans chose
to kill her inside the town.

A bullet struck her hair
and kicked her grey plait down.
My grandmother fell to the ground.
That is how she died there.

BORIS SLUTSKY
translated from the Russian by Elaine Feinstein

Boris Slutsky (1919-86) was a polemical Soviet poet whose work was often concerned with Jewish themes. He served in the Red Army from 1941 to 1945, his war experiences colouring much of his poetry.

During the 1930s **Mitsuharu Kaneko** (1875-1975) travelled widely, publishing poetry notable for its depiction of South-East Asia under colonial rule. Later he became known for his anti-war poetry which was unpublishable in Japan.

Babiy Yar

Over Babiy Yar
there are no memorials.
The steep hillside like a rough inscription.
I am frightened.
Today I am as old as the Jewish race.
I seem to myself a Jew at this moment.
I, wandering in Egypt.
I, crucified. I perishing.
Even today the mark of the nails.
I think also of Dreyfus. I am he.
The Philistine my judge and my accuser.
Cut off by bars and cornered,
ringed round, spat at, lied about;
the screaming ladies with the Brussels lace
poke me in the face with parasols.
I am also a boy in Belostok,
the dropping blood spreads across the floor,
the public-bar heroes are rioting
in an equal stench of garlic and of drink.
I have no strength, go spinning from a boot?
shriek useless prayers that they don't listen to;
with a cackle of 'Thrash the kikes and save Russia!'
the corn-chandler is beating up my mother.
I seem to myself like Anna Frank
to be transparent as an April twig
and am in love, I have no need for words,
I need for us to look at one another.
How little we have to see or to smell
separated from foliage and the sky,
how much, how much in the dark room
gently embracing each other.
They're coming. Don't be afraid.
The booming and banging of the spring.
It's coming this way. Come to me.
Quickly, give me your lips.
They're battering in the door. Roar of the ice.

Over Babiy Yar
rustle of the wild grass.
The trees look threatening, look like judges.
And everything is one silent cry.
Taking my hat off
I feel myself slowly going grey.
And I am one silent cry
over the many thousands of the buried;
am every old man killed here,
every child killed here.
O my Russian people, I know you.
Your nature is international.
Foul hands rattle your clean name.
I know the goodness of my country.
How horrible it is that pompous title
the anti-semites calmly call themselves,
Society of the Russian People.
No part of me can ever forget it.
When the last anti-semite on the earth
is buried for ever
let the International ring out.
No Jewish blood runs among my blood,
but I am as bitterly and hardly hated
by every anti-semite
as if I were a Jew. By this
I am a Russian.

YEVGENY YEVTUSHENKO
translated from the Russian by Robin Milner-Gulland & Peter Levi

Born in Siberia in 1932, **Yevgeny Yevtushenko** became one of Russia's lead-ing poets during the Soviet years. In 1961, during the Khrushchev cultural "thaw", he was able to openly publish his poem 'Babiy Yar' challenging the Soviet distortion of historical fact regarding the Nazi massacre of the Jewish population of Kiev as well as current anti-Semitism in the Soviet Union. At the time the authorities were still claiming that genocides directed against Jews during the war were Nazi killings of Soviet citizens. The massacre of 33,771 Jewish men, women and children in the ravine of Babiy Yar on 29-30 Sept-ember 1941 was followed by further mass executions, with a total of 75,000 Jews shot there by November 1941. Later victims at the killing ground included prisoners of war, Soviet partisans, Ukrainian nationalists and gypsies.

from Wind of War

1 *Oath*

May she who says farewell to her dear one today,
convert her pain into strength.
We swear to our children, swear to the graves,
that no one will force us to submit!

[Leningrad, July 1941]

2 *'They said dramatic goodbyes'*

They said dramatic goodbyes to their girlfriends,
and dressed up in new uniforms,
they kissed their mothers as they marched
away to play toy soldiers.
Not bad or good or mediocre,
they were all at their posts,
where no one is first or last...
They all went to their eternal rest.

[1943]

3 *First Long Range Shelling of Leningrad*

The quality of the city's hustle
and bustle suddenly changed.
This was neither a town
nor a country sound.
True, it was closely related
to claps of distant thunder,
but in thunder there is the wetness
of the high fresh clouds
and the longing of the meadows;
the news of the joyous cloudbursts.
But this sound was hot and dry as hell,
and my confused hearing did not want
to believe

how it spread and grew
and dispassionately brought destruction to
my child.

[September 1941]

4 *'Birds of death'*

Birds of death hover in the zenith.
Who is coming to rescue Leningrad?

Don't make any noise – Leningrad is still breathing,
it's still alive, hears everything:

its sons on the Baltic sea bed
groaning in their sleep,

their screams from the depths: 'Bread!' –
reach that seventh paradise...

But the heavens are merciless.
Death looks out of all windows.

[September 1941]

5 *Courage*

We know what now lies in the balance
and what is coming to pass.
Courage's hour has struck –
courage will not fail us.
We are not afraid to face the bullets and die,
we are not bitter at being left homeless –
we will preserve you our Russian language,
the great Russian word.
Pure and free we will uphold you
and hand you on to our children's children,
and save you from captivity
        forever!

[23 February 1942]

6-7 *In Memory of a Leningrad boy, my neighbour Valya Smirnov*

1

The lights are out.
Trenches are dug in the garden.
Petersburg's orphans
are my little children –
one can't breathe underground,
pain drills the forehead.
Through the bombing
a child's small voice is heard.

2

Knock with your little fist – I'll open up.
I always opened my door to you.
Now I've gone beyond the high mountain,
the desert, the wind and the blazing heat,
but I will never give you up...

I did not hear you crying
or asking me for bread.
Bring me a twig from the maple tree,
or just some blades of green grass
as you did last spring.
Bring me in your tiny cupped hands
some clear, cool water from our Neva,
and with my own hands I'll wipe clean
the blood from your little golden head.

[23 April 1942]

ANNA AKHMATOVA
translated from the Russian by Richard McKane

Anna Akhmatova (1889-1966) was Russia's greatest modern poet. Her poetry was banned in 1925 and mostly unpublished for over 30 years. All she wrote she committed to memory. Several trusted friends also memorised her poems. She lived in Leningrad during the 900-day siege of her city (1941-44), bearing witness to the suffering of her people in her poetry, and beginning work on her epic *Poem without a hero*, not published until 1965.

I Don't Remember Him

I don't remember him.
I never saw him
In his Moscow flat,
Trying to catch hold of his braces
From behind, to fasten them
On to his trousers at the back.
I don't remember him in the quarantine station either,
As he stood naked in line,
Waiting for the handful of liquid coal-tar soap.
I don't remember him even
In that moment of shame,
When he forgot the word 'sling swivel',
And stared dumbly at the ground,
Under the frosty gaze of the sergeant.
I don't even remember
His terrible screaming...
All I remember are his two eyes,
Looking out from under half-closed lids,
When I cradled
The stumps of his legs,
To stop them banging against the boards
Inside the jolting truck.

EVGENY VINOKUROV
translated from the Russian by Anthony Rudolf & Daniel Weissbort

Evgeny Vinokurov (1925-93) was a Russian writer who fought in the Russian army, serving on the Ukrainian front where he commanded an artillery section at the age of 17. Much of his early poetry was concerned with the war.

Edvard Kocbek (1904-81) was a controversial figure in Slovenian literature. He was a Christian Socialist founder of the Liberation Front of the Slovene Nation in 1941, working underground during the Italian occupation, but in 1943 was forced to dissolve the Christian Socialist group and to recognise the authority of the Communists on joining the Slovene Partisans. Briefly a minister in the interim Yugoslav government at the end of the war, he was denounced in 1952 after publishing a book of short stories relating to moral issues in the Partisan fight, and spent the rest of his life under constant surveillance by the secret police. His work was favourably reassessed and gained wide recognition after his death. ➤ 210

The Game

I hold a chipped bowl in my hands
and wait in the camp kitchen queue.
And when I glance forward and back
I am shocked by a marvellous insight –
only now do we see ourselves right.
Someone has changed and revealed us,
as though shuffling a pack of cards,
cheekily, naughtily, rarely,
but above all, as in all games,
the odds are mysteriously even
and he has summoned our secret truth.

He that burrowed now walks upon air,
he that declaimed speeches now stammers in his dreams,
he who slept upon straw now commands the brigade
and the quiet woodcutter is full of questions;
he that quoted Homer is building bunkers
and he that ate in Paris is shaping a spoon;
the drinker licks the dew, the singer harkens to the silence,
the sexton sows mines, the miser collects wounds,
the farmhand is a stargazer, the coward a commando,
the poet a mule driver, the dreamer a telegraphist
and the local Casanova a trusty guide.

I hold a chipped bowl in my hands
and I look to my front and look back
and I can't stop looking at images,
a procession of ghosts, spirits on pilgrimage,
the winking of truths, the revelation of fates.
Someone has changed and defined us,
as though shuffling a pack of cards,
cheekily, naughtily, rarely.
And then I see myself at last
and reel under the weight of dreams –
all are within me, as in a young mother.

EDVARD KOCBEK
translated from the Slovenian by Michael Scammell and Veno Taufer

Disintegration of Springtime

This is a damned unnatural sort of war;
The pilot sits among the clouds, quite sure
About the values he is fighting for;
He cannot hear beyond his veil of sound,

He cannot see the people on the ground;
He only knows that on the sloping map
Of sea-fringed town and country people creep
Like ants – and who cares if ants laugh or weep?

To us he is no more than a machine
Shown on an instrument; what can he mean
In human terms? – a man, somebody's son,
Proud of his skill; compact of flesh and bone
Fragile as Icarus – and our desire
To see that damned machine come down on fire.

R.N. CURREY

R.N. Currey (1907-2001) was a South African-born English poet who was a
schoolmaster in Colchester from 1934 to 1973. Called up in 1941, he was
commissioned into the Royal Artillery and posted to India, seeing active service
on the Burma frontier. His *Collected Poems* was published in 2000.

These Are Facts

These are facts, observe them how you will:
Forget for a moment the medals and the glory,
The clean shape of the bomb, designed to kill,
And the proud headlines of the papers' story.

Remember the walls of brick that forty years
Had nursed to make a neat though shabby home;
The impertinence of death, ignoring tears,
That smashed the house and left untouched the Dome.

Bodies in death are not magnificent or stately,
Bones are not elegant that blast has shattered;
This sorry, stained and crumpled rag was lately
A man whose life was made of little things that mattered;

Now he is just a nuisance, liable to stink,
A breeding-ground for flies, a test-tube for disease:
Bury him quickly and never pause to think,
What is the future worth to men like these?

People are more than places, more than pride;
A million photographs record the works of Wren;
A city remains a city on credit from the tide
That flows among its rocks, a sea of men.

[1942]

RUTHVEN TODD

Ruthven Todd (1914-78) was a Scottish poet, artist and novelist, author of
detective fiction written under the pseudonym R.T. Campbell, and editor of
the works of William Blake. During the war he was a conscientious objector.
He left Scotland in 1931, living in London, the US, and latterly on Majorca.

The Entertainment of War

I saw the garden where my aunt had died
And her two children and a woman from next door;
It was like a burst pod filled with clay.

A mile away in the night I had heard the bombs
Sing and then burst themselves between cramped houses
With bright soft flashes and sounds like banging doors;

The last of them crushed the four bodies into the ground,
Scattered the shelter, and blasted my uncle's corpse
Over the housetop and into the street beyond.

Now the garden lay stripped and stale; the iron shelter
Spread out its separate petals around a smooth clay saucer,
Small, and so tidy it seemed nobody had ever been there.

When I saw it, the house was blown clean by blast and care:
Relations had already torn out the new fireplaces;
My cousin's pencils lasted me several years.

And in his office notepad that was given me
I found solemn drawings in crayon of blondes without dresses.
In his lifetime I had not known him well.

Those were the things I noticed at ten years of age:
Those, and the four hearses outside our house,
The chocolate cakes, and my classmates' half-shocked envy.

But my grandfather went home from the mortuary
And for five years tried to share the noises in his skull,
Then he walked out and lay under a furze-bush to die.

When my father came back from identifying the daughter
He asked us to remind him of her mouth.
We tried. He said 'I think it was the one'.

These were marginal people I had met only rarely
And the end of the whole household meant that no grief was seen;
Never have people seemed so absent from their own deaths.

This bloody episode of four whom I could understand better dead
Gave me something I needed to keep a long story moving;
I had no pain of it; can find no scar even now.

But had my belief in the fiction not been thus buoyed up
I might, in the sigh and strike of the next night's bombs
Have realised a little what they meant, and for the first time been
        afraid.

ROY FISHER

Roy Fisher (*b.* 1930) is one of Britain's foremost Modernist poets of the post-war period. Born in Birmingham, he has always lived in the English Midlands and much of his poetry is deeply engaged with the city and its hinterland.

Bomb Story (Manchester, 1942)

For a year we lived like troglodytes,
Then a landmine, a near miss,
Blew in the cellar-door.
It flattened my mother's camp-bed.
She rolled under the next one
Murmured, 'How noisy',
And slept peacefully on.

The rectangle of the skeleton doorway
Framed a crimson furnace – the city on fire,
Under the lowering weight of an endless heavy roar
Of the bombers circling – 'theirs', of course;
And over that the booming racket of the ack-ack guns –
'Ours', thank heaven!

Our neighbour descended two floors in her bed
Unhurt; two others were buried.
Another, away for the night,
Rushed home and found it a steaming ruin.
Her mother's Chippendale sideboard –
A few charred fragments – was what
Caused her abandon to helpless tears.

Our windows were all shattered, every one;
The curtains shredded into long vertical strips,
Like the tattered colour of the regiment
After honourable battle.
Our neighbour's garden had a crater that would hold two buses.
He said the rich soil thrown up was most productive,
And round the perimeter he grew excellent lettuces
The next spring of the war.
Meanwhile his wife's lace corselet and her mended red jumper
Hung forty feet up in an elm
Whose leaves were scorched off.

Next morning a Pompeiian pall of dust and smoke
Loomed over all, with hosepipes snaking

Slimily in black mud across the thoroughfares.
One errant spray
Trespassing into our too, too-open windows
Unkindly moistened our National bread and marge,
Our ersatz coffee, and soya-porridge
And straw-pale tea.

But everywhere you could hear the cheerful tinkling
Of broken glass, as housewives swept it up
Into neat heaps on their garden paths;
One bemoaning her Persian carpet's ruin;
Another the grit on her drawing-room settee.
But at seven sharp the milk was on the step,
And at seven-thirty the news boy came cycling,
Zigzagging among the firemen;
Whistling, surprisingly, an air from a Nocturne of Chopin –
The most beautiful sound in the world.

MARGERY LEA

Margery Lea (*b.* 1905) worked in education in Manchester. Her wartime duties included helping evacuee children and involvement in food planning.

Manchester

A soiled light
faltered through the window,
died in the narrow room.
You lay like Eros on the shadowed bed.
I dared not look,
wanted no sight to read your darkness
nor any thought of time before or after
but a free-fall through the night.
These were the hours that could be
our last together.

The hotel
was half-destroyed by bombs,
gritty with brickdust
and everywhere abraded by hard years;
nap rubbed from the carpets,
life eroded out of the old men waiters,
the wallpaper sad fawn and blackened gilt,
chandeliers ready to fall
from their weight of dust.
We alone were young.

Two days we had.
Your train went north, mine
towards York across the Pennines.
Never before had the hills
seemed so green; in every valley
the sheltered mills shone
bright with illusory gold.

PAMELA GILLILAN

I Remember

It was my bridal night I remember,
An old man of seventy-three
I lay with my young bride in my arms,
A girl with t.b.
It was wartime, and overhead
The Germans were making a particularly heavy raid on Hampstead.
What rendered the confusion worse, perversely
Our bombers had chosen that moment to set out for Germany.
Harry, do they ever collide?
I do not think it has ever happened,
Oh my bride, my bride.

STEVIE SMITH

216

Pamela Gillilan (1918-2001) served as a WAAF meteorologist with Bomber Command in Yorkshire during the war. She published her first book of poems at the age of 68 in 1986, followed by three further collections.

Stevie Smith (1902-71) was an English writer whose poetry was characterised as combining 'caprice and doom'. Philip Larkin said her poems 'speak with the authority of sadness'. She herself spoke of death as a release from the 'pressure of despair'. As well as nine collections of poetry, she published three novels.

Flashback

I remember waking
from a sort of sleep,
khaki-clad and rigid on the canvas bed,
gas mask already slung
like an obscene shoulder-bag;
torch in one hand, tin hat in the other,
and the blasted buzzer shaking
the waking brain to jelly,
mercilessly dragging the tired body up
out of exhausted oblivion,

First out tonight.
Feet into rubber boots,
stumble down the darkened corridor,
burst through the black-out into the noisy yard
where the cars stand patiently,
their burden of stretchers
outlined against a blazing sky.

Fumble for the lock of the old Ford –
'Put out that bloody torch!'
squeeze in behind the wheel, wait for the men;
three bearers pile in the back
loud with their Cockney curses,
the leader beside me
'Now lads, remember there's a lidy in the car'.

Pull the starter, oh God make her go!
She goes. Across the yard,
double declutch at the gate, and out –
roaring down the now invisible road,
masked sidelights only –
roaring down to disaster;
where the bomb-ploughed houses wait
with their harvest of casualties.

LOIS CLARK

Lois Clark was a dancer who became an ambulance driver at the start of the war, later volunteering for civil defence work in London during the Blitz, when she drove a stretcher-party car in the Clapham and Brixton area.

from Lessons of the War

1 *Naming of Parts*

Today we have naming of parts. Yesterday,
We had daily cleaning. And tomorrow morning,
We shall have what to do after firing. But today,
Today we have naming of parts. Japonica
Glistens like coral in all of the neighbouring gardens,
    And today we have naming of parts.

This is the lower sling swivel. And this
Is the upper sling swivel, whose use you will see,
When you are given your slings. And this is the piling swivel,
Which in your case you have not got. The branches
Hold in the gardens their silent, eloquent gestures,
    Which in our case we have not got.

This is the safety-catch, which is always released
With an easy flick of the thumb. And please do not let me
See anyone using his finger. You can do it quite easy
If you have any strength in your thumb. The blossoms

Are fragile and motionless, never letting anyone see
    Any of them using their finger.

And this you can see is the bolt. The purpose of this
Is to open the breech, as you see. We can slide it
Rapidly backwards and forwards: we call this
Easing the spring. And rapidly backwards and forwards
The early bees are assaulting and fumbling the flowers:
    They call it easing the Spring.

They call it easing the Spring: it is perfectly easy
If you have any strength in your thumb: like the bolt,
And the breech, and the cocking-piece, and the point of balance,
Which in our case we have not got; and the almond-blossom
Silent in all of the gardens and the bees going backwards and forwards,
    For today we have naming of parts.

HENRY REED

Henry Reed (1914-86) was an English poet and radio dramatist who only published one book of poetry. Conscripted into the Royal Army Ordnance Corps in 1941, he published his parody of British Army basic training, 'Lessons of the War' ('Naming of Parts' is the first of its three parts), in *New Statesman and Nation* on 8 August 1942. In 1942 he was transferred to the Government Code and Cypher School at Bletchley.

'More Light! More Light!'
(for Heinrich Blücher and Hannah Arendt)

Composed in the Tower before his execution
These moving verses, and being brought at that time
Painfully to the stake, submitted, declaring thus:
'I implore my God to witness that I have made no crime.'

Nor was he forsaken of courage, but the death was horrible,
The sack of gunpowder failing to ignite.
His legs were blistered sticks on which the black sap
Bubbled and burst as he howled for the Kindly Light.

And that was but one, and by no means one of the worst;
Permitted at least his pitiful dignity;
And such as were by made prayers in the name of Christ,
That shall judge all men, for his soul's tranquillity.

We move now to outside a German wood.
Three men are there commanded to dig a hole
In which the two Jews are ordered to lie down
And be buried alive by the third, who is a Pole.

Not light from the shrine at Weimar beyond the hill
Nor light from heaven appeared. But he did refuse.
A Lüger settled back deeply in its glove.
He was ordered to change places with the Jews.

Much casual death had drained away their souls.
The thick dirt mounted toward the quivering chin.
When only the head was exposed the order came
To dig him out again and to get back in.

No light, no light in the blue Polish eye.
When he finished a riding boot packed down the earth.
The Lüger hovered lightly in its glove.
He was shot in the belly and in three hours bled to death.

No prayers or incense rose up in those hours
Which grew to be years, and every day came mute
Ghosts from the ovens, sifting through crisp air,
And settled upon his eyes in a black soot.

ANTHONY HECHT

Antony Hecht (1923-2004) was an American poet born in New York City to German-Jewish parents. Drafted into the 97th Infantry Division in 1944, he saw action in Germany and Czechoslovakia. On 23 April 1945 his division helped liberate Flossenbürg concentration camp in Bavaria, and Hecht had to interview prisoners to gather evidence: 'The place, the suffering, the prisoners' accounts were beyond comprehension. For years after I would wake shrieking.' These experiences later caused him to suffer from post-traumatic stress disorder.

The second part of this poem describes an actual incident at Buchenwald, a few miles from 'the shrine at Weimar', the home of Goethe, whose dying words Hecht uses as his title.

September Song

born 19.6.32 – deported 24.9.42

Undesirable you may have been, untouchable
you were not. Not forgotten
or passed over at the proper time.

As estimated, you died. Things marched,
sufficient, to that end.
Just so much Zyklon[1] and leather, patented
terror, so many routine cries.

(I have made
an elegy for myself it
is true)

September fattens on vines. Roses
flake from the wall. The smoke
of harmless fires drifts to my eyes.

This is plenty. This is more than enough.

GEOFFREY HILL

1. Zyklon B was a cyanide-based pesticide used to murder an estimated 1.2 million people (including around 960,000 Jews) in the gas chambers of the Nazi concentration camps during the Second World War.

Sir Geoffrey Hill (*b.* 1932) is widely regarded as Britain's greatest living poet. Hill's densely allusive poetry has earned him a reputation for 'difficulty' which he has defended as the poet's right in the face of cultural disintegration, political opportunism and media-driven mediocrity. His approach to 'difficulty' includes subjecting his own lyricism to intense interrogation and self-questioning, as in 'September Song', an early poem written for an unknown child (born the day before his own birthday) who died anonymously in one or other concentration camp. Throughout this oblique and understated poem, Hill writes with an acute awareness of how the Nazis perfected the art of misusing language to disguise the nature of their 'Final Solution', simultaneously masking and revealing the horror behind that phrase through painful irony, awful double-meanings and juxtapositions ('routine cries'), so that the meaning of each line changes, or shifts, with each line-break.

Beach Burial

Softly and humbly to the Gulf of Arabs
The convoys of dead sailors come;
At night they sway and wander in the waters far under,
But morning rolls them in the foam.

Between the sob and clubbing of gunfire
Someone, it seems, has time for this,
To pluck them from the shallows and bury them in burrows
And tread the sand upon their nakedness;

And each cross, the driven stake of tidewood,
Bears the last signature of men,
Written with such perplexity, with such bewildered pity,
The words choke as they begin –

'Unknown seaman' – the ghostly pencil
Wavers and fades, the purple drips,
The breath of the wet season has washed their inscriptions
As blue as drowned men's lips,

Dead seamen, gone in search of the same landfall,
Whether as enemies they fought,
Or fought with us, or neither; the sand joins them together,
Enlisted on the other front.

[El Alamein, October–November 1942]

KENNETH SLESSOR

Kenneth Slessor (1901-71) was an Australian poet of German Jewish descent, and a war correspondent during World War Two, reporting from Greece, Syria, Libya, Egypt and New Guinea as well as Australia. Writing of Slessor's despatches from El Alamein, Clive James rated Slessor's war correspondence – 'which far outstrips Hemingway's in the evocation of battle' – as 'at least as wealthy in vision' as his poetry.

How to Kill

Under the parabola of a ball,
a child turning into a man,
I looked into the air too long.
The ball fell in my hand, it sang
in the closed fist: *Open Open*
Behold a gift designed to kill.

Now in my dial of glass appears
the soldier who is going to die.
He smiles, and moves about in ways
his mother knows, habits of his.
The wires touch his face: I cry
NOW. Death, like a familiar, hears

and look, has made a man of dust
of a man of flesh. This sorcery
I do. Being damned, I am amused
to see the centre of love diffused
and the waves of love travel into vacancy.
How easy it is to make a ghost.

The weightless mosquito touches
her tiny shadow on the stone,
and with how like, how infinite
a lightness, man and shadow meet.
They fuse. A shadow is a man
when the mosquito death approaches.

KEITH DOUGLAS

Keith Douglas (1920-44) was the most outstanding English poet of the Second World War, best-known for his poems written during the North African Campaign, and for his posthumously published prose account *Alamein to Zem Zem* (1946). He joined up at the outbreak of war, and was posted to Cairo and Palestine in 1941. Finding himself inactive as the Second Battle of El Alamein began in October 1943, he drove to the front, was made a tank commander, and took part in the Eighth Army's sweep through North Africa. He was killed by enemy mortar fire during the Normandy invasion near Bayeux in June 1944.

Vergissmeinnicht

Three weeks gone and the combatants gone
returning over the nightmare ground
we found the place again, and found
the soldier sprawling in the sun.

The frowning barrel of his gun
overshadowing. As we came on
that day, he hit my tank with one
like the entry of a demon.

Look. Here in the gunpit spoil
the dishonoured picture of his girl
who has put: *Steffi. Vergissmeinnicht*
in a copybook gothic script.

We see him almost with content,
abased, and seeming to have paid
and mocked at by his own equipment
that's hard and good when he's decayed.

But she would weep to see today
how on his skin the swart flies move;
the dust upon the paper eye
and the burst stomach like a cave.

For here the lover and killer are mingled
who had one body and one heart.
And death who had the soldier singled
has done the lover mortal hurt.

KEITH DOUGLAS

Cairo Jag

Shall I get drunk or cut myself a piece of cake,
a pasty Syrian with a few words of English
or the Turk who says she is a princess – she dances
apparently by levitation? Or Marcelle, Parisienne
always preoccupied with her dull dead lover:
she has all the photographs and his letters
tied in a bundle and stamped *Décedé* in mauve ink.
All this takes place in a stink of jasmin.

But there are the streets dedicated to sleep
stenches and the sour smells, the sour cries
do not disturb their application to slumber
all day, scattered on the pavement like rags
afflicted with fatalism and hashish. The women
offering their children brown-paper breasts
dry and twisted, elongated like the skull,
Holbein's signature. But this stained white town
is something in accordance with mundane conventions –
Marcelle drops her Gallic airs and tragedy
suddenly shrieks in Arabic about the fare
with the cabman, links herself so
with the somnambulists and legless beggars:
it is all one, all as you have heard.

But by a day's travelling you reach a new world
the vegetation is of iron
dead tanks, gun barrels split like celery
the metal brambles have no flowers or berries
and there are all sorts of manure, you can imagine
the dead themselves, their boots, clothes and possessions
clinging to the ground, a man with no head
has a packet of chocolate and a souvenir of Tripoli.

KEITH DOUGLAS

from Elegies for the Dead in Cyrenaica

FIRST ELEGY: End of a Campaign

There are many dead in the brutish desert,
        Who lie uneasy
among the scrub in this landscape of half-wit
stunted ill-will. For the dead land is insatiate
and necrophilous. The sand is blowing about still.
Many who for various reasons, or because
        of mere unanswerable compulsion, came here
and fought among the clutching gravestones,
        shivered and sweated,
cried out, suffered thirst, were stoically silent, cursed
the spittering machine-guns, were homesick for Europe
and fast embedded in quicksand of Africa
        agonised and died.
And sleep now. Sleep here the sleep of the dust.

There were our own, there were the others.
Their deaths were like their lives, human and animal.
There were no gods and precious few heroes.
What they regretted when they died had nothing to do with
        race and leader, realm indivisible,
laboured Augustan speeches or vague imperial heritage.
(They saw through that guff before the axe fell.)
        Their longing turned to
the lost world glimpsed in the memory of letters:
an evening at the pictures in the friendly dark,
two knowing conspirators smiling and whispering secrets; or else
a family gathering in the homely kitchen
with Mum so proud of her boys in uniform:
        their thoughts trembled
between moments of estrangement, and ecstatic moments
of reconciliation: and their desire
crucified itself against the unutterable shadow of someone
whose photo was in their wallets.
Then death made his incision.

There were our own, there were the others.
Therefore, minding the great word of Glencoe's
son, that we should not disfigure ourselves
with villainy of hatred; and seeing that all
have gone down like curs into anonymous silence,
I will bear witness for I knew the others.
Seeing that littoral and interior are alike indifferent
and the birds are drawn again to our welcoming north
why should I not sing *them*, the dead, the innocent?

[...]

INTERLUDE: *Opening of an Offensive*

(A) THE WAITING

Armour has foregathered, snuffling
through tourbillions of fine dust.
The crews don't speak much. They've had
last brew-up before battle. The tawny
deadland lies in a silence
not yet smashed by salvoes.
No sound reaches us
from the African constellations.
The low ridge too is quiet.
But no fear we're sleeping,
no need to remind us
that the nervous fingers of the searchlights
are nearly meeting and time is flickering
and this I think in a few minutes
while the whole power crouches for the spring.
X–20 in thirty seconds. Then begin

(B) THE BARRAGE

Let loose (rounds)
the exultant bounding hell-harrowing of sound.
Break the batteries. Confound
the damnable domination. Slake

227

the crashing breakers-húrled rúbble of the guns.
Dithering darkness, we'll wake you! Héll's béll's
blind you. Be broken, bleed
deathshead blackness!
                    The thongs of the livid
firelights lick you
                    jagg'd splinters rend you
                                        underground
we'll bomb you, doom you, tomb you into grave's mound

(C) THE JOCKS

They move forward into no man's land, a vibrant sounding board.
                    As they advance
the guns push further murderous music.
Is this all they will hear, this raucous apocalypse?
The spheres knocking in the night of Heaven?
The drummeling of overwhelming niagara?
No! For I can hear it! Or is it?...tell
me that I can hear it! Now – listen!

                    Yes, hill and shieling
sea-loch and island, hear it, the yell
of your war-pipes, scaling sound's mountains
guns thunder drowning in their soaring swell!
– The barrage gulfs them: they're gulfed in the clumbering guns,
gulfed in gloom, gloom. Dumb in the blunderbuss black –
lost – gone in the anonymous cataract of noise.
Now again! The shrill war-song: it flaunts
aggression to the sullen desert. It mounts. Its scream
tops the valkyrie, tops the colossal
                    artillery.

Meaning that many
German Fascists will not be going home
meaning that many
will die, doomed in their false dream

We'll mak siccar! [1]
Against the bashing cudgel
against the contemptuous triumphs of the big battalions

228

mak siccar against the monkish adepts
of total war against the oppressed oppressors
mak siccar against the leaching lies
against the worked out systems of sick perversion
mak siccar
                against the executioner
against the tyrannous myth and the real terror
mak siccar

[...]

from SIXTH ELEGY: *Acroma*

No blah about their sacrifice: rather tears or reviling
of the time that took them, than an insult so outrageous.
All barriers are down: in the criss-crossed enclosures
where most lie now assembled in their aching solitude
those others lie too – who were also the sacrificed
of history's great rains, of the destructive transitions.
This one beach where high seas have disgorged them like flotsam
reveals in its nakedness their ultimate alliance.

So the words that I have looked for, and must go on looking for,
are worlds of whole love, which can slowly gain the power
to reconcile and heal. Other words would be pointless.

HAMISH HENDERSON

1. *Mak siccar* is a celebrated heroic phrase in medieval Scottish history, from an incident in 1306 when the future king Robert the Bruce stabbed the defector John Comyn in a church in Dumfries, telling his escorts 'I fear I have slain Comyn', whereupon Roger de Kirkpatrick went in to finish the job with the words: 'Aweel. I'll mak siccar!' ('Well then. I'll make sure!')

Hamish Henderson (1919-2002) was a Scottish poet, songwriter, folklorist and father of the Scottish folk revival. As a visiting student in pre-war Nazi Germany, he worked with the German resistance and helped to bring Jewish refugees out of the country. After joining the Pioneer Corps in 1940, he was shipped out to North Africa, working as an intelligence officer from 1941 with the Eighth Army in the Western desert, the setting of his *Elegies for the Dead* in *Cyrenaica*, and later helping to plan the Allied invasion of Sicily in June 1943. In Italy he captured and interrogated prisoners, and personally accepted the surrender of Italy from Marshal Graziani in May 1945. The *Elegies* were written between March 1943 and December 1947 (in North Africa, Italy and Scotland), four of them already existing in fragmentary form in autumn 1942.

Edwin Morgan (1920-2010) was one of the foremost Scottish poets of the 20th century, also renowned as a translator, and became Scotland's first Makar in 2004. During the Second World War he registered as a conscientious objector, but volunteered for the Royal Army Medical Corps, serving in Egypt, Lebanon and Palestine, the Middle East setting of *The New Divan* (1977), a long poem in 100 parts drawing on the wartime experiences of his formative years.

from The New Divan

99

I dreaded stretcher-bearing,
my fingers would slip on the two sweat-soaked handles,
my muscles not used to the strain.
The easiest trip of all I don't forget,
in the desert, that dead officer
drained of blood, wasted away,
leg amputated at the thigh,
wrapped in a rough sheet, light as a child,
rolling from side to side of the canvas
with a faint terrible sound
as our feet stumbled through the sand.

EDWIN MORGAN

from The Spoils

from III

Broken booty but usable
along the littoral, frittering into the south.
We marvelled, careful of craters and minefields,
noting a new-painted recognisance

on a fragment of fuselage, sand drifting into dumps,
a tank's turret twisted skyward,
here and there a lorry unharmed
out of fuel or the crew scattered;
leaguered in lines numbered for enemy units,
gulped beer of their brewing,
mocked them marching unguarded to our rear;
discerned nothing indigenous, never a dwelling,
but on the shore sponges stranded and beyond the reef
unstayed masts staggering in the swell,
till we reached readymade villages clamped on cornland,
empty, Arabs feeding vines to goats;
at last orchards aligned, girls hawked by their mothers
from tent to tent, Tripoli dark
under a cone of tracers.
Old in that war after raising many crosses
rapped on a tomb at Leptis; no one opened.

Blind Bashshar bin Burd saw,
doubted, glanced back,
guessed whence, speculated whither.
Panegyrists, blinder and deaf,
prophets, exegesists, counsellors of patience
lie in wait for blood,
every man with a net.
Condole with me with abundance of secret pleasure.
What we think in private
will be said in public
before the last gallon's teemed
into an unintelligible sea –
old men who toil in the bilge to open a link,
bruised by the fling of the ship and sodden
sleep at the handpump. Staithes, filthy harbour water,
a drowned Finn, a drowned Chinee;
hard-lying money wrung from protesting paymasters.

Rosyth guns sang. Sang tide through cable
for Glasgow burning:
               'Bright west,
                 pale east,
                 catfish on the sprool.'

Sun leaped up and passed,
bolted towards green creek
of quiet Chesapeake,
bight of a warp no strong tide strains. Yet
as tea's drawing, breeze backing and freshening,
who'd rather
make fast Fortune with a slippery hitch?
Tide sang. Guns sang:
      'Vigilant,
        pull off fluffed woollens, strip
        to buff and beyond.'
In watch below
meditative heard elsewhere
surf shout, pound shores seldom silent
from which heart naked swam
out to the dear unintelligible ocean.

From Largo Law look down,
moon and dry weather, look down
on convoy marshalled, filing between mines.
Cold northern clear sea-gardens
between Lofoten and Spitzbergen,
as good a grave as any, earth or water.
What else do we live for and take part,
we who would share the spoils?

BASIL BUNTING

Basil Bunting (1900-85) was a major figure in Modernist British poetry, best-known for his long poem *Briggflatts* (1966). *The Spoils* (1951) is an earlier sonata drawing on his wartime experiences. Imprisoned as a conscientious objector in 1918, Bunting volunteered for the Royal Air Force in the Second World War. From December 1940 to April 1942 he worked with barrage balloons, firstly in East Yorkshire, and latterly in Fife, the setting of the second part of this extract. In 1943 he crossed the desert in an ammunition convoy from Basra in Iraq to Libya ('a month of very hard fare'), and the first part of this extract relates to the last leg of that journey, from El Alamein to Tripoli, where he would witness the Battle of Wadi Akarit. After spells in Egypt, Malta and Italy, his knowledge of Persian languages and Islamic culture earned him promotion to Vice-Consul in Isfahan. Continuing to work for British military intelligence in Persia after the war, he was the *Times* correspondent in Tehran until his expulsion in 1952, when he returned to England.

Eighth Air Force

If, in an odd angle of the hutment,
A puppy laps the water from a can
Of flowers, and the drunk sergeant shaving
Whistles *O Paradiso!* – shall I say that man
Is not as men have said: a wolf to man?

The other murderers troop in yawning;
Three of them play Pitch, one sleeps, and one
Lies counting missions, lies there sweating
Till even his heart beats: One; One; One.
O murderers!... Still, this is how it's done:

This is a war.... But since these play, before they die,
Like puppies with their puppy; since, a man,
I did as these have done, but did not die –
I will content the people as I can
And give up these to them: Behold the man!

I have suffered, in a dream, because of him,
Many things; for this last saviour, man,
I have lied as I lie now. But what is lying?
Men wash their hands, in blood, as best they can:
I find no fault in this just man.

RANDALL JARRELL

The Death of the Ball Turret Gunner

From my mother's sleep I fell into the State,
And I hunched in its belly till my wet fur froze.
Six miles from earth, loosed from its dream of life,
I woke to black flak and the nightmare fighters.
When I died they washed me out of the turret with a hose.

RANDALL JARRELL

Losses

It was not dying: everybody died.
It was not dying: we had died before
In the routine crashes – and our fields
Called up the papers, wrote home to our folks,
And the rates rose, all because of us.
We died on the wrong page of the almanac,
Scattered on mountains fifty miles away;
Diving on haystacks, fighting with a friend,
We blazed up on the lines we never saw.
We died like aunts or pets or foreigners.
(When we left high school nothing else had died
For us to figure we had died like.)

In our new planes, with our new crews, we bombed
The ranges by the desert or the shore,
Fired at towed targets, waited for our scores –
And turned into replacements and woke up
One morning, over England, operational.
It wasn't different: but if we died
It was not an accident but a mistake
(But an easy one for anyone to make.)
We read our mail and counted up our missions –
In bombers named for girls, we burned
The cities we had learned about in school –
Till our lives wore out; our bodies lay among
The people we had killed and never seen.
When we lasted long enough they gave us medals;
When we died they said, 'Our casualties were low.'

They said, 'Here are the maps'; we burned the cities.

It was not dying – no, not ever dying;
But the night I died I dreamed that I was dead,
And the cities said to me: 'Why are you dying?
We are satisfied, if you are; but why did I die?'

RANDALL JARRELL

234

Randall Jarrell (1914-65) was a brilliant American 20th-century writer, known especially for his acerbic, witty, even cruel criticism, but was 'brutally serious about literature' (Robert Lowell), as passionate in praise or defence of good or great writing as he was ruthless in demolishing bad or pretentious poetry. As a poet he wrote with a mastery of form in a plain, colloquial style which came into its own under the pressure of war, when 'he began to write with stark, compressed lucidity' (Hayden Carruth). He enlisted in the US Army Air Force in 1942, serving for much of the war as a control tower operator.

Howard Nemerov (1920-91) was an American poet and professor who was both Poetry Consultant to the Library of Congress (1963-64) and US Poet Laureate (1988-90). He served as a pilot throughout the Second World War, firstly with the Royal Canadian Air Force and latterly in the US Army Air Force. He taught literature after the war to veterans.

The War in the Air

For a saving grace, we didn't see our dead,
Who rarely bothered coming home to die
But simply stayed away out there
In the clean war, the war in the air.

Seldom the ghosts come back bearing their tales
Of hitting the earth, the incompressible sea,
But stayed up there in the relative wind,
Shades fading in the mind,

Who had no graves but only epitaphs
Where never so many spoke for never so few:
Per ardua, said the partisans of Mars,
Per aspera, to the stars.

That was the good war, the war we won
As if there was no death, for goodness's sake.
With the help of the losers we left out there
In the air, in the empty air.

HOWARD NEMEROV

Radar

Distance is swept by the smooth
Rotations of power, its staring
Feelers multiplying our eyes for us,
Marking objects' range and bearing.

Linked to them, guns rehearse
Calculated obedience; echoes of light
Trigger the shadowing needle, determine
The arrest of the night.

Control is remote; feelings, like hands,
Gloved by space. Responsibility is shared, too.
And destroying the enemy by radar
We never see what we do.

ALAN ROSS
➤ 197

A Lullaby

For wars his life and half a world away
The soldier sells his family and days.
He learns to fight for freedom and the State;
He sleeps with seven men within six feet.

He picks up matches and he cleans out plates;
Is lied to like a child, cursed like a beast.
They crop his head, his dog tags ring like sheep
As his stiff limbs shift wearily to sleep.

Recalled in dreams or letters, else forgot,
His life is smothered like a grave, with dirt;
And his dull torment mottles like a fly's
The lying amber of the histories.

RANDALL JARRELL

Buttons

(in memory of Captain Edward Herbert)

Only buttons witnesses to the crime [1]
proved unyielding outlasting death
and as sole memorial on the grave
rise up from the depths of the earth

they are a testimony it is for God
to count them and to be merciful
but what resurrection if each body
lies in the earth a clinging particle

a bird flies over a cloud sails past
a leaf descends mallows grow lush
a mist drifts in the Smolensk forest
and up in the heights a deep hush

only buttons proved unyielding
the mighty voice of a muted chorus
only buttons proved unyielding
buttons from coats and uniforms

ZBIGNIEW HERBERT
translated from the Polish by Alissa Valles

1. 'the crime': the Katyn Forest massacres near Smolensk in Russia in April
and May 1940 – blamed on the Nazis for over 50 years – were the largest of
several mass executions of prisoners of war authorised by Stalin to neutralise
possible future opposition to Soviet occupation of Poland. Thousands of silver-
hued metal uniform coat buttons embossed with the Polish eagle were found
in the forest after working their way to the surface from the burial pits. The
total number of victims is estimated at around 22,000, including 8,000 Polish
Army officers, among these, Captain Edward Herbert, son of Herbert's
paternal uncle Marian Herbert. Soviet responsibility for the massacres was
only acknowledged in 1990. Documents released in 2013 showed that the US
Government had proof in 1943 of Soviet guilt but suppressed the findings,
probably to avoid confrontation with Stalin, then America's ally in the war.

Zbigniew Herbert (1924-98) was one of the major figures in 20th century
Polish poetry, but spent much of his life in exile, unable to publish his work
freely at home. He returned to live in Poland in 1981-86 and again in 1992,
when he could finally publish his collection *Rovigo* including 'Buttons'.

from The Pulkovo Meridian

The teeth are bared, the mouth drawn tight, the face
Is waxen and the beard like a cadaver's
(A beard the razor hardly can displace).
The walk, without a balance centre, wavers.
The pulse beneath the ashen-coloured skin
Is weak. The albumin is gone. The end sets in.

Among the women many have a swelling.
They shiver constantly (though not from frost).
Their bosoms shrink to nothingness, compelling
The once-white kerchiefs to be tighter crossed.
Who would believe that once at such a breast
A child had ever sucked himself to rest?

Like melted candles in their apathy.
All the dry summaries and indications
Are here of what by learned designations
Doctors call 'alimental dystrophy'.
Non-Latinists, non-philologues will name
It simply hunger, but it means the same.

And after that the end is very near.
The body, rolled up in a dust-grey cover
Fastened with safety-pins, and wound all over
With rope, upon a child's sled will appear,
So neatly laid out that it's plain to see
It's not the first one in the family.

[Leningrad, 1943]

VERA INBER
translated from the Russian by Dorothea Prall Radin & Alexander Kaun

Vera Inber (1890-1912) was an Odessa-born Soviet writer whose *Leningrad Diary* (1946) chronicled the daily sufferings and deprivations of her fellow citizens during the 900-day siege of the city (1941-44). She also wrote her 800-line poem 'The Pulkovo Meridian' during the siege.

Briefing for Invasion

Tomorrow, he said, is fixed for death's birthday party,
A gala show on the beaches, and all invited,
Fireworks and aerobatics and aquatic diversions;
Tomorrow you can be sure of a grand reception.

At o-four hundred hours when the night grows sickly
And the sand slips under your boots like a child's nightmare,
Clumsy and humped and shrunken inside your clothes
You will shamble up the shore to give him your greeting.

Not all those present will shake him by the hand
But none will pass on without looking into his face;
The moment may seem chaotic, but be content –
A world has laboured for this supreme occasion.

Over your heads and over all crouching Europe
The sky will be lashed with sounds too huge for hearing
But to some listening inland it will seem like
The great inarticulate word *Freedom* howled by the dead.

Your skull will be filled with the hoarse breathing of death
And the gossip and chatter of all his ghostly devices,
The dust suddenly spouting with ferocious flowers
And the air canopied with a charnel smell.

And when the white sun retches across the land
The ships will litter the sea like deer at grazing.
But other and pitiful litter along the shore
The catspaw waves will lick and leave like vomit.

O love! is it worth it? And are the dead rewarded
With a bearer bond on history's doubtful balance?
And is the loss redeemed by a sunset glory
A sweet transfusion of blood to a new-born world?

No, it will never be worth it, nor the loss redeemed.
The dead die hideously and there is no honour.

The blood that runs out in the sand can only embitter
The violence of a fate that is still unmastered.

Even though some should slip through the net of flame
And life emerge loaded with secret knowledge,
Won't they be dumb, sealed off by the awful vision?
Or should they speak, would anyone ever believe?

Only this pride we have, both now and after,
Because we have grasped the fate ourselves created,
And to have been the centre of contradiction
And not to have failed, and still to have found it hateful.

[Salerno Bay, September 1943]

RANDALL SWINGLER

Randall Swingler (1900-67) was an English poet, playwright, novelist, editor and critic, and an energetic Communist Party activist until 1956. 'Swingler's poetry provides a unique record of his times, from the romantic Communism of the early 30s and the campaigning years of the Popular Front, through the war in Italy and the anti-Fascist victory of 1945 to the disappointed hopes of Cold War Europe' (Andy Croft). ➤ 292

Saigon 1943

Not a soul on the quay.
No one had come to greet our ship.
The French town I'd dreamed of
floating on a colonial sea.
No trace here of the Orient.

Wrapped in white cloth
a corpse was carried unsteadily from the hatch –
a young army clerk
who'd killed himself with an open razor.

This was our Saigon.
France's anguish
was this city's anguish.
Could there be a connection
between the torment we as soldiers feel
and that of our fatherland?
Above the liners flying the Tricolore
was the serene blue sky
of a defeated country ripped by war.
With so many friends already dead,
so many others going off to die,
sick soldiers told the recent voiceless dead
how black the worms were
crawling beneath their living skin.

A light breeze was blowing.
With the same razor that had freed his soul
applied to our own thin throats,
we watched the dinghy carrying the stretcher
recede into the distance
parting the green water.

NOBUO AYUKAWA
translated from the Japanese by Harry & Lynne Guest and Shozo Kajima

Maritime Graves

The sea
is muddied almost to the horizon
by the waters of the Mekong.
An oil-tanker
rammed the breakwater on a lonely beach
and is belching jet-black smoke.
The crude oil spreading
reflects the five-coloured sky
after an air-raid.
At the shallow mouth of the bay

smoke-stacks jut from the water
like gravestones with numbers on them.
Huge transport ships
are lying there submerged.

As we are wounded soldiers
our uniforms are white.
We have turned into ghosts
and glide now noiselessly
over the becalmed cemetery.
To find a land of peace
you have to leave a land where there is none.
Unhappy soldiers look up at the sky;
shading their eyes they try to read the future,
gaze at the rift in the enormous rain-clouds.

This ship we've longed for,
this slow voyage –
can it take us
beyond defeat?

A look-out boat appears from nowhere.
The French pilot, hairy legs in shorts,
puffs serenely at his pipe
and three thousand tons of lousy supplies
are towed upstream on the Mekong.

NOBUO AYUKAWA
translated from the Japanese by Harry & Lynne Guest and Shozo Kajima

Nobuo Ayukawa (1920-86) was one of the founders of the Arechi (Wasteland) group of Japanese poets, and translated the work of T.S. Eliot and William Burroughs into Japanese. Ayukawa rejected traditional Japanese poetic concerns, mining his past experiences as a soldier in the Japanese Imperialist army during the Second World War and paying homage to his American and European literary influences in abstract, lyrical modernist works. During the war he kept a diary documenting acts of brutality by Japanese forces which was later published. He distanced himself from the focus of postwar Japanese poetry on protests against the atom bomb and the destruction of Hiroshima and Nagasaki, but 'unlike conservative writers, never aligned himself with those who tried to deny or whitewash Japan's prewar and wartime history' (Shoto Oketani).

Sniper

Moves in the rocks with inching fingers.
We among the feathery banana trees
Imagine for him his aim: the steel helmet
And English face filling the backsight's V.
Again as it was last time, that spurting noise,
Thud, and the writhing figure in long grass.
Until we match precision with precision:
We move ten men to one and have him then.

I saw the sniper in the afternoon. The rifle
Lay there beside him neatly like his shooting,
The grass twined all about his cap.
He had killed neatly but we had set
Ten men about him to write death in jags
Cutting and spoiling on his face and broken body.

BERNARD GUTTERIDGE

Bernard Gutteridge (1916-85) was an English poet and novelist who worked in advertising before and after the war. He served in Madagascar, India, and with the 36th Division of the British Army in Burma, where one fellow officer was Alun Lewis, whose death he recorded in his long poem 'Burma Diary'. 'Sniper' was written during the Burma Campaign in 1944. His war poems were collected in *Traveller's Eye* (1947).

Cain in the Jungle

I have killed my brother in the jungle;
Under the green liana's clammy tangle
I hid, and pressed my trigger, and he died.

Smooth as the spotted panther crept my brother,
Never a creak of his equipment's leather,
Never a leaf dislodged nor bird offended.

With his palaeozoic prototype
My mother shared her own ungainly shape
In caverns on some slow Silurian stream;

And with the cublings played my father's sons,
Shoulder to shoulder chipped their flints and bones
Or scraped a greasy ichthyosaurus hide.

And, when the floods of purple slime receded
My brother's hutments by the apes were raided,
I lay beneath my brother's legs and cried,

Yet I have fought my brother for the planets;
I have never stopped to hear the linnets,
Or watch the cocos grow against the moon.

I have only slain him in the shadows,
I have made his slant-eyed women widows
And inherited his empty meadows.

DENYS L. JONES

Denys L. Jones (*b*. 1917) went to sea before the war, and then spent seven years in the British Army. 'Cain the Jungle' was published in *Penguin New Writing* in 1946.

The Fury of Aerial Bombardment

You would think the fury of aerial bombardment
Would rouse God to relent; the infinite spaces
Are still silent. He looks on shock-pried faces.
History, even, does not know what is meant.

You would feel that after so many centuries
God would give man to repent; yet he can kill
As Cain could, but with multitudinous will,
No farther advanced than in his ancient furies

Was man made stupid to see his own stupidity?
Is God by definition indifferent, beyond us all?
Is the eternal truth man's fighting soul
Wherein the Beast ravens in its own avidity?

Of Van Wettering I speak, and Averill,
Names on a list, whose faces I do not recall
But they are gone to early death, who late in school
Distinguished the belt feed lever from the belt holding pawl.

RICHARD EBERHART

Richard Eberhart (1904-2005) was an American poet and professor who lived to the age of 101, and served in the US Naval Reserve as an aerial gunnery instructor at several bases during the Second World War. In his essay collection, *Of Poetry and Poets* (1979), he describes writing 'The Fury of Aerial Bombardment' in 1944 after being suddenly struck by how often the names of his former students appeared on the casualty lists.

from The Monk's Diary
(Monte Cassino, Italy, 1944) [1]

January 10

Dom Eusebio must make up a coffin
for the girl who died last night, but has no tacks.
A surprise from La Valletta: two women.
They tell of swarms of soldiers, columns of tanks.
Luck is with them. They have a good commandant
who calls the old ones papà and mamma. Jokes.
We need no luck, keep the Rule of Benedict.
They shake their heads. This will be an inferno.
They have seen donkeys nodding to our grottos
with monstrous loads. Even our caves speak German!
For the sick, they leave a half-sack of oranges.
For us – miraculous – winter-laying hens!
At supper, nodding content, the abbot has eggs.

January 11

The women do what they can. Glean spent olives,
press them. Wash their clothes. Even sell oranges.
In the hills no questions – if anything moves
it is shot. At noon a shell skimmed over us.
Like a button on thread it found a cave. Flesh.
The mother dead. Her child, a bundle of rags
punctured by shrapnel, scalp dressed with mud, the mash
of brain-tissue coming out. He was still warm.
Pietro wept. Wrapped the body in a sheet.
I absolved. Like bells, the shelling suddenly calmed.
Later our poor sheep, left without a shepherd,
got through the main gate. They staggered like spring lambs
through the cloisters. Blinked at frescoes. At us, famished.

January 12

So this is how men sculpt in stone their modern
civilisation! Last night at nine o'clock
the first shell struck the abbey. American.
Fault of fools who cannot see beyond a rock
and the Germans' stupid hoverings, their incessant
knocking, grinning for art. Mere moments back
in the refuge, then we shook with the impact.
Dom Oderosio was still outside. Saved
by a special protection – Saint Benedict.
Now one side of the entrance cloister is shaved
off, a rubble beach. Windows of riddled ice.
Eusebio greets two officers from the caves.
As though they are his own blood, shows them round the place.

January 20

Soon after dark, cursed firing startles us.
Down on the plain gunfire sparks and runs – orange
fireflies gliding between German and Allies.
A flare makes the banks of the Rapido bone.
Pietro stands watch with me. Eyes like a trout. Tears.

Though the shells come barely halfway up the slope
each blast sends a doe's tremor through his shoulders.
I keep vigil as night prowls, starved as the moon.
Our abbey, like a mouse in these jaws of war.
With first light, dreadful clamour. A hen – stolen.
So. Our Noah's Ark, sinking. Pietro is stood,
all shoulders. The abbot's incrimination:
the feather in his coat. Its mortal blot of blood.

MARIO PETRUCCI

1. Monte Cassino: 'a hill midway between Rome and Naples, site of the principal monastery of the Benedictines, founded by St Benedict *c*. 529. In 1944, during the Second World War, Allied forces advancing towards Rome were halted by German defensive positions to which Monte Cassino was the key; they succeeded in capturing the site only after four months of bitter fighting. The monastery, previously demolished and rebuilt several times, was almost totally destroyed, but has since been restored.' *The Oxford Reference Dictionary* (OUP, 1986).

Mario Petrucci (*b*. 1958) is an English poet of Italian parentage as well as an ecologist and physicist, and has been resident poet at the Imperial War Museum. His forthcoming collection *Monte Cassino* – from which these extracts are taken – relates to events during the Battle of Monte Cassino witnessed by his family, as told by them and by protagonists involved, as well as drawing on his own experience of growing up under the shadow of the monastery. His other books include *Heavy Water: a poem for Chernobyl* (2004).

Beyond All Calculation

We left England before dawn, flying high and easy
across the Channel, then dropped into the worst of it
behind a farmhouse near Le Mesnil; forty or fifty men
were awaiting evacuation, so we dealt with them fast,

before hundreds of others began arriving from Gold Beach.
The yard was soon like the threshold of a slaughterhouse –
bloodstained uniforms, boots, caps and helmets and berets.
The interior of the kitchen and double-parlour is best left

to the imagination. Suffice it to say we would be kept busy
for three or four days straight through without any sleep,
but we had Benzedrine, and so did the stretcher-bearers –
willing but unseasoned boys who took it the hardest,

hesitating to lift their burdens unless they could turn
their backs. They became veterans that first morning.
Anyone would have done, watching the hands working,
seeing the orderlies giving blood, the wounds excised

then dressed as soon as the bleeding was under control
and limbs immobilised. When the break-out finally came,
with the men squeezed tight together in those deep lanes
and pressing towards the horizon, they found cattle dead

in the grazing on every side, their legs up stiff like toys.
No one had milked them; it was something that had been
forgotten. In the silence afterwards, ambulances appeared.
We climbed into these with our equipment and followed on.

ANDREW MOTION

Several poems in Andrew Motion's collection *The Customs House* (2012) take
the words of soldiers (from accounts in books, interviews and meetings) to
create 'found poems' which he hopes can be read as collaborations between the
author and his source. This poem is indebted to an account in *Medicine and
Victory: British Military Medicine in the Second World War* by Mark Harrison
(Oxford University Press, 2004). ➤ 128, 558.

Carentan O Carentan

Trees in the old days used to stand
And shape a shady lane
Where lovers wandered hand in hand
Who came from Carentan.

This was the shining green canal
Where we came two by two
Walking at combat-interval.
Such trees we never knew.

The day was early June, the ground
Was soft and bright with dew.
Far away the guns did sound,
But here the sky was blue.

The sky was blue, but there a smoke
Hung still above the sea
Where the ships together spoke
To towns we could not see.

Could you have seen us through a glass
You would have said a walk
Of farmers out to turn the grass,
Each with his own hay-fork.

The watchers in their leopard suits
Waited till it was time,
And aimed between the belt and boot
And let the barrel climb.

I must lie down at once, there is
A hammer at my knee.
And call it death or cowardice,
Don't count again on me.

Everything's all right, Mother,
Everyone gets the same
At one time or another.
It's all in the game.

I never strolled, nor ever shall,
Down such a leafy lane.
I never drank in a canal,
Nor ever shall again.

There is a whistling in the leaves
And it is not the wind,
The twigs are falling from the knives
That cut men to the ground.

Tell me, Master-Sergeant,
The way to turn and shoot.
But the Sergeant's silent
That taught me how to do it.

O Captain, show us quickly
Our place upon the map.
But the Captain's sickly
And taking a long nap.

Lieutenant, what's my duty,
My place in the platoon?
He too's a sleeping beauty,
Charmed by that strange tune.

Carentan O Carentan
Before we met with you
We never yet had lost a man
Or known what death could do.

LOUIS SIMPSON

Louis Simpson (1923-2012) was a Jamaica-born American poet. He served in the Second World War with the 101st Airborne Division on active duty in France, Holland, Belgium and Germany. ➢ 266

'Carentan O Carentan' is a ballad prompted by his retrieved memory of being one of a column of American infantrymen ambushed by German soldiers during the Battle of Normandy in June 1944 near the city of Carentan. In his memoir *The King My Father's Wreck* (1995), he recalls living in Paris after the war, still traumatised by his wartime experiences: 'One night I dreamed that I was walking with other shadowy figures along what seemed to be the bank of a canal, when bullets slashed the trees and shells were falling. I woke and wrote out the dream, and as I wrote remembered [...] I had been reading Heine's ballads, and the poem took the form of a ballad. As it was a poem, not just memory, I was free to invent.'

Oradour

Oradour has no women now
Oradour has not one man now
Oradour has no leaves now
Oradour has no stones now
Oradour has no church now
Oradour has no children now

no chimneys now no laughter now
no roofs now no attics now
no mill now no love now
no wine now no singing now

Oradour, I dread to hear
Oradour, I do not dare
come near come near your wounds
your blood come near your ruins
nor bear I cannot bear
to see or hear your name.

Oradour I scream I howl
every time the butchers'
punches land a heart explodes
a terror-stricken head
two great eyes two huge red eyes
two earnest eyes two eyes as wide
as night as wide as madness
two eyes a child's eyes:
they will never not be with me.
Oradour I shall not dare now
ever read or speak your name.

Oradour mankind's shame
Oradour eternal shame
hate and shame for evermore.

Oradour has no shape now
Oradour, nor women nor men
Oradour has no children now

251

Oradour has no leaves now
Oradour has no church now
no chimneys now no girls now
no evenings or mornings now
no tears or singing now.

Oradour is no more now than a scream
and it is the harshest insult
to this once living village
and the harshest degradation
to be no more now than a scream,
a name for mankind's hate
a name for mankind's degradation
a name that through all this land
we listen to and shudder
one disembodied mouth
howling through the ages.

JEAN TARDIEU
translated from the French by Ian Higgins

Four days after the Normandy landings, on 10 June 1944, a battalion of the
Waffen-SS entered the village of Oradour-sur-Glane, near Limoges, following
a report that a German officer was being held by the Resistance in Oradour-
sur-Vayres, a nearby village. Knowing nothing about the other incident, the
inhabitants of Oradour-sur-Glane were rounded up. The women and children
were locked in the church, which was set on fire with explosives, while the
men were taken to six barns and sheds and mown down with machine-guns.
642 innocent civilians were murdered, and the village was partly razed that
evening. As a memorial to the dead, and to the way they died, the wrecked
village has been left untouched, and a museum built beside it.

Jean Tardieu (1903-95) was actively engaged with the literary Resistance
during the war, working with clandestine magazines and publishers, and
connected with other Resistance writers. His wartime poems were later pub-
lished in *Jours pétrifiés* (1948). 'Oradour' was written in September 1944. 'One
of its themes,' wrote Ian Higgins, 'is that of the tension between the
impossibility of finding words to express one's reaction to such an atrocity
and the impossibility of remaining silent about it.' One of its aims is 'to lay
bare some of the implications of reacting in words to unspeakable evil. These
implications are, ultimately, moral ones, inasmuch as, first, "Oradour" is
concerned with the creation of myth and, second, myth has a collective moral
dimension.' (*French Studies*, 1994).

Memorial

This is the house that Jacques built.

This is the tree in the sun-scorched yard
of the weather-proof house that Jacques built.

This is the car, all lacy with rust,
that waits by the linden tree in the yard
of the thick-walled house that Jacques built.

This is the baker, his bread long lost,
who was proud of the car now crumbled with rust
that slumps by the tree in the dusty yard
of the ruined house that Jacques built.

These are the children and neighbours and wives
all dead, like the baker whose life was lost,
who polished the car, now papery rust
like the oven that stands in the silent yard
of the roofless house that Jacques built.

This is the church and the blistered Christ
who couldn't protect the children and wives
who choked in each other's arms, all lost
like the prosperous baker whose car is rust
whose oven stands gaping in the yard
of the desolate house that Jacques built.

These are the soldiers who barred the doors
and torched the Christ; who erased the lives
of the more than six hundred children and wives
and men like the baker, a whole village lost
leaving prams and sewing machines to rust,
bright orange against the dust of the yards
and the stones of the houses Jacques built.

What happened later to minds as split
as those of the soldiers who locked the doors,
Christians, who extinguished the lives
of the more than six hundred children and wives

and men who had plans and loves – all lost;
and the only sign that they lived is rust
on the pans and irons in the rooms and yards
of all the houses Jacques built?

How can the linden tree still flower
from the death-soaked earth of Oradour;
and water from the well run clear,
and bees make harmony every year,
and ants run feckless over the floor?
Just as they do in Sobibor,
Haditha, Shattila, Warsaw,
in Srebrenica and Darfur...

That's how it is in Oradour.

CAROLE SATYAMURTI

Carole Satyamurti (*b*. 1939) is an English poet. Her poem 'Memorial' was
written following a visit to Oradour-sur-Glane, and published in her collection
Countdown (2011). ➢ 487

Walking Wounded

A mammoth morning moved grey flanks and groaned.
In the rusty hedges pale rags of mist hung;
The gruel of mud and leaves in the mauled lane
Smelled sweet, like blood. Birds had died or flown,
Their green and silent attics sprouting now
With branches of leafed steel, hiding round eyes
And ripe grenades ready to drop and burst.
In the ditch at the crossroads the fallen rider lay
Hugging his dead machine and did nor stir
At crunch of mortar, tantrum of a Bren
Answering a Spandau's manic jabber.
Then into sight the ambulances came,
Stumbling and churning past the broken farm,
The amputated sign-post and smashed trees,

Slow wagonloads of bandaged cries, square trucks
That rolled on ominous wheels, vehicles
Made mythopoeic by their mortal freight
And crimson crosses on the dirty white.
This grave procession passed, though, for a while,
The grinding of their engines could be heard,
A dark noise on the pallor of the morning,
Dark as dried blood; and then it faded, died.
The road was empty, but it seemed to wait –
Like a stage which knows the cast is in the wings –
Wait for a different traffic to appear.
The mist still hung in snags from dripping thorns;
Absent-minded guns still sighed and thumped.
And then they came, the walking wounded,
Straggling the road like convicts loosely chained,
Dragging at ankles exhaustion and despair.
Their heads were weighted down by last night's lead,
And eyes still drank the dark. They trailed the night
Along the morning road. Some limped on sticks;
Others wore rough dressings, splints and slings;
A few had turbanned heads, the dirty cloth
Brown-badged with blood. A humble brotherhood,
Not one was suffering from a lethal hurt,
They were not magnified by noble wounds,
There was no splendour in that company.
And yet, remembering after eighteen years,
In the heart's throat a sour sadness stirs;
Imagination pauses and returns
To see them walking still, but multiplied
In thousands now. And when heroic corpses
Turn slowly in their decorated sleep
And every ambulance has disappeared
The walking wounded still trudge down that lane,
And when recalled they must bear arms again.

VERNON SCANNELL

Vernon Scannell (1922-2007) was an English poet, novelist and boxer who
served with the Gordon Highlanders in North Africa where he deserted. He
was later wounded near Caen during the Normandy invasion, and deserted
again at the end of the war, spending two years on the run.

Seventh Eclogue

You see? As dark comes on, the barracks and the grim oak fence,
Girded with barbed-wire, dissolve: night soaks them up.
Slowly the eye relinquishes the bounds of our captivity
And the mind, only the mind, can tell how taut the wire is.
You see, dear? Even the fancy has no other way to freedom;
The broken body's released by the fair deliverer, sleep
And the whole prison-camp, then, takes flight for home.
In rags, with their heads shaven, snoring, the prisoners fly
From the blind heights of Serbia to homelands now in hiding.
Homelands in hiding! Ah, does *our* home still exist?
It might have escaped the bombs? It still is – as when we left it?
Will that man who moans on my right, and this on my left, reach home?
Is there a land still, tell me, where this verse form has meaning?

Without putting in the accents, just groping line after line,
I write this poem here, in the dark, just as I live,
Half-blind, like a caterpillar inching my way across paper.
Torches, books – the guards have taken everything –
And no post comes, just fog, which settles over the barracks.

Among false rumours and worms, we live here with Frenchmen, Poles,
Loud Italians, heretic Serbs, nostalgic Jews, in the mountains.
This feverish body, dismembered but still living one life, waits
For good news, for women's sweet words, for a life both free and human,
And the end plunged into obscurity, and miracles.

A captive beast among worms, I lie on a plank. The fleas
Once more renew their assault, though the flies have gone to rest.
It's night, you see: captivity now is a day shorter.
And so is life. The camp is asleep. Over the land
The moon shines: in its light the wires go taut again.
Through the window you can see how the shadows of armed guards
Go pacing along on the wall through the noises of the night.

The camp's asleep. You see, dear? Dreams fan their wings.
Someone starts and groans, turns in his tight space and
Is already asleep again, his face aglow. I only

Sit up awake – on my lips, instead of your kisses, the taste
Of a half-smoked cigarette; and no sleep comes bringing rest,
For I can no longer die without you, nor can I live.

[Lager Heideman, in the mountains above Žagubica, July 1944]

MIKLÓS RADNÓTI
translated from the Hungarian by Clive Wilmer and George Gömöri

Miklós Radnóti (1909-44) was a Hungarian poet born into an assimilated
Jewish family. His real stature as poet became apparent only during the
Second World War when he managed to articulate the anguish of the threat-
ened and persecuted individual in classical form and created work of great
compassion and beauty. In 1944 he was called up to a labour battalion and
sent to a labour camp in Bor, Serbia, from where he was evacuated and
forced to march towards Germany. When he grew too weak to continue his
march, he was shot dead on 10 November 1944 by militiamen accompanying
the forced labourers near the village of Abda in north-western Hungary. A
notebook of poems telling the story of his last six months was found on his
body when it was exhumed from a mass grave for reburial after the war, 18
months after his death. These included his 'Seventh Eclogue' – a love poem
written to his wife – as well as 'Forced March' [➤ 263] and 'Postcards' [➤ 263]
from this selection.

For the Martyrs of Loreto Square

I saw a new day breaking on Loreto Square
when over their red barricade the dead
climbed for the first time, still in their overalls,
bare-chested, pulsing again with blood and reason.
                              And every day,
every hour burns endlessly in this fire,
every dawn has its breast outraged by the bullets
which like lightning-strike smashed the innocent
            back against the wall.

ALFONSO GATTO
translated from the Italian by Kendrick Smithyman

Alfonso Gatto (1909-76) was an Italian poet whose early work showed Hermetic and Surrealist tendencies, but his poetry, like Quasimodo's, became more engaged after his wartime experience, which included six months in a Fascist prison. Also an occasional actor, he appeared in two Pasolini films. He was killed in a car crash.

This poem relates to the killing and public display of the bodies of fifteen civilians by Fascist squads in the Piazzale Loreto, Milan, on 10 August 1944, in retaliation for partisan actions. The following year, on 29 April 1945, the bodies of Mussolini and other high-ranking Fascists were hung upside-down from the canopy of an Esso petrol station in the same square.

He Was Lucky

(for Prof. Władysław Tatarkiewicz)

The old man
leaves his house, carries books.
A German soldier snatches his books
flings them in the mud.

The old man picks them up,
the soldier hits him in the face.
The old man falls,
the soldier kicks him and walks away.

The old man
lies in mud and blood.
Under him he feels
the books.

ANNA SWIR
translated from the Polish by Magnus Jan Krynski & Robert A. Maguire

Anna Swir [Świrszczyńska] (1909-84) was a Polish poet and dramatist known for her poetry about love, death, war, motherhood and the female body. She joined the Resistance during the Second World War and served as a military nurse during the Warsaw Uprising (1 August–2 October 1944). At one point she came within an hour of being executed before being spared.

Building the Barricade

We were afraid as we built the barricade
under fire.

The tavern-keeper, the jeweller's mistress, the barber,
all of us cowards.

The servant-girl fell to the ground
as she lugged a paving-stone, we were terribly afraid
all of us cowards –
the janitor, the market-woman, the pensioner.

The pharmacist fell to the ground
as he dragged the door of a toilet,
we were even more afraid, the smuggler-woman,
the dressmaker, the streetcar driver,
all of us cowards.

A kid from reform school fell
as he dragged a sandbag,
you see we were really
afraid.

Though no one forced us,
we did build the barricade
under fire.

ANNA SWIR
translated from the Polish by Magnus Jan Krynski & Robert A. Maguire

About war

Over roads of pine logs lorries carry war through the forest. Distant,
they raise weapons to their eyes.

On the outskirts, on stalls under yellowish awnings, they sell
apples and rainbows.

Motors hum on land, in air and on sea. This even has a certain charm from Nowy Swiat[1] one can see a deep furrow of green water with which a battleship writes out longings in the English Channel.

In a first-floor window you can also see a girl with closely cropped hair playing with a lame kitten.

Tanks climb a wall of feebly blooming bushes and rattle as though they were carrying skulls and bones.

Houses and towers fall down like hail. A grey-maned horse draws a plough up a slope, the sun and crows alight on turned up stones, and smoke from crematoria sways against a blue sky.

At the same time, at the point where the meadow meets the forest wartime cadets manoeuvre for an attack.

Now one can see a paper-tissue, an almost-white wing of an angel, who was probably freckled, drooping from telegraph wires.

Lower down a sly-faced cripple plays 'Warszawianka' on a comb.

This is the glassy surface of a still river, but in a moment one of the huge fish tossing in the depths will break the surface.

LEON STROIŃSKI
translated from the Polish by Adam Czerniawski

1. Main thoroughfare in Warsaw.

Warsaw

During the building of the barricades, the Vistula, brimming with reflections of forests, birds and white roads lined with poplars, rose, at first like a mist, then like a stiff cover of a book.

In its shade at dawn caretakers come out with huge frayed brooms to sweep up the tears which have collected during the night and lie thickly in the streets.

Already, the market women, extended to the edge of the sunlight, recommend potatoes grown on graves.

And on the horizon of the street, across the roar of grenades lying in the curves of cobblestones, the soul of the city has been moving for months.

The reflection of her face, too difficult to comprehend, has left a trace on the twisted faces of ruins as on the handkerchief of St Veronica.

Those who will come in the far, far future wanting to decipher them, drawing their cold-blue hands across features taut like strings, and who with careless fingers will poke the moan of those dried up in crevices –
will burst into prayer or blasphemy.

Here my country has come together from decimated forests and villages turned into a dog's howl. It persists in the whisper of mechanised armour.

We had to wait through so much blood and pathos in order to build from the silence of ruined monuments such a vault over a city of jazz and death.

Now lemurs from Gothic temples are thick on roofs of trams and terrify insurance officials on their way home.

The dead wander beneath the pavements and pound on bucklers which give a hollow sound, while at evening in double rows of whispers they walk arm in arm with the living, and you can tell them apart only by the skilfully folded wings, which nevertheless stick out on their backs like humps.

But in daytime huge stone capstans hum, and only around noon, when folk sit down to lunch and it's a bit quieter, can you hear more distinctly the heavy rhythmical tread of God's steel-shod boots.

LEON STROIŃSKI
translated from the Polish by Adam Czerniawski

Leon Zdzisław Stroiński (1921-44) was a Polish writer of prose poems. In May 1943 he laid a tribute wreath with two other young writers at the Warsaw statue of Copernicus (claimed by the Nazis as of German descent) in the name of the Polish Resistance. Wacek Bojarski was shot during this demonstration, Tadeusz Gajcy escaped, and Stroiński was arrested and only released after two months when his father intervened. He spent the following summer forging German documents for the Resistance, and died during the Warsaw Uprising on 16 August 1944 when the Germans blew up the house defended by the contingent he commanded. Gajcy was killed in the same engagement.

'Stroiński's prose poems deal obsessively with life under the occupation. He succeeds in capturing that eerie, bizarre and dream-like atmosphere, which perhaps only those who have experienced it can fully appreciate, by the use of startling ramified metaphors and a juxtaposition of stark realism with grim, grotesque expressionism. [...] this unorthodox, at times lyrical and almost humorous, portrayal of wartime madness is more moving and terrifying than grandiose verbal gestures importuning sympathy and pity.' (Adam Czerniawski)

A Refusal to Mourn the Death, by Fire, of a Child in London

Never until the mankind making
Bird beast and flower
Fathering and all humbling darkness
Tells with silence the last light breaking
And the still hour
Is come of the sea tumbling in harness

And I must enter again the round
Zion of the water bead
And the synagogue of the ear of corn
Shall I let pray the shadow of a sound
Or sow my salt seed
In the least valley of sackcloth to mourn

The majesty and burning of the child's death.
I shall not murder
The mankind of her going with a grave truth
Nor blaspheme down the stations of the breath
With any further
Elegy of innocence and youth.

Deep with the first dead lies London's daughter,
Robed in the long friends,
The grains beyond age, the dark veins of her mother,
Secret by the unmourning water
Of the riding Thames.
After the first death, there is no other.

[*c.* Autumn 1944; *published* 1946]

DYLAN THOMAS

Dylan Thomas (1914-53) was one of the major poets of the mid-20th century, known especially for his radio verse play *Under Milk Wood*. Avoiding conscription during the war because of a lung condition, he moved to London as the Blitz was tailing off in May 1941, living there until 1944 when the threat of German V-bombs prompted the Thomases' return to their native Wales.

Forced March

A fool he is who, collapsed,   rises and walks again,
Ankles and knees moving   alone, like wandering pain,
Yet he, as if wings uplifted him,   sets out on his way,
And in vain the ditch calls him   back, who dare not stay.
And if asked why not, he might answer   – without leaving his path –
That his wife was awaiting him,   and a saner, more beautiful death.
Poor fool! He's out of his mind: now, for a long time,
Only scorched winds have whirled   over the houses at home,
The wall has been laid low,   the plum tree is broken there,
The night of our native hearth   flutters, thick with fear.
Oh if only I could believe   that everything of worth
Were not just in my heart –   that I still had a home on earth;
If only I had! As before,   jam made fresh from the plum
Would cool on the old verandah,   in peace the bee would hum,
And an end-of-summer stillness   would bask in the drowsy garden,
Naked among the leaves   would sway the fruit trees' burden,
And there would be Fanni waiting,   blonde, by the russet hedgerow,
As the slow morning painted   slow shadow over shadow, –
Could it perhaps still be?   The moon tonight's so round!
Don't leave me friend, shout at me: I'll get up off the ground!

[15 September 1944]

MIKLÓS RADNÓTI
translated from the Hungarian by Clive Wilmer and George Gömöri
➤ 257

Postcards

I

From Bulgaria, wild and swollen, the noise of cannon rolls:
It booms against the ridge, then hesitates, and falls.
Men, animals, carts, thoughts pile up as they fly;
The road rears back and whinnies, maned is the racing sky.
But you in this shifting chaos are what in me is constant:

263

In my soul's depth forever, you shine – you are as silent
And motionless as an angel who marvels at destruction,
Or a beetle burrowing in a hollow tree's corruption.

[In the mountains, 30 August 1944]

II

No more than six or seven miles away
Haystacks and houses flare;
There, on the meadow's verges, peasants crouch,
Pipe-smoking, dumb with fear.
Here still, where the tiny shepherdess steps in,
Ripples on the lake spread;
A flock of ruffled sheep bend over it.
And drink the clouds they tread.

[Cservenka, 6 October 1944]

III

Blood-red, the spittle drools from the oxen's mouths,
The men stooping to urinate pass blood,
The squad stands bunched in groups whose reek disgusts.
And loathsome death blows overhead in gusts.

[Mohács, 24 October 1944]

IV

I fell beside him. His body, which was taut
As a cord is when it snaps, spun as I fell.
Shot in the neck. 'This is how you will end,'
I whispered to myself. 'Keep lying still.
Now, patience is flowering into death.'
'*Der springt noch auf*,' said someone over me.
Blood on my ears was drying, caked with earth.

[Szentkirályszabadja, 31 October 1944]

MIKLÓS RADNÓTI
translated from the Hungarian by Clive Wilmer and George Gömöri
➤ 257

Rhine Jump, 1944

They dropped us on the guns, left us in a flaring
lurch of slipstream kicking like sprayed flies –
till canopies shook sudden heads, inhaled, held a breath –
alive again we slanted down,
too many, into their doomed sights.

On scrambled moment it was red, green,
dragging to the door of the Douglas then
falling through a monstrous aviary roof
on Guy Fawkes Night (only this was day)
into shrill scarifying glory...

then Germany, the Fatherland, a zooming field –
banged down on it, stood up among the chaos, with
fingers flopped like rubber gloves trying
to slap one's box, slough the afterbirth of chute,
make somehow that snatch of wood.

There were chutes already in those trees, caught:
battalion boys who'd dropped too late or drifted...
harness-ravelled, cocooned there –
like silkworms, moveless, wet...
so easy, against all that white.

But not so many resistive earthworms –
the early birds had seen to that.
Soon, it was rendezvous: a stodgy farm.
The war was folding: fight-thin.
Prisoners happened; columned, toneless.

Next day it was hearing tales again,
having a kip in a pigsty, scouting the dropping-zone
to get silk (knickers for sweethearts, wives);
maybe a green envelope, speculation
about leave, Japan.

Oh and a gun-pit by the way, an 88:
bodiless, nothing special –

only the pro's interest in other's kit:
grey slacks for the use of, old, ersatz;
with a brown inside stripe: non–ersatz.

GEOFFREY HOLLOWAY

Geoffrey Holloway (1918-97) was an English poet who became a mental health worker after the war. A pacifist by nature and by conviction, he joined the Royal Army Medical Corps in 1939, serving in a field ambulance, a general hospital and in 225 Para Field Ambulance. He parachuted into France on D-day and later took part in the Rhine landings.

from **The Runner**

8

October, and the sky was turning gray.
The battle line had settled. Every night
The bombers flew, going to Germany
At a great height. And back the other way
The V-1's came. The soldiers in their holes
Heard them droning and saw the rhythmic flames
Carrying woe to Antwerp and to England.

They dozed or watched. Then it began to rain,
And always rained. It seemed they were never dry.
Winter was in the air. Paths turned to mud.
By day and night the shells came shrieking in;
They got so they could tell a dying fall
And pay the rest no mind. They lived with mud.
They cooked and ate their rations in the can,
And tried to dry their socks between two rains.
Cold and sullen, under a raincoat roof,
They shivered in their holes.

                              One moonlit night
Dodd was returning on his way alone.
There was a wind; the haunted shadows stirred,
And rainpools glimmered in the moonlit fields.

There was a field the runner loathed to cross.
A place of horrors. Here, on the first day,
There'd been fierce charges, combats at close range,
And the dead were mixed as they had fallen.
Here crouched the German soldier with his *schmeisser*
Close to the parachutist in his rage –
Putrid things, never to be forgotten.
The field was swelling, shining with an aura
Of pale corruption.

　　　　　　　To avoid it, Dodd
Went by another path he did not know,
Leading, it seemed, back to the company.
But in a while a fearful premonition
Stopped him. In a shadow, cold with dread,
He stood listening. The branches stirred,
And all at once there was a clash of arms,
The sounds of footsteps. Stealthily he turned
To slip away.

　　　　'Wer geht da?'

　　　　　　　He ran.
He plunged into the darkness, blind with panic.
A storm of shots erupted at his back.
Brambles tore at his legs. He climbed a bank,
Clawing, and stumbled down the other side.
Then, as he ran, he shouted out the password.
'Ohio!' like a dog drenched with hot water.
His rifle fell. He left it where it was.
'Ohio!' He collided with a branch
And staggered. At his back the storm increased.
Red tracers streaked the air. Across a ditch
He leaped. And ran across the road beyond.
A hole was in his way; he cleared it with
A stride, and the dark figure starting up
Out of the hole. He kept on running, shouting
'Ohio!' A shape standing in the path
Snatched at him; he swerved out of its grasp.
There was a maze of holes. He stumbled, reeled,
And fell. His helmet flew off with a clang.

Feet were approaching. He lay still as death.
'It's Dodd,' said a voice.

                              At last, he looked up
Into the faces of the third platoon.
Fisher. Others. They looked down in wonder.

LOUIS SIMPSON

Louis Simpson (1923-2012) was a Jamaica-born American poet. He served in
the Second World War with the 101st Airborne Division on active duty in
France, Holland, Belgium and Germany. As a ground soldier in the Battle of
the Bulge in 1944, he had to take messages across the battlefield as a runner,
an experience he draws on 'The Runner', a long poem in 12 parts, written in
the third person with a soldier called Dodd as its protagonist. The writing of
the poem in Rome, as late as 1957, was part of an attempt to come to terms
with his war experiences. He described it as 'fiction; the episodes and characters
are imaginary. But the fiction is based on the following history...' The other
characters in the poem may be conflations of fellow soldiers, but Dodd quite
clearly *is* Simpson. What happens to Dodd in the poem happened to Simpson.

➤ 248

November

It was three weeks since I had walked the street.
Even now it was just for a single day
I crept from the dusky piebald library.
The sky was black, a thoroughly black November.
People in town were occupied in looting,
Policemen, soldiers, Arrow Cross militia,
Both Germans and Hungarians. In handcarts
In large laden trucks, in wheelbarrows,
They dragged their booty off into the Vár[1]
And other places. Now and then explosions
And heavy guns boomed out their *mene-tekels*[2]
To shattered townsfolk who were used to it
And continued to swarm across the makeshift
Wooden bridge with idiotic indifference.
It was the first time I saw Margaret Bridge,
The pointlessly imploring messenger

Of Pest's destruction, knee-bent in the river.
Just for a day I left my hiding place,
Wanting a glimpse, if no more, of Hold utca,[3]
Of Szabadság tér,[4] cafés, Chain Bridge. But
There was no time for even that. I saw
My mother. She could barely keep in step
With others driven along. Then suddenly
A ten-year-old boy leapt clear of the queue,
Looking to run: a young lout with a rifle
Took aim at him and fired, and he collapsed.
His mother ran to him but she was merely
Wounded. A woman on the pavement said
To her son, 'Look there! See, they're driving out
The Jews!' The child just stared. There were few
Swabians among the guards. Most had local accents
from Vas county, the lowlands or from Nógrád
cheerfully goading their captives, moving quickly.
By the time I caught a ferry over to Buda
They were all there, each with a small bundle.
I saw my mother too in the pouring rain,
Dressed in black, her tiny body labouring
Towards Ujlak out of breath, in the foul dark.
That night the company – perhaps as consolation –
Was busily discussing who should hang.
I'd sooner have imagined mama lying
Dead in the mud, a merciful bullet in her.
Maybe the woman I'd met in the afternoon
Would soon be saying to her son, 'See there?
They're driving out the fascists!' I also thought
I might survive ten or twenty more years,
And how being condemned to be Hungarian
Was a life sentence. After midnight the rain
Came down so heavily we could hear it inside,
And I knew that the same rain was beating hard
On my mother in the open factory-brickyard.
But we had fire. Busily drinking and eating.
Meat and red wine. Marika did my weeping.

ISTVÁN VAS
translated from the Hungarian by George Szirtes

1. Vár: the Castle District. 2. *mene-tekels:* biblical words of warning from the writing on the wall. 3. Hold utca: street in Budapest. 4. Szabadság tér: *lit.* Liberty Square the largest square in Budapest.

István Vas (1910-91) was a Hungarian poet, prose writer and translator of English poetry (Shakespeare, Donne, T.S. Eliot). During the war he went into hiding to escape deportation to a concentration camp: this poem describes events in Budapest in November 1944. He worked for a publishing house from 1946.

Johannes Bobrowski (1917-65) was a German lyric poet, narrative writer and essayist. Born in Tilsit, East Prussia, the son of a railway official, he was the great-great nephew of Joseph Conrad. Conscripted into the German Army in 1939, he was a lance corporal throughout the war in Poland, France and the Soviet Union. He began to write poetry on the Eastern Front in 1941, and was a prisoner of war, forced to work in a coal mine in Russia, from 1945 until 1949, when he returned to Germany. He lived in East Berlin and worked as a reader for publishing houses until his death in 1965 from a perforated appendix.

Report

Bajla Gelblung,
escaped in Warsaw
from a transport from the Ghetto,
the girl took to the woods,
armed, was picked up
as partisan
in Brest-Litovsk,
wore a military coat (Polish),
was interrogated by German
officers, there is
a photo, the officers are young
chaps faultlessly uniformed,
with faultless faces,
their bearing
is unexceptionable.

JOHANNES BOBROWSKI
translated from the German by Ruth and Matthew Mead

They Took Away the Gypsies

They took away the Gypsies, took them all,
to dig enormous ditches.
The ditch grows deep, deeper and wider
till they stand in muddy water.

Poor lads – they're just the same as us.
The gendarmes harry, goad and beat them,
squeeze them in an iron grip.
Stragglers feel their rifle butts.

What's it for, this ditch they're digging,
this ditch so dark and fathomless?
They've no idea – how could they know?
The gendarmes won't be telling them!

If only they knew why they were digging
a ditch so vast – for them and others.
It gapes for them and for their fellows,
even for children and their mothers.

The evening of the day that follows
the blue sky wears a hem of red,
brightest red, the blood of Gypsies,
who've paid the price with their clean hearts.

Never forget that day, my brothers,
Gypsy friends, remember always
that darkest day of grief,
the darkest dawn of endless mourning.

JÓZSEF CHOLI DARÓCZI
translated from the Hungarian by Jamie McKendrick & Mari Gömöri

József Choli Daróczi (*b.* 1939) has lived in Budapest since 1956. A poet who writes in both Hungarian and Lovari, a Romani dialect, he has also worked on academic research into the life of the Roma in Hungary, edited a Gypsy-Hungarian dictionary, and translated the New Testament into Lovari.

Robbery, Naked

You won't be needing these, he said,
and flung my mother's photograph
among his booty, and my shirt.
I still retained heaped on my blanket
the things I had to bring: a mess-tin,
my boots and socks, warm underclothes,
a bar of shaving-soap – and I had
that irremovable mark on my finger
in the place of my looted wedding ring.

Letter from Nusi

And now at last we are quite certain
we shall be taken shortly – but where?
Kolozsvár? Várad? Újfalu?
And then the wagons? Where from there?
But you don't need to fret about us,
outside, the bags are all prepared,
the basket of food, a pot of honey,
a pair of backpacks, the bedding linen –
the cart is waiting by the portal
for grandma's ride (poor gran's old feet!)
and mum has sent a card to dad.
No time left. Still, what really matters,
the place is tidied up for winter.
Sanyikám, darling, I take my leave.
And tell our father he's in my heart.
Whatever our lot, we shall be safe –
God shall provide.

[Derecske, 6 June 1944]

272

Statistics

No cry of anguish, no manner of wailing
is more heartrending than the sheer numbers:
147 trains
for the transportation in 51 days
of 434,000
provincial Jews by 200 SS troops
aided by 5,000 Hungarian
gendarmes and hundreds of volunteers –
they were detained at first in the ghettoes,
they were then taken into the brick-works
already stripped of their family savings,
then caged in cattle-trucks, 80 in each, and
conveyed without water and food to Mengele
from the first day of the occupation –
processed by people obeying orders
who never outdid the German commands
but willingly obliged the commanders –

Nearly half a million provincial Jews:
Nearly 10% of them stayed alive.

Jason

She carefully unlaced her grandmother's boots,
then kicked off her own. Before the pair: the river.
Behind them: Jason, the neighbours' son from the square
lit by the frozen snow – and his machinegun.
Jason, discharging his first-ever magazine.
Jason, standing stunned as the tumbling bodies
are whisked away and gone with the turbulent current.
…Had he done that? Was there so little to life?

Gustav!

Feinstein, a Jew from Memel,
recognised his neighbour
in the execution squad.
And he cried out to him:
Gustav! aim
straight between the eyes!

Tally

Counting heads at the gate,
the Düsseldorf guard kept tally.
Beneath a detailed statement
about the deportation,
1,007 lives
are described on the sheet
by groups of vertical lines
crossed out.

Towards the Dniester

As the marchers dragged themselves forward,
the bare-footed peasants by the road
picked out the choicest boots and trousers
and, at their bidding, the guards
shot down the occasional well-clad prisoner
in exchange for a handful of notes.
The death-march stumbled on towards Orhei.
The peasants collected their wares.

ANDRÁS MEZEI
translated from the Hungarian by Thomas Ország-Land

Between 18 March 1944 and 4 April 1945, half a million Hungarian Jews, Roma, homosexuals and political dissidents were transported to extermination camps, mostly in Poland and Austria. Tens of thousands were enslaved in labour camps. Nearly three-quarters of Hungary's Jewish population perished. The Jewish-Hungarian poet **András Mezei** (1930-2008) survived the Holocaust as well as the three-month siege of Budapest. His life was inevitably shaped by these events. Throughout his long writing career, he returned repeatedly to the terrible experiences of his childhood, assembling a poetic collage of eye-witness accounts. In 2010, Thomas Orzág-Land, himself a Holocaust survivor, published *Christmas in Auschwitz*, his translation of Mezei's most important poems about the Hungarian Holocaust.

Ravens

They untangle, lug, stack and kindle the dead.
Chosen on the platform for brawn, broken in
Hell for leather, men clubbed and goaded
As still among the bodies they recognise kin.
Shirkers are shot. Others harden to endure
As stokers of hell, well-fed privileged caste
High on their pickings. A three-month tour
Of duty before they in their turn are gassed.
Sonderkommando, Levi's 'crematorium ravens'
Fallen beyond his compassion's greyest zone;
Soiled by fellow blood, vultures and cravens,
Cain sucking his marrow from Abel's bone.
Pity these ravens for what driven ravens do;
Bitter complicity that Jew should oven Jew.

MICHEAL O'SIADHAIL

Micheal O'Siadhail (*b.* 1947) is a prolific Irish poet whose books include *The Gossamer Wall: Poems in witness to the Holocaust* (2002). The fruit of many years of immersion in the testimonies of survivors, this episodic book-length sequence tells the stories of victims and perpetrators from many parts of Europe involved in different phases and aspects of the Holocaust.

If I only knew

If I only knew
On what your last look rested.
Was it a stone that had drunk
So many last looks that they fell
Blindly upon its blindness?

Or was it earth,
Enough to fill a shoe,
And black already
With so much parting
And with so much killing?

Or was it your last road
That brought you a farewell from all the roads
You had walked?

A puddle, a bit of shining metal,
Perhaps the buckle of your enemy's belt,
Or some other small augury
Of heaven?

Or did this earth,
Which lets no one depart unloved,
Send you a bird-sign through the air,
Reminding your soul that it quivered
In the torment of its burnt body?

NELLY SACHS
translated from the German by Ruth & Matthew Mead

Nelly Sachs (1891-1970) was a Jewish German poet and dramatist. In May 1940, she fled from Germany to Sweden where she started a new life as translator and author. In her first book of poems, *In the Habitations of Death*, published in her mid-50s in 1967, and in later volumes, she gave voice to the Jewish victims of the Holocaust. She was joint winner of the Nobel Prize in Literature in 1966.

Shemà

You who live secure
In your warm houses,
Who return at evening to find
Hot food and friendly faces:

> Consider whether this is a man.
> Who labours in the mud
> Who knows no peace
> Who fights for a crust of bread
> Who dies at a yes or a no.
> Consider whether this is a woman,
> Without hair or name
> With no more strength to remember
> Eyes empty and womb cold
> As a frog in winter.

Consider that this has been:
I commend these words to you.
Engrave them on your hearts
When you are in your house, when you walk on your way,
When you go to bed, when you rise.
Repeat them to your children.
Or may your house crumble,
Disease render you powerless,
Your offspring avert their faces from you.

[written 10 January 1946]

PRIMO LEVI
translated from the Italian by Ruth Feldman & Brian Swann

Primo Levi (1919-67) was an Italian Jewish chemist and writer who survived a year's imprisonment in Auschwitz, from February 1944 until the camp was liberated on 27 January 1945, but did not reach home in Turin until October, after spending months in a Soviet transit camp and then travelling through war-wrecked Europe. His works include *If This Is a Man* (1947) and *The Truce* (1963), his memoirs of Auschwitz and his return; *The Periodic Table* (1975), stories from from his life and from science; and *Collected Poems* (1984).

Deathfugue

Black milk of daybreak we drink it at evening
we drink it at midday and morning we drink it at night
we drink and we drink
we shovel a grave in the air where you won't lie too cramped
A man lives in the house he plays with his vipers he writes
he writes when it grows dark to Deutschland your golden hair Margareta[1]
he writes it and steps out of doors and the stars are all sparkling he whistles
        his hounds to stay close
he whistles his Jews into rows has them shovel a grave in the ground
he commands us play up for the dance

Black milk of daybreak we drink you at night
we drink you at morning and midday we drink you at evening
we drink and we drink
A man lives in the house he plays with his vipers he writes
he writes when it grows dark to Deutschland your golden hair Margareta
Your ashen hair Shulamith[2] we shovel a grave in the air where you won't lie
        too cramped

He shouts dig this earth deeper you lot there you others sing up and play
he grabs for the rod in his belt he swings it his eyes are so blue
stick your spades deeper you lot there you others play on for the dancing

Black milk of daybreak we drink you at night
we drink you at midday and morning we drink you at evening
we drink and we drink
a man lives in the house your goldenes Haar Margareta
your aschenes Haar Shulamith he plays with his vipers
He shouts play death more sweetly this Death is a master from Deutschland
he shouts scrape your strings darker you'll rise up as smoke to the sky
you'll then have a grave in the clouds where you won't lie too cramped

Black milk of daybreak we drink you at night
we drink you at midday Death is a master aus Deutschland
we drink you at evening and morning we drink and we drink
this Death is ein Meister aus Deutschland his eye it is blue
he shoots you with shot made of lead shoots you level and true
a man lives in the house your goldenes Haar Margarete

he looses his hounds on us grants us a grave in the air
he plays with his vipers and daydreams der Tod ist ein Meister
　　　　aus Deutschland

dein goldenes Haar Margarete
dein aschenes Haar Sulamith

[*c.* 1944; *published* 1947]

PAUL CELAN
translated from the German by John Felstiner

1. *Margareta:* Faust's beloved in Goethe's drama. 2. *Shulamith:* Hebrew maiden in Song of Songs (the German is *Sulamith*).

Aspen Tree

Aspen tree, your leaves glance white into the dark.
My mother's hair never turned white.

Dandelion, so green is the Ukraine.
My fair-haired mother did not come home.

Rain cloud, do you linger at the well?
My soft-voiced mother weeps for all.

Rounded star, you coil the golden loop.
My mother's heart was hurt by lead.

Oaken door, who hove you off your hinge?
My gentle mother cannot return.

[1945]

PAUL CELAN
translated from the German by John Felstiner

Paul Celan was born Paul Antschel in 1920 in a part of Romania now in Ukraine to German-speaking Jewish parents who later perished in Nazi death camps. Surviving a forced labour camp, he eventually settled in Paris. He wrote his poetry in German, and became one of the major writers of the Holocaust, committing suicide in 1970 by jumping from a bridge into the Seine. His work is characterised by a sense of horror, a belief that poetry must be open to the unexpected and unpredictable, and by his search for a redefinition of reality.

from Prussian Nights

– Burn the houses down, my brothers!
Ah, look how it's taking hold!
The walls won't catch? – Well, start the rafters!
Fire the rafters first, you dolt!
No point in driving on – eh, fellows? –
Unless we leave them some mementoes?
Without orders, as it takes us,
Here, there, everywhere, look – scores
Of smoky-red, dark-gleaming fires!
Well, now we're getting our revenge, lads,
We've hit him good and hard, the foe!
Everything's aflame. – Night-quarters?
We'll have to spend it in the snow.
Oh, well, that's bad! But all the same,
We've given *them* a tougher time
The whole district sees a dawn
The like of which it's never known!
Our columns pour ahead like lava
With wild cries, whistling, headlamps' glare
– Klein Koslau, Gross Koslau –
Every village – is now a fire!
Everything flames. Locked in their burning
Cowsheds, how the cows are bellowing –
            – Ah, poor creatures
            But you're not ours!
What's more, we have ourselves to save...
For right and left, on either side
What serpents rush and dance and glide!
On either side what columns rise,
On either side roofs meet the skies

– Made of fiery dust, of stars,
Of embers, glimmerings and sparks
Which shower down on our bended necks.
In the school the fiery wind
Hunts hungrily among the books.
And there's only rough tarpaulin
We made ourselves, on my six trucks.
Better watch *we* don't catch fire!
On the running board. It's funny and grim.

[…]

Zweiundzwanzig, Höringstrasse.
It's not been burned, just looted, rifled.
A moaning by the walls, half-muffled:
The little daughter's on the mattress,
Dead. How many have been on it?
A platoon, a company, perhaps?
A girl's been turned into a woman,
A woman turned into a corpse.
It's all come down to simple phrases:
Do not forget! Do not forgive!
Blood for blood! A tooth for a tooth!

[…]

Some soldiers have gathered round
A pram that's been abandoned,
                              Blue,
        Lace trimmings, too:
        'Look, a little 'un.
        Still, he's a German!
He'll grow and put a helmet on.
Deal with him now, d'you think?
The order from Supreme Command
Is *Blood for Blood!* Give no quarter!'
'To talk like that! What, are you drunk?
Are you Herod? Is your priest
Some abominable beast?'
'It's not me, grandpa! – Moscow's order!'

'Board!' Forward the column goes
Once more. No time to rest or doze.
We roll on and on over Europe
As in a strange kaleidoscope.
From lack of sleep and drunkenness
We've turned daring, we've grown wings.
Everything's mixed up, everything's
Double – crossroads, signposts, faces,
Explosions, meetings, wounds and mines,
Evil and good, fears and delights,
The silver of the Prussian noons,
The crimson of the Prussian nights.
Two logs stand crossed upon the road
To signal detour. Iron fate's
Changed its route. Dreamlike there floats
Before us, somewhere to the side,
Silent, trackless, deep in snows,
Someone's solitary house
With the virgin woods behind.
Someone's noisy column turned
Towards smoke rising from the hearth.
They've hardly cut the engines' noise
When they're out to find some warmth.
Slapping their shoulders, they reach the house.
Now they're in. She stands there, numb.
They laugh. 'Get us some eggs then, Mum!'
And the housewife does her best,
Brings them apples, ripe and brittle,
They grabbed them, walked around a little,
A crunch between their teeth like frost.
And then they shot the housewife first,
Spattering with blood the carpet's pile.
The husband was bedridden, ill:
They cured him with a carbine burst.
Only the grandson, a young boy,
In a flash managed to escape
– Out of the window and away
Over the fence with a leap! With a leap!
          Like a wild creature,
          Like a little hare,
Across the field towards the wood

Running, ducking, dodging aside.
The whole troop, nearly, rushed from the road,
Firing anyhow, in pursuit:
      'I'll get him!' 'Winged him!' 'He's down!'
      'He's away!' '– Shoot! Shoot!'
      'Ah, the brute,
He's got away. Well, when he's grown...'

ALEKSANDR SOLZHENITSYN
translated from the Russian by Robert Conquest

Prussian Nights was written, or rather composed in Solzhenitsyn's head, while he was serving his sentence of forced labour. A poem, a verse narrative, it is not autobiography in any strict sense. But it is based on his own war experience.

Solzhenitsyn's battery formed part of the Second Byelorussian Front, which invaded East Prussia from the south in January 1945. The attack reached Neidenburg (now Nidzica) on January 20; Allenstein (now Olsztyn) on January 22; and the Baltic – cutting off the German armies in East Prussia – on January 26. Solzhenitsyn was arrested in this area in early February, three weeks after the beginning of the offensive. [...]

The Second World War is the one major experience of Solzhenitsyn's life of which he has written little, although elsewhere in his work he has made passing comments which gloss or clarify certain points in the text of *Prussian Nights* – on his affection for the soldiers under his command, 'people of a kind I had become attached to during the war years because I myself was more complex and worse'; on rape and shooting in East Prussia; on the justified gloom of the newly released Russian prisoners of war marching home in formation; on his loot of a hundred Faber pencils... [Tr.]

Aleksandr Solzhenitsyn (1918-2008) was one of the foremost Russian writers of the 20th century, awarded the Nobel Prize in Literature in 1970. He grew up during the Russian civil war, and during the Second World War he was an artillery officer in the Red Army. While serving in East Prussia – following the events described in *Prussian Nights* – he was arrested for complaining about the treatment of civilians and for making derogatory comments about Stalin in letters to a friend and sentenced to eight years in a labour camp. These experiences formed the basis for his novella *One Day in the Life of Ivan Denisovich* (1962), his only major work published in the Soviet Union until 1990. His later books include his historical study, *The Gulag Archipelago* (*ca.* 1958-68), and the novels *Cancer Ward* (1968) and *August 1914* (1971), the latter an historical novel about Imperial Russia's defeat at the Battle of Tannenberg in East Prussia during the First World War. *Prussian Nights* was not published in Russian until 1974 – in Paris – and first published in German in 1976 and in English in 1977.

Ordeal by Fire

Führer's order: the German woman does
Not smoke. (DANZIG MENACED BY RUSSIANS.)
Females born '25, the paper says,
Must honour their obligations.

The Propaganda Minister spat
Sixteen lines in praise of The Girls.
In the smoke and flak of Berlin's ack-ack,
In the ordeal by fire, who falls?...

Hanna Preuss, 20, soldier's wife.
Four weeks she'd been with her soldier.
She'd sworn to be true to the colours for life,
Wearing field-grey, at the altar.

Elvira, a warden, her surname was Klaus,
Sole child of a coal stockholder.
Seventeen, says the gravestone near their house:
She'd gone and enlisted as older.

Anna Simon, who cried, before she died,
'Who's stitched us up, betrayed us?
I never was one for an ack-ack gun,
Never wanted to join the soldiers.'

Four dead girls, one hadn't a face,
Laid out by the gunnery crew.
One soldier took for a souvenir
A bloodsoaked feminine shoe.

INGE MÜLLER
translated from the German by Timothy Adès

Inge Müller (1925-66) was an East German author. She served in the Reichs-arbeitsdienst (Reich Labour Service) during the war, and was deeply affected by the deaths of her parents in an air strike, buried under rubble for three days with their dog. After the war she collaborated with her husband, play-wright Heiner Müller, on radio drama and theatre pieces, but her own work was only fully published in 1976, twenty years after her death by suicide at 41.

Five minutes after the air raid

In Pilsen,
twenty-six Station Road,
she climbed to the third floor
up stairs which were all that was left
of the whole house,
she opened her door
full on to the sky,
stood gaping over the edge.

For this was the place
the world ended.

Then
she locked up carefully
lest someone steal
Sirius
or Aldebaran
from her kitchen,
went back downstairs
and settled herself
to wait
for the house to rise again
and for her husband to rise from the ashes
and for her children's hands and feet to be stuck back in place.

In the morning they found her
still as stone,
sparrows pecking her hands.

MIROSLAV HOLUB
translated from the Czech by George Theiner

Miroslav Holub (1923-98) was the Czech Republic's most important postwar poet, and also one of her leading immunologists. His fantastical and witty poems give a scientist's bemused view of human folly and other life on the planet. Mixing myth, history and folktale with science and philosophy, his plainly written, sceptical poems are surreal mini-dramas often pivoting on paradoxes. During the war he was conscripted to work on the railways. His poetry was banned for many years after the Soviet invasion of Czechoslovakia in 1968 when he was deemed to be a 'non-person'. ➤ 338, 345, 350

Never Again

A hundred houses were in ruins,
nearly a thousand had been damaged
by aerial bombs,
No, I didn't count them myself.
I worked my way through the rubble
and circumnavigated the craters.
They were frightening
like gaping gates to fiery hell.

Speedily they cleared away the debris
but it was three days before
they broke into the little house
in Šverma Street,
the house of Mr Hrnčíř.
The whole family was dead.

Only the rooster, that fighting cock
whom the Apostle Peter did not
greatly love,
alone had saved himself.
Over the bodies of the dead he'd climbed
onto a pile of rubble.

He looked about the scene of the disaster
and spread his wings
to shake the heavy dust
from his golden feathers.

And I repeated softly to myself
what I had found written
in letters of grief and in letters of pain
upon the faces of the Kralupy people.

And into that silence of death
I screamed in a loud voice,
so loud the war should hear it:
Never again, war!

The rooster looked at me
with its black beady eye
and burst into horrible laughter.
He laughed at me
and at my pointless screaming.
Besides, he was a bird
and sided with the planes.
The bastard!

JAROSLAV SEIFERT
translated from the Czech by Ewald Osers

Jaroslav Seifert (1901-86) was a leading Czech avant-garde poet awarded the
Nobel Prize in Literature in 1984. He worked as a journalist and editor before
the war. During the German occupation, he was editor of the daily *Národní
práce* and after 1945, of the trade-union daily *Práce*. Expelled from the Com-
munist Party in 1929 for signing a manifesto against Bolshevik tendencies, he
was one of the signatories of Charter 77 in 1977, the petition challenging human
rights abuses by Czechoslovakia's post-1968 Communist government.

Roads

Choked sunset glow
Of crashing time.
Roads. Roads.
Intersections of flight.
Cart tracks across the ploughed field
That with the eyes
Of killed horses
Saw the sky in flames.

Nights with lungs full of smoke,
With the hard breath of the fleeing
When shots
Struck the dusk.
Out of a broken gate
Ash and wind came without a sound,

A fire
That sullenly chewed the darkness.

Corpses,
Flung over the rail tracks,
Their stifled cry
Like a stone on the palate.
A black
Humming cloth of flies
Closed their wounds.

PETER HUCHEL
translated from the German by Michael Hamburger

Peter Huchel (1903-81) was an East German poet who edited the influential poetry magazine *Sind und Form* from 1949 until forced to resign in 1962 after the building of the Berlin Wall. He spent the next ten years in isolation under Stasi surveillance until 1971, when he was allowed to leave the country and move, first to Rome, then to West Germany. During the war he was conscripted into the Heer (German army) and taken prisoner by the Russians in 1945. This poem probably relates to his journey through the war-torn landscapes of Eastern Europe, either on his way to the prison camp or returning home at the end of the war.

War Dead

With grey arm twisted over a green face
The dust of passing trucks swirls over him,
Lying by the roadside in his proper place,
For he has crossed the ultimate far rim
That hides us from the valley of the dead.
He lies like used equipment thrown aside,
Of which our swift advance can take no heed,
Roses, triumphal cars – but this one died.

Once war memorials, pitiful attempt
In some vague way regretfully to atone
For those lost futures that the dead had dreamt,

Covered the land with their lamenting stone –
But in our hearts we bear a heavier load:
The bodies of the dead beside the road.

[Near La Spezia, Italy, April 1945]

GAVIN EWART

On the Willow Boughs

And we, how could we sing
with a foreign foot on our heart,
among dead abandoned in the squares
on the grass hard with ice,
to the lamb bleat of children,
the black howl of the mother
going towards her son
crucified on a pole?
On the willow boughs as an offering
even our lyres were hung
and lightly swayed in the sad wind.

SALVATORE QUASIMODO
translated from the Italian by Jack Bevan

Salvatore Quasimodo (1901-68) was one of Italy's great Modernist poets, and a leading figure, with Giuseppe Ungaretti and Eugenio Montale, in the Ermetismo (Hermeticism) grouping during the 1930s. His experiences of living through the war under Fascist rule and German occupation led to his poetry becoming more social or public in its address. He was awarded the Nobel Prize in Literature in 1959 'for his lyrical poetry, which with classical fire expresses the tragic experience of life in our own times'. ➤ 293

Gavin Ewart (1916-95) was an English poet of Scottish descent known for his formally brilliant comic verse relating to English society, sexual foibles and human behaviour – irreverent, highly entertaining, and often quite shocking at the time of publication. His first book was published just before his 23rd birthday in February 1939. He served as a captain in the Royal Artillery from 1940 to 1946, fighting in North Africa and in Italy. ➤ 569

Pilot Station, Harwich

Landmarks of sorts there always were,
Flamborough Head, Immingham, Southwold –
Sea-marks as well, the buoys
Marking the channel where E-boats,
Engines idling, waited for us, all contacts
Muffled. But they were mere signposts,
Not aspects of arrival –

No, the real landmark that made
The pulse quicken, coming up on deck
On a summer morning, was the black
And white pagoda of the Trinity House
Pilot Station, exotic to us as Konorak
Or Madurai. Anchoring there,
We could look down from above
At the launches swishing up the estuary
With signals and mail. Wrens at the helm
In bell-bottoms, their lovely hair flying.
It was the nearest we ever got to love.

ALAN ROSS
➤ 197

The Lines

After the centers' naked files, the basic line[1]
Standing outside a building in the cold
Of the late or early darkness, waiting
For meals or mail or salvage, or to wait
To form a line to form a line to form a line;
After the things have learned that they are things,
Used up as things are, pieces of the plain
Flat object-language of a child or states;
After the lines, through trucks, through transports, to the lines

290

Where the things die as though they were not things –
But lie as numbers in the crosses' lines;
After the files that ebb into the rows
Of the white beds of the quiet wards, the lines
Where some are salvaged for their state, but some
Remanded, useless, to the centers' files;
After the naked things, told they are men,
Have lined once more for papers, pensions – suddenly
The lines break up, for good; and for a breath,
The longest of their lives, the men are free.

RANDALL JARRELL
➤ 235

1. *basic line:* queue in basic training camp.

Mail Call

The letters always just evade the hand.
One skates like a stone into a beam, falls like a bird.
Surely the past from which the letters rise
Is waiting in the future, past the graves?
The soldiers are all haunted by their lives.

Their claims upon their kind are paid in paper
That establishes a presence, like a smell.
In letters and in dreams they see the world.
They are waiting: and the years contract
To an empty hand, to one unuttered sound –

The soldier simply wishes for his name.

RANDALL JARRELL

The Day the War Ended...

On the day the war ended
The sun laced the avenues with lime-tree scent
The silver birches danced on the sidewalk
And the girls came out like tulips in their colours:

Only the soldiers were caught, like sleepwalkers
Wakened unaware, naked there in the street.
Fatuous in flowers, their tanks, tamed elephants,
Wallowed among the crowds in the square.

There is a moment when contradictions cross,
A split of a moment when history twirls on one toe
Like a ballerina, and all men are really equal
And happiness could be impartial for once –

Only the soldier, snatched by the sudden stop
In his world's turning, whirled like a meteor
Through a phoenix night of stars, is falling, falling

And as his trajectory bows and earth begins
To pull again, his hollow ears are moaning
With a wild tone of sorrow and the loss, the loss...

[Gradisca, Yugoslav-Italian border, May 1945]

RANDALL SWINGLER
➤ 240

Midnight: May 7th, 1945

Thunder gathers all the sky,
Tomorrow night a war will end,
Men their natural deaths may die
And Cain shall be his brother's friend.

From the lethal clouds of lead
Thickening hatred shall descend
In fruitful rain upon the head:
Tomorrow night a war will end.

Thunder, mock not Abel's cry:
Let this symbolic storm expend
The sum of man's malignity!
– And Cain shall be his brother's friend.

There are no words to be said:
Let the future recommend
The living to the luckless dead.
Tomorrow night a war will end.

PATRIC DICKINSON

Patrick Dickinson (1914-94) was an English lyric poet, maverick classicist and influential broadcaster who was born in India. He served in the Artists' Rifles in the first year of the war and joined the BBC after being invalided out of the Army in 1940. His father, a regular officer in the Indian Army, was killed in 1915 ('not ever a blank in our lives, but a living absence').

Man of My Time

You are still the one with stone and sling,
man of my time. You were there in the cockpit,
with evil wings, the sundials of death,
– I have seen you – in the fire-chariot, at the gallows,
at the torture wheels. I have seen you: it was you
with your knowledge precisely extermination-guided,
loveless, Christless. You have killed again
as before, as your fathers killed, as the beasts
killed when first they saw you.
And this blood smells as it did on the day
when the brother said to the other brother:
Let us go into the fields. And that chill, clinging echo

has reached down even to you, within your day.
Forget, O sons, the blood clouds
risen from earth, forget the fathers:
their tombs sink down in the ashes,
the black birds, the wind, are covering their hearts.

SALVATORE QUASIMODO
translated from the Italian by Jack Bevan
➤ 289

June, July, and August, 1945

Do you remember? No! Let me help you:
they were months of scorching heat, ruins, and dust
moistened only in places where women watered flowers
at hastily built little memorials,
but children already played at being barricade fighters and generals in
        bunkers,
and shrilled like the recently silenced alarm sirens,
and yelled loudly that an air raid is reported,
while street loudspeakers called: 'Relatives of the missing
should visit the *Collecting Centre for Corpses* in such-and-such district,
or else the dead will be buried in a common grave!' –
It was freedom, yes, it was freedom,
but with all its still murky massive features,
there was some wind here and there, and it blew loathingly,
as if it had found a German hair between two pages of a brand-new book,
every large square was sick at heart,
scabby buses from concentration camps arrived there:
'Kadel, my love!... Annie!... All right, Mary,
stop crying! You're back home, you know?... One more, one more
        kiss, Jenda!'
I'm telling you, they were months of scorching heat, ruins and dust
moistened only by the tears of the returned ones, the welcoming ones,
they all stood there, absolutely free, like at a time
when we don't want anything else,
after a brief sorrowful moment
the memory of the dead began searching in pockets
for tangible keepsakes: a woman's lock of hair,

and a man's red censor's pencil of shame
deleting the carved wrinkles on the face of a tragedy
and transforming it into a smile of self-denial.
They were standing there, in a brotherhood so unanimous
you could hardly grasp that they could return to their sentimental
      homes,
return with the desire to catch up on all the missed Christmas Eves,
yes, and when a streetcar moved jerkily,
and some girls grabbed the handrails,
their sleeves pulled up and you could see, just above their wrists,
prisoners' tattooed numbers...
They hunted for wide bracelets to cover them,
but it isn't easy to find such a bracelet, my dear!
And even now, the gates in a Prague street are wide open, May-like,
with scribbled words: DO NOT ENTER! SHOOTING GOING ON!
Do you remember? No! I don't want to remember any more, either,
but I can still see the splendid Red Army girls,
who at the crossroads of our new destiny
started signalling with their flags
the safe life that's allowed to keep its spontaneity,
the spontaneity of a miracle and love...
And I can see a little boy and girl.
She said: 'Show me! You got blue teeth?'
But he didn't, he took out another paper bag
and they both dug into more blueberries...

VLADIMÍR HOLAN
translated from the Czech by C.G. Hanzlicek & Dana Hábová

Vladimír Holan (1905-80) was a Czech poet whose work was attacked for its 'decadent formalism' in 1948 and banned until 1963. He survived on a small pension during the war, and spent his last years living in reclusive poverty in a small flat on the island of Kampa on the Vitava river in central Prague.

The next six poems in this selection relate to the atomic bombing of the Japanese city of Hiroshima on 6 August 1945, followed by the destruction of Nagasaki three days later. The combined death toll from both attacks is thought to have been higher than 200,000.

Nobuyuki Saga (1902-97) was a Japanese poet and publisher. After the war, he was editor-in-chief of *Shigaku* (Poetry Studies), one of the most important post-war magazines in Japan because it published poets from across different factions and groups.

The Myth of Hiroshima

What are they looking for,
running to the summit of lost time?
Hundreds of people vaporised instantly
are walking in mid-air.

> 'We didn't die.'
> 'We skipped over death in a flash and became spirits.'
> 'Give us a real, human death.'

One man's shadow among hundreds is branded on stone steps.

> 'Why am I imprisoned in stone?'
> 'Where did my flesh go, separated from its shadow?'
> 'What must I wait for?'

The twentieth-century myth is stamped with fire.
Who will free this shadow from the stone?

NOBUYUKI SAGA
translated from the Japanese by Hajime Kajima

this is a Human Being

this is a human being
look what an A-bomb has done to it
the flesh swells so horribly
and both men and women are reduced to one form
'Help me!' says the faint cry
leaking from the swelled lips, the terribly
burned mess of a festered face
this, this is a human being
this is a man's face

TAMIKI HARA
translated from the Japanese by Geoffrey Bownas & Anthony Thwaite

Glittering Fragments

Glittering fragments
Ashen embers
Like a rippling panorama,
Burning red then dulled.
Strange rhythm of human corpses.
All existence, all that could exist
Laid bare in a flash. The rest of the world
The swelling of a horse's corpse
At the side of an upturned train,
The smell of smouldering electric wires.

TAMIKI HARA
translated from the Japanese by Geoffrey Bownas & Anthony Thwaite

Tamiki Hara (1905-51) was a Japanese author who survived the bombing of Hiroshima, one of the main themes of his postwar writing, notably *Summer Flowers*, written shortly after 6 August 1945. Despondent at the outbreak of the Korean War and the prospect of further nuclear warfare, he committed suicide in 1951.

At a First Aid Post

You
Who have no channels for tears when you weep
No lips through which words can issue when you howl
No skin for your fingers to grip with when you writhe in torment
You
Your squirming limbs all smeared with blood and slimy sweat and
       lymph
Between your closed lids the glaring eyeballs show only a thread
       of white
On your pale swollen bellies only the perished elastic that held up
       your drawers
You who now can no longer feel shame at exposing your sheltered
       sex

O who could believe that
Only minutes ago
You were all schoolgirls fresh and appealing

In scorched and raw Hiroshima
Out of dark shuddering flames
You no longer the human creatures you had been
Scrambled and crawled one after the other
Dragged yourselves along as far as this open ground
To bury in the dusts of agony
Your frizzled hair on skulls almost bare as heads of Buddhist saints

Why should you have to suffer like this
Why suffer like this
What is the reason
What reason
And you
Do not know
How you look nor
What your humanity has been turned into

You are remembering
Simply remembering
Those who until this morning were
Your fathers mothers brothers sisters
(Would any of them recognise you now if they met you)
Remembering your homes where you used to sleep wake eat
(In a single flash all the flowers on their hedges were blasted
And no one knows where their ashes lie)
Remembering remembering
Here with your fellow-creatures who one by one gradually moving
Remembering

Those days when
You were daughters
Daughters of humankind.

SANKICHI TOGE
translated from the Japanese by James Kirkup

To Miss...

You live on deep in the ditch of an alley in the slums
At the bomb-blasted site of the Transport Corps
The stony road haunted by a vision of horses
Kicking the air above their torn bellies.

Only a year ago, rainy days would allow you to go out
To the hospital, because you could hide then behind your umbrella.
But now that you never come out to expose to our view
The memory of that flash the shadow of the B29
That thundered down upon your face your eyes your nose

One arm ripped away by an avalanching house
the other remaining for you to make a living by...
What sad stitches you keep knitting day by day
When bitter blood stains your fingers
In this quiet corner of the town
Humming softly with windmills
The voices of children playing in vegetable plots.

Never have I dared to call on you.
But today I am coming to see you
Along this ruined path.

Welts like serpents
Your skin's sickly lustre baldly naked
Bring back to me my native feelings of compassion for you
As you sit there before me caked with oozing pus
In this hole of constant pain
The heart once of a tender girl now shrivelled to a stone
In the rosy light of the setting sun.

O let me tell you now my hear
Of this burning wish we have that wells up from our souls
Of this passion fierce enough to melt the coldest heart
Of the desperate battle in which thousands of your pictures
Shall overcome the powers of darkness in this world
(Under the droning shadows that even now
Keep looking over us again)

Of that hard-won moment when
Our indignation
And your curse
Shall open into radiance of loveliest flowers!

SANKICHI TOGE
translated from the Japanese by James Kirkup

The Shadow

Cheap movie theatres, saloons, fly-by-night markets,
burned, rebuilt, standing, crumbling, spreading like the itch –
the new Hiroshima,
head shiny with hair oil,
barefaced in its resurgence,
already visible all over the place,
in growing numbers, billboards in English;
one of these: 'Historic A-Bomb Site.'

Enclosed by a painted fence
on a corner of the bank steps,
stained onto the grain of the dark red stone:
a quiet pattern.

That morning
a flash tens of thousands of degrees hot
burned it all of a sudden onto the thick slab of granite:
someone's trunk.

Burned onto the step, cracked and watery red,
the mark of the blood that flowed as intestines melted to mush:
a shadow.

Ah! If you are from Hiroshima
and on that morning,
amid indescribable flash and heat and smoke,
were buffeted in the whirlpool of the glare of the flames, the shadow
        of the cloud,

crawled about dragging skin that was peeling off,
so transformed that even your wife and children
would not have known you,
this shadow
is etched in tragic memory
and will never fade.

Right beside the street where the people of the city come and go,
well-meaning but utterly indifferent,
assaulted by the sun, attacked by the rain, covered over by dust,
growing fainter year by year: this shadow.

The bank with the 'Historic Site' sign at the foot of its steps
dumped out into the street pieces of stone and glass, burned gritty,
completed a major reconstruction,
and set the whole enormous building sparkling in the evening sun.
In the vacant lot diagonally across,
drawing a crowd: a quack in the garb of a mountain ascetic.

Indifferent, the authorities say: 'If we don't protect it with glass or
         something,
it will fade away,' but do nothing.
Today, too,
foreign sailors amble up in their white leggings,
come to a stop with a click of their heels,
and, each having taken a snapshot, go off;
the shoeshine boy who followed them here
peers over the fence, wonders why all the fuss,
and goes on his way.

SANKICHI TOGE
translated from the Japanese by Richard H. Minear

Sankichi Toge (1917-53) was a Japanese poet and peace activist who had com-
posed three thousand tanka and even more haiku by 1945. He was in Hiroshima
when the bomb was dropped, and was very soon writing startlingly different
kinds of poetry, culminating in his 1951 collection *Genbaku shishu* (Poems of
the Atomic Bomb). A lifelong sufferer from bronchiectasis, he died on the
operating table in Hiroshima in 1953.

That Year's Paper Korean Flags

Japan surrendered at midday on 15 August, 1945.
It was unconditional surrender,
nay,
conditional surrender,
leaving the emperor in place.
From that day
paper Taegeukgis [1] fluttered across the Korean peninsula.
People waved them, sometimes just with a yin-yang symbol
and the four divination signs added
to the Japanese flag.

On 20 August, 1945,
a declaration was issued by the Soviet Army:

We, the Red Army, will provide all the conditions
for the Korean people
to have freedom and creativity.
The Korean people themselves
should create their own happiness.

On 2 September, 1945
General Order No. 1 was issued from America's MacArthur
          headquarters

The Korean people must immediately obey all the orders
issued under my authority.
All acts of resistance to the occupying forces
and any act of disturbing public peace will be severely
punished.

Taegeukgis that had been hidden since March 1919 were fluttering
          everywhere.
Taegeukgis that had been buried until August 1945 were fluttering
          again.
They were not a liberation army
but an occupying army.
Paper Taegeukgis were fluttering for them.

Chin Mu-gil of Yongtun village, Miryong-ri, Mi-myeon, Okku-gun,
     in North Jeolla
was good at painting paper Taegeukgis.
He drew fifty a day.
He even took some over the hill to Okjeong-ri.
He sent some to Mijei village, too.

On 6 October 1945
an American jeep appeared in Yongtun village.
The villagers welcomed the big-nosed soldiers
carrying Taegeukgis in their hands.

Who knew that the soldiers would start hunting women?
All the village's pigtailed young women
hid in fireholes,
crept under the floors,
hid in bamboo groves,
but from their hiding places they were dragged up the hill behind
     the village.

In Hamgyeong Province in northern Korea, too,
it was said the Soviet troops robbed people of their watches
and hunted for women.

Jin Mu-gil's cousin, a tall girl, in Okjeong-ri
locked her door
and huddled all night in the closet, as a cripple, as a hunchback.

KO UN
translated from the Korean by Brother Anthony of Taizé & Lee Sang-Wha
➤ 324

1. The Taegeukgi (or Taegukgi) was the national flag of Korea from 1883 until
1948 when the present version was adopted by South Korea. Japan occupied
and imposed colonial rule on Korea from annexation in 1910 until Japanese
forces surrendered in August 1945.

The Morning After

FROM *Sonnets for August 1945*

I

The fire left to itself might smoulder weeks.
Phone cables melt. Paint peels from off back gates.
Kitchen windows crack; the whole street reeks
of horsehair blazing. Still it celebrates.

Though people weep, their tears dry from the heat.
Faces flush with flame, beer, sheer relief
and such a sense of celebration in our street
for me it still means joy though banked with grief.

And that, now clouded, sense of public joy
with war-worn adults wild in their loud fling
has never come again since as a boy
I saw Leeds people dance and heard them sing.

There's still that dark, scorched circle on the road.
The morning after kids like me helped spray
hissing upholstery spring wire that still glowed
and cobbles boiling with black gas tar for VJ.

II

The Rising Sun was blackened on those flames.
The jabbering tongues of fire consumed its rays.
Hiroshima, Nagasaki were mere names
for us small boys who gloried in our blaze.

The blood-red ball, first burnt to blackout shreds,
took hovering batwing on the bonfire's heat
above the Rule Britannias and the bobbing heads
of the VJ hokey-cokey in our street.

The kitchen blackout cloth became a cloak
for me to play at fiend Count Dracula in.
I swirled it near the fire. It filled with smoke.
Heinz ketchup dribbled down my vampire's chin.

That circle of scorched cobbles scarred with tar 's
a night-sky globe nerve-rackingly all black,
both hemispheres entire but with no stars,
an Archerless zilch, a Scaleless zodiac.

TONY HARRISON
➤ 503

'The last foot soldier has already fallen...'

The last foot soldier has already fallen;
The last pilot chuted into the sea.
On railroad tracks the piled-up ties are smoking;
The wire of fences withers rustily.

    This tank that sticks its steel out of the water,
    This broken bridge, kneeling upon its knees...
    They now are silent – these who saw the horror,
    And they forget the fight and war's disease.

But Earth's wakening day is full of labour;
The cranes in harbours start to turn once more,
The houses hoist themselves up on their crutches...
The cities treat and heal each open sore.

    Here they will build, and break again, rebuilding,
    While down the road to his home walks someone.
    He'll knock – and his mother will come to open –
    She'll open the doors to her grečiřy-haired son.

IVAN ELAGIN
translated from the Russian by Vladimir Markov & Merrill Sparks

Ivan Elagin [Matveyev] (1918-87) was a Jewish Russian émigré poet, originally
from Vladivostok in Siberia, who studied medicine in Kiev and served in the
war as a medic. After several years in displaced persons camps, he moved to
the US and taught Russian language and literature at the University of Pitts-
burgh from 1971. Most of his poetry was written in exile.

War has been brought into disrepute

I hear it is being said in respectable circles
That from the moral point of view the Second World War
Did not come up to the First. The *Wehrmacht*
Is said to deplore the means by which the SS
Effected the extermination of certain peoples. In the Ruhr
It seems, the Captains of Industry regret the bloody razzias
That filled their mines and factories with slaves. The intelligentsia
So I hear, condemn the industrialists' demand for such slave workers
And their shabby treatment. Even the Bishops
Are distancing themselves from this way of waging war. In short
On all sides there is a feeling that unfortunately
The Nazis have done us a disservice and that war
Of itself a natural and necessary thing, by being conducted
On this occasion in so heedless and indeed inhuman a fashion
Has been, and will be for quite some time
Discredited.

[1945]

BERTOLT BRECHT
translated from the German by David Constantine
➤ 160

Return

He was a man coming home again
a singing very god inside him
a bushful of birds in his hands
eye light-lidded and wide awake
mouth greedy for good things
                    and a step
that had the animals turn and look

He was so heavy in the dark
but so frail in the sunshine
rising early weighing little

and his voice ready in his throat
lovely as currant-juice

Women followed him now and then
as people follow soldiers
for no reason with silly songs
he was covered in dust
but so fine-looking when the wind blew
and took the real light of him
into even the remotest cottage

He was a man coming home again
His papers were in order
                              and nobody
seized him and marched him back.

[1946]

JEAN CAYROL
translated from the French by Ian Higgins

Jean Cayrol (1911-2005) was a French writer and publisher. After service in
the Navy, he joined a Resistance network in 1941, but was betrayed and
arrested in June 1942, and deported in 1943. He spent the last two years of
the war in the concentration camps of Mauthausen and Gusen. The dominant
theme in his poetry is that of Lazarus, man rising again out of destruction. He
wrote numerous novels and also film scripts, notably that for Alain Resnais'
1955 documentary *Nuit et brouillard* (Night and Fog) about the camps and
secret deportations. After the war he was an influential publisher with Le
Seuil, credited with discovering authors such as Roland Barthes.

Pigtail

When all the women in the transport
had their heads shaved
four workmen with brooms made of birch twigs
swept up
and gathered up the hair

Behind clean glass
the stiff hair lies
of those suffocated in gas chambers
there are pins and side combs
in this hair

The hair is not shot through with light
is not parted by the breeze
is not touched by any hand
or rain or lips

In huge chests
clouds of dry hair
of those suffocated
and a faded plait
a pigtail with a ribbon
pulled at school
by naughty boys.

[The Museum, Auschwitz, 1948]

TADEUSZ RÓŻEWICZ
translated from the Polish by Adam Czerniawski

The survivor

I am twenty-four
led to slaughter
I survived.

The following are empty synonyms:
man and beast
love and hate
friend and foe
darkness and light.

The way of killing men and beasts is the same
I've seen it:
truckfuls of chopped-up men
who will not be saved.

Ideas are mere words:
virtue and crime
truth and lies
beauty and ugliness
courage and cowardice.

Virtue and crime weigh the same
I've seen it:
in a man who was both
criminal and virtuous.

I seek a teacher and a master
may he restore my sight hearing and speech
may he again name objects and ideas
may he separate darkness from light.

I am twenty-four
led to slaughter
I survived.

TADEUSZ RÓŻEWICZ
translated from the Polish by Adam Czerniawski

Tadeusz Różewicz (1921-2014) was one of Poland's four great 20th century poets, a Polish poet, as well as an innovative dramatist. During the war he was a soldier in the Polish underground Home Army, along with his brother who was executed by the Gestapo in 1944.

Erich Fried (1921-88) was an Austrian-born poet, writer and translator known for his political poetry and love poems. Born to Jewish parents in Vienna, he fled to London after his father was murdered by the Gestapo after the *Anschluss* with Nazi Germany, but was able to arrange for his mother and many other Jews to come to Britain. He remained in London after the war, working for the BBC's German Service. ➢ 90, 310, 311

Conversation with a Survivor

What did you do in those days
that you shouldn't have done?
'Nothing'

What did you not do
that you should have done?
'This and that:
a few things'

Why did you not do it?
'Because I was afraid'
Why were you afraid?
'Because I didn't want to die'

Did others die
because you didn't want to?
'I think
they did'

Have you got anything else to say
about what you didn't do?
'Yes: to ask you
what you would have done in my place?'

I do not know
and cannot sit in judgment on you.
Only one thing I know:
Tomorrow none of us
will stay alive
if today
we again do nothing

ERICH FRIED
translated from the German by Stuart Hood

On Certain Survivors

When the man
Was dragged out from under
The debris
Of his shelled house,
He shook himself
And said:
Never again.

At least, not right away.

GÜNTER KUNERT
translated from the German by Michael Hamburger

Günter Kunert (*b*. 1929) is a versatile German writer from Berlin whose work embraces a wide range of different literary forms. He left the GDR for West Germany in 1979 after falling out of favour with the authorities over his support for Wolf Biermann.

What Happens

It has happened
and it goes on happening
and will happen again
if nothing happens to stop it

The innocent know nothing
because they are too innocent
and the guilty know nothing
because they are too guilty

The poor do not notice
because they are too poor
and the rich do not notice
because they are too rich

The stupid shrug their shoulders
because they are too stupid
and the clever shrug their shoulders
because they are too clever

The young do not care
because they are too young
and the old do not care
because they are too old

That is why nothing happens
to stop it
and that is why it has happened
and goes on happening and will happen again

ERICH FRIED
translated from the German by Stuart Hood

'First they came for the Jews...'

First they came for the Jews.
and I did not speak out –
because I was not a Jew.

Then they came for the Communists
and I did not speak out –
because I was not a Communist.

Then they came for the Trade Unionists.
and I did not speak out –
because I was not a Trade Unionist.

Then they came for the Catholics.
and I did not speak out –
because I was a Protestant.

Then they came for me –
and there was no one left
to speak out for me.

attributed to MARTIN NIEMÖLLER
translated from the German

Draft of a Reparations Agreement

All right, gentlemen who cry blue murder as always,
nagging miracle-makers,
quiet!
Everything will be returned to its place,
paragraph after paragraph.
The scream back into the throat.
The gold teeth back to the gums.
The terror.
The smoke back to the tin chimney and further on and inside
back to the hollow of the bones,
and already you will be covered with skin and sinews and you will
        live,
look, you will have your lives back,
sit in the living room, read the evening paper.
Here you are. Nothing is too late.
As to the yellow star: immediately
it will be torn from your chest
and will emigrate
to the sky.

DAN PAGIS
translated from the Hebrew by Stephen Mitchell

Dan Pagis (1930-86) was an Israeli poet. Born in Bukovina, Romania, he was imprisoned for three years during his adolescence in a concentration camp in Ukraine, but managed to escape in 1944. He was able to reach Israel in 1946, where he later worked as a schoolteacher in a kibbutz and then as a lecturer in medieval Hebrew literature.

How did they bury them all, who died in the war?

How did they bury them all, who died in the war?
From near and far the tidy packed masses were neatly
Disposed, laid straight, boxed and buried; in a soil
Crowded already and crammed with the old wars'
Great litter of lives spilt. And they buried them all
As the gardener after the autumn fall
Digs in the apples to rot. So the summer's spoil
Wastes down to mud and the sweetness goes rotten.
They buried them all, and the trees have already forgotten.

VALENTINE ACKLAND

The End and the Beginning

After every war
someone's got to tidy up.
Things won't pick
themselves up, after all.

Someone's got to shove
the rubble to the roadsides
so the carts loaded with corpses
can get by.

Someone's got to trudge
through sludge and ashes,
through the sofa springs,
the shards of glass,
the bloody rags.

Someone's got to lug the post
to prop the wall,
someone's got to glaze the window,
set the door in its frame.

No sound bites, no photo opportunities
and it takes years.
All the cameras have gone
to other wars.

The bridges need to be rebuilt,
the railroad stations, too.
Shirt sleeves will be rolled
to shreds.

Someone, broom in hand,
still remembers how it was.
Someone else listens, nodding
his unshattered head.
But others are bound to be bustling nearby
who'll find all that
a little boring.

From time to time someone still must
dig up a rusted argument
from underneath a bush
and haul it off to the dump.

Those who knew
what this was all about
must make way for those
who know little.
And less than that.
And at last nothing less
than nothing.

Someone's got to lie there
in the grass that covers up
the causes and effects
with a cornstalk in his teeth,
gawking at clouds.

WISŁAWA SZYMBORSKA
translated from the Polish by Stanislaw Baranczak and Clare Cavanagh
➤ 568

KOREAN WAR | 1950–1953

TOTAL DEATHS: OVER 2 MILLION

After Japan annexed Korea in 1910, colonial rule was imposed, including the banning of Korea's language, culture and flag. In his poem 'That Year's Paper Korean Flags' [➤ 302], Ko Un celebrates the occasion when his whole country was briefly free at the end of the Second World War. But one occupation soon gave way to others, as the country north of the 38th parallel was taken over by Soviet Russia and what became the Republic of Korea to the south was controlled from Japan by the US military under General Douglas MacArthur.

After several years of frontier clashes, the North Korean People's Army invaded the Republic on 25 June 1950, sweeping rapidly south until the United Nations intervened, authorising the deployment of a UN force to assist South Korea, eventually made up of 88% American troops plus soldiers from 20 other countries (including 100,000 from Britain). After months of hard-fought confrontation, the North Koreans were forced back across the frontier and pursued almost to the Chinese border to the north, whereupon China entered the war, the UN forces recoiled in disorder and by the new year were defending a line well to the south of the 38th parallel, with Seoul, the South Korean capital, in enemy hands for the second time during the war. Rallying in March 1951, UN troops pushed the Chinese and North Koreans back, and for the next two years from July 1951 both sides fought near-static campaigns from heavily fortified positions in the general area of the 38th parallel until American air supremacy brought about a ceasefire 27 July 1953.

After three years of brutal fighting with millions of casualties, the final truce line of 1953 corresponded almost exactly to the positions held by the two sides at the start of the war. North Korea, officially the Democratic People's Republic of Korea, has since been ruled by the hereditary dictatorship of the Kim family, founded in 1948 by Kim Il-sung, who launched the Korean War.

Over a million Americans fought in Korea, with almost as many killed there as would die later in the much longer conflict in Vietnam, but once the war was over, returning veterans met with little appreciation of what they had endured. Literary responses to the Korean War likewise did not find an eager readership, with a handful of novels maintaining any interest: Pat Franks's *Hold Back the Night* (1951), James Michener's *The Bridges at Toko-Ri* (1953) and Richard Condon's *The Manchurian Candidate* (1959), along with the later *M*A*S*H* (1968), made into a film and TV series which most viewers took to be "really" about the Vietnam War, not the Korean War.

The impact on Korean literature was far greater, with poets including Ku Sang and Ko Un giving voice to the immense sufferings of their people in this savage, national war. Yet despite the large numbers of Americans from all walks of life involved, the amount of significant poetry relating to their war experiences has been small and not widely published. Vietnam veteran W.D. Ehrhart [➤ 358] has done much to redress this, most notably with his 1999 anthology, *Retrieving Bones: Stories and Poems of the Korean War* (edited with Philip K. Jason), to which this selection is much indebted.

316

from **Even the Knots on Quince Trees Tell Tales**

27

I reckon that anyone who experienced the shock and despair of
        June 25, 1950
would be less at a loss if confronted with the end of the world.

Accompanying the Korean army, transformed into a defeated remnant
in the space of a day, in its so-called retreat, it was only in Suwon,
on hearing reports that a UN force had entered the war,
that I felt able to breathe freely again, as if I had boarded Noah's Ark.

Assigned at Daejeon to the political section of military intelligence,
returning from witnessing an execution of Communists by firing squad
I was drinking *soju* at a small roadside store while Staff-sergeant Kim,
who had been involved in the execution, poured out his thoughts:

'Before Liberation I was living in Japan, in Hiroshima,
and in those days, if you met a fellow countryman along the road
you felt so happy, and now those same fellow countrymen
get shot dead, mark you, with my own hand
and a whole heap of them, too…
this Ism of people condemned to die…what the hell is it,
this spooky Ism?…
And those fellows' Ism is the enemy….'
and he began to weep noisily.

While experiencing warfare, and today too, thirty years later,
I have heard no more striking view of what happened on June 25 [1]
than that outburst of Staff-sergeant Kim:

'This Ism of people condemned to die…what the hell is it,
this spooky Ism?…
And those fellows' Ism is the enemy….'

28

From Daejeon we skirted Geumsan,
and then, as we left the Yeongdong highway
we came under attack from a Communist guerrilla unit.

Hastily abandoning the jeep I was in,
I crouched behind the bank of a field beside the road
and pointed the M1 rifle I had never once fired
in the direction of the enemy.

Just then I noticed the seeds from a dried dandelion
right before my eyes being carried away in a gust of wind.

The question:
'Now once my flesh is scattered like that,
where will the seeds of my life go
to give birth to new flowers?'

and the realisation that
'I am eternally wrapped in a profound mystery'

came to my mind in a flash,
making all fear and apprehension vanish
and drawing me into a rapture I cannot name.

29

I am left behind in Daegu as part of the last defensive regiment.

Like a pursued animal that will crawl into any kind of hole,
hearing the enemy bombardments, now they have come very near,
I crouch in our darkened barracks in the blackout.

We may have been overrun by the Communists by morning,
we can't tell if the leftist brigands may not soon control everything,
and is really the only task I can fulfil as I die
simply to help make up for the small number of soldiers?

'I must become an avenging spirit, a ghost
with a knife held in his bloody lips
I must get rid of the reds with my own two hands.'

In all my life, only then
did I feel a lust for revenge.

1. *June 25, 1950:* the day when the North Korean forces launched a surprise
attack on the South, beginning the Korean War.

36

On the frozen ground of my heart
a bitter Siberian wind bites the flesh.

In a field of dry tangled weeds
a garbage dump
of gaping cans, smashed ration-boxes,
pages from Stars and Stripes, broken-necked bottles,
and in one corner the cadaver of a hairy dog, shot dead;
along the ridges bitten into the fields by tanks
the dry stiff carcass of a cat;

in front of a tent like a plastic hot-house
behind a barbed-wire fence hung with blood-stained slacks,
a GI is coming and going;
whenever he whistles, peep-peep,
wretched urchins pop up their heads, like frogs,
from holes in the ground like those where *kimch'i* is kept,
wrapped in coloured scarves,
yellow, red and blue.

The sky suddenly
begins to spew black mist
and a cluster of crows flaps off
over the sullen hills –

this itch in my back that drives me mad,
this rising bile that dilates my breast,
who can it be directed at?

from **39**

The allied forces go crawling upward.
There are black private soldiers among them.
Penetrating the hail of shells and bullets
one of our private soldiers reaches the top
and hurls a grenade.
A black soldier follows him up
and hurls a grenade.
Red heat, explosion after explosion, hand-to-hand...
As day breaks, at the summit

the South Korean flag is waving ghostlike.
The corpses of allies and foes lie side by side.
The name-tag fallen from the neck of one black soldier
glistens exceptionally bright in the morning sunlight.

KU SANG
translated from the Korean by Brother Anthony of Taizé

Ku Sang (1919-2004) was one of South Korea's leading poets. Born in Seoul of Catholic parents, he grew up in Wonsan, in South Hamgyeong Province, now situated in North Korea, and fled south after the end of the Second World War when his first poetry publications were severely criticised by the Communist authorities. He served as assistant director of the writers' group deployed to cover the activities of the South Korean military during the Korean War. The poems in his book *Choto-ui shi* (Wastelands of Fire, 1956) bore witness to the suffering of his people during the Korean War. His later work is notable for its fusion of Christian faith, Buddhist contemplation and Taoist thought.

Middle School Classmates

Korea was a battlefield, everywhere.
The battlefront
swept down to the south of the peninsula.
Then the battlefront
swept up to the north of the peninsula.
The battlefront,
not leaving even one corner alone,
scoured and ransacked
every nook and cranny.

Moreover, the battlefront was not only in the battlefront.
In the rear too
there was hatred between one and another,
deceit between one and another,
plunder between one and another.

Back under the Japanese rule, foolish people were friends among
        themselves.
But now in this battlefield
even foolish people turned into one another's enemies.

Yeom Gi-uk informed on Baek U-jong,
saying that he met the younger brother of Kim Chin-gu
who'd gone north after Liberation.
But Kim Chin-gu had already died in the Bodoyeonmaeng[1]
and his younger brother had gone north, so he'd never met him.
Yeom was Baek's middle-school classmate
and Baek once refused a favour Yeom asked
so Baek U-jong was denounced.
False or not
if you denounced someone as a spy, you got a reward.
All the guys you disliked were spies.

KO UN
translated from the Korean by Brother Anthony of Taizé & Lee Sang-Wha

1. After Liberation in 1945 and before the Korean War the South government
tried to convert Communist sympathisers; the organisation composed of such
people was called the Bodoyeonmaeng (the Bodo League) and most of them
were killed by the police of the South government when the South Korean
forces were retreating for the second time on 4 January 1951; that was when
Koreans began killing each other indiscriminately. [Tr.]

Old Sim Yu-seop

War widows need to smoke cigarettes, if they can.
When you miss someone, you need to have a cigarette.
When the person you miss has disappeared,
you need to have a cigarette.
There have to be cigarettes for widows,
and for widowers.
There have to be cigarettes for friends they were separated from
        forever.

One nation was divided into two.
And from that moment,
people became enemies.
Naturally,
inevitably,
absurdly
war broke out.

For a few months the front line moved farther south.
It engulfed even the west of South Gyeongsang Province.

The American fighter planes changed
from second-world-war propellor-driven Grumman Hellcats
to jet-propelled Sabers.

Then the front line shot up northward.
The retreating lines of North Korean troops increased.
First came the North's unhindered advance,
and then the South's unhindered advance.

The whole country was turned into scorched ground
from carpet bombing by the US air force.
Was that scorched ground what we wanted?
Were the ruins
what we wanted so ardently?

While the fighting moved up
and down,

the rice was ripening
in the fields round Jochiwon in South Chungcheong Province.

Sixty-five year-old
Sim Yu-Seop,
after giving the paddy fields a triple summer weeding,
was waiting for the autumn harvest
wordlessly.

His heart was entirely preoccupied with his two sons.

While the country shifted from
the Republic of Korea
to the People's Republic,
and then from the People's Republic
back to the Republic of Korea,

his elder son was a soldier for the South,
the younger left as a volunteer soldier for the North.

Even when the dog wagged its tail,
Old Sim's lips wouldn't open.
It would soon be third anniversary of his wife's death.
'Thin-as-a-post' as he was known felt lonely.

More than the old fellow himself,
his shadow was 'thin-as-a-post.'
In all his sixty years of life
he had only ever told three or four lies.
He, too, had to chain-smoke cigarettes made from dried tobacco leaves.

KO UN
translated from the Korean by Brother Anthony of Taizé & Lee Sang-Wha

3 October 1950

Seoul belonged to the enemy for three months
under the rule of the North Korean People's Republic.
The American airforce's bombing raids
went on day after day.
Seoul was in ruins.
Grass grew
between the broken bricks in the ruins.

South Korean troops
recaptured Seoul.
The Northern flag was lowered
from the flagstaff of the Government Building,

the American flag was raised,
followed by the South Korean flag and they fluttered there.

Seoul was under martial law.
From seven in the evening
until five the next morning
was curfew time,
the time for the mice.
Checkpoints stood here and there
in the ruins.
The police that had come back
set about arresting those who had collaborated during the past
          three months,
including children less than ten years old.

The kid of the noodle bar in Juja-dong, central Seoul,
got to know about the harsh world
from early on.
He got to know all about
the world of beaters
and beaten,
the world where there were thieves
amidst all that fear,
the world where even robbers
and thieves were arrested and beaten with clubs.

He was envious of robbers, envious of thieves.

KO UN
translated from the Korean by Brother Anthony of Taizé & Lee Sang-Wha

Ko Un was born in 1933 in Gunsan, North Jeolla Province, Korea. After
immense suffering during the Korean War, he became a Buddhist monk. His
first poems were published in 1958, his first collection in 1960. A few years
later he returned to the world. After years of dark nihilism, he became a leading
spokesman in the struggle for freedom ančiřd democracy during the 1970s
and 1980s in South Korea, when he was often arrested and imprisoned. He
has published more than 150 volumes of poems, essays and fiction, including
the monumental seven-volume epic *Mount Paekdu* and the 30-volume
Maninbo (Ten Thousand Lives) series. He is now Korea's foremost living
writer, with his work translated into more than 20 languages.

The January–May 1951 Slaughter

I'm sick. They didn't stop coming,
And we wouldn't stop firing.

At the beginning, in January
It looked like the Chongchon action for us again,
But we stopped them.
Brutally.

I passed on the beer ration again.
Drink? I don't even want to eat...
Our counter-offensive started on January 21;
        Happy Birthday, Rafe.

In February, it was just as bad. If possible: it was worse.
No one talks about the cold anymore, nor about the dead,
Theirs or ours, but mostly theirs.
Also, we never seem to run out of shells.

March, and Seoul's been retaken. We took our time.
I don't want to look at the Chinese dead.
There are hundreds of them out there. They died in the city,
They died in the fields and in the hillsides.
They died everywhere.

At one point,
It was artillery against artillery in the city.
It's early April.
I am not going to talk about this again, and so I will say it
This once:
    We fired twelve thousand rounds of 105mm in twenty-four hours
In support of the Second Div.
    I don't see how people can understand what
I am saying when I say
    12,000 rounds of 105s in 24 hours.

It means this:

Seventeen of us were wounded. Minor wounds they were,
And all wounds bleed, but we kept firing.
There was no pain...the blood caked and we kept up the fire.
We're animals,
But then, so are they.

At the aid station, Sonny Ruiz said it best:

'They came at the infantry down there like pigs in a chute,
    And we just cut their necks off from up here.'

The officers are now ordering us to eat,
But we notice that their appetite hasn't improved either.

May, and I'm overdue for an R&R; I'm one of the medicals;
Personally, I think it's mental.

ROLANDO HINOJOSA

Roland Hinojosa (*b.* 1929) enlisted in the US Army in 1946, served two years, started college, but was called back and sent to Korea in early July 1950, nine days before the North Korean invasion. He served as a tank crewman with a reconnaissance unit in Korea, sustaining two minor wounds. His father was Mexican-American, and Hinojosa has written in both Spanish and English, much of his work being concerned with Chicano identity, but because his army experience wasn't lived in Spanish, he preferred to write about it in English.

Restoration Again

In June 1950
Seoul was occupied by the enemy.
In September 1950
Seoul was recaptured by our forces.
In January 1951
Seoul was again occupied by the enemy.
In March 1951
Seoul was again recaptured by our forces.

On winter nights
people chopped up wooden telegraph poles to make fire,
set fire to thatched-roof houses to keep themselves warm.

Yi Sang-Ho,
who looked after his younger brother Yi Sang-Un in prison
both before
and after Liberation,
survived in that Seoul.
He survived.
In April 1951
he passed away as the cherry trees on Mount Namsan were
blossoming.

Yi Sang-Un, a student of English literature in the Japanese
colonial period,
was sent to prison for anti-Japanese activities
and again for leftist activities,
and then went missing permanently.

His brother Yi Sang-Ho died alone.
He had a long-ridged nose.
His eyebrows were bushy.
Beneath those eyebrows
his eyes stayed wide open as he died.

There were no more occupations,
no more recapturings.
In the colossal ruins
dictatorship grew fierce.

We can't take it! We want change! the opposition cried,
but the dictatorship in the divided land grew fiercer.

KO UN
translated from the Korean by Brother Anthony of Taizé & Lee Sang-Wha
➤ 324

I Remember

I remember the time
Black got it
incoming knocked him back
into a snowbank
      buried him
      he was Missing in Action
      all winter

spring thaw & we were
back on the same hill &
the Lt. stumbled on him
cracked his shin-bone on
Black's helmet & looked
down at Black, preserved like
a fresh side of beef
      all winter

'You Sonofabitch,' he said
to Black's stiff corpse

'You Sonofabitch, if you'd
been more careful I
wouldn't hafta write
all those Goddam letters'číř

'You Sonofabitch' & he spit

but I'd seen his eyes
watering before he looked
straight up into the sun

WILLIAM WANTLING

William Wantling (1933-74) enlisted in the Marines after leaving high school, arriving in Korea in 1952. Discharged after being seriously wounded, he turned to crime and served five and half years for narcotics and forgery in San Quentin Prison, where he discovered poetry. After his release he studied at Illinois State University, but never escaped the drug dependency that started with morphine in hospital. A selection of his work appeared in *Penguin Modern Poets* (1968).

Shellshock

I am MacFatridge as he was then,
torn by the mine he was defusing;
at the aid-tent door his arm fell off,
and a Medic stooped to retrieve it
and stood as though lugging a melon
that had burst in the sun.

There are those of us who are not tough
despite all they told us. If I cry
now, no one seems to care, but before
I would have been punished with a laugh.
I wish that underneath the green sky
of this room, images of terror
would come again: that the emerald door
I can't pass would let me out to sleep.

WILLIAM CHILDRESS

William Childress (*b.* 1933) grew up in a family of sharecroppers and migrant cottonpickers, joining the US Army at 18. Sent to Korea in 1952, he served as a demolitions expert and secret courier. He later re-enlisted as a paratrooper, twice narrowly escaping death from parachute malfunctions. He is a widely published writer and photojournalist, the author of three books of poetry.

Memory of a Victory

Off the Korean Coast, beyond Wonsan
waiting for invasion soft winds blew
the scent of squid drying in the sun,
homely smells of rice paddies, cooking fires.

It was a picture world with low hills
much like New Mexico, except for water,
the strange smells. Little plumes of smoke.
Here & there, the glint of steel.

Under the waiting guns lay peachblossoms.
I could see them with my binoculars.
The planes still had not come, all eternity
waited beneath the sweep second hand.

Then the crackling radio commanded
'Fire!' and a distant world I could have loved
went up in shattering bursts, in greyblack explosions,
the strange trees that suddenly grew on the hillside.

They fired their rifles, light howitzers
back. After a while we sent boats into the silence.

KEITH WILSON

Keith Wilson (1927-2009) went to Korea in 1950 as an ensign fresh out of
the US Naval Academy, but felt betrayed after three tours in 1953: 'When I
found out that Korea was all a very dirty and murderous joke, I was silenced
for many years. [...] I started writing *Graves Registry* in the winter of 1966 in
anger that our government was again fighting an undeclared war that I, from
my experiences in Korea, knew we could never win. [...] I had it buried inside.
It took the pressure of rage and fear for the young men [of the Vietnam
generation] that made me write it and it poured out, page after page.' [quoted
in *Retrieving Bones*] Wilson went into academia after leaving the navy, teaching
for many years at New Mexico State University.

A Mouse

After the bombing
a gaunt mouse came along.
He was glad.

How hungry you must be!

Legless Gi-cheol threw his wooden pillow
at the animal.
He cooked and ate it.

330

He cooked and ate the scream the mouse made
as it died.

When would the war end?

KO UN
translated from the Korean by Brother Anthony of Taizé & Lee Sang-Wha

Ode for the American Dead in Asia

1

God love you now, if no one else will ever,
Corpse in the paddy, or dead on a high hill
In the fine and ruinous summer of a war
You never wanted. All your false flags were
Of bravery and ignorance, like grade school maps:
Colors of countries you would never see –
Until that weekend in eternity
When, laughing, well armed, perfectly ready to kill
The world and your brother, the safe commanders sent
You into your future. Oh, dead on a hill,
Dead in a paddy, leeched and tumbled to
A tomb of footnotes. We mourn a changeling: you:
Handselled to poverty and drummed to war
By distinguished masters whom you never knew.

2

The bee that spins his metal from the sun,
The shy mole drifting like a miner ghost
Through midnight earth – all happy creatures run
As strict as trains on rails the circuits of
Blind instinct. Happy in your summer follies,
You mined a culture that was mined for war:
The state to mold you, church to bless, and always
The elders to confirm you in your ignorance.
No scholar put your thinking cap on nor
Warned that in dead seas fishes died in schools
Before inventing legs to walk the land.

331

The rulers stuck a tennis racket in your hand,
An Ark against the flood. In time of change
Courage is not enough: the blind mole dies,
And you on your hill, who did not know the rules.

3

Wet in the windy counties of the dawn
The lone crow skirls his draggled passage home:
And God (whose sparrows fall aslant his gaze,
Like grace or confetti) blinks and he is gone,
And you are gone. Your scarecrow valor grows
And rusts like early lilac while the rose
Blooms in Dakota and the stock exchange
Flowers. Roses, rents, all things conspire
To crown your death with wreaths of living fire.
And the public mourners come: the politic tear
Is cast in the Forum. But, in another year,
We will mourn you, whose fossil courage fills
The limestone histories: brave: ignorant: amazed:
Dead in the rice paddies, dead on the nameless hills.

THOMAS McGRATH

Thomas McGrath (1916-90) grew up on a farm in North Dakota, and served in the Aleutian Islands with US Army Air Forces during World War II. A distinguished leftist academic, he was blacklisted during the McCarthy era. Much of his Whitmanesque poetry relates to social concerns, notably his epic narrative *Letter to an Imaginary Friend*, published in sections between 1957 and 1985 and as a complete work in 1997.

The Long March

North from Pusan,
trailing nooses of dust,
we dumbly followed
leaders whose careers
hung on victory.

The road might
have been the Appian Way
except for
the children lining it.
We gave what we could

to hold back the grave,
but in Pusan the dead-truck
snuffled through frozen dawns
retrieving bones in thin sacks,
kids who would never beg again.

When we bivouacked
near Pyongtaek, a soldier
fished a bent brown stick
from a puddle. It was
the arm of someone's child.

Not far away, the General
camps with his press corps.
Any victory will be his.
For us, there is only
the long march to Viet Nam.

WILLIAM CHILDRESS
➤ 329

333

THE COLD WAR | 1947–1991

TOTAL DEATHS: UNKNOWN

The Cold War began in the aftermath of the Second World War and continued until the break-up of the Soviet Union. A significant factor in the overall balance of power was the Communist victory in the second part of the Chinese Civil War (1946-50) at a cost of two million lives. While there was never any large-scale fighting directly between the West (US and NATO) and the Eastern Bloc (Soviet Union and Warsaw Pact allies), millions more people were killed in the two major regional wars in Korea [➤ 316] and Vietnam [➤ 351]; and both superpowers were heavily armed in preparation for the all-out nuclear world war imagined in poems such as those by Peter Porter, Miroslav Holub and Edwin Muir [➤ 343, 345, 347], which convey the climate of fear felt by many during the Cold War in the West and East. Robert Lowell's 'Fall 1961' [➤ 342] was written at a time of mounting tension, when the building of the Berlin Wall in August 1961 was to be followed by the Cuban missile crisis of 1962.

The USSR consolidated its hold over the Eastern Bloc in the postwar years, crushing the Hungarian Uprising of 1956 (see poems by László Nagy and Györgi Petri ➤ 348, 349) and invading Czechoslovakia in 1968 after the Prague Spring attempt at liberalisation (Holub ➤ 350). Other poems included here by Auden, Holub, Reiner Kunze and Gyula Illyés [➤ 346, 338, 338, 341] give a chilling sense of the atmosphere of daily life under totalitarian regimes requiring subjugation and total conformity of the individual.

The US and USSR and their allies opposed and defied each other in other conflicts during the span of the Cold War, such as the Greek Civil War (1946-49: total deaths 158,000), when the Greek government, supported by the UK and the US, defeated a communist takeover, but with anti-communist feeling opening the way for the military coup of 1967 and later polarisation. In 1956, Egypt successfully challenged Britain, France and Israel with Soviet support over control of the Suez Canal (total deaths approximately 3000).

In 1978 the People's Democratic Party of Afghanistan seized power in Afghanistan, leading to a civil war between a communist government helped by thousands of Soviet military advisors and guerrilla *mujahideen* trained by Pakistan and assisted by the US (whose troops were to be attacked by the same men or their sons in the US-led war in Afghanistan from 2001). In 1979, the assassination of Afghan president Nur Muhammad Taraki by political rivals was followed by the Soviet invasion [➤ 543].

Every Day

War is no longer declared,
but rather continued. The outrageous
has become the everyday. The hero
is absent from the battle. The weak
are moved into the firing zone.
The uniform of the day is patience,
the order of merit is the wretched star
of hope over the heart.

It is awarded
when nothing more happens,
when the bombardment is silenced,
when the enemy has become invisible
and the shadow of eternal weapons
covers the sky.

It is awarded
for deserting the flag,
for bravery before a friend,
for the betrayal of shameful secrets
and the disregard
of every command.

INGEBORG BACHMANN
translated from the German by Peter Filkins

Ingeborg Bachmann (1926-73) was an Austrian poet, dramatist and novelist associated with post-war Germany's Gruppe 47 movement. Aged 12 she witnessed the march of Nazi troops into Klagenfurt after the annexation of Austria, returning to this period both in her memoir *Youth in an Austrian Town* (1961) and in her unfinished novel *The Book of Franza*. After completing her doctorate thesis on Heidegger in Vienna in 1949, she found herself more engaged by Wittgenstein and the philosophy of language, significant influences on her later writing, which included collaborations on opera libretti with Hans Werner Henze.

The Shield of Achilles

        She looked over his shoulder
            For vines and olive trees,
        Marble well-governed cities
            And ships upon untamed seas,
        But there on the shining metal
            His hands had put instead
        An artificial wilderness
            And a sky like lead.

A plain without a feature, bare and brown,
    No blade of grass, no sign of neighborhood,
Nothing to eat and nowhere to sit down,
    Yet, congregated on its blankness, stood
    An unintelligible multitude,
A million eyes, a million boots in line,
Without expression, waiting for a sign.

Out of the air a voice without a face
    Proved by statistics that some cause was just
In tones as dry and level as the place:
    No one was cheered and nothing was discussed;
    Column by column in a cloud of dust
They marched away enduring a belief
Whose logic brought them, somewhere else, to grief.

        She looked over his shoulder
            For ritual pieties,
        White flower-garlanded heifers,
            Libation and sacrifice,
        But there on the shining metal
            Where the altar should have been,
        She saw by his flickering forge-light
            Quite another scene.

Barbed wire enclosed an arbitrary spot
    Where bored officials lounged (one cracked a joke)
And sentries sweated for the day was hot:
    A crowd of ordinary decent folk

Watched from without and neither moved nor spoke
As three pale figures were led forth and bound
To three posts driven upright in the ground.

The mass and majesty of this world, all
    That carries weight and always weighs the same
Lay in the hands of others; they were small
    And could not hope for help and no help came:
    What their foes liked to do was done, their shame
Was all the worst could wish; they lost their pride
And died as men before their bodies died.

            She looked over his shoulder
                For athletes at their games,
            Men and women in a dance
                    Moving their sweet limbs
            Quick, quick, to music,
                But there on the shining shield
            His hands had set no dancing-floor
                But a weed-choked field.

A ragged urchin, aimless and alone,
    Loitered about that vacancy; a bird
Flew up to safety from his well-aimed stone:
    That girls are raped, that two boys knife a third,
    Were axioms to him, who'd never heard
Of any world where promises were kept,
Or one could weep because another wept.

            The thin-lipped armourer,
                Hephaestos, hobbled away,
            Thetis of the shining breasts
                Cried out in dismay
            At what the god had wrought
                To please her son, the strong
            Iron-hearted man-slaying Achilles
                Who would not live long.

[1956]

W.H. AUDEN
➤ 189

The corporal who killed Archimedes

With one bold stroke
he killed the circle, tangent
and point of intersection
in infinity.

On penalty
of quartering
he banned numbers
from three up.

Now in Syracuse
he heads a school of philosophers,
squats on his halberd
for another thousand years
and writes:

one two
one two
one two
one two

[1960]

MIROSLAV HOLUB
translated from the Czech by Ian & Jarmila Milner
➤ 285

The Bringers of Beethoven
(for Ludvik Kundera)

They set out to bring Beethoven
to everyone.
And as they had a record with them
they played for speedier understanding
Symphony no. 5, in C minor, opus 67

But the man M. said
it was too loud for him, he
was getting old

In the night the bringers of Beethoven put
up poles in streets and squares
hooked up cables, connected
loudspeakers, and with the dawn
for more thorough acquaintance came the strains of
Symphony no. 5, in C minor, opus 67,
came loud enough to be heard
in the mute fields.

But the man M. said he had a headache,
went home about noon, closed
doors and windows and praised
the thickness of the walls

Thus provoked, the bringers of Beethoven strung
wire on to the walls and hung
loudspeakers over the windows, and in
through the panes came
Symphony no. 5, in C minor, opus 67

But the man M. stepped out of the house and denounced
the bringers of Beethoven;
they all asked him what he had
against Beethoven

Thus attacked, the bringers of Beethoven knocked
on M.'s door and when they opened up they
forced a foot inside; praising the neatness of the place
they went in.
The conversation happened to turn
to Beethoven,
and to enliven the subject they happened
to have with them
Symphony no. 5, in C minor, opus 67

But the man M. hit the bringers
of Beethoven with an iron ladle.
He was arrested just in time.

M.'s act was called homicidal
by lawyers and judges of the bringers of Beethoven.
But they must not give up hoping.
He was sentenced
to Symphony no. 5, in C minor, opus 67,
by Ludwig van Beethoven

M. kicked and screamed,
until the loudspeakers stopped
beyond the mute fields

He was just too old, the bringers of Beethoven said.
But by M.'s coffin, they said,
are his children

And his children demanded
that over the coffin of
the man M. should be played
Symphony no. 5, in C minor, opus 67

REINER KUNZE
translated from the German by Gordon & Gisela Brotherston

Reinzer Kunze (*b.* 1933) is a German writer and former GDR dissident who
was forced to move to West Germany in 1979 due to his 'counter-revolutionary
activities', which would have included the writing of *The Lovely Years* (1976),
an indictment of life under the Communist regime.

While the Record Plays

They heated hatchet blades over gas fires in roadside workshops
and hammered them into cleavers.

They brought wooden blocks on trucks and carried them across
these new provinces grimly, quickly, and steadily: almost
according to ritual.

Because at any time – at noon or midnight – they would arrive at
one of these impure settlements,

where women did not cook nor make beds as theirs did, where men
did not greet one another as they did, where children and
the whole damned company did not pronounce words as
they did, and where the girls kept apart from them.

They would select from these insolent and intolerable people twelve
men, preferably young ones, to take to the marketplace,

and there – because of *blah-blah-blah* and moreover *quack-quack-
quack* and likewise *quack-blah-quack* – would beat and
behead them,

of historical necessity – because of *twaddle-twiddle* and *twiddle-diddle*,
and expertly, for their occupations would be different one
from the other,

agronomist and butcher, bookbinder and engineer, waiter and
doctor, several seminarists, cadets from military academies,
a considerable number of students,

those familiar with Carnot, Beethoven and even Einstein, displaying
their finest talents,

because, after all, nevertheless, *blah-blah-blah* and *twiddle-dee-dee*,

while through loudspeakers records played – music and an
occasional gruff order, and they, the zealous ones, wiped
their foreheads and turned aside every now and then to
urinate since excitement affects the kidneys;

then having washed the blocks and hauled down the large tricolour
which on such occasions always waved above their heads,

they too would march on into the broad future,

past the heads, carefully placed in a circle,

then out of the settlement where now also

and forever and ever,

reason, comfort, and hope would be no –

wrr-wrr-wrr – that is to say – *we-wp, wa-rp*, the sound (by now
the only one

without music or words) that the needle makes as the record
grinds on.

GYULA ILLYÉS
translated from the Hungarian by William Jay Smith

Gyula Illyés (1902-83) was a Hungarian poet and novelist. A founding member
of the anti-fascist March Front movement (1937-39), he went into hiding after
the Nazi invasion of Hungary in 1944. After the war he became a leader of the
National Peasant Party for two years until the Communist takeover.

Fall 1961

Back and forth, back and forth
goes the tock, tock, tock
of the orange, bland, ambassadorial
face of the moon
on the grandfather clock.

All autumn, the chafe and jar
of nuclear war;[1]
we have talked our extinction to death.
I swim like a minnow
behind my studio window.

Our end drifts nearer,
the moon lifts,
radiant with terror.
The state
is a diver under a glass bell.

A father's no shield[2]
for his child.
We are like a lot of wild
spiders crying together,
but without tears.

Nature holds up a mirror.
One swallow makes a summer.
It's easy to tick
off the minutes,
but the clockhands stick.

Back and forth!
Back and forth, back and forth –
my one point of rest
is the orange and black
oriole's swinging nest!

ROBERT LOWELL

1. 'Across the nation last week, there was endless conversation about the threat of nuclear war' between the United States and the Soviet Union (*Time*, 29 September 1961); opposing troops engaged in a stand-off as the Berlin Wall was built, and both countries resumed nuclear testing. 2. *shield:* the North American Defense Command engaged in an exercise called 'Sky Shield II' against a simulated Russian attack on 14 October 1961. [Bidart/Gewanter]

Robert Lowell (1917-77) was one of America's greatest modern poets. His biographer Paul Mariani called him 'the poet-historian of our time' and 'the last of [America's] influential public poets'. He was a conscientious objector and served several months in prison during the Second World War. ➤ 381

Your Attention Please

The Polar DEW[1] has just warned that
A nuclear rocket strike of
At least one thousand megatons
Has been launched by the enemy
Directly at our major cities.
This announcement will take
Two and a quarter minutes to make,
You therefore have a further
Eight and a quarter minutes
To comply with the shelter

Requirements published in the Civil
Defence Code – section Atomic Attack.
A specially shortened Mass
Will be broadcast at the end
Of this announcement –
Protestant and Jewish services
Will begin simultaneously –
Select your wavelength immediately
According to instructions
In the Defence Code. Do not
Take well-loved pets (including birds)
Into your shelter – they will consume
Fresh air. Leave the old and bed-
ridden, you can do nothing for them.
Remember to press the sealing
Switch when everyone is in
The shelter. Set the radiation
Aerial, turn on the geiger barometer.
Turn off your television now.
Turn off your radio immediately
The Services end. At the same time
Secure explosion plugs in the ears
Of each member of your family. Take
Down your plasma flasks. Give your children
The pills marked one and two
In the CD green container, then put
Them to bed. Do not break
The inside airlock seals until
The radiation All Clear shows
(Watch for the cuckoo in your
perspex panel), or your District
Touring Doctor rings your bell.
If before this, your air becomes
Exhausted or if any of your family
In critically injured, administer
The capsules marked 'Valley Forge'
(Red pocket in No. 1 Survival Kit)
For painless death. (Catholics
Will have been instructed by their priests
What to do in this eventuality.)
This announcement is ending. Our President

Has already given orders for
Massive retaliation – it will be
Decisive. Some of us may die.
Remember, statistically
It is not likely to be you.
All flags are flying fully dressed
On Government buildings – the sun is shining.
Death is the least we have to fear.
We are all in the hands of God,
Whatever happens happens by His Will.
Now go quickly to your shelters.

[1961]

PETER PORTER

1. *DEW:* Distant Early Warning, the radar system for tracking intercontinental ballistic missiles.

Peter Porter (1929-2010) was a prolific Australian-born poet who moved to London from 1951, becoming one of the most influential British poets of the post-war period and a central figure in The Group during the 1950s and 60s. This poem gained some notoriety after Denys Hawthorne's reading of it in the style of a radio announcer on the BBC's Third Programme in 1961 was so convincing that listeners believed Britain actually was under nuclear attack.

The end of the world

The bird had come to the very end of its song
and the tree was dissolving under its claws.

And in the sky the clouds were twisting
and darkness flowed through all the cracks
into the sinking vessel of the landscape.

Only in the telegraph wires
a message still
crackled:

C·—·—·o——m—e· h···o——m—e·
y—·—o——u··— h···a·—v···—e·
a·— s···o——n—.

[1963]

MIROSLAV HOLUB
translated from the Czech by Ewald Osers
➤ 285

The Horses

Barely a twelvemonth after
The seven days war that put the world to sleep,
Late in the evening the strange horses came.
By then we had made our covenant with silence,
But in the first few days it was so still
We listened to our breathing and were afraid.
On the second day
The radios failed; we turned the knobs; no answer.
On the third day a warship passed us, heading north,
Dead bodies piled on the deck. On the sixth day
A plane plunged over us into the sea. Thereafter
Nothing. The radios dumb;
And still they stand in corners of our kitchens,
And stand, perhaps, turned on, in a million rooms
All over the world. But now if they should speak,
If on a sudden they should speak again,
If on the stroke of noon a voice should speak,
We would not listen, we would not let it bring
That old bad world that swallowed its children quick
At one great gulp. We would not have it again.
Sometimes we think of the nations lying asleep,
Curled blindly in impenetrable sorrow,
And then the thought confounds us with its strangeness.
The tractors lie about our fields; at evening
They look like dank sea-monsters couched and waiting.
We leave them where they are and let them rust:

'They'll moulder away and be like other loam.'
We make our oxen drag our rusty ploughs,
Long laid aside. We have gone back
Far past our fathers' land.
                                        And then, that evening
Late in the summer the strange horses came.
We heard a distant tapping on the road,
A deepening drumming; it stopped, went on again
And at the corner changed to hollow thunder.
We saw the heads
Like a wild wave charging and were afraid.
We had sold our horses in our fathers' time
To buy new tractors. Now they were strange to us
As fabulous steeds set on an ancient shield
Or illustrations in a book of knights.
We did not dare go near them. Yet they waited,
Stubborn and shy, as if they had been sent
By an old command to find our whereabouts
And that long-lost archaic companionship.
In the first moment we had never a thought
That they were creatures to be owned and used.
Among them were some half-a-dozen colts
Dropped in some wilderness of the broken world,
Yet new as if they had come from their own Eden.
Since then they have pulled our ploughs and borne our loads,
But that free servitude still can pierce our hearts.
Our life is changed; their coming our beginning.

EDWIN MUIR

Edwin Muir (1887-1959) was a poet and novelist from Orkney. With his wife
Willa Muir he also published significant translations of the work of Kafka
and several German-language writers. 'The Horses', his best-known poem,
was first published in his 1956 collection *One Foot in Eden*.

László Nagy (1925-78) was a poet and translator. His poem 'Squared by Walls',
published only in 1965, is about the Hungarian uprising of 1956 and his guilt
at remaining a mere observer rather than an active participant in those mom-
entous events. ➤ 348

Squared by Walls

Couldn't you have died,
or at least bled,
instead of pacing the floor
stunned with despair?
You kept clear of the trouble –
bullets, armoured track, emblazoned
girls' screams. Nor for you broken
wheels, scattering rooftiles,
grim gangs of working lads,
and soot-brindled petals.
You did not spill one drop
of blood, and when it stopped,
you had only gone grey and mad.

In usual winter weather
you stand here; no other
but yourself, and wide awake,
squared by walls that echo
a cough like raking
gunfire. It's not merely
your flesh that's cold;
mind and heart are frozen, – crowned
by knives of ice.
You are ashamed of your melting phrases;
as if you had lost the right
to think of spring
and lilacs, – the lung-like trees blossoming.
What agony for a Lord of Life!
Yet, deep in the secret places
of your being, furtive with guilt,
you are breathing on the frosted pane,
that you may look out at the world again.

LÁSZLÓ NAGY
translated from the Hungarian by Tony Connor & George Gömöri

To Imre Nagy

You were impersonal, too, like the other leaders,
bespectacled, sober-suited; your voice lacked
sonority, for you didn't know quite what to say

on the spur of the moment to the gathered multitude. This urgency
was precisely the thing you found strange. I heard you,
old man in pince-nez, and was disappointed,
not yet to know

of the concrete yard where most likely the prosecutor
rattled off the sentence, or
of the rope's rough bruising, the ultimate shame.

Who can say what you might have said
from that balcony? Butchered opportunities
never return. Neither prison nor death
can resharpen the cutting edge of the moment

once it's been chipped. What we can do, though, is remember
the hurt, reluctant, hesitant man
who nonetheless soaked up
anger, delusion
and a whole nation's blind hope,

when the town woke to gunfire
that blew it apart.

GYÖRGY PETRI
translated from the Hungarian by Clive Wilmer & George Gömöri

György Petri (1943-2000) was a dissident Hungarian poet known his uncom-
promising stance and disquieting, disenchanted poetry.

Imre Nagy was Prime Minister of the short-lived revolutionary Government
of Hungary, October-November 1956. Petri's poem telescopes two events:
Nagy's speech from the balcony of the Parliament building in Budapest on
23 October, when the uprising began, and his execution by order of the Kádár
regime in June 1958. The last two lines refer to the second Soviet attack on
the Government and its supporters, 4 November 1956. [CW/GG]

The Prague of Jan Palach

And here stomp Picasso's bulls.
And here march Dalí's elephants on spidery legs.
And here beat Schönberg's drums.
And here rides Señor de la Mancha.
And here the Karamazovs are carrying Hamlet.
And here is the nucleus of the atom.
And here is the cosmodrome of the Moon.
And here stands a statue without the torch.
And here runs a torch without the statue.
And it's all so simple. Where
Man ends, the flame begins –
And in the ensuing silence can be heard the crumbling
of ash worms. For
those milliards of people, taken by and large,
are keeping their traps shut.

[1969]

MIROSLAV HOLUB
translated from the Czech by George Theiner
➤ 285

Jan Palach, a young student, set himself on fire in Wenceslas Square on 16
January 1969 in protest at the crushing of the 'Prague Spring' after the 1968
Soviet invasion. Following the publication of this translation, in Britain, in
1969, Holub's work was banned in Czechoslovakia for the next 12 years.

VIETNAM WAR | 1956–1975

TOTAL DEATHS: 1–3.8 MILLION

The Vietnam War was the longest war – and the first defeat – in American history. But for many Vietnamese, this was the American War, a continuation of the First Indochina War, or Anti-French Resistance War (1946-54: total deaths 400,00–900,000), which followed Viet Minh leader Ho Chi Minh's declaration of an independent Democratic Republic of Vietnam in September 1945. The opening poem by Pham Po [➤ 352] in this selection is from the earlier conflict. Vietnam had been a French colony since 1886, with French involvement continuing even during the Second World War when Vichy French collaborated with the Japanese occupying forces [➤ 240-42].

Independence was granted to Cambodia, Laos and Vietnam after the 1954 ceasefire, with Vietnam partitioned at the 17th parallel, the Viet Minh under Ho taking control of North Vietnam with backing from China and a US-supported anti-Communist government installed in a separate State of Vietnam in the south under Ngô Đình Diệm. An insurgency by South Vietnamese rebels – the National Liberation Front or Viet Cong (VC) – helped destabilise the increasingly divisive and corrupt regime of Diệm, who was eventually ousted and executed in a military coup in the same month as US President Kennedy's assassination, November 1963. By then the insurgency had grown into a full-scale war between nationalist forces and the South Vietnamese army supported by a swelling number of US military "advisors". Under the new US President, Lyndon B. Johnson, American involvement escalated, with the despatch of US Marines to South Vietnam in 1965 marking the beginning of the American ground war. Many of the poems which follow are by writers then engaged in fighting that ground war on either side.

As well as US air strikes on strategic targets in South Vietnam, towns and cities in North Vietnam were heavily bombed, as were Laos [➤ 375] and Cambodia in parallel "secret wars". By the late 60s, atrocities like My Lai [➤ 381] and the napalming of civilians had made the conflict deeply unpopular in the US. Veterans were joining protests against a war viewed by many as unwinnable. The withdrawal of American military support made the eventual defeat of South Vietnamese forces inevitable. A total of 58,220 Americans died in the war, along with 500 Australians (see Bruce Dawe's 'Homecoming' ➤ 386).

The opposite, Vietnamese perspective was set out by Nguyen Ba Chung in *Mountain River* (1998): 'During the war, support for the fight was overwhelming. Pham Tien Duat's 'The Fire in the Lamps' [➤ 359] presents the fight as a natural consequence of an ancient identity. [...] These lines, like many other poems of resistance, resonate deeply in Vietnam – they suggest the soul of a man who can find himself at home only after he has fought off his adversaries. They invoke a sense of selfless heroism and an iron determination that rise out of an unfathomable depth – the impassioned individual facing insurmountable odds with almost reckless abandon, not out of hatred but out of love. They are the authors' call to arms, not for themselves, but in defense of others, in defense of their own identity, in defense of their reasons for existence.'

Beautiful and Loving Days Gone By

I shot him.
The beautiful and loving days gone by
Could not stop me.
Perhaps he had forgotten those days,
But I remember still
The rice fields of my village, the endless sea of rice,
The morning dew like pearls on the sides of the road,
And the two of us,
Our school books together in one bag,
Our clothes rumpled by sleep,
Our bare feet moving side by side.
In our swinging hands, the handful of rice
Our mothers rolled into a leaf of the areca palm.
Our wide conical hats had long chin straps.
In our pockets, a matchbox, a cricket inside...
How beautiful, how gentle the days gone by.
And yet those days held no future for us.
Many years ago
He left our village to join the enemy.
I'm sad and I'm angry.
I met him.
I shot him.
The beautiful and loving days gone by
Could not stop me.

His body lay on the dike,
No longer the boy I had known.
I looked at his face
Grieved for the boy I had lost.

[1950]

PHAM HO
translated from the Vietnamese by Nguyen Ba Chung,
Nguyen Quang Thieu & Bruce Weigl

Bombing at Seng Phan

Far from Seng Phan
I hear bombs exploding day and night,
Sounds of low howling planes
Echo in my head.

Closer, I hear a slow rumble,
Trees wrenched from the ground.
Cups and glasses shake,
Kerosene lamps tremble,
Bombs fall like wild beasts.

I stand at Seng Phan,
But greater than the sounds of bombs is the music from the caves,
Is the sound of the mines of the combat engineers exploding,
The sound of the slow drawing of the water pipe,
The sound of the great whine of the trucks heading up the road.

In the battle zone,
The sound of bombing seems so small.

[Seng Phan, December 1963]

PHAM TIEN DUAT
translated from the Vietnamese by Nguyen Quang Thieu,
Nguyen Ba Chung & Kevin Bowen

Pham Tien Duat (1941-2007) was born in Phu Tho town, Phu Tho province.
His father taught Chinese and French; his mother was an illiterate peasant.
Joining the army after graduating from college, he lived, wrote and fought
American troops along the Truong Son Trail (Ho Chi Minh Trail) throughout
the Vietnam War, producing hundreds of poems relating to the war between
1964 and 1975. ➤ 359, 385

Pham Ho (1926-2007) was a much celebrated writer for children, the author
of numerous books of poems and stories, of plays and cartoons, as well as a
painter. Born into a Confucian family in the village of Nhan Am, An Nho'n
district, Binh Dinh province, he became a cultural activist during the war of
resistance against the French, moving to North Vietnam, and later helped found
the Vietnam Writers' Association.

The Green Beret

He was twelve years old,
and I do not know his name.
The mercenaries took him and his father,
whose name I do not know,
one morning upon the High Plateau.
Green Beret looked down on the frail boy
with the eyes of a hurt animal and thought,
a good fright will make him talk.
He commanded, and the father was taken away
behind the forest's green wall.
'Right kid tell us where they are,
Tell us where or your father – dead.'
With eyes now bright and filled with horror
the slight boy said nothing.
'You've got one minute kid,' said Green Beret,
'tell us where or we kill father'
and thrust his wrist-watch against a face all eyes,
the second-hand turning, jerking on its way.
'OK boy ten seconds to tell us where they are.'
In the last instant the silver hand shattered the
sky and the forest of trees.
'Kill the old guy' roared Green Beret
and shots hammered out
behind the forest's green wall
and sky and trees and soldiers stood,
in silence, and the boy cried out.
Green Beret stood
in silence, as the boy crouched down
and shook with tears,
as children do when their father dies.
'Christ,' said one mercenary to Green Beret,
'he didn't know a damn thing
we killed the old guy for nothing.'
So they all went away,
Green Beret and his mercenaries.

And the boy knew everything.
He knew everything about them, the caves,

the trails, the hidden places and the names,
and in the moment that he cried out,
in that same instant,
protected by frail tears
far stronger than any wall of steel,
they passed everywhere
like tigers
across the High Plateau.

HO THIEN
translated from the Vietnamese

A copy of **Ho Thien**'s poem 'The Green Beret' is said to have been found on his body in Vietnam somewhere near the Cambodian border in 1966. Nothing is known of him.

Tran Da Tu was born in 1940 in Hai Duong, northern Vietnam. He published two volumes of poems in Vietnam, *The Time of Writing Love Poetry* (1960) and *Declaration of Love in the Night* (1965), before receiving political asylum and moving to the United States. 'Love Tokens' was written in Saigon in 1964.

Love Tokens

I'll give you a roll of barbwire
A vine for this modern epoch
Climbing all over our souls
That's our love, take it, don't ask

I'll give you a car bomb
A car bomb exploding on a crowded street
On a crowded street exploding flesh and bones
That's our festival, don't you understand

I'll give you a savage war
In the land of so many mothers
Where our people eat bullets and bombs instead of rice
Where there aren't enough banana leaves to string together
To replace mourning cloths for the heads of children

I'll give you twenty endless years
Twenty years seven thousand nights of artillery
Seven thousand nights of artillery lulling you to sleep
Are you sleeping yet or are you still awake

On a hammock swinging between two smashed poles
White hair and whiskers covering up fifteen years
A river stinking of blood drowning the full moon
Where no sun could ever hope to rise

I'm still here, sweetie, so many love tokens
Metal handcuffs to wear, sacks of sand for pillows
Punji sticks to scratch your back, fire hoses to wash your face
How do we know which gift to send each other
And for how long until we get sated

Lastly, I'll give you a tear gas grenade
A tear gland for this modern epoch
A type of tear neither sad nor happy
Drenching my face as I wait.

TRAN DA TU
translated from the Vietnamese by Linh Dinh

Garden Fragrance

Last night a bomb exploded on the veranda
But sounds of birds sweeten the earth this morning.
I hear the fragrant trees, look in the garden,
Find two silent clusters of ripe guavas.

LAM THI MY DA
translated from the Vietnamese by Martha Collins & Thuy Dinh

Lam Thi My Da (*b.* 1949) is from Le Thuy District, Quang Binh Province, in central Vietnam, and now lives in Hué. She served in Quang Tri and Thua Thien with North Vietnam's youth brigades and women's engineering units. She has published several collections in Vietnam as well as *Green Rice* (2005), an English translation of her poetry by Martha Rhodes and Thuy Dinh.

Noon: Taking Aim

Stalking through jungles
this the the way
you hold your M-16

muzzle down
sniffing
like a hundred-dollar dog.

Keep it on automatic.
Anything moves in the bushes
you open fire:

this damn '16
will rise for you
and point the bastard out.

Kind of pull it sideways,
like this
Don't aim the damn thing:

point it.
And don't forget: just a touch
on the trigger.

If you're holding it
like this
it'll get him.

WALTER McDONALD

Walter McDonald (*b.* 1934) served in the US Air Force from 1957 to 1971, was a pilot in Vietnam and an instructor at the Air Force Academy, retiring as a major. He has published many books, and from 1971 to 2002 taught at Texas Tech University, where he is the Paul Whitfield Horn Professor Emeritus.

The Next Step

The next step you take
may lead you into an ambush.

The next step you take
may trigger a tripwire.

The next step you take
may detonate a mine.

The next step you take
may tear your leg off at the hip.

The next step you take
may split your belly open.

The next step you take
may send a sniper's bullet through your brain.

The next step you take.
The next step you take.

The next step.
The next step.

The next step.

W.D. EHRHART

W.D. Ehrhart (*b.* 1948) enlisted in the US Marines in 1966 at the age of 17, and fought in Vietnam with the First Battalion, First Marines, receiving a Purple Heart, two Presidential Unit Citations, and promotion to sergeant. He later became active in Vietnam Veterans Against the War, and has published numerous books and written extensively on poetry from the Korean and Vietnam Wars, including the anthologies *Carrying the Darkness: The Poetry of the Vietnam War* (1985) and (with Philip K. Jason) *Retrieving Bones: Stories and Poems of the Korean War* (1999). ➢ 316, 383

Mines

In Vietnam I was always afraid of mines:
North Vietnamese mines, Vietcong mines,
American mines,
whole fields marked with warning signs.

A bouncing betty comes up waist high –
cuts you in half.
One man's legs were laid
alongside him in the Dustoff:
he asked for a chairback, morphine.
He screamed he wanted to give
his eyes away, his kidneys,
his heart...

BRUCE WEIGL
➤ 365

The Fire in the Lamps

1 *The Lamps*

You and I, we are crossing to the other side of the bridge,
to a country where the land is peaceful,
where fruit hangs thick from trees
and red blossoms shimmer among dark leaves
like signal lamps that promise summer.
Here the tomato is a small lantern
to warm the long winter night,
the pepper, the flame of an oil lamp,
so hot it will burn your tongue.
Our land, so filled with life,
one branch might light a field.
But men travel across oceans,
their planes swarm through night fog,

loom out in the darkness
like fireflies over fresh dug graves.
Seven hundred meters up,
they can see the light of a
match shine on a human face.

One thousand meters up,
they can see the small oil lamps.
Eight thousand meters,
the sparks of the welding stick.
But no matter how far,
they dive and bomb,
the land flares up,
bombs blow out lights,
blood oozes.

Still, night after night we light the lamps.
Lamps to return a thousand years of fire.
Fire, from the time of our first struggling life,
kept from generation to generation
in the rice husks and ashes of household fires.
The flames in the lamps,
half our life is there.
They try to take it away,
try to take our hearts away.

2 *The Blackout*

You and I, we are crossing to the other side of the bridge
where there are peaceful country lands,
where night after night the blackout makes
the earth and sky grow larger
and we can see nothing
as darkness covers all.

The yellow bamboo to show its charm – must
ask for the wind's help.
A girl to show her grace must
reach for words.
A flower to show its ways must
have sweet fragrance.

Here darkness covers all
to cover the enemy's eyes.

In the blackout the tractors grind,
they tow our guns up to the high fields.
The voice of the commander
yells out the guns' positions.
The soldier's call from the sighting tube
tells where the gun pits are.
It carves out a rhythm, sways in time to the rice pestle's cadence,
calling across the battle.

In the blackout, ruts
mark out the roads.
Endless convoys, trucks rumbling down,
moving, one after the other,
like children playing
dragon and snake,
one child humming behind the other.

In the blackout, there are songs.
Young volunteers raise their voices
as they break rocks, repair roads,
the smell of cordite
still hanging in the air.

In the blackout, on the roads
the troops are marching.
Shock troops pass.

Darkness is everywhere.
In the bomb crater, immense darkness.
A curtain conceals the coming campaign.

Night in Viet Nam
is an intermission between two acts,
home to many transformations.
Darkness covers all.
Nothing can be seen.
We move forward through what fantastic sounds.

3 Lighting the Lamps

You and I, we are crossing to the other side of the bridge
where there are peaceful country lands
the enemy bombs and strafes day and night.
Within the land, we light the lamps,
the lamps crawl into the bamboo tubes
so children can go to school at night
the lamps crawl into the mountain caves
light for the night shifts, the lamps crawl under the blankets
for the young village women to read letters from lovers.

Let's light the lamps on the peaks of the mountains
for the enemy to drop bombs to blow off rocks
we'll use for bridges and for roads.
Let's switch on the headlights of our trucks,
then amid the flares and shells, switch them off, turn back
to confuse the planes, then go on driving.

Tomorrow, tomorrow, when we win
I'll hold your hand and we'll walk beneath the moon and stars.
We'll light up our lamps and watch the moon from the veranda,
we'll light our lanterns, our five-pointed stars.

Together, we'll walk to the house, decorate it with these shining
        lanterns.
Our wedding-hall. We'll make a shadow lamp
cut shapes of these men and women,
these scenes, troops in the darkness, their images
to march forever on the walls
by the light of our burning lanterns.

[1967]

PHAM TIEN DUAT
translated from the Vietnamese by Nguyen Quang Thieu & Kevin Bowen
➤ 353

The Way of Tet

Year of the monkey, year of the human wave,
the people smuggled weapons in caskets through the city
in long processions undisturbed
and buried them in Saigon graveyards.
At the feet of their small Buddhas
weary bar girls burned incense
before the boy soldiers arrived
to buy them tea and touch them
where they pleased. Twenty years
and the feel of a girl's body
so young there's no hair
is like a dream, but living is a darker thing,
the iron burning bee who drains the honey,
and he remembers her
twisting in what evening
light broke into the small room in the shack
in the labyrinth of shacks
in the alley where the lost and corrupted kept house.
He undressed her for the last time,
each piece of clothing
a sacrifice she surrendered to the war
the way the world had become.
Tomorrow blood would run in every province.
Tomorrow people would rise from tunnels everywhere
and resurrect something ancient from inside them, and the boy
who came ten thousand miles to touch her small self lies beside
the girl whose words he can't
understand, their song a veil between them.

She is a white bird in the bamboo, fluttering.
She is so small he imagines
he could hold all of her
in his hands and lift her to the black
sky beyond the illumination round's white light
where she would fly from her life
and the wounds from the lovers would heal,
the broken skin grow back.

But he need only touch her, only
lift the blanket from her shoulders
and the automatic shape of love unfolds,
the flare's light burning down on them,
lost in a wave that arrives
after a thousand years of grief
at their hearts.

BRUCE WEIGL

On the Anniversary of Her Grace

Rain and low clouds blown through the valley,
rain down the coast raising the brackish
rivers at their high tides too high,
rain and black skies that come for you.

Not excellent and fair,
I wake from a restless night of dreams of her
whom I will never have again
as surely as each minute passing
makes impossible another small fulfilment
until there's only a lingering
I remember, a kiss I had imagined
would come again and again to my face.

Inside me the war had eaten a hole.
I could not touch anyone.
The wind blew through me to the green place
where they still fell in their blood.
I could hear their voices at night.

I could not undress in the light
her body cast in the dark rented room.

I could keep the dragons at the gate.
I could paint my face and hide
as shadow in the triple-canopy jungle.

I could not eat or sleep then walk all day
and all night watch a moonlit path for movement.

I could draw leeches from my skin
with the tip of a lit cigarette
and dig a hole deep enough to save me
before the sun bloodied the hills we could not take
even with our lives
but I could not open my arms to her
that first night of forgiveness.
I could not touch anyone.
I thought my body would catch fire.

BRUCE WEIGL

Bruce Weigl (*b.* 1949) enlisted in the US Army at 18 and served for three years, including a year in Vietnam from December 1967. His many books include *The Circle of Hanh: A Memoir* (1999), and thirteen books of poetry in which Vietnam at war and in peace has been his central concern, the latest of which, *The Abundance of Nothing* (2012), was a Pulitzer Prize finalist.

Selective Service

We rise from the snow where we've
lain on our backs and flown like children,
from the imprint of perfect wings and cold gowns,
and we stagger together wine-breathed into town
where our people are building
their armies again, short years after
body bags, after burnings. There is a man
I've come to love after thirty, and we have
our rituals of coffee, of airports, regret.
After love we smoke and sleep
with magazines, two shot glasses
and the black and white collapse of hours.
In what time do we live that it is too late
to have children? In what place
that we consider the various ways to leave?

There is no list long enough
for a selective service card shriveling
under a match, the prison that comes of it,
a flag in the wind eaten from its pole
and boys sent back in trash bags.
We'll tell you. You were at that time
learning fractions. We'll tell you
about fractions. Half of us are dead or quiet
or lost. Let them speak for themselves.
We lie down in the fields and leave behind
the corpses of angels.

CAROLYN FORCHÉ

Carolyn Forché (*b.* 1950) is one of America's leading poets and an outspoken human rights activist known especially for writing and championing poetry of witness. She has published four collections of poetry, including *The Country Between Us* (1981), which drew on her experiences in El Salvador during the civil war, *The Angel of History* (1994), and *Blue Hour* (2003), as well as translations of Claribel Alegría, Mahmoud Darwish and Robert Desnos, the landmark anthology *Against Forgetting: Twentieth-Century Poetry of Witness* (1993), and most recently, *Poetry of Witness: The Tradition in English: 1500-2001* (with Duncan Wu, 2014). ➤ See also 22

Doug Anderson (*b.* 1943) served in Vietnam as a corpsman with a Marine infantry battalion in 1967. His books include *Keep Your Head Down: Vietnam, the Sixties, and a Journey of Self-Discovery* (2009), and poetry collections including *The Moon Reflected Fire* (1994), from which these two poems are taken. He has taught at colleges including the William Joiner Center for the Study of War and Its Social Consequences, and latterly, Emerson College, Boston.

Bamboo Bridge

We cross the bridge, quietly.
The bathing girl does not see us
till we've stopped and gaped like fools.
There are no catcalls, whoops,
none of the things that soldiers do;
the most stupid of us is silent, rapt.

She might be fourteen or twenty,
sunk thigh deep in the green water,
her woman's pelt a glistening corkscrew,
a wonder, a wonder she is; I forgot.
For a moment we all hold the same thought,
that there is life in life and war is shit.
For a song we'd all go to the mountains,
eat pineapples, drink goat's milk,
find a girl like this, who cares
her teeth are stained with betel nut,
her hands as hard as feet.
If I can live another month it's over,
and so we think a single thought,
a bell's resonance.
And then she turns and sees us there,
sinks in the water, eyes full of hate;
the trance broken.
We move into the village on the other side.

DOUG ANDERSON

Night Ambush

We are still, lips swollen with mosquito bites.
A treeline opens out onto paddies
quartered by dikes, a moon in each,
and in the center, the hedged island of a village
floats in its own time, ribboned with smoke.
Someone is cooking fish.
Whispers move across water.
Children and old people. Anyone between
is a target. It is so quiet
you can hear a safety clicked off
all the way on the other side.
Things live in my hair. I do not bathe.
I have thrown away my underwear.
I have forgotten the why of everything.

I sense an indifference larger than anything
I know. All that will remain of us
is rusting metal disappearing in vines.
Above the fog that clots the hill ahead
a red tracer arcs and dims.
A black snake slides off the paddy dike
into the water and makes the moon shiver.

DOUG ANDERSON

Night Crossing

The boat was coming in the dead of night,
Clusters of bamboo, rising tide.
The oars shook the starry sky,
A stray bird circled above,
Noiselessly the boat came in the dark,
As searchlights swept the tops of the palms.
Guns loaded, eyes wide open,
We waited.

The sampan girl had rolled up the legs of her trousers,
A cold wind blew in from the shore,
As she helped load our packs on board,
Bringing the scent of flowers and dry grass
From the forests and mountains.
As our hands touched we imagined her cheeks blushed red,
I felt her warm breath, sensed her quick gestures.

Heavily laden, the boat pulled.
'May we help you, Comrade?' I asked.
She shook her head and made the sampan turn fast.
Living in the midst of enemy posts and blockhouses,
She was used to containing joy and sorrow.

The boat went out into the darkness,
As the tide kept rising.

The oars again shook heaven and stars,
On the other bank, the palms beckoned us.
The sampan girl kept her eyes fixed
On the distant watchtower at the village entrance.
Her nimble hands worked the oars,
Her slender silhouette loomed over the river.
A few more strokes! The bank was now close,
Tender joy welled up in our hearts.
A burst of gunfire tore the night,
Sparks flew in the darkness.
'Sit still,' she said, 'don't move!'
The boat kept advancing towards the enemy.
It gave a lurch, bullets whizzed overhead,
Her silhouette towered over the waves.
'Sit down, sister, we will row,' we pleaded.
'No, brothers, don't worry.' Again the boat moved forward.

The whole dark sky was in turmoil,
Our hearts ached, our eyes shone with anger
Enemy slugs swept the river,
In our hands, our rifles burned with hatred.

The boat was now safely moored to a tree,
We were forced to leave quickly,
But slowly shook the girl's hand,
'Thank you,' we whispered.
A smile lighted her face as she shook her head,
'I'm a member of the Revolutionary Youth,' she said,
'I've only done my duty.'
Her figure faded in the night.
As we marched across the village,
We still heard her muffled steps.

Valiant girl, your memory
Is alive in our hearts
As we press on to other battles.

GIANG NAM
translated from the Vietnamese by Don Luce, John Schafer & Jacqui Chagnon
➤ 371

Starlight Scope Myopia

Gray-blue shadows lift
shadows onto an oxcart.

Making night work for us,
the starlight scope brings
men into killing range.

The river under Vi Bridge
takes the heart away

like the Water God
riding his dragon.
Smoke-colored

Viet Cong
move under our eyelids,

lords over loneliness
winding like coral vine through
sandalwood & lotus,

inside our lowered heads
years after this scene

ends. The brain closes
down. What looks like
one step into the trees,

they're lifting crates of ammo
& sacks of rice, swaying

under their shared weight.
Caught in the infrared,
what are they saying?

Are they talking about women
or calling the Americans

beaucoup dien cai dau?
One of them is laughing.
You want to place a finger

to his lips & say 'shhhh'.
You try reading ghost talk

on their lips. They say
'up-up we go', lifting as one.
This one, old, bowlegged,

you feel you could reach out
& take him in your arms. You

peer down the sights of your M-16,
seeing the full moon
loaded on an oxcart.

YUSEF KOMUNYAKAA

Yusef Komunyakaa (*b*. 1949) served in the US Army from 1968 to 1971, with one tour of duty in Vietnam (1969-70) as a combat reporter and editor for the military paper, *Southern Cross*, covering actions and stories, interviewing fellow soldiers, and publishing articles on Vietnamese history, which earned him a Bronze Star. The son of a carpenter, he later went to university on the GI Bill, graduating in 1975. He is a highly influential American poet known for his poetry's fusion of jazz rhythms and vernacular speech and for poems drawing on his experiences in Vietnam as a black soldier fighting alongside white men and on the struggles of African Americans in his native Louisiana.

Giang Nam (*b*. 1929) joined the Vietnamese Resistance in 1945, and first wrote poetry for friends and comrades in prison: 'From my experience as an activist fighting against the French during the nine years of resistance and then staying in the South to continue the struggle against the US, I have become a poet. I know one thing: this struggle is the source of my inspiration, the instigator of both the joy and the sadness in my poems.' [quoted in *Mountain River*] ➤ 369

Facing It

My black face fades,
hiding inside the black granite.
I said I wouldn't,
dammit: No tears.
I'm stone. I'm flesh.
My clouded reflection eyes me
like a bird of prey, the profile of night
slanted against morning. I turn
this way – the stone lets me go.
I turn that way – I'm inside
the Vietnam Veterans Memorial
again, depending on the light
to make a difference.
I go down the 58,022 names,
half-expecting to find
my own in letters like smoke.
I touch the name Andrew Johnson;
I see the booby trap's white flash.
Names shimmer on a woman's blouse
but when she walks away
the names stay on the wall.
Brushstrokes flash, a red bird's
wings cutting across my stare.
The sky. A plane in the sky.
A white vet's image floats
closer to me, then his pale eyes
look through mine. I'm a window.
He's lost his right arm
inside the stone. In the black mirror
a woman's trying to erase names:
No, she's brushing a boy's hair.

YUSEF KOMUNYAKAA

Thanks

Thanks for the tree
between me & a sniper's bullet.
I don't know what made the grass
sway seconds before the Viet Cong
raised his soundless rifle.
Some voice always followed,
telling me which foot
to put down first.
Thanks for deflecting the ricochet
against that anarchy of dusk.
I was back in San Francisco
wrapped up in a woman's wild colors,
causing some dark bird's love call
to be shattered by daylight
when my hands reached up
& pulled a branch away
from my face. Thanks
for the vague white flower
that pointed to the gleaming metal
reflecting how it is to be broken
like mist over the grass,
as we played some deadly
game for blind gods.
What made me spot the monarch
writhing on a single thread
tied to a farmer's gate,
holding the day together
like an unfingered guitar string,
is beyond me. Maybe the hills
grew weary & leaned a little in the heat.
Again, thanks for the dud
hand grenade tossed at my feet
outside Chu Lai. I'm still
falling through its silence.
I don't know why the intrepid
sun touched the bayonet,

but I know that something
stood among those lost trees
& moved only when I moved.

YUSEF KOMUNYAKAA

Overheard over S.E. Asia

'White phosphorus, white phosphorus,
mechanical snow,
where are you falling?'

'I am falling impartially on roads and roofs,
on bamboo thickets, on people.
My name recalls rich seas on rainy nights,
each drop that hits the surface eliciting
luminous response from a million algae.
My name is a whisper of sequins. Ha!
Each of them is a disk of fire,
I am the snow that burns.
                                        I fall
wherever men send me to fall –
but I prefer flesh, so smooth, so dense:
I decorate it in black, and seek
the bone.'

DENISE LEVERTOV

Born in England, **Denise Levertov** (1923-97) became one of America's greatest modern poets. Throughout her life, she worked also as a political activist, campaigning tirelessly for civil rights and environmental causes, and against the Vietnam War, the Bomb and US-backed regimes in Latin America. Her poems in collections such as *To Stay Alive* (1971) and *The Freeing of the Dust* (1975) focus on the suffering of the Vietnamese people. During the Second World War she volunteered as a nurse in Blitz-torn London. ➤ 195

James Fenton (*b.* 1949) is a leading English poet and former Oxford Professor of Poetry. His 1982 collection *The Memory of War* includes poems drawing on his experiences as a war reporter in Vietnam and Cambodia during the 1970s.

Cambodia

One man shall smile one day and say goodbye.
Two shall be left, two shall be left to die.

One man shall give his best advice.
Three men shall pay the price.

One man shall live, live to regret.
Four men shall meet the debt.

One man shall wake from terror to his bed.
Five men shall be dead.

One man to five. A million men to one.
And still they die. And still the war goes on.

JAMES FENTON

Laos

The *Stars and Stripes* says
'Nixon promises no war in Laos!'

I stand in the Aerial Port,
on my way to Nah Trang,
and there's a line of grunts
a mile long,
a snake full of killing evil,
waiting in line.

I've never seen a line like this,
in eleven months,
and ask a friendly looking,
blond grunt,
'What's happening?'

He says,
'Laos'
and spits at my feet,
looks the other way
so I know he's had enough
of talking about the War.

They all died.
Every one of them died,
before anyone knew they were there.

DAVID WIDUP

David Widup served with the US Air Force in 1969-70, and was honourably discharged in 1972. He has said that the Vietnam veterans parade in New York City in 1985 marked the beginning of his writing career and his recovery from the war. 'I can't remember what it feels like to not have the war in my bones. [...] I have woken up afraid almost every morning since I went to Vietnam over 25 years ago.[...] I have never read a poem, read a story, or seen a movie that tells what it was like to be there. Many are true as impressions, but they are false in tone, fact and mood. Others are lacking in the details, the specifics. And I know why. It is those details that pull the trigger that drag us back into hell. It takes a crazy person to pull them out like a rotted skeleton and put them on a page and make them real again – for all the world to see and smell. I have made myself sick writing about Vietnam. And I haven't even started. Not really.' [David Widup, *In Country*, 1994]

Elliot Richman published his first poem many years after his service in Vietnam, in 1984, when he was 42. He has since published several collections, including *A Bucket of Nails: Poems from the Second Indochina War* (1990), *Honorable Manhood* (1994), *Walk on Trooper* (1994) and *The World Dancer* (2004).

The Woman He Killed

I was doorgunner in a Huey
flak-jacketed,
visor down,
when a VC lady leaped from high grass

in a hot LZ
amid swirling dust
and bellowing rotor blades.

Lurching off the earth
in the frenzied buck of the chopper
we stared face to face.

Black hair waving in Laotian wind,
blouse rustling in updraft
she looked so young and beautiful
even as she attempted to blow me
away with a handgun,
the only weapon she had.

And I who didn't want to bust
even one cap in her heart
fired my weapon on Rock & Roll.

So the dance we did
was under tracer light
with mad machine-gun music,
her black blouse unbuttoning,
torso sawing in half
as if caressed by a chain saw
before sinking
into sheets of dust.

ELLIOT RICHMAN

Blood Trail

I had a man in my sights
and I pulled the trigger.
I knew he would fall,
but I didn't think
he would get back up
and run like a wounded deer.

We followed the blood trail
and found only an abandoned pack.
The Lieutenant grabbed the cash,
the men divided the food,
Intelligence was sent the love letters
and I took the credit
for a probable kill.
Intelligence reported the letters
were from a woman in the southern provinces.
Which meant she was arrested,
beaten, raped, locked in a tiger cage,
forced to eat her own excrement
and beaten again.

If she confessed, she was executed.
If she refused to confess, she was executed.
It was a funny war.
I shot a man.
I killed a woman.

JON FORREST GLADE

Jon Forrest Glade was drafted into the US infantry and served with the 101st Airborne in and around the A Shau Valley in northern South Vietnam in 1969 before leaving aboard a hospital plane four and half months later.

Food for Thought, 3:00 A.M.

They moved in unison
like dancers in a ballet,
the spider, twenty inches from my rifle,
the VC, twenty feet farther out, in line,
each slowly sliding a leg forward.
I let the man take one more step
so as not to kill the bug.

DAVID CONNOLLY

David **Connolly** served in Vietnam with the 11th Armored Cavalry Regiment. He is proud of having been – and continues to be – a Vietnam Veteran against the War (VVAW), and appeared in the documentary film *Voices in Wartime* (2005): 'I try to write a poem, write a piece of poetry that would point out to you the absolute inhumanity of combat.[…] What I tried to do there was to give you this vision of looking down my rifle, you know, and give you the feeling of how hard-hearted I was at the time, that I could put this spider's life up above this, really, my contemporary, you know? He may have been my enemy, but I'm sure he was a 19-year-old kid, too, you know?' [*Voices in Wartime*].

Wearing Faces

Stand down, guard duty on the bunker line,
Weed-rapping about the last operation.

And someone said: Ya 'memba
That little dude got blown away
In that shitstorm of RPGs?[1]

Then someone cried
And none of us could hold it.

For a while afterwards
It seemed easier for us
To act like we were men.

DAVID CONNOLLY

1. *RPGs:* rocket-propelled grenades.

No Lie, GI

We had a deal, he and I,
of no bullshit between us.
If one of us got wounded,
the other wouldn't lie.

So when he got hit
and he asked me,
'How's my leg?'
I looked him straight in the eye
and told him, 'It's fine.'
It looked fine to me,
laying over there,
looked as good as new.

DAVID CONNOLLY

Corporal Charles Chungtu, U.S.M.C.

This is what the war ended up being about:
we would find a VC village,
and if we could not capture it
or clear it of Cong,
we called for jets.
The jets would come in, low and terrible,
sweeping down, and screaming,
in their first pass over the village.
Then they would return, dropping their first bombs
that flattened the huts to rubble and debris.
And then the jets would sweep back again
and drop more bombs
that blew the rubble and debris
to dust and ashes.
And then the jets would come back once again,
in a last pass, this time to drop napalm
that burned the dust and ashes to just nothing.
Then the village
that was not a village anymore
was our village.

BRYAN ALEC FLOYD
➤ 381

Women, Children, Babies, Cows, Cats

'It was at My Lai or Sonmy or something,[1]
it was this afternoon... We had these orders,
we had all night to think about it –
we was to burn and kill, then there'd be nothing
standing, women, children, babies, cows, cats....
As soon as we hopped the choppers, we started shooting.
I remember... as we was coming up upon one area
in Pinkville, a man with a gun... running – this lady...
Lieutenant LaGuerre[2] said, "Shoot her." I said,
"You shoot her, I don't want to shoot no lady."
She had one foot in the door... When I turned her,
there was this little one-month-year-old-baby
I thought was her gun. It kind of cracked me up.'

ROBERT LOWELL

1. American troops commanded by Lt William Calley murdered 104 unarmed Vietnamese civilians at Son My, a hamlet near the village of My Lai, on 16 March 1968. The massacre was covered up, but Calley eventually stood trial and was sentenced to life imprisonment with hard labour, yet only served three and half years' house arrest following President Nixon's intervention, challenged by Lowell in his article 'Judgment Deferred on William Calley' in *The New York Review of Books* (6 May 1971). Lowell's poem draws on Calley's testimony at his court-martial: 'I was ordered to go in there and destroy the enemy [...] I did not sit down and think in terms of men, women, and children. They were all classified the same [...] everything went into a body count – VC [Viet Cong], buffalo, pigs, cows.' 2. Calley is personified as *LaGuerre*, the War, in this dramatic monologue in the voice of one of Calley's men, based on the testimony of Paul Meadlo, who balked at his orders before joining in.

Robert Lowell (1917-77) was one of America's greatest modern poets, and a prominent opponent of the Vietnam War. ➢ 343

Bryan Alec Floyd (*b.* 1966) graduated from Seattle University before serving in the Marine Corps from 1966 to 1968. His books include *The Long War Dead* (1976), 'which treats the Vietnam War in the manner of the *Spoon River Anthology*: portraits (often posthumous) of 47 marines who served in Vietnam and what the war did to them; violent, sentimental, sometimes grimly comic' [*Los Angeles Herald Examiner*].

A Bummer

We were going single file
Through his rice paddies
And the farmer
Started hitting the lead track[1]
With a rake
He wouldn't stop
The TC[2] went to talk to him
And the farmer
Tried to hit him too
So the tracks went sideways
Side by side
Through the guy's fields
Instead of single file
Hard On, Proud Mary
Bummer, Wallace, Rosemary's Baby
The Rutgers Road Runner
And
Go Get Em–Done Got Em
Went side by side
Through the fields
    If you have a farm in Vietnam
And a house in hell
Sell the farm
And go home

MICHAEL CASEY

1. *track:* tracked vehicle (each with its army name).   2. *TC:* track commander.

Michael Casey (*b.* 1947) was drafted into the US Army after graduating from college in 1968, and served in Vietnam as a military police officer in Quang Ngai province. His debut collection, *Obscenities* (1972), was chosen for the Yale Series of Younger Poets by Stanley Kunitz, who wrote of Casey's work: 'He has had the original insight and the controls to produce a kind of anti-poetry that befits a kind of war empty of any kind of glory.' His other books include *Millrat* (1999), *The Million Dollar Hole* (2001) and *Raiding a Whorehouse* (2004).

Guerrilla War

It's practically impossible
to tell civilians
from the Viet Cong.

Nobody wears uniforms.
They all talk
the same language
(and you couldn't understand them
even if they didn't).

They tape grenades
inside their clothes,
and carry satchel charges
in their market baskets.

Even their women fight.
And young boys.
And girls.

It's practically impossible
to tell civilians
from the Viet Cong;

after awhile,
you quit trying.

W.D. EHRHART
➤ 358

Stop

Stop!...
He ran three steps ahead of me,
a ranger with the face of a child.
His shot just missed my temple.

My fingers tightened on the trigger,
the AK's clip pressed to my stomach.
Only half a second.
No! Only a tenth of a second.
If my finger moved half a millimeter
he'd be dead.

Stop!
He kept running.
I kept running after him, rifle ready.
Chasing him was much harder
than pulling the trigger. A tenth of a second was all it would take.

I knew that so well.
Just as I knew
if the situation had been reversed,
and I ran in front empty handed,
and he ran behind, M-16 in hand,
very likely I'd have been dead.
Life and death crossing in a tenth of a second.

The clip pressed hard to my stomach,
beating harder, a disquieting thought:
'It's easy to kill him,
to save him is harder...'
'It's easy to kill him,
save him, it's harder...'

The thought ran forward through me,
forward...
forward.
With all my strength,
I forced him
to stop!

[Quang Tri Campaign, 1972]

NGUYEN DUY
translated from the Vietnamese by Nguyen Ba Chung

384

White Circle

Bomb smoke rises in black circles.
White circles hover along the ground.
My friend and I walk on in silence,
The silence expected after war.
No loss greater than death.
The white mourning band takes the shape of a zero.
My friend, inside that white circle
A head burns with fire.

[1972]

PHAM TIEN DUAT
translated from the Vietnamese by Nguyen Quang Thieu
➤ 353

'White Circle' – written by Pham Tien Duat in 1971 and published in the
Thanh Nien journal in 1972 – immediately created a firestorm. Because of its
emphasis on the tragic consequences of the war, it was criticised [in North
Vietnam] for undermining the war effort. In a trip back to the rear in 1971,
Pham Tien Duat stopped at a friend's village. It was one of thousands of
nondescript villages in the North whose special trade was to make mosquito
nets for the army. Everywhere the village was covered with pieces of white
cloth, left out in the sun to be dried, before being dyed camouflage green.
What deeply shocked Pham Tien Duat was that half of the young women
and children in the villages wore white bands on their foreheads – a sign of
mourning for those who never returned from battle.[...] This was the first sign
of division in what had been total dedication to and identification with the
national cause. A fissure had begun to open; in the postwar period, it would
widen. [Nguyen Ba Chung, *Mountain River: Vietnamese Poetry from the Wars:
1948-1993* (1998)]

Nguyen Duy (*b.* 1948) served as a militia squad leader in 1965, defending the
area of Hàm Ròng-Thanh Hóa from American attacks. In 1966, he joined the
signal corps, fighting in various battlefields including Khe Sanh and along
Route 6, south of Laos. He left the army in 1976 and studied Vietnamese
linguistics and literature in Hô Chí Minh City, where he still lives. Born into
a peasant family in a village in Thanh Hóa province, he is one of Vietnam's
most celebrated poets, credited with breathing new life into *luc bat*, the poetic
style used in Vietnamese folk poetry. Nguyen Ba Chong's translation of his
work, *Distant Road: Selected Poems*, was published in the US in 1999. ➤ 387

385

Homecoming

All day, day after day, they're bringing them home,
they're picking them up, those they can find, and bringing them home,
they're bringing them in, piled on the hulls of tanks, in medevacs, in
        convoys,
they're zipping them up in green plastic bags,
they're tagging them now in Saigon, in the mortuary coolness
they're giving them names, they're rolling them out of
the deep-freeze lockers – on the tarmac at Tan Son Nhut
the noble jets are whining like hounds,
they are bringing them home
– curly-heads, kinky-hairs, crew-cuts, balding non-coms
– they're high, now, high and higher, over the land, the steaming *chow mein*,
their shadows are tracing the blue curve of the Pacific
with sorrowful quick fingers, heading south, heading east,
home, home, *home* – and the coasts swing upward, the old ridiculous
        curvatures
of earth, the knuckled hills, the mangrove-swamps, the desert emptiness...
in their sterile housing they tilt towards these like skiers
– taxiing in, on the long runways, the howl of their homecoming rises
surrounding them like their last moments (the mash, the splendour)
then fading at length as they move
on to small towns where dogs in the frozen sunset
raise muzzles in mute salute,
and on to cities in whose wide web of suburbs
telegrams tremble like leaves from a wintering tree
and the spider grief swings in his bitter geometry
– they're bringing them home, now, too late, too early.

BRUCE DAWE

Bruce Dawe (*b.* 1930) is one of Australia's leading poets. After leaving school at 16, he did a variety of jobs. He joined the Royal Australian Air Force in 1959, initially as a trainee telegraphist but re-mustered as an education assistant, and was posted to Malaysia for six months. Leaving the RAAF in 1968, he went into teaching. He has published numerous books including two editions of *Sometimes Gladness: Collected Poems* in 1978 and 2006.

Quang Tri

Everywhere we dug there were white bones.
What could we do? Could we just leave them?
What kind of foundation would they make for our house?
My friends were perplexed. Were they our bones or their bones?
No, I told them, there are no American bones here.
The Americans left years ago and took their bones with them.
These skeletons, scattered all over our land,
Belong only to Vietnamese.

[Quang Tri, 1974]

VAN LE
translated from the Vietnamese by Nguyen Ba Chung with Bruce Weigl

Van Le (*b.* 1949) is a film director, poet, novelist and short story writer. He joined the army after leaving school and fought in major battles against US and South Vietnamese forces. After working as a journalist and in the Documentary Film Studio in Hô Chí Minh City, he rejoined the army during the Cambodian-Vietnamese War, returning to the studio when that war ended in 1978.

Red Earth – Blue Water

Bombs ploughed into the red earth, berry red
Scorching sunlight burned the noon air like kiln fire

Bomb-raked funnels turned into rose water wells
A noiseless stream of blue water gushing up

That's our country isn't it friend.
The maddening agony, the honey comes from within.

[Quang Binh, 1975]

NGUYEN DUY
translated from the Vietnamese by Nguyen Ba Chung
➤ 385

ISRAEL, PALESTINE & LEBANON | 1947–present

The poems in this section relate to the wars and conflicts involving Israel, Palestine, Lebanon, neighbouring Arab states and militant groups summarised below, as well as to continuing daily conflict in these countries and territories. Difficult conditions and conflicting claims are responsible for the wide range in some of the figures which include both civilian and military casualties.

1948 Palestine War ('The Catastophe' in Arabic, 'War of Independence' in Hebrew): 30 November 1947 – 20 July 1949. DEATHS: Israel 6,373; Egypt, Jordan and Syria, 4,000–15,000. Two phases:
(1) 1947–48 Civil War in Mandatory Palestine between the Jewish and Arab communities of Palestine still under British rule.
(2) 1948 Arab–Israeli War after 15 May 1948, end of British Mandate: Transjordan, Egypt, Syria and Iraq against the new State of Israel. Israel kept the area allotted to it under the UN Partition Plan but also took control of almost 60% of the area allotted to the proposed new Palestinian Arab state. Transjordan occupied the remainder of the West Bank, Egypt military took control of the the Gaza Strip. No Arab Palestinian state was created. Around 700,000 Palestinian Arabs fled or were expelled from the area that became Israel.

Six-Day War: 5–10 June 1967. Israel against Egypt, Syria, Jordan and Iraq. Israel captured the Gaza Strip and the Sinai Peninsula from Egypt, the West Bank (including East Jerusalem) from Jordan, and the Golan Heights from Syria. DEATHS: Israel 796–1003; Arab states 23,560,

Yom Kippur War: 6–25 October 1973. Coalition of Arab states led by Egypt and Syria against Israel. DEATHS: Israel 7,250–8,800; Arab states 8,000–18,500.

War of Attrition: 1 July 1967 – 7 August 1970. Conflict between Israel and Egypt. DEATHS: Israel 721–1,551; Egypt, PLO and allies, 13,000 approx.

Black September: Jordanian Civil War, September 1970 – July 1971. Conflict between Jordan and Palestine Liberation Organisation (PLO) ending with their expulsion to Lebanon. DEATHS: Jordan 82; PLO and Syrians 4,000–20,600+.

Lebanese Civil War: 13 April 1975 – 13 October 1990. Conflict between factions backed by Israel or Syria. DEATHS: 120,000–150,000.

1982 Lebanon War: 6 June 1982 – June 1985. Israeli invasion of southern Lebanon resulting in the expulsion of the PLO. DEATHS: Israel 657; Syrians and Palestinians 19,085 (plus 800–3,500 killed in Sabra and Shatila massacre).

First Intifada: 8 December 1987 – 13 September 1993. Palestinian uprising against Israeli occupation of the Palestinian territories. DEATHS: Israel 160; Palestinians 2162.

Operation Grapes of Wrath (April War): 11–27 April 1996. Israeli offensive against Lebanon to end shelling of northern Israel by Hezbollah (DEATHS: Israel 3, Hezbollah 14, civilians 170), including First Qana massacre. ➤ 406

Second Intifada: 28 September 2000 – 8 February 2005. Palestinian uprising against Israeli occupation of the Palestinian territories. DEATHS: Israel 1,010; Palestinians 3,354.

2006 Lebanon War: 12 July – 14 August 2006. Conflict in the Golan Heights between Israel and Hezbollah. DEATHS: Israel 163, Hezbollah 500, others 1300.

April the Twentieth, 1948

My mother in the morning
on April the twentieth in the morning,
was drowsily reading the newspapers
my father in the morning
gave her with her glass of tea.

And drowsily thus
did my mother and peacefully
read
holding the glass of tea in her hand
in the third
line
in the paper the death
of her son.

DAHLIA KAVEH
translated from the Hebrew by Jean Nordhaus

Yitzhak and Amalya

It hurt us terribly.
Six thousand young men fell

in the war.
In the field between Magdal and Ashdod

red poppies flamed,
briars grew.

There my brother Yitzhak fell too,
my big brother.

Nineteen years old,
his body still not found.

His name is carved on a communal headstone
in the Military Plot at Kefar Warburg.

Only a few letters remain
wrapped in sackcloth,

bearing only his
initials

embroidered with blue wool thread,
and with love

his girlfriend 'for life'
Amalya.

YISRAEL PINCAS
translated from the Hebrew by Laura Fargas

War

I, too, have declared war:
You'll need to divert part of the force
deployed to wipe out the Arabs –
to drive them out of their homes
and expropriate the land –
and set it against me.
You've got tanks and planes,
and soldiers by the batallion;
you've got the rams' horn in your hands
with which to rouse the masses;
you've got men to interrogate and torture;
you've got cells for detention.
I have only this heart
with which I give shelter
to an Arab child.
Aim your weapon at it;
even if you blow it apart
it will always,
always mock you.

AHARON SHABTAI
translated from the Hebrew by Peter Cole

Dahlia Kaveh teaches biology in Jerusalem. Her first book of poetry, published in 1990, received the Hebrew University's Harry Hershon Prize. [➤ 389]

Yisrael Pincas was born in 1935 in Sofia, Bulgaria, and emigrated to Palestine in 1944. He has published several books of poetry. [➤ 389]

Aharon Shabtai (*b.* 1939) is one of Israel's leading poets, the foremost Hebrew translator of Greek drama, and an outspoken critic of Israeli policies in the Palestinian territories and of human rights violations against Palestinians. He has published over 20 books of poetry in Israel, and two selections in the US, *Love & Selected Poems* (1997) and *J'Accuse* (2003), both translated into English by Peter Cole, who writes that the poems in *J'Accuse* 'fulfil not only the traditional functions of political poetry – witnessing, remembrance, protest – but also, in their audacity, serve as a poet's mirror held up to his people: one designed to show the nation its true reflection, now and in days to come.' [➤ 390]

Yehuda Amichai (1924-2000) was Israel's greatest modern poet, and one of the first to write in colloquial Hebrew. Born in Wurzburg, Germany, and raised speaking both Hebrew and German, he emigrated with his Orthodox Jewish family to Mandate Palestine in 1935. As a young man he volunteered for the British Army during the Second World War, later fighting in the 1948 Palestine War, and served again with the Israel Defence Forces in 1956 and 1973. Within ten years of publishing his first book of poetry in Hebrew, in 1955, he was widely regarded as Israel's leading poet, first coming to international attention when Ted Hughes and Daniel Weissbort included his work in their first issue of *Modern Poetry in Translation* in 1965. He won many major literary awards, including the Israel Prize in 1982, his country's highest state honour, for effecting 'a revolutionary change in both the subject matter and the language of poetry'. ➤ 391, 396, 397, 409

Jerusalem

On a roof in the Old City
laundry hanging in the late afternoon sunlight:
the white sheet of a woman who is my enemy,
the towel of a man who is my enemy,
to wipe off the sweat of his brow.

In the sky of the Old City
a kite.
At the other end of the string,
a child
I can't see
because of the wall.

We have put up many flags,
they have put up many flags.
To make us think that they're happy.
To make them think that we're happy.

YEHUDA AMICHAI
translated from the Hebrew by Chana Bloch & Stephen Mitchell

Jerusalem

I

Stone cries to stone,
Heart to heart, heart to stone,
And the interrogation will not die
For there is no eternal city
And there is no pity
And there is nothing underneath the sky
No rainbow and no guarantee –
There is no covenant between your God and me.

II

It is superb in the air.
Suffering is everywhere
And each man wears his suffering like a skin.
My history is proud.
Mine is not allowed.
This is the cistern where all wars begin,
The laughter from the armoured car.
This is the man who won't believe you're what you are.

III

This is your fault.
This is a crusader vault.
The Brook of Kidron flows from Mea She'arim.
I will pray for you.
I will tell you what to do.
I'll stone you. I shall break your every limb.

Oh I am not afraid of you
But maybe I should fear the things you make me do.

IV

This is not Golgotha.
This is the Holy Sepulchre,
The Emperor Hadrian's temple to a love
Which he did not much share.
Golgotha could be anywhere.
Jerusalem itself is on the move.
It leaps and leaps from hill to hill
And as it makes its way it also makes its will.

V

The city was sacked.
Jordan was driven back.
The pious Christians burned the Jews alive.
This is a minaret.
I'm not finished yet.
We're waiting for reinforcements to arrive.
What was your mother's real name?
Would it be safe today to go to Bethlehem?

VI

This is the Garden Tomb.
No, *this* is the Garden Tomb.
I'm an Armenian. I am a Copt.
This is Utopia.
I came here from Ethiopia.
This hole is where the flying carpet dropped
The Prophet off to pray one night
And from here one hour later he resumed his flight.

VII

Who packed your bag?
I packed my bag.
Where was your uncle's mother's sister born?
Have you ever met an Arab?
Yes I am a scarab.
I am a worm. I am a thing of scorn.
I cry Impure from street to street
And see my degradation in the eyes I meet.

I am your enemy.
This is Gethsemane.
The broken graves look to the Temple Mount.
Tell me now, tell me when
When shall we all rise again?
Shall I be first in that great body count?
When shall the tribes be gathered in?
When, tell me, when shall the Last Things begin?

IX

You are in error.
This is terror.
This is your banishment. This land is mine.
This is what you earn.
This is the Law of No Return.
This is the sour dough, this the sweet wine.
This is my history, this my race
And this unhappy man threw acid in my face.

X

Stone cries to stone,
Heart to heart, heart to stone.
These are the warrior archaeologists.
This is us and that is them.
This is Jerusalem.
These are the dying men with tattooed wrists.
Do this and I'll destroy your home.
I have destroyed your home. You have destroyed my home.

JAMES FENTON
➤ 374

In Jerusalem

In Jerusalem, and I mean within the ancient walls,
I walk from one epoch to another without a memory
to guide me. The prophets over there are sharing

the history of the holy... ascending to heaven
and returning less discouraged and melancholy, because love
and peace are holy and are coming to town.
I was walking down a slope and thinking to myself: How
do the narrators disagree over what light said about a stone?
Is it from a dimly lit stone that wars flare up?
I walk in my sleep. I stare in my sleep. I see
no one behind me. I see no one ahead of me.
All this light is for me. I walk. I become lighter. I fly
then I become another. Transfigured. Words
sprout like grass from Isaiah's messenger
mouth: 'If you don't believe you won't believe.'
I walk as if I were another. And my wound a white
biblical rose. And my hands like two doves
on the cross hovering and carrying the earth.
I don't walk, I fly, I become another,
transfigured. No place and no time. So who am I?
I am no I in ascension's presence. But I
think to myself: Alone, the prophet Muhammad
spoke classical Arabic. 'And then what?'
Then what? A woman soldier shouted:
Is that you again? Didn't I kill you?
I said: You killed me... and I forgot, like you, to die.

MAHMOUD DARWISH
translated from the Arabic by Fady Joudah

Mahmoud Darwish (1942-2008) was the poetic voice of the Palestinian people.
One of the most acclaimed contemporary poets in the Arab world, he was also
a prominent spokesman for human rights. Born in the village of al-Birweh in
Galilee, Palestine, he spent most of his life in exile. His family fled to Lebanon
in 1948 when the Israeli Army destroyed their village, returning secretly to the
newly created state of Israel after a year. From 1970 to 1996 he lived in Mos-
cow, Cairo, Beirut, Cyprus and Paris, finally settling in Ramallah. A member
of the PLO's Executive Council, he wrote the 1988 Palestinian Declaration of
Independence, resigning in opposition to the Oslo accords. His many honours
included the Lenin Peace Prize, the Lannan Prize for Cultural Freedom, the
French medal for Knight of Arts and Letters and the Prinz Claus Award from
the Netherlands. When he died in hospital in the US from complications
following heart surgery, Palestinian President Mahmoud Abbas immediately
declared three days of national mourning. ➤ 407, 418

395

from **Patriotic Songs**

1

Our baby was weaned in the first days
of the war. And I ran out to stare
at the terrible desert.

At night I came back again to see him
asleep. Already he's forgetting
his mother's nipples, and he'll go on forgetting
till the next war.

And so, while he was still small,
his hopes were closed, and his complaints
opened wide – never to close again.

2

The war broke out in autumn at the empty border
between sweet grapes and oranges.

The sky is blue, like veins in a woman's tormented thighs.

The desert is a mirror for those looking at it.

11

The town I was born in was destroyed by shells.
The ship in which I sailed to the land of Israel was drowned later in
          the war.

The barn at Hammadia where I had loved was burned out.
The sweet shop at Ein-Gedi was blown up by the enemy.
The bridge at Ismailia, which I crossed to and fro on the eve of my loves,
has been torn to pieces.

Thus my life is wiped out behind me according to an exact map:

How much longer can my memories hold out?

The girl from my childhood was killed and my father is dead.

That's why you should never choose me
to be a lover or a son, or a bridge-crosser
or a citizen or a tenant.

15

Even my loves are measured by wars:
I am saying this happened after the Second
World War. We met a day before the
Six-Day War. I'll never say
before the peace '45–'48 or during
the peace '56–'67.

But knowledge of peace
passes from country to country,
like children's games,
which are so much alive, everywhere.

YEHUDA AMICHAI
translated from the Hebrew by Yehuda Amichai & Ted Hughes
➤ 391

The Place Where We Are Right

From the place where we are right
flowers will never grow
in the spring.

The place where we are right
is hard and trampled
like a yard.

But doubts and loves
dig up the world
like a mole, a plow.
And a whisper will be heard in the place
where the ruined
house once stood.

YEHUDA AMICHAI
translated from the Hebrew by Stephen Mitchell

Interviews with My Father: Those Times

The war was long and took many turns.
They got so smart killing people – sending one bomb in,
waiting for the flood of help, then bombing again.

They stopped you anywhere, checkpoints like weeds
sprouting from a road you'd just driven. You learned who
ran what part of where because you only wanted your family to win.

Even kids during that summer's ceasefire, we knew
our volleyball tournament in a Maronite town meant a name change
for our teammate Muhammad while sunlight scowled over the dirt court.

But the fighting didn't stop long. Eventually some leader
would be killed and whole villages were leveled by sundown.
Recruiters always dogging us, offering each boy

a machine gun, two packs of smokes, and five dollars daily.
Some bullied us. Others wielded guilt:
we were cowards and traitors and deserters.

They used the whistling bombs you couldn't see coming,
but you heard the beehive rounds, whirring
metal wings, flechettes flying angry and low,

fusing their hum to the air, until we could feel
that drone in our skulls, until we could see
how easily bees peel skin away.

Only Israelis had fighter jets, passing so close, like clippers
raking the tips of our hair. Our hearts sawing, the reeling contrails
made of our robbed breath. And when they kidnapped my cousin,

her father let his beard grow long as though
it would bring her back, a chin full of tinder for smoke signals
or the threads groomed the air for signs of her.

Those times. I can still taste the singed dust of buildings.
The sky like fiberglass. Everything brought together,
furious, ignited. At least we had that –
the common tongue of chaos.

RUTH AWAD

Ruth Awad (*b.* 1987) is a poet, tattoo artist and copywriter with an MFA
from Southern Illinois University Carbondale. She recently completed her
first book-length collection, much of it written in response to her father's
stories of growing up in war-torn Lebanon and emigrating to the US.

Desert

The cities dissolve, and the earth is a cart loaded with dust
Only poetry knows how to pair itself to this space.

No road to this house, a siege,
and his house is graveyard.
     From a distance, above his house
     a perplexed moon dangles
     from threads of dust.

I said: this is the way home, he said: No
     you can't pass, and aimed his bullet at me.
Very well then, friends and their homes
     in all of Beirut's are my companions.

Road for blood now –
     Blood about which a boy talked
     whispered to his friends:
          nothing remains in the sky now
          except holes called 'stars'.

The city's voice was too tender, even the winds
would not tune its strings –

The city's face beamed
like a child arranging his dreams for nightfall
bidding the morning to sit beside him on his chair.

They found people in bags:
      a person   without a head
      a person   without hands, or tongue
      a person   choked to death
      and the rest had no shapes and no names.
          – Are you mad? Please
                    don't write about these things.
A page in a book
      bombs mirror themselves inside of it
      prophecies and dust-proverbs mirror themselves inside of it
      cloisters mirror themselves inside of it, a carpet made of
            the alphabet disentangles thread by thread
falls on the face of the city, slipping out of the needles of memory.
A murderer in the city's air, swimming through its wound –
its wound is a fall
that trembled to its name – to the haemorrhage of its name
and all that surrounds us –
houses left their walls behind
            and I am no longer I.

Maybe there will come a time in which you'll accept
to live deaf and mute, maybe
they'll allow you to mumble: death
            and life
            resurrection
            and peace unto you.

From the wine of the palms to the quiet of the desert...et cetera
from a morning that smuggles its own intestines
      and sleeps on the corpses of the rebels...et cetera
from streets, to trucks
      from soldiers, armies...et cetera
from the shadows of men and women...et cetera
from bombs hidden in the prayers of monotheists and infidels...et
   cetera

from iron that oozes iron and bleeds flesh...et cetera
from fields that long for wheat, and grass and working hands...et
    cetera
            and heap darkness upon us...et cetera
from legends of the dead who pronounce life, who steer our life...
    et cetera
from talk that is slaughter   and slaughter   and slitters
    of throats...et cetera
from darkness to darkness to darkness
I breathe, touch my body, search for myself
            and for you, and for him, and for the others

and I hang my death
between my face and this haemorrhage of talk...et cetera

You will see –
        say his name
        say you drew his face
        reach out your hand toward him
        or smile
        or say I was happy once
        or say I was sad once
        you will see:
                there is no country there.

Murder has changed the city's shape – this stone
                        is a child's head –
and this smoke is exhaled from human lungs.
Each thing recites its exile...   a sea
                    of blood – and what
do you expect on these mornings except their arteries set to sail
into the darkness, into the tidal wave of slaughter?

Stay up with her, don't let up –
she sits death in her embrace
and turns over her days
                tattered sheets of paper.

Guard the last pictures
of her topography –
she is tossing and turning in the sand
in an ocean of sparks –
on her bodies
are the spots of human moans.

Seed after seed are cast into our earth—
fields feeding on our legends,
guard the secret of these bloods.
                    I am talking about a flavor to the seasons
                    and a flash of lightning in the sky.

Tower Square – (an engraving whispers its secrets
                                to bombed-out bridges...)
Tower Square – (a memory seeks its shape
                                among dust and fire...)
Tower Square – (an open desert
                                chosen by winds and vomited... by them...)
Tower Square – (It's magical
                        to see corpses move/their limbs
                        in one alleyway, and their ghosts
                        in another/and to hear their sighs...)
Tower Square – (West and East
                        and gallows are set up—
                        martyrs, commands...)
Tower Square – (a throng
        of caravans: myrrh
                        and gum Arabica and musk
                                and spices that launch the festival...)
Tower Square – (let go of time...
                        in the name of place)

– Corpses or destruction,
        is this the face of Beirut?
– and this
        a bell, or a scream?
– A friend?
– You? Welcome.

Did you travel? Have you returned? What's new with you?
– A neighbour got killed…/

. . . .

A game /
– Your dice are on a streak.
– Oh, just a coincidence /

. . . .

> Layers of darkness
> and talk dragging more talk.

[Beirut, 1982]

ADONIS
translated from the Arabic by Khaled Mattawa

Adonis [Ali Ahmad Said Esber] was born in 1930 in the village of Al Qassabin, Latakia, Syria, to an Alawite family, and taught to read and to memorise poems by his father while working on the family farm. He took his writing name at the age of 17 'to alert napping editors to his precocious talent and his pre-Islamic, pan-Mediterranean muses'. Imprisoned for membership of the Syrian Social Nationalist Party in 1955, he moved to Beirut on his release, later emigrating to France in 1980 to escape the Lebanese Civil War. He has lived in Paris since then. Widely regarded as the greatest living poet writing in Arabic, he has been nominated several times for the Nobel Prize. His particular, highly innovative achievement has been to overturn the formalism of traditional Arabic poetry, using free verse, variable metrics and prose poetry to address themes of exile and transformation.

Corporal Rabinovitch's Corpse

'Corporal Rabinovitch's corpse
has been laid to eternal rest.'

His corpse was granted rest.
His corpse applied for a furlough;
the application, favourably despatched.

'Corporal Rabinovitch's corpse
has been laid to eternal rest
at the Military Cemetery in Kiryat Shaul.'

But the paperwork created discrimination.
Corporal Rabinovitch's restless soul
has been trying since last Friday to hitchhike

back from Lebanon to his parents' apartment
in Tel Aviv and just can't get a lift.

ASSIA MARGULIS
translated from the Hebrew by Elaine Magarrell

Assia Margulis (*b.* 1949) emigrated from Russia to Israel in 1972. A member
of Kibbutz Negbah, she teaches mathematics, and has worked to help with the
absorption of Russian immigrants. She has published several books of poetry.

Exodus

The street is empty
as a monk's memory,
and faces explode in the flames
like acorns –
and the dead crowd the horizon
and doorways.
No vein can bleed
more than it already has,
no scream will rise
higher than it's already risen.
We will not leave!

Everyone outside is waiting
for the trucks and the cars
loaded with honey and hostages.
We will not leave!

The shields of light are breaking apart
before the rout and the siege;
outside, everyone wants us to leave.
But we will not leave!

Ivory white brides
behind their veils
slowly walk in captivity's glare, waiting,
and everyone outside wants us to leave,
but we will not leave!

The big guns pound the jujube groves,
destroying the dreams of the violets,
extinguishing bread, killing the salt,
unleashing thirst
and parching lips and souls.
And everyone outside is saying:
'What are we waiting for?
Warmth we're denied,
the air itself has been seized!
Why aren't we leaving?'
Masks fill the pulpits and brothels,
the places of ablution.
Masks cross-eyed with utter amazement;
they do not believe what is now so clear,
and fall, astonished,
writhing like worms, or tongues.
We will not leave!

Are we in the inside only to leave?
Leaving is just for the masks,
for pulpits and conventions.
Leaving is just
for the siege-that-comes-from-within,
the siege that comes from the Bedouin's loins,
the siege of the brethren
tarnished by the taste of the blade
and the stink of crows.
We will not leave!

Outside they're blocking the exits
and offering their blessings to the impostor,
praying, petitioning
Almighty God for our deaths.

[1983]

TAHA MUHAMMAD ALI
translated from the Arabic by Peter Cole, Yahya Hijazi & Gabriel Levin

Taha Muhammad Ali (1931-2011) was a much celebrated Palestinian poet
whose work is driven by a storyteller's vivid imagination, disarming humour
and unflinching honesty. Born in rural Galilee, Muhammad Ali was left without
a home when his village was destroyed during the Arab-Israeli War of 1948. Out
of this history of shared loss and survival, he created art of the first order. An
autodidact, he owned a souvenir shop now run by his sons in Nazareth. ➢ 412

Grapes of Wrath

It happens on a Thursday, just after 2pm,
when ancient cultures and beliefs conspire
and vultures spiral above a peacekeepers' camp,
where cedars age slowly and the *Litani* River
caresses the ground where Jesus turned water
into wine, where artillery salvos rip the air
on their long flight and bite deep, deep into
that place of safety vaporising its concrete
walls and burning and blistering and tearing
apart the mass of terrified flesh and innocent blood
seeking refuge from the hate of man.

A soldier climbs from the rubble limbs
and discarded faces, his eyes caked black with tears,
his hands at arm's length clutching the newborn baby
that looks like a headless doll.

[First Qana Massacre, 18 April 1996]

MICHAEL J. WHELAN

During 'Operation Grapes of Wrath' Israeli Defence Force artillery shells struck a Fijian UN compound in South Lebanon protecting 800 civilians fleeing the fighting, killing approximately 120 people.

Michael J. Whelan (*b.* 1970) is a soldier, poet, writer and historian living in Tallaght, Co. Dublin, with over 24 years service in the Irish Defence Forces. He was deployed as a United Nations Peacekeeper in South Lebanon and with K.FOR in Kosova during the 1990s. ➤ 391, 494

He Embraces His Murderer

He embraces his murderer to win him over.
Will you be furious if I survive?
My brother... my brother...
What can I possibly have done to make you destroy me?
Look, two birds are flying above our heads –
aim at them instead! aim this hell away from me!
Why don't we go to my mother's place where she'll cook beans for us –
What do you say? Why not?
You're fed up with my embrace and sick of my smell?
Aren't you worn out by the fear that's inside me?
So chuck that pistol in the river!
How about it? Yes?
An enemy on the riverbank has got us covered with a machinegun?
So shoot him instead!
Then we'll both escape his fire, and you'll be released from this crime.
What do you think?
You're going to kill me and let the enemy go home – to our home?
And then you'll return to the law of the jungle?
What did you do with my mother's coffee – with our mother's coffee?
What did I do to make you destroy me... my brother?
I won't let you out of my arms.
I will never release you.

[1986]

MAHMOUD DARWISH
translated from the Arabic by Sarah Maguire & Sabry Hafez
➤ 395

407

Fears

1

We spent another spring in peace.
Now it's autumn, and the tom-tom drums
slowly thunder from the far North.
A war. Tank carriers again travel northwards
and twenty-year-old Yonni, Yishai and Rafi
are donning their bulletproof vests on the borders.
Perhaps before the Holidays. Perhaps in a time
like Yom Kippur. Again we'll see the taliths
like white flags on the backdrop of khaki and blood.
The sound of drums steadily becomes stronger
from newscast to newscast.
Like the Northstar, a flare bomb;
tomorrow night, the siren will wail.
I hear war.

2

At night, aircraft fly through Jerusalem's skies.
Watchmen! What of the night?
The same *khamsin* blows as it did that Yom Kippur
when a squadron of Phantom airplanes crossed the border
of holiness, and later sounded the huge noise –
'awful-awful-awful' –
I have set watchmen on thy walls, oh Jerusalem,
who shall never hold their peace, day or night.
Over their heads fly the F-16s,
while Gai and Eviatar are illuminated
in the pilots' canopies, as if under wedding chuppas.
Now, when they fly through September darkness,
going out eastward, climbing northwards –
oh watchman, what of the night?
Soon it will be rent by the broken sounds
of the holiday shofar: we will genuflect and say
'holy-holy-holy' – but someone at the Military Rabbinate
already will have prepared the flag-covered coffins.
And the graves.

3

I'm beset by fears,
as if though fog
silently float the faces
of Yuval, Shai, and Ittai.
I love them.
Gabbi and Amir slowly turn
their heads away from me,
as if they know my blessings
won't help them, as they didn't help
five years ago.
I cry out in a choked voice –
Lay not, lay not Thine Hand upon the lad –
not another time, not now –
but again I see the fire,
the kindling, the knife,
and there's no ram caught in the thicket.

Who, who this time will be
your son, your only son, Isaac?

[September 1986]

RA'AYA HARNIK
translated from the Hebrew by Maurya Simon

Ra'aya Harnik (*b.* 1933) was brought from Berlin to Mandate Palestine as a
child in 1936. She has published poetry, children's books and non-fiction,
and edited documentary programmes for Israel Radio for several years. Since
her retirement she has worked as a volunteer at the Spielberg Foundation.

The Diameter of the Bomb

The diameter of the bomb was thirty centimetres
and the diameter of its effective
range – about seven metres.
And in it four dead and eleven wounded.

And around them in a greater circle
of pain and time are scattered
two hospitals and one cemetery.
But the young woman who was
buried where she came from
over a hundred kilometres away
enlarges the circle greatly.
And the lone man who weeps over her death
in a far corner of a distant country
includes the whole world in the circle.
And I won't speak at all about the crying of orphans
that reaches to the seat of God
and from there onward, making
the circle without end and without God.

YEHUDA AMICHAI
translated from the Hebrew by Yehuda Amichai & Ted Hughes
➤ 391

The Night after the Surgeries

This is the night after the surgeries:
everyone is lying sedated with morphine,
and the screws extracted from them
have been transferred to the Secret Service.
As usual, everything is closed up there
in the hospital – just as the operating rooms
are closed, and the extracted nails and screws
are sealed up in a special evidence bag,
in case the Secret Service expresses an interest in them,
in case they want to know from which
village hardware store
they were taken
to fulfil their purpose.

DAHLIA FALAH
translated from the Hebrew by Rachel Tzvia Back

And Today Is a Holiday

And today is a holiday, but
'shoot only if shot at'
and today is a holiday, but
'if they flee, shoot above their heads'
and today is a holiday
'if they continue running
it is all right to aim at their legs'
a holiday that's ended
'don't aim at the head'
a holiday no one would recall
'no shooting children'
and no one would forget the scent
'avoid women'
the scent rising from distant houses
'keep away from mosques'
an odour penetrating to the capillaries
opening memory like a rose.
In the voyages of jasmine
and olive oil,
in the shimmering essences we
arrive at the valley of difference
like leaves of a black tree
plucked, drifting with the wind.

VARDA GINOSSAR
translated from the Hebrew by Jean Nordhaus

Varda Ginossar (*b.* 1943) was brought to Israel from Egypt as a child. She has been artistic director and curator of the Artists Residence, an arts and culture centre in Herzliya, since 1995, and has published several books of poetry.

Dahlia Falah is the pseudonym of an Israeli writer whose identity has been kept secret by her publisher. Her first poems appeared in the late 70s. Her first collection, *Poems* (1997), was followed by her second and most recent book, entitled *2003*, in 2003.

Fooling the Killers

Qasim,
I wonder now
where you are...
I haven't forgotten you
after all these years,
long as the graveyard
wall is long.
I always
ask the grass of the field
about you, and the dirt paths.

Are you alive,
with your poise,
your cane, and memories?
Did you marry?
Do you have a tent of your own,
and children?
Did you make it to Mecca?
Or did they kill you
at the foot of the Hill of Tin?

Or maybe you never grew up,
Qasim, and managed to hide,
behind your mere ten years,
and you're still the same old Qasim,
the boy who runs around
and laughs
and jumps over fences,
who likes green almonds
and searches for birds' nests.

But even if they did it,
Qasim,
if, shamelessly,
they killed you,
I'm certain
you fooled your killers,

just as you managed
to fool the years.
For they never discovered
your body at the edge of the road,
and didn't find it
where the rivers spill,
or on the shelves
at the morgue,
and not on the way to Mecca,
and not beneath the rubble.

As no one saw you
concealing your corpse,
so no one will ever set eyes on you,
and no earthly breeze
encounter a bone of your body,
a finger of your hand,
or even a single shoe
that might fit you.
Qasim, you fooled them.

I always envied you, Qasim,
your skill at hiding
in the games of hide-and-seek we played –
barefoot at dusk – forty years ago –
when we were little boys.

[1988]

TAHA MUHAMMAD ALI
translated from the Arabic by Peter Cole, Yahya Hijazi & Gabriel Levin
➤ 406

A Night Unlike Others

His finger almost touches the bell,
the door, unbelievably slowly,
opens.

413

He enters.

He goes to his bedroom.
Here they are:
his picture next to his little bed,
his schoolbag, in the dark,
awake.
He sees himself sleeping
between two dreams, two flags.

He knocks on the doors of all the rooms
– he almost knocks. But he does not.
They all wake up:
'He's back!
By God, he's back!' they shout,
but their clamour makes no sound.

They stretch their arms to hug Mohammed
but do not reach his shoulders.

He wants to ask them all
how they are doing
under the night shelling;
he cannot find his voice.

They too say things
but find no voice.

He draws nearer, they draw nearer,
he passes through them, they pass through him,
they remain shadows
and never meet.

They wanted to ask him if he'd had his supper,
if he was warm enough over there, in the earth,
if the doctors could take the bullet and the fear
out of his heart.

Was he still scared?
Had he solved the two arithmetic problems

in order not to disappoint his teacher
the following day?

Had he...?

He, too, simply wanted to say:
I've come to see you
to make sure you're all right.
He said:
Dad will, as usual, forget to take his hypertension pill.
I came to remind him as I usually do.
He said:
my pillow is here, not there.

They said.
He said.
Without a voice.

The doorbell never rang,
the visitor was not in his little bed,
they have not seen him.

The following morning neighbours whispered:
it was all a delusion.
His schoolbag was here
marked by the bullet holes,
and his stained notebooks.

Those who came to give their condolences
had never left his mother.

Moreover, how could a dead child
come back, like this, to his family,
walking,
calmly
under the shelling
of such a very long
night?

MOURID BARGHOUTI-PALESTINE
translated from the Arabic by Radwa Ashour

415

Silence

Silence said:
truth needs no eloquence.
After the death of the horseman,
the homeward-bound horse
says everything
without saying anything.

MOURID BARGHOUTI-PALESTINE
translated from the Arabic by Radwa Ashour

Mourid Barghouti-Palestine: 'When I started the opening two lines of this very short poem, I realised I was talking to myself, not to my readers, as if to solidify my hatred of rhetoric and eloquence and my love for simplicity and concrete language. As a Palestinian with a negated history and a threatened geography, craving world attention and understanding, I was hesitant to have the poem published. But I decided to publish it because I needed to be its reader. I was trying to convince Mourid Barghouti that pain, even the Palestinian pain, does not mean shouting loudly.' [*Guardian*, 13 December 2008.]

Mourid Barghouti-Palestine (*b.* 1944) grew up in Ramallah, and was studying in Cairo when the Six-Day War of 1967 erupted. Prevented then like many Palestinians from returning home to the West Bank, he has spent much of his life in exile. In 1976, he was banished from Egypt, and later also from Lebanon and Jordan, and was only allowed to return to Ramallah following the Oslo Accords of 1996. He now lives in Cairo. As well as his poetry, published in English translation in *Midnight and Other Poems* (2008), his books include two memoirs, *I Saw Ramallah* (1997; UK, 2003), which Edward Said called 'one of the finest existential accounts of Palestinian displacement', and *I Was Born Here, I Was Born There* (UK, 2011). Originally Mourid Barghouti, he now wishes to be published as Mourid Barghouti-Palestine.

Agi Mishol was born in 1947 in Transylvania, the daughter of Hungarian-speaking Holocaust survivor parents, and emigrated with them to Israel as a child. During her military service she worked as a clerk at the nuclear facility in Dimona and started studying literature at Ben-Gurion University in Be'er Sheva, later enrolling at the Hebrew University in Jerusalem where she joined Yehuda Amichai's writing workshop. She has worked for much of her life as a teacher and lecturer, as well as farming peaches, persimmons and pomegranates with her husband where they live at Kfar Mordechai. She is one of Israel's most popular poets, the author of 16 collections in Hebrew and of two books translated into English, *The Swimmers* (1998) and *Look There* (2006).

Shaheeda[1]

The evening grows dim
and you're only twenty.
NATAN ALTERMAN, 'A Souk Evening'

You're only twenty
and your first pregnancy is a bomb.
Bearing explosives and metal shards
under the wide skirt,
you advance through the souk,
you, Andaleeb Takatka,[2] ticking among passersby.

Someone has screwed with the bolts in your head
and despatched you into town,
and you, who came from Bethlehem,[3] chose
a bakery no less. There, you pulled
from yourself the safety latch
and together with the Sabbath challahs
the poppy seeds and the sesame seeds
blew yourself up to the skies.

You flew with Rivka Fink,
and Yelena Konreiv from Caucasia,
Nissim Cohen from Afghanistan,
Suhila Hushi from Iran,
and two Chinese men as well
you swept along with you
to your death.

Since then other incidents
have overshadowed yours
yet I keep talking and talking
articulating nothing.

AGI MISHOL
translated from the Hebrew by Tsipi Keller

---

1. *Shaheeda:* in Arabic, female martyr. 2. Recruited by Tanzim, a militant Fatah faction, Andaleeb Tatatka was a 20-year-old Bethlehem woman who detonated an explosive belt at a Jerusalem bus stop in April 2002, killing herself and six others and injuring sixty. 3. In Hebrew, *Beit Lechem* means House of Bread.

from A State of Siege

Here, by the downslope of hills, facing the sunset
and time's muzzle,
near gardens with severed shadows,
we do what the prisoners do,
and what the unemployed do:
we nurture hope

*   *   *

A country on the verge of dawn,
we have become less intelligent,
because we stare into victory's hour:
no night in our artillery-glistened night
our enemies are sleepless,
and our enemies ignite the light for us
in the blackness of shelters
Here, after Job's poems we waited for no one...

*   *   *

The soldiers measure the distance between being
and nonbeing
with a tank's scope...

*   *   *

We measure the distance between our bodies
and mortar shells... with the sixth sense

*   *   *

You standing at the doorsteps, enter
and drink Arabic coffee with us
(you might sense you're human like us)
you standing at the doorsteps of houses,
get out of our mornings,
we need reassurance that we
are human like you!

*   *   *

We find time for entertainment:
we throw dice or flip through our papers
for news of yesterday's wounded,
and read the horoscope column: In the year
two thousand and two the camera smiles
for those born in the sign of siege

*   *   *

When the fighter planes disappear, the doves fly
white, white. Washing the sky's cheek
with free wings, reclaiming splendour and sovereignty
of air and play. Higher and higher
the doves fly, white white. I wish the sky
were real (a man passing between two bombs told me)

*   *   *

(To a killer:) If you'd contemplated the victim's face
and thought, you would have remembered your mother in the gas
chamber, you would have liberated yourself from the rifle's wisdom
and changed your mind: this isn't how identity is reclaimed!

*   *   *

(To another killer:) Had you left the foetus
for thirty days, the possibilities would have changed:
the occupation might end and that suckling
would not remember the time of siege,
and he'd grow up a healthy child, become a young man
and study in the same institution with one of your daughters
the ancient history of Asia
and they might fall together in passion's net
and beget a girl (and she'd be Jewish by birth)
so what have you done then?
Now your daughter has become a widow
and your granddaughter an orphan?
What have you done to your fugitive family
and how did you strike three doves with one shot?

*   *   *

Our losses: from two martyrs to eight
every day,
and ten wounded
and twenty homes
and fifty olive trees,
in addition to the structural defect
that will afflict the poem and the play and the incomplete painting

* * *

(To death:) We know from which tank
you came. We know what you want... so go back
missing one ring. And apologise to the soldiers and their officers,
and say: The newlyweds caught me looking
their way, so I hesitated then returned the tearful bride
to her kin... alone

[Ramallah, 2002]

MAHMOUD DARWISH
translated from the Arabic by Fady Joudah
➤ 395

Black Horses

The enemy's dead think mercilessly of me in their eternal sleep
while ghosts take to the stairs and house corners
the ghosts that I picked off the road and gathered like necklaces
from others' necks and sins.

Sin goes to the neck... there I raise my ghosts, feed them
and they swim like black horses in my sleep.

With the energy of a dead person the last blues song rises
while I think of jealousy
the door is a slit open and breath enters through the cracks, the river's
respiration, the drunks
and the woman who wakes to her past in the public garden

and when I fall asleep
I find a horse grazing grass
whenever I fall asleep
a horse comes to graze my dreams.

On my desk in Ramallah there are unfinished letters and photos
of old friends,
a poetry manuscript of a young man from Gaza, a sand hourglass,
and poem beginnings that flap like wings in my head.

I want to memorise you like that song in elementary school
the one I carry whole without errors
with my lisp and tilted head and dissonance...

the little feet that stomp the concrete ground with fervor
the open hands that bang on desks

All died in war, my friends and classmates...
and their little feet, their excited hands, remained
stomping the classroom floors, the dining tables and sidewalks,
the backs and shoulders of pedestrians...
wherever I go
I hear them
I see them.

[*2003*]

GHASSAN ZAQTAN
translated from the Arabic by Fady Joudah

Ghassan Zaqtan was born in Beit Jala, near Bethlehem, in 1954, his family
having been driven out of Zakariyya by Israeli forces in 1948. He eventually
moved to Jordan, then Beirut, Damascus and Tunis, before returning to
Palestine in 1994, and lives in Ramallah. Now widely regarded as Palestine's
most important poet, he has edited the Palestine Liberation Organisation's
literary magazine, *Bayader*, as well as the poetry journal *Al-Soua'ra* and the
literary page of the Ramallah newspaper *Al-Ayyam*. Founding director of the
House of Poetry in Ramallah, Zaqtan has also served as director general of
the Palestinian Ministry of Culture's Literature and Publishing Department.
Fady Joudah's translation of his tenth collection, *Like a Straw Bird It Follows
Me* (with selected earlier poems), published in 2012, was the International
Winner of the Griffin Poetry Prize 2013.

For Mohammed Zeid of Gaza, Age 15

There is no *stray* bullet, sirs.
No bullet like a worried cat
crouching under a bush,
no half-hairless puppy bullet
dodging midnight streets.
The bullet could not be a pecan
plunking tin roof,
not hardly, no fluff of pollen
on October's breath,
no humble pebble at our feet.

So don't gentle it, please.

We live among stray thoughts,
tasks abandoned midstream.
Our fickle hearts are fat
with stray devotions, we feel at home
among bits and pieces,
all the wandering ways of words.

But this bullet had no innocence, did not
wish anyone well, you can't tell us otherwise
by naming it mildly, this bullet was never the friend
of life, should not be granted immunity
by soft saying – friendly fire, straying death-eye,
why have we given the wrong weight to what we do?

Mohammed, Mohammed, deserves the truth.
This bullet had no secret happy hopes,
it was not singing to itself with eyes closed
under the bridge.

NAOMI SHIHAB NYE

The '*stray* bullet' which killed teenager Mohammed Zeid in October 2002 was
fired by an Israeli army officer, Captain Zvi Kurtzky, convicted over the death
by a military court in 2004.

Befouled Language

Confirming a Kill	—A bullet to the head
Exposing the Enemy	—Uprooting olive groves
Collateral Damage	—Every neighbour's life imperilled
Encirclement	—A city under siege
Closure	—Jailing civilians in their homes
Targeted Eliminations	—Killing the good with the bad
Administrative Detention	—Imprisonment without trial
Bargaining Chips	—Toying with human life
Roadblocks	—Breaking a people's spirit
Delimiting Village Expansion	—Banishing a man to the wilderness
Family Unification Plan	—Separating husbands from their wives
Trial	—Distinguishing between blood and blood
Emigration Directorate	—Arresting men in their sleep
Human Resource Company	—Robbing the foreigner of his livelihood
Urban Development	—Building new prisons
Settlement Outposts	—Deluding the world
An Isolationist Nation	—Sonic booms over neighbouring countries
Geneva Accords	—The murder of a seven-year-old boy

NATAN ZACH
translated from the Hebrew by Rachel Tzvia Back

Natan Zach was born in Berlin in 1930 to a German father and an Italian mother, emigrating to Mandate Palestine with his family in 1936, and served in the Israeli Defence Force as an intelligence clerk during the 1948 Arab-Israeli War. With work translated into more than 20 languages, he is one of Israel's most internationally renowned and innovative poets. Credited with helping to revolutionise Hebrew poetry during the 1950s and 60s, he led the rebellion of the modernist *Likrat* (towards) group of poets against the Zionist traditionalists, and has been an influential editor, critic and translator (notably of Else-Lasker-Schüler and Allen Ginsberg).

Naomi Shihab Nye (*b.* 1952) is a wandering poet – for over 30 years she has travelled America and the world to read and teach. Born in Missouri to a Palestinian father and an American mother, she grew up in St Louis, Jerusalem and San Antonio. Drawing on her Palestinian-American background, the cultural diversity of Texas, and her experiences in the Middle East and elsewhere, her poetry 'reflects this textured heritage, which endowed her with an openness to the experiences of others and a sense of continuity across borders' (Bill Moyers). Her many books include *Tender Spot: Selected Poems* (UK, 2008).

You and We

You and we are the sauce of Western delicacies
so the baby herring in Amsterdam will be more tender
so the nostrils of the taster in the Bordeaux winery will dilate in rapture
so the sculptures which faded in Paris and London will be gilded again
so Scandinavian design will challenge Italian design
so fresh salmon steak will glow in splendour in Scotland
so top fashion houses can innovate each season
so major league teams will get an ultramodern stadium
so abandoned power stations will house fabulous museums
so Belgium will have countless brands of beer
so Venice won't sink and Berlin can return to its former glory
so dark-red Spanish dried ham and German sausage won't disappoint their fans
so hunters in England won't be deprived of their hobby –
you and we must become bloodthirsty beasts:
you must blow yourself up aboard buses crawling in our cities
turn wretched people and tender girls into steaks
and we must shoot smart missiles from helicopters through your alleys
to blast cars into dust and passers-by into coal-dolls
you must shoot rounds of fire at infants in highchairs in restaurants
divide our poor world into *dar-al-islam* and *dar-al-harb*[1]
to rouse in your tender children eternal hatred and a drugged rapture for death
and we must stop women in labour from getting to doctors until the foetus dies
and shoot bent-over fathers sneaking across to find day work
we must uproot olives at harvest blow up houses of the poor
rave over our revelries in Hebron
polarise local humanity into Jew and Goy
two breeds of dogs – trained to kill.

MEIR WIESELTIER
translated from the Hebrew by Shirley Kaufman
➤ 426

1. *dar-al-islam* and *dar-al-harb* are Islamic terms used by extremist ideologists, meaning 'the house of Islam' and 'the house of war', the idea being that the world is divided into two: those territories which are Islamic already and those that true believers should conquer or Islamicise by *jihad* or holy war.

News About No One

Those who are
         never in the news,
whom no one remembers –
what wind erased their traces
as if they never walked the earth;
my father, all the others, where
         O where...?

What happened to the
         neighbourhood carpenter
maker of solid beds, and dressers
         for brides?
How he worshipped the wood!

Where is the silent shoemaker
who hugged his anvil, and bit the bitter nails
between his teeth? Did a 'smart' bomb
demolish his hole-in-the-wall
crammed to the ceiling
with battered shoes?

Where the coppersmith,
         where the golden tray?

The ear of wheat around the saint's image?
The horseshoe above the door?
What happened to Umm Youssef, the midwife?
How many babies were dragged
   out of the warm darkness of the womb
into the starkness of this world
   by her dextrous hands
sending them on their way
   with a slap on their bare bottoms
through the crooked valleys of
         their destinies, soldiers who fight
         in dubious battles
         and unjust wars?...

After they got tired
slaving in the mills of poverty
to fill the granaries of the tyrant
did they feel ashamed of the way
        this world is made?

After the sieges, after the wars
beyond hunger, beyond
        enemies, out of the reach
of the executioner's hand –
        did they go to sleep
  at last?
To sleep, and hug the dust.

SARGON BOULUS
translated from the Arabic by the author

Sargon Boulus (1944-2007) remains one of the best-known and influential of contemporary Arab poets. Born into an Assyrian Iraqi family, he started publishing his own work in 1961 in the ground-breaking *Shi'r* (Poetry) magazine in Beirut. After leaving Iraq and settling in San Francisco in the late 1960s, he became an unstoppable translator of modern English-language poets into Arabic and dedicated his life to reading, writing and translating poetry, every so often making forays to Europe to meet up with fellow exiles and to perform at festivals. He started assembling his posthumously published *Knife Sharpener: Selected Poems* (2009) in the months before he died – in hospital in Berlin – translating all the poems himself.

Meir Wieseltier was born in Moscow in 1941, and spent his early childhood as a refugee in Siberia and Europe. He arrived in Israel in 1949, and has lived in Tel Aviv since 1955. The central figure of the Tel Aviv Poets group in the early 60s, he has published over a dozen books of poetry and translated English, French and Russian poetry into Hebrew as well as novels by Dickens, Forster, Malcolm Lowry and Virginia Woolf. Shirley Kaufman's translation, *The Flower of Anarchy: Selected Poems*, was published in the US in 2003. A master of both comedy and irony, Wieseltier has written powerful poems of social and political protest in Israel. His non-conformist voice is anarchic and involved, angry and caring, trenchant and lyric. ➢ 424

426

THE TROUBLES | 1966–1999

TOTAL DEATHS: 3,636

The Troubles was the popular name given to the political and sectarian conflict in Northern Ireland involving Irish nationalists and republicans mostly from the Catholic community who wanted a united Ireland and unionists and loyalists from the Protestant community who wanted Northern Ireland to remain part of the United Kingdom, and the British Government and its security forces. When the Irish Free State was established in 1922, Northern Ireland, with its Protestant majority and unionist-dominated Parliament, remained within Britain, while the rest of the island became politically independent. [> 130]

The tipping point came in 1969 as a new civil rights campaign to end long-standing discrimination against Catholic nationalists, and preferential treatment for Protestant unionists in housing, employment and politics, met opposition from loyalists. In October 1968 civil rights protesters in Derry were attacked by police officers from the Royal Ulster Constabulary (RUC), which was around 90% Protestant; and when a loyalist order of Orangemen, the Apprentice Boys, was allowed to march through Derry in August 1969, they were attacked by nationalists, prompting the RUC to try to storm the Catholic Bogside area of the city. Days of rioting ensued, and spread to Belfast and elsewhere, with loyalists invading nationalist districts, burning houses and businesses, and RUC officers opening fire and killing several civilians and wounding many others. The unrest only ended, temporarily, when British troops were deployed.

The 1970s saw a huge upsurge in violence, with the British Army taking over responsibility for law and order, assisted by a reformed police force; the newly re-formed Provisional Irish Republican Army (IRA) waging 'armed struggle' against British rule in Northern Ireland; and loyalist paramilitaries (the Ulster Volunteer Force, or UVF, and the Ulster Defence Association, or UDA) carrying out a campaign of assassinations. There were numerous bombings and attacks by republican and loyalist paramilitaries on people and property as well as the security forces, and the British Army was responsible for the deaths of many civilians, most notoriously in the shootings of 13 unarmed civilians on 'Bloody Sunday' in Derry on 30 January 1972. The republican cause was later boosted by the 1981 Hunger Strike when ten republican prisoners, including Bobby Sands (elected as an MP in jail), starved themselves to death, helping Sinn Féin to gain recognition as a mainstream political party. The Good Friday Agreement of 1998 largely brought an end to the Troubles with devolved multi-party power-sharing within a local Assembly, the decommissioning of weapons and a *de facto* end to the Republic of Ireland's claim to Northern Ireland.

Throughout the Troubles writers were pressured to take sides, to condemn or endorse actions by the IRA, UDA, UVF, RUC or the British Army, and/or to declare support for political parties. The selection which follows shows how leading Irish poets resisted demands to 'write about the Troubles' or to make political statements, choosing instead to write about the human cost of three decades of conflict and bloodshed in poems expressing their abhorrence of violence from whatever faction or side.

Claudy [1]

(for Harry Barton, a song)

The Sperrins surround it, the Faughan flows by,
at each end of Main Street the hills and the sky,
the small town of Claudy at ease in the sun
last July in the morning, a new day begun.

How peaceful and pretty if the moment could stop,
McIlhenny is straightening things in his shop,
and his wife is outside serving petrol, and then
a girl takes a cloth to a big window-pane.

And McCloskey is taking the weight off his feet,
and McClelland and Miller are sweeping the street,
and, delivering milk at the Beaufort Hotel,
young Temple's enjoying his first job quite well.

And Mrs McLaughlin is scrubbing her floor,
and Artie Hone's crossing the street to a door,
and Mrs Brown, looking around for her cat,
goes off up an entry – what's strange about that?

Not much – but before she comes back to the road
that strange car parked outside her house will explode,
and all of the people I've mentioned outside
will be waiting to die or already have died.

An explosion too loud for your eardrums to bear,
and young children squealing like pigs in the square,
all faces chalk-white and streaked with bright red,
and the glass and the dust and the terrible dead.

For an old lady's legs are ripped off, and the head
of a man's hanging open, and still he's not dead.
He is screaming for mercy, and his son stands and stares
and stares, and then suddenly, quick, disappears.

And Christ, little Katherine Aiken is dead,
and Mrs McLaughlin is pierced through the head.
Meanwhile to Dungiven the killers have gone,
and they're finding it hard to get through on the phone.

JAMES SIMMONS

1. Three IRA car bombs exploded on the Main Street of the village of Claudy, Co. Derry, on 31 July 1972, killing nine people and injuring 30. The men who planted the bomb were said to have tried to telephone a warning from the nearby town of Dungiven, but phones there were out of order due to an earlier bombing of a telephone exchange. A local priest was implicated in the attacks.

James Simmons (1933-2001) was a poet and singer-songwriter from Derry who founded and led The Resistance Cabaret, a satirical revue combining poetry, songs and political comment, during the early 70s in Northern Ireland. He founded *The Honest Ulsterman* in 1968 and edited 17 of its first issues.

Wounds

Here are two pictures from my father's head –
I have kept them like secrets until now:
First, the Ulster Division at the Somme
Going over the top with 'Fuck the Pope!'
'No Surrender!': a boy about to die,
Screaming 'Give 'em one for the Shankill!'
'Wilder than Gurkhas' were my father's words
Of admiration and bewilderment.
Next comes the London-Scottish padre
Resettling kilts with his swagger-stick,
With a stylish backhand and a prayer.
Over a landscape of dead buttocks
My father followed him for fifty years.
At last, a belated casualty,
He said – lead traces flaring till they hurt –
'I am dying for King and Country, slowly.'
I touched his hand, his thin head I touched.

Now, with military honours of a kind,
With his badges, his medals like rainbows,
His spinning compass, I bury beside him
Three teenage soldiers, bellies full of
Bullets and Irish beer, their flies undone.
A packet of Woodbines I throw in,
A lucifer, the Sacred Heart of Jesus
Paralysed as heavy guns put out
The night-light in a nursery for ever;
Also a bus-conductor's uniform –
He collapsed beside his carpet-slippers
Without a murmur, shot through the head
By a shivering boy who wandered in
Before they could turn the television down
Or tidy away the supper dishes.
To the children, to a bewildered wife,
I think 'Sorry Missus' was what he said.

MICHAEL LONGLEY

Michael Longley was born in Belfast in 1939 of English parentage and has spent most of his life in Belfast and at his second home at Carrigskeewan on the coast of Co. Mayo. His father served in the British Army in both world wars. Longley's poetry is formally inventive and precisely observed, spanning and blending love poetry, war poetry, nature poetry, elegies, satires, verse epistles, art and the art of poetry. He has extended the capacity of the lyric to absorb dark matter: the Great War, the Holocaust, the Troubles; and his translations from classical poets speak to contemporary concerns. ➤ 22, 162, 429, 445, 445, 449, 454, 458.

The Tollund Man

I

Some day I will go to Aarhus
To see his peat-brown head,
The mild pods of his eyelids,
His pointed skin cap.

In the flat country nearby
Where they dug him out,
His last gruel of winter seeds
Caked in his stomach,

Naked except for
The cap, noose and girdle,
I will stand a long time.
Bridegroom to the goddess,

She tightened her torc on him
And opened her fen,
Those dark juices working
Him to a saint's kept body,

Trove of the turfcutters'
Honeycombed workings.
Now his stained face
Reposes at Aarhus.

II

I could risk blasphemy,
Consecrate the cauldron bog
Our holy ground and pray
Him to make germinate

The scattered, ambushed
Flesh of labourers,
Stockinged corpses
Laid out in the farmyards,

Tell-tale skin and teeth
Flecking the sleepers
Of four young brothers, trailed
For miles along the lines.

III

Something of his sad freedom
As he rode the tumbril
Should come to me, driving,
Saying the names

Tollund, Grauballe, Nebelgard,
Watching the pointing hands
Of country people,
Not knowing their tongue.

Out there in Jutland
In the old man-killing parishes
I will feel lost,
Unhappy and at home.

SEAMUS HEANEY

Seamus Heaney (1939-2013) was awarded the Nobel Prize in Literature in 1995 for 'for works of lyrical beauty and ethical depth, which exalt everyday miracles and the living past'. Born into a Catholic farming family in Mossbawn, Co. Derry, he left Northern Ireland in 1972 and lived in America, Wicklow and Dublin. His concerns for the land, language and troubled history of Ireland run through all his work. In 'Bogland', for example, the first in his 'bog poem' series (*Door into the Dark* (1969), he digs up collective history in Ireland's unfenced, crusting boglands ('Every layer they strip | Seems camped on before').

When the Troubles began in 1969, Heaney started looking for 'images and symbols adequate to our predicament', finding them in recently published accounts of mummified bodies found in Danish peat bogs. But with the Troubles getting worse with almost daily bombings and shootings, Heaney's subsequent bog poems – published in *Wintering Out* (1972) and *North* (1975) – were read by some, simplistically, as endorsing republicanism, with James Simmons later accusing him of 'a culpable ambiguity in [his] responses to atrocity' ('The Trouble with Seamus', 1992). Yet the parallels in 'The Tollund Man' [➤ 430] between Iron Age ritual or justice in 'the old man-killing parishes' of Jutland (part III) and atrocities by Black and Tans [➤ 432] in the 1920s (part II) are contained in a profoundly religious poem whose symbolism is clearly redemptive. Similarly, Heaney's position in 'Punishment' ('I who have stood dumb | when your betraying sisters | cauled in tar | wept by the railings | would connive | in civilised outrage | yet understand the exact | and tribal, intimate revenge') may be ambiguous but doesn't endorse the IRA's tarring and feathering of Catholic girls for going out with British soldiers.

Other poems in this selection only need to describe the actions of both the British Army and terrorists from both sides to show Heaney's abhorrence of all violence, notably 'The Strand at Lough Beg' [➤ 440] (on the UVF murder of his cousin Colum McCartney) and 'Casualty' [➤ 442] (the death of his friend, eel fisherman Louis O'Neill, in a pub bombing initially blamed on the IRA but later thought to have been a UVF attack) from *Field Work* (1979), and 'Keeping Going' [➤ 450] (his brother Hugh's resilience following the shooting of a local man, an RUC reservist) and the sestina 'Two Lorries' [➤ 452] (the IRA's bombing of Magherafelt) from *The Spirit Level* (1994).

In Memory: The Miami Showband –
Massacred 31 July 1975 [1]

Beautiful are the feet of them that preach the gospel of peace,
Of them that bring glad tidings of good things

In a public house, darkly lit, a patriotic (sic)
Versifier whines into my face: 'You must take one side
Or the other, or you're but a fucking romantic.'
His eyes glitter hate and vanity, porter and whiskey,
And I realise that he is blind to the braille connection
Between a music and a music-maker.
'You must take one side or the other
Or you're but a fucking romantic':
The whine is icy
And his eyes hang loose like sheets from poles
On a bare wet hillside in winter
And his mouth gapes like a cave in ice;
It is a whine in the crotch of whose fear
Is fondled a dream gun blood-smeared;
It is in war – not poetry or music –
That men find their niche, their glory hole;
Like most of his fellows
He will abide no contradiction in the mind.
He whines: 'If there is birth, there cannot be death'
And – jabbing a hysterical forefinger into my nose and eyes –
'If there is death, there cannot be birth.'
Peace to the souls of those who unlike my fellow poet
Were true to their trade
Despite death-dealing blackmail by racists:
You made music, and that was all: You were realists
And beautiful were your feet.

PAUL DURCAN

1. On 31 July 1975 a group of UVF paramilitaries including serving soldiers
from the British Army's Ulster Defence Regiment stopped the Miami Show-
band's minibus on the A1 road north of Newry, Co. Down. Two of the gun-
men were killed when they tried to plant a time bomb in the vehicle, where-
upon the others opened fire on the band members standing in the road, killing
three of the musicians and wounding two.

Paul Durcan was born in 1944 in Dublin and grew up there and in Turlough, Co. Mayo. His father was a judge and his mother the niece of Yeats's great love, Maude Gonne (whom he knew as a child) and John MacBride, one of the leaders of the Easter Rising executed by the British [➤ 133, *n* 5 & 6].

'His work is aggressively satirical, dedicated to exposing a range of Irish ills [...] Where Durcan has perhaps been most outspoken, however, is in his condemnation of sectarian violence in Ireland. He has been commended by some critics for his continued attention to the crisis in Northern Ireland from the 1970s onwards, and noted for his rigorous castigation of both paramilitary and government wrong-doing. [...] And throughout his later work, he has continued to document in his poetry the atrocities of Northern Ireland, stamping each collection with an incisive political relevance.' [Eve Patten] ➤ 455

The War Horse

This dry night, nothing unusual
About the clip, crop, casual

Iron of his shoes as he stamps head
Like a mint on the innnocent coinage of earth.

I lift the window, watch the ambling feather
Of hock and fetlock, loosed from its daily tether

In the tinker camp on the Enniskerry Road,
Pass, his breath hissing, his snuffling head

Down. He is gone. No great harm is done.
Only a leaf of our laurel hedge is torn –

Of distant interest like a maimed limb,
Only a rose which now will never climb

The stone of our house, expendable, a mere
Line of defence against him, a volunteer

You might say, only a crocus its bulbous head
Blown from growth, one of the screamless dead.

But we, we are safe, our unformed fear
Of fierce commitment gone; why should we care

If a rose, a hedge, a crocus are uprooted
Like corpses, remote, crushed, mutilated?

He stumbles on like a rumour of war, huge,
Threatening; neighbours use the subterfuge

Of curtains; he stumbles down our short street
Thankfully passing us. I pause, wait,

Then to breathe relief lean on the sill
And for a second only my blood is still

With atavism. That rose he smashed frays
Ribboned across our hedge, recalling days

Of burned countryside, illicit braid:
A cause ruined before, a world betrayed.

EAVAN BOLAND

Eavan Boland was born in Dublin in 1944. Her father was a diplomat and her mother a noted Irish painter, Frances Kelly. She has mostly worked as a university lecturer, in Dublin and for the past 20 years as Professor of English at Stanford University in the US. While much of her poetry is concerned with domestic life, family, love, myth, love, history and Irish landscape, its treatment of these areas is often subversive, offering fresh perspectives old themes, especially in relation to the role of women in Irish life, history and culture.

from Whatever You Say Say Nothing

I

I'm writing just after an encounter
With an English journalist in search of 'views
On the Irish thing'. I'm back in winter
Quarters where bad news is no longer news,

Where media-men and stringers sniff and point,
Where zoom lenses, recorders and coiled leads
Litter the hotels. The times are out of joint
But I incline as much to rosary beads

As to the jottings and analyses
Of politicians and newspapermen
Who've scribbled down the long campaign from gas
And protest to gelignite and Sten,

Who proved upon their pulses 'escalate',
'Backlash' and 'crack down', 'the provisional wing',
'Polarisation' and 'long-standing hate'.
Yet I live here, I live here too, I sing,

Expertly civil-tongued with civil neighbours
On the high wires of first wireless reports,
Sucking the fake taste, the stony flavours
Of those sanctioned, old, elaborate retorts:

'Oh, it's disgraceful, surely, I agree.'
'Where's it going to end?' 'It's getting worse.'
'They're murderers.' 'Internment, understandably...'
The 'voice of sanity' is getting hoarse.

III

'Religion's never mentioned here,' of course.
'You know them by their eyes,' and hold your tongue.
'One side's as bad as the other,' never worse.
Christ, it's near time that some small leak was sprung

In the great dykes the Dutchman made
To dam the dangerous tide that followed Seamus.
Yet for all this art and sedentary trade
I am incapable. The famous

Northern reticence, the tight gag of place
And times: yes, yes. Of the 'wee six' I sing
Where to be saved you only must save face
And whatever you say, you say nothing.

Smoke-signals are loud-mouthed compared with us:
Manoeuvrings to find out name and school,
Subtle discrimination by addresses
With hardly an exception to the rule

That Norman, Ken and Sidney signalled Prod
And Seamus (call me Sean) was sure-fire Pape.
O land of password, handgrip, wink and nod,
Of open minds as open as a trap,

Where tongues lie coiled, as under flames lie wicks,
Where half of us, as in a wooden horse
Were cabin'd and confined like wily Greeks,
Besieged within the siege, whispering morse.

IV

This morning from a dewy motorway
I saw the new camp for the internees:
A bomb had left a crater of fresh clay
In the roadside, and over in the trees

Machine-gun posts defined a real stockade.
There was that white mist you get on a low ground
And it was déjà-vu, some film made
Of Stalag 17, a bad dream with no sound.

Is there a life before death? That's chalked up
In Ballymurphy. Competence with pain,
Coherent miseries, a bite and sup,
We hug our little destiny again.

SEAMUS HEANEY

➤ 432

Lunch with Pancho Villa

I

'Is it really a revolution, though?'
I reached across the wicker table
With another $10,000 question.
My celebrated pamphleteer,
Co-author of such volumes
As *Blood on the Rose*,
The Dream and the Drums,
And *How It Happened Here*,
Would pour some untroubled Muscatel
And settle back in his cane chair.

'Look, son. Just look around you.
People are getting themselves killed
Left, right and centre
While you do what? Write rondeaux?
There's more to living in this country
Than stars and horses, pigs and trees,
Not that you'd guess it from your poems.
Do you never listen to the news?
You want to get down to something true,
Something a little nearer home.'

I called again later that afternoon,
A quiet suburban street.
'You want to stand back a little
When the world's at your feet.'
I'd have liked to have heard some more
Of his famous revolution.
I rang the bell, and knocked hard
On what I remembered as his front door,
That opened then, as such doors do,
Directly on to a back yard.

II

Not any back yard, I'm bound to say,.
And not a thousand miles away
From here. No one's taken in, I'm sure,
By such a mild invention.

But where (I wonder myself) do I stand,
In relation to a table and chair,
The quince-tree I forgot to mention,
That suburban street, the door, the yard –
All made up as I went along
As things that people live among.

And such a person as lived there!
My celebrated pamphleteer!
Of course, I gave it all away
With those preposterous titles.
The Bloody Rose? The Dream and the Drums?
The three-day-wonder of the flowering plum!
Or was I desperately wishing
To have been their other co-author?
Or, at least, to own a first edition
Of *The Boot Boys and Other Battles?*

'When are you going to tell the truth?'
For there's no such book, so far as I know,
As *How it Happened Here*,
Though there may be. There may.
What should I say to this callow youth
Who learned to write last winter –
One of those correspondence courses –
And who's coming to lunch today?
He'll be rambling on, no doubt,
About pigs and trees, stars and horses.

PAUL MULDOON

Paul Muldoon was born into a Catholic family in 1951 on a farm in a pre-dominantly Protestant area of Co. Armagh. He worked for the BBC in Belfast during some of the worst years of the Troubles (1973-86) and now teaches at Princeton University in the US. Both playful and serious, his poetry is noted for its technical virtuosity, wordplay and wit. Countering criticisms of his work as self-indulgent and evasive in 'Lunch with Pancho Villa' – from *Mules* (1977) – he ridicules the idea that poetry should make political statements. Similarly, in 'The Boundary Commission' [➤ 446], from *Why Brownlee Left* (1980), he refuses to take sides. But while rejecting calls to endorse or condemn, his poetry can still express his personal sense of being haunted by the Troubles, even in America, as in 'Wire' [➤ 456], from *Hay* (1998).

The Toome Road

One morning early I met armoured cars
In convoy, warbling along on powerful tyres,
All camouflaged with broken alder branches,
And headphoned soldiers standing up in turrets.
How long were they approaching down my roads
As if they owned them? The whole country was sleeping.
I had rights-of-way, fields, cattle in my keeping,
Tractors hitched to buckrakes in open sheds,
Silos, chill gates, wet slates, the greens and reds
Of outhouse roofs. Whom should I run to tell
Among all of those with their back doors on the latch
For the bringer of bad news, that small-hours visitant
Who, by being expected, might be kept distant?
Sowers of seed, erectors of headstones...
O charioteers, above your dormant guns,
It stands here still, stands vibrant as you pass,
The invisible, untoppled omphalos.

SEAMUS HEANEY

The Strand at Lough Beg
(in memory of Colum McCartney)

> *All round this little island, on the strand*
> *Far down below there, where the breakers strive*
> *Grow the tall rushes from the oozy sand.*
>
> DANTE, *Purgatorio*, I, 100–103

Leaving the white glow of filling stations
And a few lonely streetlamps among fields
You climbed the hills toward Newtownhamilton
Past the Fews Forest, out beneath the stars –
Along the road, a high, bare pilgrim's track
Where Sweeney fled before the bloodied heads,
Goat-beards and dogs' eyes in a demon pack

440

Blazing out of the ground, snapping and squealing.
What blazed ahead of you? A faked road block?
The red lamp swung, the sudden brakes and stalling
Engine, voices, heads hooded and the cold-nosed gun?
Or in your driving mirror, tailing headlights
That pulled out suddenly and flagged you down
Where you weren't known and far from what you knew:
The lowland clays and waters of Lough Beg,
Church Island's spire, its soft treeline of yew.

There you used hear guns fired behind the house
Long before rising time, when duck shooters
Haunted the marigolds and bulrushes,
But still were scared to find spent cartridges,
Acrid, brassy, genital, ejected,
On your way across the strand to fetch the cows.
For you and yours and yours and mine fought the shy,
Spoke an old language of conspirators
And could not crack the whip or seize the day:
Big-voiced scullions, herders, feelers round
Haycocks and hindquarters, talkers in byres,
Slow arbitrators of the burial ground.

Across that strand of yours the cattle graze
Up to their bellies in an early mist
And now they turn their unbewildered gaze
To where we work our way through squeaking sedge
Drowning in dew. Like a dull blade with its edge
Honed bright, Lough Beg half shines under the haze.
I turn because the sweeping of your feet
Has stopped behind me, to find you on your knees
With blood and roadside muck in your hair and eyes,
Then kneel in front of you in brimming grass
And gather up cold handfuls of the dew
To wash you, cousin. I dab you clean with moss
Fine as the drizzle out of a low cloud.
I lift you under the arms and lay you flat.
With rushes that shoot green again, I plait
Green scapulars to wear over your shroud.

SEAMUS HEANEY

Casualty

I

He would drink by himself
And raise a weathered thumb
Towards the high shelf,
Calling another rum
And blackcurrant, without
Having to raise his voice,
Or order a quick stout
By a lifting of the eyes
And a discreet dumb-show
Of pulling off the top;
At closing time would go
In waders and peaked cap
Into the showery dark,
A dole-kept breadwinner
But a natural for work.
I loved his whole manner,
Sure-footed but too sly,
His deadpan sidling tact,
His fisherman's quick eye
And turned, observant back.

Incomprehensible
To him, my other life.
Sometimes, on the high stool,
Too busy with his knife
At a tobacco plug
And not meeting my eye,
In the pause after a slug
He mentioned poetry.
We would be on our own
And, always politic
And shy of condescension,
I would manage by some trick
To switch the talk to eels
Or lore of the horse and cart
Or the Provisionals.

But my tentative art
His turned back watches too:
He was blown to bits
Out drinking in a curfew
Others obeyed, three nights
After they shot dead
The thirteen men in Derry.
PARAS THIRTEEN, the walls said,
BOGSIDE NIL. That Wednesday
Everyone held
Their breath and trembled.

II

It was a day of cold
Raw silence, wind-blown
surplice and soutane:
Rained-on, flower-laden
Coffin after coffin
Seemed to float from the door
Of the packed cathedral
Like blossoms on slow water.
The common funeral
Unrolled its swaddling band,
Lapping, tightening
Till we were braced and bound
Like brothers in a ring.

But he would not be held
At home by his own crowd
Whatever threats were phoned,
Whatever black flags waved.
I see him as he turned
In that bombed offending place,
Remorse fused with terror
In his still knowable face,
His cornered outfaced stare
Blinding in the flash.

He had gone miles away
For he drank like a fish

Nightly, naturally
Swimming towards the lure
Of warm lit-up places,
The blurred mesh and murmur
Drifting among glasses
In the gregarious smoke.
How culpable was he
That last night when he broke
Our tribe's complicity?
'Now, you're supposed to be
An educated man,'
I hear him say. 'Puzzle me
The right answer to that one.'

III

I missed his funeral,
Those quiet walkers
And sideways talkers
Shoaling out of his lane
To the respectable
Purring of the hearse...
They move in equal pace
With the habitual
Slow consolation
Of a dawdling engine,
The line lifted, hand
Over fist, cold sunshine
On the water, the land
Banked under fog: that morning
When he took me in his boat,
The screw purling, turning
Indolent fathoms white,
I tasted freedom with him.
To get out early, haul
Steadily off the bottom,
Dispraise the catch, and smile
As you find a rhythm
Working you, slow mile by mile,
Into your proper haunt
Somewhere, well out, beyond...

Dawn-sniffing revenant,
Plodder through midnight rain,
Question me again.

SEAMUS HEANEY
➤ 432

Wreaths

The Civil Servant

He was preparing an Ulster fry for breakfast
When someone walked into the kitchen and shot him:
A bullet entered his mouth and pierced his skull,
The books he had read, the music he could play.

He lay in his dressing gown and pyjamas
While they dusted the dresser for fingerprints
And then shuffled backwards across the garden
With notebooks, cameras and measuring tapes.

They rolled him up like a red carpet and left
Only a bullet hole in the cutlery drawer:
Later his widow took a hammer and chisel
And removed the black keys from his piano.

The Greengrocer

He ran a good shop, and he died
Serving even the death-dealers
Who found him busy as usual
Behind the counter, organised
With holly wreaths for Christmas,
Fir trees on the pavement outside.

Astrologers or three wise men
Who may shortly be setting out
For a small house up the Shankill

Or the Falls, should pause on their way
To buy gifts at Jim Gibson's shop,
Dates and chestnuts and tangerines.

The Linen Workers

Christ's teeth ascended with him into heaven:
Through a cavity in one of his molars
The wind whistles: he is fastened for ever
By his exposed canines to a wintry sky.

I am blinded by the blaze of that smile
And by the memory of my father's false teeth
Brimming in their tumbler: they wore bubbles
And, outside of his body, a deadly grin.

When they massacred the ten linen workers
There fell on the road beside them spectacles,
Wallets, small change, and a set of dentures:
Blood, food particles, the bread, the wine.

Before I can bury my father once again
I must polish the spectacles, balance them
Upon his nose, fill his pockets with money
And into his dead mouth slip the set of teeth.

MICHAEL LONGLEY
➤ 430

The Boundary Commission

You remember that village where the border ran
Down the middle of the street,
With the butcher and baker in different states?
Today he remarked how a shower of rain

446

Had stopped so cleanly across Golightly's lane
It might have been a wall of glass
That had toppled over. He stood there, for ages,
To wonder which side, if any, he should be on.

PAUL MULDOON
➤ 439

Nails

The black van exploded
Fifty yards from the hotel entrance.
Two men, one black-haired, the other red,
Had parked it there as though for a few moments
While they walked around the corner
Not noticing, it seemed, the children
In single file behind their perky leader,
And certainly not seeing the van
Explode into the children's bodies.
Nails, nine inches long, lodged
In chest, ankle, thigh, buttock, shoulder, face.
The quickly-gathered crowd was outraged and shocked.
Some children were whole, others bits and pieces.
These blasted crucifixions are commonplace.

BRENDAN KENNELLY
➤ 141

Belfast Confetti

Suddenly as the riot squad moved in, it was raining exclamation marks,
Nuts, bolts, nails, car-keys. A fount of broken type. And the explosion
Itself – an asterisk on the map. This hyphenated line, a burst of
        rapid fire...
I was trying to complete a sentence in my head, but it kept stuttering,
All the alleyways and side-streets blocked with stops and colons.

447

I know this labyrinth so well – Balaklava, Raglan, Inkerman, Odessa
    Street –
Why can't I escape? Every move is punctuated. Crimea Street. Dead
    end again.
A Saracen, Kremlin-2 mesh. Makrolon face-shields. Walkie-talkies.
    What is
My name? Where am I coming from? Where am I going? A fusillade
    of question-marks.

CIARAN CARSON

Campaign

They had questioned him for hours. Who exactly was he? And when
He told them, they questioned him again. When they accepted who he
    was, as
Someone not involved, they pulled out his fingernails. Then
They took him to a waste-ground somewhere near the Horseshoe Bend,
    and told him
What he was. They shot him nine times.

A dark umbilicus of smoke was rising from a heap of burning tyres.
The bad smell he smelt was the smell of himself. Broken glass and
    knotted Durex.
The knuckles of a face in a nylon stocking. I used to see him in the
    Gladstone Bar,
Drawing pints for strangers, his almost perfect fingers flecked with scum.

CIARAN CARSON

Ciaran Carson was born in 1948 to an Irish-speaking family in Belfast, where
he has always lived. Many of his poems are written in a long line style he took
over from a mixture of sources (Louis MacNeice, C.K. Williams, Irish *sean-
nós* songs) and turned into a new kind of storytelling verse mode in which
language echoes the sounds of a city plagued by sectarian violence, riots and
bombings. Also a traditional musician, novelist and translator, Carson has said:
'I'm not that interested in ideologies. I'm interested in the words, and how
they sound to me, how words connect with experience.'

Jump Leads

As the eggbeater spy in the sky flickered overhead, the TV
    developed a facial tic
Or as it turned out, the protesters had handcuffed themselves to
    the studio lights.
Muffled off-camera, shouts of *No*. As I tried to lip-read the
    talking head
An arms cache came up, magazines laid out like a tray of wedding
    rings.
The bomb-disposal expert whose face was in shadow for security
    reasons

Had started very young by taking a torch apart at Christmas to
    see what made it tick.
Everything went dark. The killers escaped in a red Fiesta
    according to sources.
Talking, said the Bishop, is better than killing. Just before the
    Weather
The victim is his wedding photograph. He's been spattered with
    confetti.

CIARAN CARSON

The Ice-cream Man

Rum and raisin, vanilla, butterscotch, walnut, peach:
You would rhyme off the flavours. That was before
They murdered the ice-cream man on the Lisburn Road
And you bought carnations to lay outside his shop.
I named for you all the wild flowers of the Burren
I had seen in one day: thyme, valerian, loosestrife,
Meadowsweet, twayblade, crowfoot, ling, angelica,
Herb robert, marjoram, cow parsley, sundew, vetch,
Mountain avens, wood sage, ragged robin, stitchwort,
Yarrow, lady's bedstraw, bindweed, bog pimpernel.

MICHAEL LONGLEY

Keeping Going

(for Hugh)

The piper coming from far away is you
With a whitewash brush for a sporran
Wobbling round you, a kitchen chair
Upside down on your shoulder, your right arm
Pretending to tuck the bag beneath your elbow,
Your pop-eyes and big cheeks nearly bursting
With laughter, but keeping the drone going on
Interminably, between catches of breath.

*

The whitewash brush. An old blanched skirted thing
On the back of the byre door, biding its time
Until spring airs spelled lime in a work-bucket
And a potstick to mix it in with water.
Those smells brought tears to the eyes, we inhaled
A kind of greeny burning and thought of brimstone.
But the slop of the actual job
Of brushing walls, the watery grey
Being lashed on in broad swatches, then drying out
Whiter and whiter, all that worked like magic.
Where had we come from, what was this kingdom
We knew we'd been restored to? Our shadows
Moved on the wall and a tar border glittered
The full length of the house, a black divide
Like a freshly opened, pungent, reeking trench.

*

Piss at the gable, the dead will congregate.
But separately. The women after dark,
Hunkering there a moment before bedtime,
The only time the soul was let alone,
The only time that face and body calmed
In the eye of heaven.
                              Buttermilk and urine,
The pantry, the housed beasts, the listening bedroom.
We were all together there in a foretime,

450

In a knowledge that might not translate beyond
Those wind-heaved midnights we still cannot be sure
Happened or not. It smelled of hill-fort clay
And cattle dung. When the thorn tree was cut down
You broke your arm. I shared the dread
When a strange bird perched for days on the byre roof.

*

That scene, with Macbeth helpless and desperate
In his nightmare – when he meets the hags agains
And sees the apparitions in the pot –
I felt at home with that one all right. Hearth,
Steam and ululation, the smoky hair
Curtaining a cheek. 'Don't go near bad boys
In that college that you're bound for. Do you hear me?
Do you hear me speaking to you? Don't forget!'
And then the potstick quickening the gruel,
The steam crown swirled, everything intimate
And fear-swathed brightening for a moment,
Then going dull and fatal and away.

*

Grey matter like gruel flecked with blood
In spatters on the whitewash. A clean spot
Where his head had been, other stains subsumed
In the parched wall he leant his back against
That morning like any other morning,
Part-time reservist, toting his lunch-box.
A car came slow down Castle Street, made the halt,
Crossed the Diamond, slowed again and stopped
Level with him, although it was not his lift.
And then he saw an ordinary face
For what it was and a gun in his own face.
His right leg was hooked back, his sole and heel
Against the wall, his right knee propped up steady,
So he never moved, just pushed with all his might
Against himself, then fell past the tarred strip,
Feeding the gutter with his copious blood.

*

My dear brother, you have good stamina.
You stay on where it happens. Your big tractor
Pulls up at the Diamond, you wave at people,
You shout and laugh about the revs, you keep
Old roads open by driving on the new ones.
You called the piper's sporrans whitewash brushes
And then dressed up and marched us through the kitchen,
But you cannot make the dead walk or right wrong.
I see you at the end of your tether sometimes,
In the milking parlour, holding yourself up
Between two cows until your turn goes past,
Then coming to in the smell of dung again
And wondering, is this all? As it was
In the beginning, is now and shall be?
Then rubbing your eyes and seeing our old brush
Up on the byre door, and keeping going.

SEAMUS HEANEY

Two Lorries

It's raining on black coal and warm wet ashes.
There are tyre-marks in the yard, Agnew's old lorry
Has all its cribs down and Agnew the coalman
With his Belfast accent's sweet-talking my mother.
Would she ever go to a film in Magherafelt?
But it's raining and he still has half the load

To deliver farther on. This time the lode
Our coal came from was silk-black, so the ashes
Will be the silkiest white. The Magherafelt
(Via Toomebridge) bus goes by. The half-stripped lorry
With its emptied, folded coal-bags moves my mother:
The tasty ways of a leather-aproned coalman!

And films no less! The conceit of a coalman...
She goes back in and gets out the black lead
And emery paper, this nineteen-forties mother,
All business round her stove, half-wiping ashes
With a backhand from her cheek as the bolted lorry
Gets revved and turned and heads for Magherafelt

And the last delivery. Oh, Magherafelt!
Oh, dream of red plush and a city coalman
As time fastforwards and a different lorry
Groans into shot, up Broad Street, with a payload
That will blow the bus station[1] to dust and ashes...
After that happened, I'd a vision of my mother,

A revenant on the bench where I would meet her
In that cold-floored waiting room in Magherafelt,
Her shopping bags full up with shovelled ashes.
Death walked out past her like a dust-faced coalman
Refolding body-bags, plying his load
Empty upon empty, in a flurry

Of motes and engine-revs, but which lorry
Was it now? Young Agnew's or that other,
Heavier, deadlier one, set to explode
In a time beyond her time in Magherafelt...
So tally bags and sweet-talk darkness, coalman,
Listen to the rain spit in new ashes

As you heft a load of dust that was Magherafelt,
Then reappear from your lorry as my mother's
Dreamboat coalman filmed in silk-white ashes.

SEAMUS HEANEY

➢ 432

1. Much of the town centre of Magherafelt, Co. Derry, was extensively damaged by an IRA van bomb detonated outside the bus station on Broad Street on Sunday 23 May 1993.

Ceasefire

I

Put in mind of his own father and moved to tears
Achilles took him by the hand and pushed the old king
Gently away, but Priam curled up at his feet and
Wept with him until their sadness filled the building.

II

Taking Hector's corpse into his own hands Achilles
Made sure it was washed and, for the old king's sake,
Laid out in uniform, ready for Priam to carry
Wrapped like a present home to Troy at daybreak.

III

When they had eaten together, it pleased them both
To stare at each other's beauty as lovers might,
Achilles built like a god, Priam good-looking still
And full of conversation, who earlier had sighed:

IV

'I get down on my knees and do what must be done
And kiss Achilles' hand, the killer of my son.'[1]

MICHAEL LONGLEY

➤ 430

1. Conflating several passages from Homer's *Iliad*, 'Ceasefire' was published in *The Irish Times* two days after the start of the August 1994 ceasefire in Northern Ireland; the last couplet recalls the words of Gordon Wilson, the father from Enniskillen whose daughter was one of eleven people killed when an IRA bomb exploded at a Remembrance Day ceremony in 1987, who publicly forgave her murderers on television in one simple sentence which has never been forgotten in Ireland.

The Bloomsday Murders, 16 June 1997 [1]

– A nation? says Bloom. A nation is the same people
living in the same place.
Ulysses, Bodley Head edition, 1960, p.489

Not even you, Gerry Adams, deserve to be murdered:
You whose friends at noon murdered my two young men,
David Johnston and John Graham;
You who in the afternoon came on TV
In a bookshop on Bloomsday signing books,
Sporting a trendy union shirt
(We vain authors do not wear collars and ties.)

Instead of the bleeding corpses of David and John
We were treated to you gazing up into camera
In bewilderment fibbing like a spoilt child:
'Their deaths diminish us all.'
You with your paterfamilias beard,
Your Fidel Castro street-cred,
Your Parnell martyr-gaze,
Your Lincoln gravitas.
O Gerry Adams, you're a wicked boy.

Only on Sunday evening in sunlight
I met David and John up the park
Patrolling the young mums with prams.
'Going to write a poem about us, Paul?'
How they laughed! How they saluted!
How they turned their backs! Their silver spines!

Had I known it, would I have told them?
That for next Sunday's newspaper I'd compose a poem
How you, Gerry Adams, not caring to see,
Saw two angels in their silver spines shot.

I am a citizen of the nation of Ireland –
The same people living in the same place.
I hope the Protestants never leave our shores.
I am a Jew and my name is Bloom.

You, Gerry Adams, do not sign books in my name.
May God forgive me – lock, stock and barrel.

PAUL DURCAN

1. Two RUC constables were shot dead by IRA gunmen in Lurgan, Co.
Armagh, on 16 June 1997, the same day that Sinn Féin leader Gerry Adams
was seen on television signing copies of his books. This was also Bloomsday,
when Dubliners remember James Joyce, who set his novel *Ulysses* on 16 June
1904. Joyce's Leopold Bloom is his Jewish everyman figure who parallels
Ulysses (Odysseus) in Homer. The comparison of Adams with Joyce's political
hero Charles Stewart Parnell and with Abraham Lincoln is one of the poem's
many bitter ironies. When Durcan's poem was published at the end of the
same week in an Irish Sunday newspaper, the poet received death threats.

➤ 434

Wire

As I roved out this morning at daybreak
I took a short cut
through the pine forest, following the high-tension wires
past the timber line
till I stumbled upon a makeshift hide or shooting-box
from which a command-wire seemed to run

intermittently along the ski-run
or fire-break.
I glanced into the hideout. A school lunch-box.
A pear so recently cut
I thought of Ceylon. A can of Valvoline.
Crocodile clips. Sri Lanka, I mean. A hank of wire

that might come in handy if ever I'd want to hot-wire
a motor and make a run
for the border. From just beyond my line
of vision I glimpsed something, or someone, break
cover for an instant. A shaved head, maybe, or a crew-cut.
Jumping up like a jack-in-the-box

before ducking back down. Then a distant raking through the
        gear-box
of a truck suddenly gone haywire
on this hillside of hillsides in Connecticut
brought back some truck on a bomb run,
brought back so much with which I'd hoped to break –
the hard-line

yet again refusing to toe the line,
the bullet and the ballot box,
the joy-ride, the jail-break,
Janet endlessly singing 'The Men behind the Wire',[1]
the endless re-run
of Smithfield,[2] La Mon,[3] Enniskillen,[4] of bodies cut

to ribbons as I heard the truck engine cut
and, you might have read as much between the lines,
ducked down here myself behind the hide. As if I myself were on
        the run.
The truck driver handing a box-
cutter, I'm sure, to the bald guy. A pair of real live wires.
I've listened to them all day now, torn between making a break

for it and their talk of the long run, the short term, of boxing clever,
fish or cut bait, make or break,
the end of the line, right down to the wire.

PAUL MULDOON

1. *'The Men behind the Wire'*: Paddy McGuigan's song (which reached No.1 in the Irish charts) about the men held without trial at Long Kesh and Magilligan prison camps and aboard HMS *Maidstone* after internment was imposed in 1971. 2. *Smithfield:* On 21 July 1972 ('Bloody Friday'), 26 IRA bombs were set off in the space of 80 minutes in Belfast, the first of these at Smithfield bus station, killing eleven people and injuring 130. 3. *La Mon:* On 17 February 1978, an IRA incendiary bomb was set off in Gransha, Co. Down, blasting a fireball into the La Mon restaurant, killing twelve people and injuring thirty. 4. *Enniskillen:* On 8 November 1987, an IRA bomb exploded at a Remembrance Day ceremony in Enniskillen, Co. Fermanagh, killing eleven people and injuring 63; see also Michael Longley's 'Ceasefire' [➤ 454].

All of These People

Who was it who suggested that the opposite of war
Is not so much peace as civilisation? He knew
Our assassinated Catholic greengrocer who died
At Christmas in the arms of our Methodist minister,
And our ice-cream man whose continuing requiem
Is the twenty-one flavours children have by heart.
Our cobbler mends shoes for everybody; our butcher
Blends into his best sausages leeks, garlic, honey;
Our cornershop sells everything from bread to kindling.
Who can bring peace to people who are not civilised?
All of these people, alive or dead, are civilised.

MICHAEL LONGLEY
➤ 430

Progress

They say that for years Belfast was backwards
and it's great now to see some progress.
So I guess we can look forward to taking boxes
from the earth. I guess that ambulances
will leave the dying back amidst the rubble
to be explosively healed. Given time,
one hundred thousand particles of glass
will create impossible patterns in the air
before coalescing into the clarity
of a window. Through which, a reassembled head
will look out and admire the shy young man
taking his bomb from the building and driving home.

ALAN GILLIS

Alan Gillis was born in Belfast in 1973. He is a lecturer in English at Edinburgh University and editor of *Edinburgh Review*, and has published three collections of poetry.

YUGOSLAV WARS OF SUCCESSION | 1991–1999

TOTAL DEATHS: 140,000+

The Yugoslav Wars of Succession were a series of four ethno-national wars which led to the break-up of Tito's federal Yugoslavia, the first three precipitated by Serbia's attempts to annex new territories from other constituent republics that had declared independence (Slovenia, Croatia and Bosnia), followed by a fourth that culminated in the effort to expel most of the non-Serbian population (Kosova). Often portrayed in the media as a continuing war in the Balkans during the 1990s, they were in fact separate if interrelated wars, like the two earlier Balkan Wars which preceded the First World War in 1912-13.

The **Slovenian Independence War** (27 June – 7 July 1991) saw immediate victory by Slovenia over the Serb-controlled Yugoslav People's Army (JNA).

The **Croatian War of Independence** (3 March 1991 – 12 November 1995) included a ceasefire in January 1992 followed by intermittent combat during the last three years when Croats and Serbs were involved in the Bosnian War. The poems on pages 462-70 relate to this war and its aftermath.

The main belligerents in the **Bosnian War** (6 April 1992 – 14 December 1995) were the forces of the Republic of Bosnia and Herzegovina and those of the self-declared Bosnian Serb and Bosnian Croat entities within Bosnia and Herzegovina, Republika Srpska (VRS) and Herzeg-Bosnia, led and supplied by Serbia and Croatia respectively. Two million people were displaced with VRS forces responsible for the "ethnic cleansing" of Muslim Bosniak and Croat populations. Other major events included the Siege of Sarajevo (by JNA and later by VRS forces), which lasted from 5 April 1992 to 29 February 1996, a year longer than the Siege of Leningrad, and the Srebenica massacre (July 1995), when over 8,000 men and boys were slaughtered by VRS forces under General Ratko Mladić in a UN "safe area" under the protection of Dutch UN peacekeepers. The poems on pages 470-90 relate to the Bosnian War.

The **Kosova War** (28 February 1998 – 11 June 1999) was fought between the Federal Republic of Yugoslavia (the federation of Serbia and Montenegro under Slobodan Milošević), which controlled Kosova before the war, and the Kosova Liberation Army (KLA) supported by NATO and Albania. Nearly a million people were displaced and thousands massacred until a ten-week NATO bombing campaign (March – June 1999) against Yugoslavia finally forced the Serbs to withdraw their forces from Kosova. The poems on pages 491-94 relate to the Kosova War. ('Kosovo' is the Serbian spelling, 'Kosova' the Albanian.)

The poets whose work appears in this section include writers who served during these conflicts in the different armies as conscripts or volunteers or who witnessed events as civilians or journalists. Several of them lived in Sarajevo during the siege. A number of poems relate to particular events, happenings and incidents which came to be associated especially with the brutal Yugoslav Wars: the Siege of Sarajevo, snipers shooting civilians in bread queues, massacres (notably here, those at Srebenica and in Kosova), concentration camps, ethnic cleansing, rape (and "rape camps" were also set up to enforce Serb male ethnicity), and neighbours from different ethnic communities turning on each other in times of war.

My Death in the Trenches

Throw this body out of the trench!
Take his weapons
Take the clothes off him

And peel off the skin listen
He's one of ours!

So the other side don't make shoeleather of him

He's one of ours cut off his head too!

So they can't make a scarecrow
Listen

He's one of ours

And suck out the eyes

And our vision of the world
take

take it with you
away from them

While you still can...

He's one of ours

ILIJA LADIN
translated from the Bosnian by Ken Smith & Igor Klikovac

Ilija Ladin (a *nom de plume* for Ilija Kozić) was born in 1929 in Stratinska, near Banja Luka, and studied French literature at Sarajevo. A member of the 60s generation of poets, he was highly influential among the 'rock' generation of poets that emerged in the early 80s.

Essential Serbo-Croat

Guraj	Push
Pomozi mi	Help me
Boli	It hurts
Boli me	I have a pain
Boli me ovdje	I have a pain here
Bole me grudi	I have a pain in my breast
Bole me prsa	I have a pain in my chest
Boli me oko	I have a pain in my eye
Boli me stopalo	I have a pain in my foot
Boli me glava	I have a pain in my head
Hitno je	It's urgent
Ozbiljno je	It's serious
Boli me ovdje	It hurts here
Boli puno	It hurts a lot
To je jaka bol	It's a sharp pain
To je tupa bol	It's a dull pain
To je uporna bol	It's a nagging pain
Večinom vremena	Most of the time
Vrti mi se u glavi	I feel dizzy
Zlo mi je	I feel sick
Slabo mi je	I feel weak
Nije dobro	It's no good
Izgubio sam sve	I have lost everything
Ne mogu vam pomoči	I can't help you

KEN SMITH

Ken Smith (1938-2003) was an influential English poet whose work shifted territory from Yorkshire, America and London to war-ravaged Eastern Europe. He was working in Berlin when the Wall came down, writing a book which turned into *Berlin: Coming in from the* Cold (1990), and edited the anthology *Klaonica: poems for Bosnia* (1993) with Judi Benson.

Cow

Members of the household driven away, house taken, windows smashed. The cow dragged to the barn, the door bolted, they set it on fire. Dousing themselves with brandy, they listened to her mooing a long bovine eternity.

Shelter

The siren switches day for night, kneads time into shapeless lumps. Inside each lump crouches a person alone, hours for weeks, months for years. Between the rumbling and the bodily echoes, between night and day, no nights or days are spent. If the siren does end with a shriek of postponed fear, it's never the same city that the shelter exits open to.

The far road to Dalj

An abrupt surplus of angels, an angelic tempest on the tip of the needle of paradise. Stabbing, insensate.

God and the Croats exchange hostages: heads propped with rifle butts, carved ribs, hammered nails, extracted hearts like gingerbread, scapulars, powermongers – they bolster us by coming to light from the other side.

In refrigerator trucks the rose-fingered forewarnings take us back from whatever the wintry future.

In the slaughtered transubstantiations of bread and wine – Faith, Hope, Love will be made as sacrifices as long as there will be kin and generations.

It is snowing over the Madonna's gouged eyes among tearful slopes.

It's time, Dalj, coming closer.

How much homeland on the soles of shoes! Croatia is bursting like a meteor, and its shards are falling far outside this chilled world.

Belfries

Built one hundred, two hundred, three hundred years back, each goes to its own shell, the belfries have seen too much.

Belfries, once a bond between land and sky, now remind the sky of land that is no more, former belfries.

Belfries upright in name only, remembered in their lightning.

Pyramids, cones, spindles, arches, approached the skies too cautiously, moved aside at the boldest step, prevailing in idea alone.

Belfries which will never leave us again no matter where we go.

Singed earth

Where there were house, sheaves of grain, glade of trees in advance they saw gashes, smoking ruins, char.

Where there were man, woman, child, they saw bloody stain. Dust, a draft, they heard, not speech. Eyes blinded in advance, ears deafened in advance, by flash, by blast.

Where sheep, cows, horses grazed, they saw carcass.

Where they smelled blood, they saw jet, stream, river.

Where they heard song, they harkened to scream.

Where there were people, they opened black earth, in advance.

[1992]

ZVONIMIR MRKONJIĆ

translated from the Croatian by Ellen Elias-Bursac

Zvonimir Mrkonjić is a leading poet, playwright and critic, the author of numerous books of poetry and essays. Born in Split, Croatia in 1938, he has lived in Zagreb for most of his life.

nothing else

no, i was not at the square when a grenade hit
yes, someone dear to me was hit there
no, i did not sleep in a cellar
yes, i phone every night those who were sleeping there
no, i was not a man and they did not take me to the camp
yes, i met someone coming out of the wires with a bullet in his chest
no, i did not see anyone dying
yes, i saw the corpses floating along the river
no, i did not starve
yes, i sold a wedding ring and bought bread and milk
no, nobody forced me out of my home
yes, someone changed the locks and lay in my bed
no, i did not buy a tiny pistol i spotted in the shop
yes, i liked it, it would fit in my wallet
no, i did not choose the river bank i happened to be at
yes, i know, i could learn to swim
no, i was not scared
yes, i did cry watching the planes passing by
no, they did not hear me, i was far below
yes, i knew they would drop a bomb in your backyard
no, in fact i did not know, i worried they might do that
yes, i remember everything
no, it was not cold, it was a beautiful summer
i walked my baby in a stroller and sang to her
the whole day
what did i sing?
about a cloud and a bird,
a wish and a star,
la la la,
yes, nothing else

TATJANA LUKIĆ

Tatjana Lukić (1959-2008) was born in Osijek, Croatia, and lived there and in Bosnia, Serbia and the Czech Republic until 1992 when she arrived in Australia as a refugee with a young family. Already a poet published in the former Yugoslavia, she learned English and switched to writing in English. Her English poems were published posthumously in her collection *la, la, la* (2009).

In Circles

Sometimes it seems as if I'm living on borrowed time
my friends are dead and scattered across graveyards
wiped off the slate just like that, none of them even thirty
those people I used to break bread with
those people I slept in the same bunkers with
those people I walked the same grass with, climbing onto tanks and
      falling down
hitting my face against the ground showered with bullets and shells
(oh sweet quiet earth you know our prayers)
their ghosts still come back with the last of the echoing voices:
is there more juice? asks one who will die in an attack
take care of my brother, says another who will be killed by tank
the third one is trying to remember who he is and where he's coming
      from
while his brain slowly switches off (he'd been hit in the head)
what's over there? asks the fourth clutching a glass of red watered wine
his gaze fixed over the hill where an ambush has already been set up
      for him
and a fifth is silent but his eyes are able to pronounce:
Death.

sometimes it feels as if I'd broken off the chain
I wake up in the middle of the night gasping for air
hearing the hum of fourteen storeys through the open window
(the smell of burnt flesh rising out of wooden caskets)
Christ the Redeemer is a lasting fresh wound among the black clouds
electric fireflies scurry, curse and celebrate
the time when pigs fed on human flesh
down there is a house that once, a hundred years ago, used to be blue
now it is a roofless ruin with frameless windows like empty eye sockets
the inside is all wrecked but somehow at night it becomes alive
the forgotten balconies fill up with flowers and light
while round black women with turbans lean against
corroded fence and tiny echoes of their conversation
whisper that there are three hundred thousand dead people on those
      fields
where my boots lost their soles

where my eyes drowned into the mud of the universe
where my heart was like an iron rope cut off from its anchor
whizzing through the air in blind circles:
aimless, aimless.

TOMICA BAJSIĆ
translated from the Croatian by Damir Šodan

from The Wounded Man is Tempting God

I wandered around the forest of the enemy kingdom
and stumbled upon a piece of wire hidden in the grass
it was a buried PROM2 tripwire-activated
bounding anti-personnel mine
and in the split second before the explosion
I wanted God to make that cup pass me by
but when the detonation threw me in into the air I saw pieces
of iron, pieces of my uniform, pieces of my flesh whirling
in orbit / sand stars porcelain four winds tartan
razors ice / Joseph Conrad proposing to Freya the girl from
the Seven Islands / my enemies cats stealing the planet oxygen
digging through garbage / all lighthouses ablaze all the way
from the New Hebrides to the Pepper Coast / the President of Zimbabwe
Canaan Banana listening to the German radio / thousands of mummified
         fish heads
prophesying in alien tongues / Wolfgang Amadeus Mozart
making airplanes out of a piece of a newspaper –
I never liked Mozart and that's what threw me down on the ground
while the Vienna Boys' Choir sang:
'a jug goes to the water until it breaks
a jug goes to the water until it breaks'

God let that cup pass me by I thought there in the ambulance
let me live for a little bit longer at least for another 100 years
I don't want to die now that our time has come
I wanted my medals to shine like oil platforms
lighting up the night flights over the Atlantic
and my veteran's charisma to become electric

let my limousine slide through the crowd like Moby Dick
slid before the eyes of helpless captain Ahab
I never said I did not want to sell my soul
I was only negotiating the price
let me be invited at the presidential party
there are so many dishes I never tasted
there are so many people on this Earth whose destiny
I never took in my hands
[...]

TOMICA BAJSIĆ
translated from the Croatian by Damir Šodan

Tomica Bajsić was born 1968 in Zagreb, Croatia, and is a poet, prose writer, graphic designer, editor and translator. The author of six books of poetry and prose, he is editor for translated poetry in the Croatian magazine *Poezija*, and founder editor of Druga Priča Publishing. He did his compulsory military service with the 63rd Parachutist Brigade of the JNA (Yugoslav National Army), and served in the special forces of the HV (Croatian Army) General Staff, receiving the second highest Croatian medal of honour, the Order of Nikola Šubić Zrinski, for acts of heroism in saving human lives, and the Order of the Croatian Cross for sustaining severe wounds in action as well as several commendations for his work in instructing reconnaissance-sabotage units.

Boraja

We stopped by the first tavern
along the road and took
the table under the red parasol
with a Karlovac beer logo on it
we laid down our arms
and took off our jackets
we stank of sweat
and engine oil

The owner passed the brandy
to the liberating army
the waiter asked for our orders
five kilos of roast lamb

and a crate of beer
for starters

As for this Chetnik here [1]
I said
pulling his head out of the bag
I kept beside the chair
and putting it in the middle of the table
a little red wine for him
he looks a bit anaemic

The waiter laughed
everybody laughed
and the owner said
he'll get it on the house
if he asks politely

Well he did I replied
the last thing he said was

For God's sake please.

BORIS DEŽULOVIĆ
translated from the Croatian by Hamdija Demirović

1. Historically, Chetniks were Serbian self-styled monarchist elite military units established before World War I. In World War II, they sided with the fascists and fought against Tito's partisans. In the early 1990s they resurfaced as right-wing nationalist paramilitaries responsible for many atrocities committed in the territory of the former Yugoslavia. [Damir Šodan]

Boris Dežulović was born in Split in 1968. He is, or has been, a poet, novelist, illustrator, cartoonist, investigative journalist, reporter and columnist, winner of the European Press Prize 2013, and one of the founding editors of the satirical weekly, the *Feral Tribune*. This poem is from his 2005 collection *Pjesme iz Lore* (Poems from Lora), published at a time when the conduct of Croatian forces during the war was being seriously questioned following official confirmation of reports that Serbian prisoners had been badly tortured in the Lora prison camp at Split. The poems in this collection are especially shocking because they read like confessional poetry – like a Croatian Randy Newman writing in character – with gloating accounts of torture and degradation relayed in a racy, laddish style using soldiers' slang.

Hijra '92

anyway, those days they cracked down [1]
on our people damn hard.
Hasan's kid was killed right before his eyes
when they brought him to the camp to identify his dad.

but they really took offence with me
because I was a doctor, a bachelor, I had studied abroad.
plus my parents worked in Germany
and I owned three motorcycles: a Yamaha DT175, a Laverda 750s

and that old Zündapp with a passenger sidecar
that I called 'the Kraut!' but as soon as the bus
stopped at the gates I realised if I passed that guard
post – it was all over for me!

maybe some lucky fellow would stand a chance, but not me!
that's why I waited to be the last in line, lingering
for a while on the other side of the bus, pretending to tie my shoelace
and when I saw the last man walking through

and those heavy iron gates closing behind him,
I slowly stood up, and with my hands in the pockets
of my leather Avirex pilot jacket,
started walking slowly down the road.

I remember it as clearly as if it had happened today.
I even whistled so they wouldn't figure me out,
that tune by Denis & Denis:
'I'll be your computer program!' [2]

God knows why that song came to me
because as local pop goes, I always preferred Atomsko Sklonište [3]
and that crippled singer of theirs
because somehow they sounded honest and raw;

so there I was, walking like that for a while
light as a feather, though my feet were as heavy
as a two-ton refrigerator truck!
and then, coming upon the first bend, I dashed

into a cornfield where I spent the next five days.
what did I eat? the bark off trees
munching it like the Partisans did – ha ha – only there weren't
any trees in sight, let alone a Partisan.

so I stumbled one morning onto the asphalt road
and collapsed, luckily, a bunch of international humanitarians
came by and picked me up and then –
onward to Zagreb! *Via Zagabria!* and there

long lines at counters, huge crowds and pissing rain
for a good seven days. as for the bikes – they never found them;
one remained in the garage at my aunt's and the other two
are still rotting beneath the tarpaulin in the barn.

DAMIR ŠODAN
translated from the Croatian by the author

1. This poem is based on the story told by a man who through an act of desperate bravery escaped from a Serbian concentration camp for Muslims in northwestern Bosnia in 1992. 2. *Denis & Denis*: a popular 1980s electropop duo in the former Yugoslavia. 3. *Atomsko Sklonište* (Atomic Shelter): a 1970s Croatian hard rock band known for their strong antiwar lyrics.

Damir Šodan (*b.* 1964) is a poet, playwright, editor and translator. Born in Split, Croatia, he studied English Literature and History at Zagreb University, and works as a translator for the UN War Crimes Tribunal for the former Yugoslavia in The Hague, where he has lived for many years. He is an associate editor of *Poezija* and *Quorum* magazines in Zagreb, and has published four books of poetry, two collections of plays and an anthology of contemporary Croatian 'neorealist' poetry, *Walk on the Other Side* (2010).

Kalesija Flash: The Ballad of a Boy from My Band

he stuttered as a child and thus spoke little
one late summer he heard *house of the rising sun*
on the radio and thereafter we saw him less and less
in school and more and more in the garage
plucking at the thick strings of a white bass guitar

if you want blood you've got it
thin and hunched with a joint stuck behind his ear
he shook his hips on stage where our music
sounded as bad as *never mind the bollocks*
I heard he stopped stuttering during the war
yet he still spoke less and less and smoked more and more
trading freshly cut-off human ears
for stale cigarettes
shining his kalashnikov like a fender guitar
singing a duke sinđelić[1] song in tom waits' voice
cold cold ground my brother
cold cold ground

DRAGOSLAV DEDOVIĆ
translated from the Bosnian by Damir Šodan

1. Stevan Sinđelić (1771-1809) was a Serbian military commander who came to prominence during the First Serbian Uprising (1804-13) against the Ottoman rule. He is an often celebrated figure in Serbian heroic folk songs. [Tr.]

Dragoslav Dedović was born in Zemun, Serbia, in 1963, and grew up in Bosnia where he worked as a journalist and editor. He publicly stood up against the war and the use of force to settle the disputes between the Yugoslav nations; and when war broke out in Bosnia in 1992, he emigrated to the West. A widely published poet and short story writer, he now works as an editor at Deutsche Welle Radio in Germany.

Hagiographic Joke

the country where I was born
at war with my mother's motherland
my mother's fatherland at war
with my sister's homeland
too many corpses I think
for an ordinary family feud
I shall leave and my son will be born
in the promised land whose language
my father learned in a concentration camp
during the previous war

the same language I will whisper good night in
to the woman I love

sometimes I will use that language
to tell my life's story
because I am endlessly amused
by that frozen uncomprehending look
on a person's face

if someone
would tell me a story like that
I would die laughing

DRAGOSLAV DEDOVIĆ
translated from the Bosnian by Damir Šodan

Palais Jalta

a Catholic priest from Boka
plays piano as the stoned veteran
curses the mother of the ample-chested émigré
– he is an undiscovered author
and she knows some German publishers –
the sarma[1] tastes great and the wine is Spanish
etc.
Jasko, the former left-handed midfielder
with Kalesija Jedinstvo
watches me from somewhere above
his brother identified him
on the truck full of corpses
thanks to his *Nike* sneakers

DRAGOSLAV DEDOVIĆ
translated from the Bosnian by Damir Šodan

1. Sarma is a dish of vine, cabbage or chard leaves stuffed usually with mince.
It can be found in most cuisines of the former Ottoman Empire, from the
Middle East to the Balkans. [Tr.]

I would call her my girlfriend

but they tell me the word is patronising,
and it's true she was in her thirties
with two young children
and she turned old so quickly.

When I found her with the rest of her village
she was older than my grandmother
and just as dead due to the butcher knife
sticking in her vagina.

And then there was her daughter
whom I had carried on my shoulders that morning,
she was old too, like a great aunt,
and shrivelled with bullets.

Then the son – God knows where he is,
probably in a hole somewhere dug for a dead fighter,
because he was old enough to be a fighter
being about ten, and there were fighters

that age in Bosnia, plenty of them.
So they're quite right, I shouldn't patronise
and call her my girlfriend
because she was too old

old as death. Even her little daughter
was older than me when I dragged them both
to the ditch where all the others were laid out
and kicked earth over them.

COLIN MACKAY

Colin Mackay (1951-2003) was a Scottish poet and novelist. He was working as a nightwatchman at Edinburgh's Meadowbank football stadium when he decided he had to help the people of Bosnia, driving to the war-torn country with a friend taking a van load of provisions. There he met and fell in love with Svetlana, the widow of a Bosnian Muslim who'd been killed in the war, and was trying to arrange for her and her two children to go to Scotland with

him when the family was slaughtered along with her whole village. He found
her body and that of her daughter Ludmilla; the body of her son Ahmad was
discovered later. This poem is from his sequence telling that story in *Cold
Night Lullaby* (1998). Colin Mackay later took his own life.

The Minutes of Hasiba

(from an interview on 6 November 1992)

They came at night with their flashlights
Through PARTISANS' HALL
They took me with them and we drove
To a bridge over the Drina
On the bridge stood
Ten older women Tied up
And fifteen soldiers They yelled
Here comes one of yours See how we love her
Then they did everything with me All fifteen of them
Afterwards they smoked and put out their cigarettes
In my hair Then one soldier took
His knife and slit a farmer's throat
Not quite through So that his head stayed on his shoulders
It didn't bother me anymore I had
Seen so much already I didn't care
Then he tore his head off entirely and they played
Soccer with it and laughed and laughed
I knew the farmers They were
Neighbours colleagues relatives
Just a few weeks ago I knew most
Of the soldiers too They were
Neighbours colleagues relatives They were
Men like you

HOLGER TESCHKE
translated from the German by Margitt Lehbert

Holger Teschke (*b.* 1958) is a German poet, dramatist and essayist, born in
East Germany, who was dramaturg at the Berliner Ensemble from 1987 to
1999. He has since taught theatre directing in the US and worked as a free-
lance writer in Berlin.

Luck in Sarajevo

In Sarajevo
in the spring of 1992,
everything is possible:

you go stand in a bread line
and end up in an emergency room
with your leg amputated.

Afterwards, you still maintain
that you were very lucky.

IZET SARAJLIĆ
translated from the Bosnian by Charles Simic

Izet Sarajlić (1930-2002) was one of the most popular and widely translated writers of the former Yugoslavia: a poet, historian, philosopher, essayist, editor, journalist and translator. Born in Doboj, he lived in Sarajevo from 1945, where he remained during the siege (and was wounded by a shell). In 1971 he became president of the Writers Union of Bosnia-Herzegovina, but was dismissed 17 days later and subsequently expelled from the Communist Party.

War Game

on the top of the highest tower
of the Old Town
a sharpshooter
has his nest
the distance between
him and the place
where we
are crossing
is about fifty
metres in a straight
line

if for a moment
you forget
that you need to run fast
bullets warn you
and if they don't
it means you're dead.

FARUK ŠEHIĆ
translated from the Bosnian by Vesna Stamenković

Faruk Šehić was born in Bihać, western Bosnia, in 1970, grew up in Bosanska Krupa, and was studying veterinary medicine in Zagreb until the outbreak of war in 1992. He served in the Army of Bosnia-Herzegovina from 1992 to 1995, leading a unit of 130 men as a lieutenant. He writes poetry, prose, essays and literary reviews. He has published six books of poetry, most recently *Street Epistles* (2009). He now lives in Sarajevo.

Rules and Duties

at night you listen
you're on the lookout during the day
those are your duties
on the line
there's nothing
in between
you eat when there's
food and time
you smoke with gusto
you rarely sleep
you've become
just a bunch
of sharpened senses
you also count
on the luck factor
and something else
you wear a charm
for protection

in spite of it all
you believe you won't
survive
you're getting used to death
and that's exactly what keeps you
alive.

FARUK ŠEHIĆ
translated from the Bosnian by Vesna Stamenković

The Corpse

On the bridge we slowed down,
and watched dogs in the snow along Miljacka
tearing apart a human corpse.
Then we went on.

Nothing in me changed.
I listened to the snow spattering under tyres
like when teeth crush an apple;
and felt this wild desire

to laugh at you
because you call this place 'hell'
and run away; telling yourself
that outwith Sarajevo, death is unknown.

SEMEZDIN MEHMEDINOVIĆ
translated from the Bosnian by Kathleen Jamie & Antonela Glavinić

Born in 1960 near Tuzla, **Semezdin Mehmedinović** is a poet, filmmaker
and journalist. With its urban inflection and focus on everyday life, his early
work (along with that of Ranko Sladojević) marked an influential turning-point
in contemporary Bosnian poetry. When war broke out in 1992, he remained
in Sarajevo, publishing *Sarajevo Blues*, poems and stories from the city under
siege. With Benjamin Filipović he co-wrote and co-directed *Mizaldo, Kraj
Teatra* (Mizaldo, End of Theatre, 1994), one of the first Bosnian films made
during the war. He emigrated to the US in 1996.

The Pillow

Why is this pillow black,
The little boy wonders, lying back.
Inside him, a bullet. How did it enter?
Through the window, crazy splinter!

And the window itself, how black it is!
Nothing can be seen outside
Or in the room. Behind his eyes
It's blackout, Lights Out, time has died.
Call that a game? To get up, go out,
For the bombs to stop, for the silly war
Not to be such a bore...

Is there anything sweet?
Only some sugar. He'd kill for an ice cream!
Only the voice-overs, and the screams.

RANKO SLADOJEVIĆ
translated from the Bosnian by Harry Clifton & Antonela Glavinić

Ranko Sladojević was born in 1951 in Fojnica, near Sarajevo, and studied German language and literature at Sarajevo University where he taught in the German department until the outbreak of war. Influenced by the 'new subjectivity' of German writing in the 60s and early 70s, his early work was experimental, while his later war poems showed a return to traditional forms. He is a distinguished critic of contemporary literature in the former Yugoslavia and Germany, and has translated poetry and philosophy from the German. He now lives in Heidelberg.

Lunch on Day Seventy-seven

A typical conversation with the neighbours –
What will be the outcome of all this?
Hopefully, solutions will be found,
The quicker the better. Really, as it is,

Excitement's killing everyone. Who knows
When next we see our missing sons and daughters
Whether they'll be recognisable?
Danger around us, like a gambler's throw,

But it has been asked of us to linger here
Eating winter lunch off summer plates.
Still, the Great One gives us our desserts –

If only He would let the suffering stop! –
And coffee for afters. Not what you'd call good cheer
But better than nothing – food, and talking shop.

RANKO SLADOJEVIĆ
translated from the Bosnian by Harry Clifton & Antonela Glavinić

Immortal Instant

The sniper at work over the street corner acts.
Two girls, breathless after the dash across,
radiate heat and bouquets, as when ironing
silken delicates. With one, in place of a chignon,
goosefleshed Christmas wheat.[1] She explodes, rages,
curses the sniper; at the window, seemingly,
I'm watching a beautiful storm. From the other, words
Like a sun-umbrella's flutterings, in the morning,
on an Adriatic beach. Now and again, she flicks her head
back: just for us. As she well knows: flicked hair
sweetens the air. Beauty, always forthcoming, never
misses a half-smile. As they well know: making us happy
costs them nothing. Those half-smiles saying
you aren't just one fact among others – not at all,
not for them – even banishing the hex of that fact
if any other woman's glacial look had magicked it up.
The air smelt strongly of my distant youth
when every boulevard led to the end of the world,
when life was not yet 'threadbare as a proverb'.

Now they're going, leaving such tenderness in me
as engulfs you when looking too long at the heavens
into which snowflakes are swarming.
So they disappeared chattering, not girls
but breezes, blown lightly, surprisingly,
through the St John's heat of siege. The St John's heat
of being.

MARKO VEŠOVIĆ
translated from the Bosnian by Chris Agee

1. *Christmas wheat:* the Orthodox tradition of growing wheat in a small pot,
for the Christmas season.

When the Shells Thunder

the eye observes only trifles:
grey tuft of hair sprouting from an old man's ear,
a hand stubbing a butt into bits of ashes
        in a yellow ashtray,
black half-moon under a neighbour's thumbnail,
a bent tack in dust,
a plate with two biscuits seeming
    yellow stars from a Jewish sleeve,
a spider suspended over a chasm like a mountaineer on a rope,
a woman's shoes, slush-stained, retaining
    white markings resembling a map of the Adriatic coast:
reality unstrings itself,
spills into trifles as if under the enlargement of a magnifying glass,
shatters into splinters from which the World
has simply disappeared: those aren't children in a cellar
but young in a den; that's no longer woman's hair
but split ends on a skull (through dead as a wig);
shells blow reality to smithereens,
evaporating at once all unifying forces;
detonation, all meaning sucked from the earthly,

'backwards the shaped world begins to move,
     melts the metal of ancient plate':[1]
while all around us lie the ruins, not of Sarajevo
     but of Jericho.

MARKO VEŠOVIĆ
translated from the Bosnian by Chris Agee

1. The quoted verse is from Goethe.

Stray

> *When the sail suddenly droops as the mast breaks.*
>   DANTE

Squatting, on the staircase, to the cat belonging to no one
I feed and stroke. Eyes older than the world –
looking at me, from the long-long ago. The thought flashes:
if I had one drop of happiness, I wouldn't survive.
Yet evil, or God, isn't permitted me. What's more, he said,
I'm not tormenting you, up here in my office,
as much as I planned. What's more, I'm not through mocking
your enthusiasms. Supposing each evil must have
its good: now amidst the indifference of a different people
I rest from that excessive and wearying love
lavished upon me by my own people. I look deeply
into the cat's eyes, as if studying distance
across a seascape: all's empty from here
to the childhood soul – the sacked church
of Saint Francis in Matavulj's novel.[1]
And living queasy as dandruff on the shoulders
of an old bachelor. Hollow nights spent
above papers, as if ministering to a gravely ill patient.
Wherever I go – always – I'm dogged
by futility arriving a half-hour before.
Life is a nightmare with a stone for a cushion.
My enthusiasms were ridiculous, like the walk of characters

481

in a silent film. All the world traffics itself
into my soul. It's late, late for everything:
sense and nonsense, joy, sorrow.
Time seems swifter than a smuggler's high-speed powerboat
no naval launch could possibly overtake.
I'm left feeding cats in Sarajevo,
or conversing with people as if fanning a fire
out of sodden wood, at the end of a century in which Evil,
like the altars of Easter, spread wide its doors.
When one looks straight into a cat's eyes, one sees far off
into first tears. Even farther. To the wax candle
on the wake-table. Even farther. To the earthen grave
no higher than a camel's hump. Well, living is sad –
sad as the caged song of a blind goldfinch. And bitterer still
the soul in its monkish cell, where truth was born, belonging to
        no one,
like the street's cats. Mine were the succours
of the ashtray. Mine are enthusiasms justly mocked:
fervours, eagernesses, resembling that opera-singer
forced, in Buchenwald, to sing his big aria
while the laager-people are beaten to death.

MARKO VEŠOVIĆ
translated from the Bosnian by Chris Agee

1. *Simo Matavulj:* an 19th-century Serbian writer from Dalmatia.

Marko Vesović was born in 1945 in Pape, Montenegro, and has lived in Sarajevo since the early 60s. He studied at Sarajevo University, where he taught literature for many years. Suffused with an ironic, Rabelaisian wit, his early poetry both mocks an imperfect world and celebrates the enchantments of childhood memory with gentleness and ardour. Also a highly respected critic and novelist, and an influential opponent of Serb nationalism, he published articles and essays in the journal *Slobodna Bosna* (Free Bosnia) during the siege of Sarajevo. *Polish Cavalry*, his collection of poems written during the siege, appeared in 2002.

Fahrudin Zilkić was born in 1968 in Plav, Montenegro, and has lived in Sarajevo since 1981. He was mobilised during the war, and has since worked as a journalist for *Oslobodjenje*. His first book of poems appeared in 1995.

Ricochet

It's when you define the world's sides,
when you run across a section of road
between two bushes.

It's when you hear the shot,
and while you're lying flat on your
face you're spattered with gravel.

Ricochet –
it's when a year later
you recognise the scar on the stone
where your life went on again.

FAHRUDIN ZILKIĆ
translated from the Bosnian by Francis R. Jones

People Talking

> *They never said a bad word about the people who did this*
> *to them. Except for expressing disbelief at what was done to them.*
>
> JEAN-RENÉ RUEZ, Chief Investigator for Srebrenica
> speaking about the survivors

Ignorance

He says: Cross yourself!
And I cross myself.
But I didn't know
so I used my whole hand.
And then he takes
the blunt edge of the axe
to my hand.
But, believe me, girl,
I didn't know.

Natural disaster

They brought us here
to a complex:
a bunch of houses and
garages.
You go into one, into another,
into a third.
And then you come out dead.

Revenge

I know who killed my wife and
son and
daughter.
I know, one of them came back.
Opened a bakery.
But I make sure
I never buy anything there.

Showering

They sway like algae
as the guards wash them with
fire hoses.
About thirty men I
don't know. All naked.
And Hajra, the bank
teller, among them.
To this day,
as far as I know,
the bodies have not been found.

Occupation

I used to be a lawyer.
Today, I'm a victim.

Birthday

We all gathered
there. In front
of the car battery factory.
And it was hot, July.
Next to me
on the asphalt
at the same time
a child was being born.

Survivors

Twice
quietly
so mother wouldn't hear
and get a fright
I took father
off
the gallows.

(Ključ, Sanski Most, Prijedor, Foča, Sarajevo, Srebrenica)
Noted down by Adisa Bašić, Sarajevo.

ADISA BAŠIĆ
translated from the Bosnian by Ulvija Tanović

Poet and journalist **Adisa Bašić** was born in 1979 in Sarajevo. She has pub-
lished three poetry collections, and is an Assistant Professor of Poetry and
Creative Writing at the Department of Comparative Literature and Library
Science, Sarajevo Faculty of Philosophy.

The Field-mouse

Summer, and the long grass is a snare drum.
The air hums with jets.
Down at the end of the meadow,
far from the radio's terrible news,
we cut the hay. All afternoon
its wave breaks before the tractor blade.
Over the hedge our neighbour travels his field
in a cloud of lime, drifting our land
with a chance gift of sweetness.

The child comes running through the killed flowers,
his hands a nest of quivering mouse,
its black eyes two sparks burning.
We know it will die and ought to finish it off.
It curls in agony big as itself
and the star goes out in its eye.
Summer in Europe, the field's hurt,
and the children kneel in long grass,
staring at what we have crushed.

Before day's done the field lies bleeding,
the dusk garden inhabited by the saved, voles,
frogs, a nest of mice. The wrong that woke
from a rumour of pain won't heal,
and we can't face the newspapers.
All night I dream the children dance in grass
their bones brittle as mouse-ribs, the air
stammering with gunfire, my neighbour turned
stranger, wounding my land with stones.

GILLIAN CLARKE

Gillian Clarke (*b.* 1937) became the third National Poet of Wales in 2008. She lives in rural Ceredigion. Her poem 'The Field-mouse' was written during hay-making time in Wales, during the Bosnian War: 'It seemed far away, yet it was in Europe, as we are too. All over the European countryside the same seasonal work must be done.'

Striking Distance

Was there one moment when the woman
who's always lived next door turned stranger
to you? In a time of fearful weather
did the way she laughed, or shook out her mats
make you suddenly feel as though
she'd been nursing a dark side to her difference
and bring that word, in a bitter rush
to the back of the throat – *Croat/Muslim/*
Serb – the name, barbed, ripping
its neat solution through common ground?

Or has she acquired an alien patina
day by uneasy day, unnoticed
as fallout from a remote explosion?
So you don't know quite when you came to think
the way she sits, or ties her scarf,
is just like a Muslim/Serb/Croat;
and she uses their word for water-melon
as usual, but now it's an irritant
you mimic to ugliness in your head,
surprising yourself in a savage pleasure.

Do you sometimes think, she could be you,
the woman who's trying to be invisible?
Do you have to betray those old complicities –
money worries, sick children, men?
Would an open door be too much pain
if the larger bravery is beyond you
(you can't afford the kind of recklessness
that would take, any more than she could);
while your husband is saying you don't understand
those people/Serbs/Muslims/Croats?

One morning, will you ignore her greeting
and think you see a strange twist to her smile –
for how could she not, then, be strange to herself
(this woman who lives nine inches away)
in the inner place where she'd felt she belonged,

which, now, she'll return to obsessively
as a tongue tries to limit a secret sore?
And as they drive her away, will her face
be unfamiliar, her voice, bearable:
a woman crying, from a long way off?

CAROLE SATYAMURTI

➤ 254

The Black Swans

(for Eddie, who served in Bosnia as a UN peacekeeper)

Through a panel of glass in the back of the wagon
the country went past. You clean your weapon,
make camp, drive around, stand guard, stand down.
Sit with a gun in your hand and your thumb up your arse.
Or you try to get shot at – just for a laugh.

Nineteen, fighting the boredom, wearing a blue lid.
Then one day the kid who gets smokes for the lads
walks into the woods and never comes back.
Then one day the Black Swans[1] drive by in a van –
a death squad of Bennies[2] in bobble hats, wielding Kalashnikovs,
smirking, running their fingers across their throats.
Not to be checked or blocked. A law unto themselves.

Walk in the valley. Walk in the shadow of death
in the wake of the Black Swans, treading the scorched earth.
Houses trashed and torched. In a back yard
a cloud of bluebottles hides a beheaded dog.
This woman won't talk, standing there open-mouthed,
tied to a tree, sliced from north to south.
In the town square, a million black-eyed bullet-holes stare
and stare. Crows lift from the mosque. Behind the school,
flesh-smoke – sweet as incense – rises and hangs
over mounds of soil planted with feet and hands.

SIMON ARMITAGE

488

1. The Black Swans were Bosnian Muslim paramilitaries. 2. *Bennies:* British army slang, originally referring to Falkland islanders, many of whom wore woollen caps like the character Benny in the TV soap *Crossroads*.

Simon Armitage (*b.* 1963) is a well-known English poet who has worked on many radio and TV documentaries. This poem and 'Remains' [➤ 537] are based on the testimonies of traumatised veterans of the Gulf War and the Balkan conflicts (as well as the Malaya Emergency) who appeared with him in *The Not Dead*, a film shown on Channel Four in 2007. Eddie served in Bosnia as a UN peacekeeper:

'A born soldier, he expected to shoot and be shot at – that's what he was trained for. Instead, he lifted the barrier at the checkpoint to wave through the death squads. A couple of days later he'd be a member of the party that went in to witness the horror and clean up the mess. [...] There are other things he won't describe, he says, because they are worse. After returning home, to try and cure his nerves and overcome his paranoid reaction to loud bangs, he took a revolver into the middle of a field and fired several blank rounds against his head. He also tried to hang himself from a tree. [...] And the last word came not from a man but from the voice of Laura, Eddie's wife. Tracing the scar of a bullet that took away part of her husband's face before pinballing through his body, she describes the slow and painful process of trying to reach him, touch him, love him, and make him human again. In the film, the scene provides an obvious, ironic contrast with Britain itself, its majors and generals bemused, irritated and embarrassed by these broken men, the mother country washing her hands of those soldiers who escape death only to return home as "untouchables", as haunted and haunting ghosts.' [SA]

Horror

Broken streets. Broken footsteps.
Broken cages for birds and animals called – people
Broken youths in broken cars
Broken skulls in broken hospitals
Broken brains on broken tables
Broken girlish giggles in a broken cellar
Broken foetuses in broken wombs
Broken mothers on broken burial mounds
Broken breath in the broken government air
Broken heart on the broken threshold
Broken thoughts in broken dustbins
Broken God in his broken temple

Broken earth under the broken cupola of heaven
Broken self.

Smashed skulls on smashed spines
Smashed clavicle
Smashed pelvic bone on the woman who just gave birth
Smashed young bones in young flesh
Smashed bullets by a smashed wall
Smashed vowels in smashed exhalations
Smashed child's knee on the smashed arm of his father
Smashed instruments in the smashed hands of the doctor
Smashed rose petals in smashed garden ornaments
Smashed prayers in smashed tongues
Smashed self.

Frightened beasts in their frightened lairs
Frightened children in frightened games
Frightened shoppers for bread in the frightened square
Frightened passengers on the frightened bus
Frightened voices of speakers on the frightened news
Frightened candles in frightened cellars
Frightened lungs in the frightened air
Frightened blossom on the frightened branches
Frightened soldiers, frightened guns at the ready
Frightened citizens in frightened offices
Frightened articles in frightened newspapers
Frightened voices of relatives in frightened neighbouring countries
Frightened water in the kettle in the frightened evenings
Frightened anaesthetics in frightened glass cupboards
Frightened backs under frightened cudgels
Frightened vagina of a frightened schoolgirl
Frightened souls cowering in frightened flesh
Frightened self.

STEVAN TONTIĆ
translated from the Bosnian by Mary Radosavljević

Stevan Tontić is a prolific poet and translator. Born in 1946 in Sanski Most,
he studied philosophy and sociology in Sarajevo. He has published numerous
poetry collections and anthologies. He left Sarajevo in 1993, living in Berlin
for nine years, but returned in 2001.

Search and Destroy

'They came in the night,'
Besa said, holding the buggy tight.
'We were scared, hiding between
buildings and under floors.
We ran from house to house
through holes in walls,
it was dangerous to go through doors!

They burned our homes,
with our people inside,
and there by the stream,
see there is Mendi and Teki,
my cousins with the others
forming a hill of corpses
and in the old marketplace
you will see the broken cobbles
filled with blood.

I am alive – see, this is my child.
I covered her mouth with my hand
like this, till the shooting ended,
I am alive but I am not happy.'

[Djakovica massacre, Kosova, March 1999]

MICHAEL J. WHELAN

Michael J. Whelan (*b.* 1970) is a soldier, poet, writer and historian living in
Tallaght, Co. Dublin, with over 24 years service in the Irish Defence Forces.
He was deployed as a United Nations Peacekeeper in South Lebanon and with
KFOR in Kosova during the 1990s. ➤ See also 406, 494.

Mass Grave, Padalishtë

A tiny mound. Nine fresh graves. For the second time
In two days in the killing fields
Inner tears —— It was clear

That little Afrim, commemorated on the hill behind,
Had been buried here. Mother and Father, his six sisters
In a row narrowing to his five year old smallness:

The whole Imeraj clan
Whose names and ages I had just jotted down
In sight of their cousins' graves down a grassy knoll –

Tape fluttering, a lone trainer on the rise –
Still cloying the air with the sickly sweetish
Dead flesh reek

Yesterday's Spanish [1] had unearthed. I am sweating,
Dust has coated my boots,
I have followed the others down a highway bend

To this gash of earth on a verge
Of thorny pasturage, on from
The abstract pathos of the wooden sign

Where I felt plunged into
The inward isobar of a sudden profundity,
August in Kosova,

This hour's whole archipelago of beauty and terror
That felt burnt like some high kingdom of the ur-moment
Through the ozone of consciousness. Where MUP had descended

From the passes to Serbia
Like mountainous evil in a Finnish epic,
Where Abraham might have slaughtered his seed,

We stand before the simple fact
In silence, eyes meeting, *catastrophe* murmured
In Albanian. I squat, fingering

The clods as if touching his tragedy,
Thinking somehow of his boy's perspirant brow,
How much he was loved,

The unbelievableness of sinking a bullet
Like a sink head
Into the same skull. Rising,

Inner tears...
As if the inner was tearing, listening
To the crunch, inside, of our steps on the dirt road

Towards the burnt houses and rolling uplands
Where their lives ended,
Where high hay is aflush with wildflowers and luminescence,

Where sleepers of shadow dapple the road;
Picking up, on the way back,
From the clods, a bit of jumper

Blanched like a dishrag's threads; from a thorn
Near Afrim's mound, a shoelace tied to plastic twine;
From a few paces, a scrap of sock.

CHRIS AGEE

1. *Yesterday's Spanish:* a patrol of Spanish NATO soldiers.

Chris Agee (*b.* 1956) is an American-born poet and editor who was in Sarajevo at the end of the siege, an experience recounted in his essay 'A Week in Sarajevo'. He was arrested by the Yugoslav Army in June 1999 during the Kosova War, and returned immediately to its killing fields as NATO took control of the country. His anthology, *Scar on the Stone: Contemporary Poetry from Bosnia* (1998), was described by Stephen Schwartz as 'one of the most important volumes in English brought into print as a result of the worldwide attention paid to the Bosnian War'. He divides his time between Ireland and his house near Dubrovnik, Croatia.

Roadside Bomb

Torn into shreds, metal fused to flesh and flesh
to metal borne, veins and skin dripping,
unwrapping from bones,
legs hanging from roof windows,
arms stretched out as if shaking hands with their
murderer or waving, others swimming in boiling
blood pooling between half bodied seats
and broken conversations,
their own bewildered faces looking on.

We had felt the tremor but took no notice,
you get used to that after a while, though we heard
the details later, how they'd timed it perfectly under
a bus full of mourners, ripping it apart in the centre
of a convoy of peacekeepers as it crossed over
the border to a cemetery where their loved ones lived
safely, under the ground in one piece,
waiting, on the old.

[17 February 2001]

MICHAEL J. WHELAN
➤ 491

Serbian Orthodox Church's annual Day of the Dead: a Serbian bus is blown
up while being escorted into Kosova by NATO armoured vehicles. [MJW]

IRAQ WARS | 1980–2011

Iran-Iraq War: 22 September 1980 – 20 August 1988

Following a long history of border disputes, and amid fears that that the Iranian Revolution in 1979 would inspire insurgency among its long-suppressed Shia majority, Iraq's leader Saddam Hussein ordered his forces to invade Iran, but they were quickly repelled. A conflict similar to the First World War continued for the next six years involving trench warfare and the use by Iraq of chemical weapons, also used in the genocidal al-Anfal Campaign [➤ 500] against the Kurdish people (and other non-Arab populations) in northern Iraq during the latter part of the war and responsible for the deaths of 182,000 civilians.

DEATHS: Iran forces, 200,000–800,000; Iraqi forces, 105,000–375,000; civilians on both sides, 100,000+ (excludes al-Anfal)

Gulf War: 2 August 1990 – 28 February 1991

The Gulf War was fought by a coalition of forces led by the US against Iraq following Iraq's invasion of the neighbouring oil-rich state of Kuwait. After five weeks of fierce aerial bombardment, a ground assault was launched on 24 February which resulted in heavy Iraqi losses and the destruction of hundreds of tanks and other military vehicles. The war received massive media coverage, with live television footage of planes taking off from aircraft carriers and missiles hitting their targets beamed into homes around the world, and graphic pictures of war and destruction published in the press [➤ 504, 511]. Many of the writers responding to the war drew upon these sources, with some poets also borrowing the military jargon of the time to expose whatever horrors were being hidden or obscured by such terminology [➤ 513].

DEATHS: Coalition forces, 482; Kuwait, 200; Iraqi forces, 20,000–35,000; civilians 4000+.

Iraq War: 20 March 2003 – 15 December 2011

The second invasion of Iraq, led by the US and supported by the UK and their allies, resulted in regime change and the overthrow and later execution of Saddam Hussein, but was initially approved by Congress and Parliament because of claims (later proved unfounded) that Iraq held and intended to use weapons of mass destruction (WMD). Attempts to rebuild the country have since been hampered by a continuing insurgency against the occupiers and the new Iraqi government as well as by scandals such as the human rights violations at Abu Ghraib prison, where US Army military police and CIA personnel were abusing and torturing prisoners in 2003-04. Saadi Youssef's poem 'The Wretched of the Heavens' was written in response to this [➤ 525], while Macdara Woods's 'Driving to Charleston' is concerned with the morally ambiguous reaction to the scandal in the US [➤ 526]. Torture methods used at Abu Ghraib and elsewhere included "waterboarding" [➤ 530].

DEATHS: Coalition forces and Iraqi Security Forces (post-Saddam), 24,219; Iraqi combatants (invasion period), 7,600–11,000; insurgents (post-Saddam), 21,221–26,405; civilians, 115,598–126,166.

The Sky in a Helmet

I was bewildered before the bullet –
both of us together
there beneath the flattened sky,
                              dreading death
I gathered my life's pieces into my rucksack....
                    and portioned it out:
                              for my son...
                              for my library...
                              for the trenches

(for childhood, an orphaning...
and for my woman, poetry
                    and poverty...
for the war, this chronic bleeding....
and for memory... just ashes)

Now what is left to you of the life
you used to carry between bunker and hope
always fearing this shrapnel of time.
The sergeant said:
This is death &
it doesn't deal in addition, subtraction
so choose a hole the size of your desire
this is the time for holes & for heads...
Or...
run for it
right now...
          from such impossible death
(– for there's no way out...
the earth is narrower than we thought
...narrower than that miser's palm...
and who'll take the orphan to safety
where the horizon goes dark ...
and the face of morning blacks out).
....
No worries
I piled together what was left of me

496

and charged ahead...
– but where to...?!
Between you & death there's an invisible muzzle
and the question two small children asked:
                    – 'Daddy, when are you coming back...?'
I turned round...
The sergeant yelled: This is your homeland now...
my heart shuddered, white with weakness
I choked with tears of humiliation:
– O sky of Iraq...
                    is there air to breathe
I looked everywhere...
Iraq's sky was punctured with shrapnel
and it was ....

....
I tripped on a rock
saw my burst boot laughing at me...
(– No worries...
let the fat clerks who sit behind their desks write
                    about – the fat of the land)
....

In a room, twenty years ago
She used – fearfully – to mend my worn trousers
Washing off her shame with her tears
....
– Father, where is my pocket money...?!
my friends have gone to school already...
....
(My friends have gone to their bullets
such destinies are deaf...)
My friends...
my friends...
my fri...
I fell...
and my homeland gathered me in...
and we raced to the barricade
challenging death together
Which of us will protect –

O my homeland –
> his own head...?

We have just one helmet...
> just one.

[Baghdad, 1986]

ADNAN AL-SAYEGH
translated from the Arabic by Stephen Watts & Marga Burgui-Artajo

Adnan al-Sayegh was born in al-Kufa, Iraq, in 1955, and is from the gener-
ation of Iraqi poets known as the Eighties Movement. He was conscripted to
serve in the army during the Iran-Iraq War, when this poem was written. In
1993 his criticisms of Saddam Hussein's oppressive rule led to his exile in
Jordan and Lebanon, and in 1996 he was sentenced to death *in absentia* for his
poem 'Uruk's Anthem'. After living in Sweden for many years, he moved to
London in 2004. In 2006 he returned to Iraq to read at a poetry festival, but
was forced to leave in haste when threatened with death or having his tongue
cut out after his poems upset the armed militia in Basra. ➤ 516

The spoils, 1988
(for the 182,000 victims of Anfal, Kurdistan, Iraq)

Anfal came!
The little sparrows stopped practising their first flight.
The sheep died drinking from the water they trusted.
The caves were choked in gas.
The houses were flattened.

The villagers were taken, separated,
those who cried were shot because they cried,
those who didn't were shot because they didn't.
They were kept in the southern sands.
Those who survived the desert
were buried together, alive.

Anfal came!
The soldiers spoke a foreign language.

The villagers thought they were Muslim brothers
but they spat at the Qura'an the imams held before them,
pissed on the engraved name of Allah,
bulldozed the village mosques.

Anfal came and some survived it.
Of those who survived
some went back and rebuilt their houses.
They washed the roads, perfumed the air,
replanted the trees.

Some couldn't bear to return.
They left for unknown destinations
and started their lives in a new land
speaking in a foreign language.
They got remarried, had new children, found jobs,
laughed and danced as before.

But sometimes, on very hot days
when the land smelt a particular way
listening to music
they would remember Anfal.

CHOMAN HARDI

Dropping gas: 16th March 1988

It is not quiet in Halabja, though it should be.
I return from the mountains with the rest.
What is it about wanting to know?
Wanting to see so that you believe?
What is it about not being able to just let go?

Half of the houses are still standing
and the rest, you can see what they were made of –
bricks and cement, windows and doors
flesh and blood.

There are screams and cries everywhere
of those discovering the bodies of their loved ones –
children who managed to escape their courtyards
and died outside on the steps,
a man's back and the face of his baby under his arm.

My neighbour says, *They are all dead.*
He wants to show me his family.
There are some journalists taking photos,
some men robbing the dead bodies
and a clear sky –
it's all dead now, cannot be killed any more.

I stand detached from everything,
observing, believing and not believing.
My neighbour will lose his mind and kill himself next week,
a woman who does not find her daughter
will search for her till the day she dies,
the man who left his family behind
will live in a hell of his own
and the Imam who always called for prayers
will soon take to drink.

I stand here watching, crying and not crying.
I know that I don't know anything,
that I will never know anything
and I know that this ruin
is the only knowledge I will ever have.

CHOMAN HARDI

Choman Hardi (*b*. 1974) is a Kurdish poet and academic. In 1975 her family fled to Iran after the Algiers Accord, returning home after a general amnesty in 1979, but were forced to leave again in 1988 during Saddam Hussein's al-Anfal campaign against the Kurdish people when up to 182,000 civilians were killed. This campaign included ground offensives, aerial bombing (including the use of chemical weapons), firing squads, deportations and demolition of settlements. She arrived in the UK in 1993 as a refugee and studied at Oxford, London and Kent. After publishing three collections of poetry in Kurdish, her first English collection, *Life for Us*, was published by Bloodaxe Books in 2004.

Chemical Weapon

The Kurds of March were in the hush of impossibility.
Their clothes were the colours of spring,
their faces were spring,
and the singer was murdered.

The clouds that dropped black mustard in the lungs,
the clouds that looped death's throttle around a beautiful morning,
the clouds that clotted our children's blood,
the clouds that leavened Satan's bread
with the hues of twilight,
will they cross the cypress woods
and reach the date palms?

The Kurds of March were in the hush of impossibility.

[Nicosia, 23 March 1989]

SAADI YOUSSEF
translated from the Arabic by Khaled Mattawa
➤ 526

Escape Journey, 1988

They force you to crawl, these mountains,
even if you are only fourteen.
Who made the first journey over them?
Whose feet created this track?

The exhausted mules carry us
along with the smuggled goods.
Sitting on their backs, climbing mountains
feels much safer than going down.
The steepness makes me lean backwards,
my back nearly touching the mule's,
then holding on becomes impossible

501

and I dismount.
It is easier, safer to walk sideways.

And from high up, I can see the white valley.
'A valley of plaster,' I tell my sister.
The mule owner says: 'It is snow.'
But I cannot imagine being rescued from this rough mountain
only to walk over the snow, covering the river.
I cannot imagine listening to the rushing water
passing by holes where the river exposes itself.

'You are too young to complain,'
the mule owner says,
and I look at my father, his little body,
and listen to his difficult breathing.
But then again, he's been here before.

CHOMAN HARDI

Initial Illumination

Farne cormorants with catches in their beaks
shower fishscale confetti on the shining sea.
The first bright weather here for many weeks
for my Sunday G-Day train bound for Dundee,
off to St Andrew's to record a reading,
doubtful, in these dark days, what poems can do,
and watching the mists round Lindisfarne receding
my doubt extends to Dark Age Good Book too.
Eadfrith the Saxon scribe/illuminator
incorporated cormorants I'm seeing fly
round the same island thirteen centuries later
into the *In principio*'s initial I.
Billfrith's begemmed and jewelled boards got looted
by raiders gung-ho for booty and berserk,
the sort of soldiery that's still recruited
to do today's dictators' dirty work,
but the initials in St John and in St Mark

graced with local cormorants in ages,
we of a darker still keep calling Dark,
survive in those illuminated pages.
The word of God so beautifully scripted
by Eadfrith and Billfrith the anchorite
Pentagon conners have once again conscripted
to gloss the cross on the precision sight.
Candlepower, steady hand, gold leaf, a brush
were all that Eadfrith had to beautify
the word of God much bandied by George Bush
whose word illuminated midnight sky
and confused the Baghdad cock who was betrayed
by bombs into believing day was dawning
and crowed his heart out at the deadly raid
and didn't live to greet the proper morning.

Now with noonday headlights in Kuwait
and the burial of the blackened in Baghdad
let them remember, all those who celebrate,
that their good news is someone else's bad
or the light will never dawn on poor Mankind.
Is it open-armed at all that victory V,
that insular initial intertwined
with slack-necked cormorants from black laquered sea,
with trumpets bulled and bellicose and blowing
for what men claim as victories in their wars,
with the fire-hailing cock and all those crowing
who don't yet smell the dunghill at their claws?

TONY HARRISON

Tony Harrison (*b*. 1937) is Britain's leading film and theatre poet. Much of his poetry addresses social and humanitarian issues, most famously his controversial long poem *v*. (1985). He has published a number of poems written in immediate response to war in *The Guardian*, including 'Initial Illumination' (5 March 1991), and 'A Cold Coming' [➤ 504] (18 March 1991), prompted by a photograph by Kenneth Jarecke published in *The Observer* with the caption: 'The charred head of an Iraqi soldier leans through the windscreen on his burned-out vehicle, February 28. He died when a convoy of Iraqi vehicles retreating from Kuwait City was attacked by Allied Forces.' In 1995 he was sent to Bosnia by *The Guardian* to write poems about the war. ➤ 304, 504

A Cold Coming

A cold coming we had of it.

T.S. ELIOT, 'Journey of the Magi'

I saw the charred Iraqi lean
towards me from bomb-blasted screen,

his windscreen wiper like a pen
ready to write down thoughts for men,

his windscreen wiper like a quill
he's reaching for to make his will.

I saw the charred Iraqi lean
like someone made of Plasticine

as though he'd stopped to ask the way
and this is what I heard him say:

'Don't be afraid I've picked on you
for this exclusive interview.

Isn't it your sort of poet's task
to find words for this frightening mask?

If that gadget that you've got records
words from such scorched vocal chords,

press RECORD before some dog
devours me mid-monologue.'

So I held the shaking microphone
closer to the crumbling bone:

'I read the news of three wise men
who left their sperm in nitrogen,

three foes of ours, three wise Marines
with sample flasks and magazines,

504

three wise soldiers from Seattle
who banked their sperm before the battle.

Did No. 1 say: God be thanked
I've got my precious semen banked.

And No. 2: O praise the Lord
my last best shot is safely stored.

And No. 3: Praise be to God
I left my wife my frozen wad?

So if their fate was to be gassed
at least they thought their name would last,

and though cold corpses in Kuwait
they could by proxy procreate.

Excuse a skull half roast, half bone
for using such a scornful tone.

It may seem out of all proportion
but I wish I'd taken their precaution.

They seemed the masters of their fate
with wisely jarred ejaculate.

Was it a propaganda coup
to make us think they'd cracked death too,

disinformation to defeat us
with no post-mortem millilitres?

Symbolic billions in reserve
made me, for one, lose heart and nerve.

On Saddam's pay we can't afford
to go and get our semen stored.

Sad to say that such high tech's
uncommon here. We're stuck with sex.

If you can conjure up and stretch
your imagination (and not retch)

the image of me beside my wife
closely clasped creating life...

(I let the unfleshed skull unfold
a story I'd been already told,

and idly tried to calculate
the content of ejaculate:

the sperm in one ejaculation
equals the whole Iraqi nation

times, roughly, let's say, 12.5
though that .5's not now alive.

Let's say the sperms were an amount
so many times the body count,

2,500 times at least
(but let's wait till the toll's released!).

Whichever way Death seems outflanked
by one tube of cold bloblings banked.

Poor bloblings, maybe you've been blessed
with, of all fates possible, the best

according to Sophocles i.e.
'the best of fates is not to be'

a philosophy that's maybe bleak
for any but an ancient Greek

but difficult these days to escape
when spoken to by such a shape.

When you see men brought to such states
who wouldn't want that 'best of fates'

or in the world of Cruise and Scud
not go kryonic if he could,

spared the normal human doom
of having made it through the womb?)

He heard my thoughts and stopped the spool:
'I never thought life futile, fool!

Though all Hell began to drop
I never wanted life to stop.

I was filled with such a yearning
to stay in life as I was burning,

such a longing to be beside
my wife in bed before I died,

and, most, to have engendered there
a child untouched by war's despair.

So press RECORD! I want to reach
the warring nations with my speech.

Don't look away! I know it's hard
to keep regarding one so charred,

so disfigured by unfriendly fire
and think it once burned with desire.

Though fire has flayed off half my features
they once were like my fellow creatures',

till some screen-gazing crop-haired boy
from Iowa or Illinois,

equipped by ingenious technophile
put paid to my paternal smile

and made the face you see today
an armature half-patched with clay,

an icon framed, a looking glass
for devotees of "kicking ass",

a mirror that returns the gaze
of victors on their victory days

and in the end stares out the watcher
who ducks behind his headline: GOTCHA!

or behind the flag-bedecked page 1
of the true to bold-type-setting SUN!

I doubt victorious Greeks let Hector
join their feast as spoiling spectre,

and who'd want to sour the children's joy
in Iowa or Illinois

or ageing mothers overjoyed
to find their babies weren't destroyed?

But cabs beflagged with SUN front pages
don't help peace in future ages.

Stars and Stripes in sticky paws
may sow the seeds for future wars.

Each Union Jack the kids now wave
may lead them later to the grave.

But praise the Lord and raise the banner
(excuse a skull's sarcastic manner!)

Desert Rat and Desert Stormer
without scars and (maybe) trauma,

the semen-bankers are all back
to sire their children in their sack.

With seed sown straight from the sower
dump second-hand spermatozoa!

Lie that you saw me and I smiled
to see the soldier hug his child.

Lie and pretend that I excuse
my bombing by B52s,

pretend I pardon and forgive
that they still do and I don't live,

pretend they have the burnt man's blessing
and then, maybe, I'm spared confessing

that only fire burnt out the shame
of things I'd done in Saddam's name,

the deaths, the torture and the plunder
the black clouds all of us are under.

Say that I'm smiling and excuse
the Scuds we launched against the Jews.

Pretend I've got the imagination
to see the world beyond one nation.

That's your job, poet, to pretend
I want my foe to be my friend.

It's easier to find such words
for this dumb mask like baked dogturds.

So lie and say the charred man smiled
to see the soldier hug his child.

This gaping rictus once made glad
a few old hearts back in Baghdad,

hearts growing older by the minute
as each truck comes without me in it.

I've met you though, and had my say
which you've got taped. Now go away.'

I gazed at him and he gazed back
staring right through me to Iraq.

Facing the way the charred man faced
I saw the frozen phial of waste,

a test-tube frozen in the dark,
crib and Kaaba, sacred Ark,

a pilgrimage of Cross and Crescent
the chilled suspension of the Present.

Rainbows seven shades of black
curved from Kuwait back to Iraq,

and instead of gold the frozen crock's
crammed with Mankind on the rocks,

the congealed geni who won't thaw
until the World renounces War,

cold spunk meticulously jarred
never to be charrer or the charred,

a bottled Bethlehem of this come-
curdling Cruise/Scud-cursed millennium.

I went. I pressed REWIND and PLAY
and I heard the charred man say:

TONY HARRISON
➤ 503

Poem on the Obliteration of 100,000 Iraqi Soldiers

They are hiding away in the desert,
hiding in sand which is growing warm
with the hot season,

they are hiding from bone-wagons
and troops in protective clothing
who will not look at them,

the crowds were appalled on seeing him,
so disfigured did he look
that he seemed no longer human.

That killed head straining through the windscreen
with its frill of bubbles in the eye-sockets
is not trying to tell you something –

it is telling you something.
Do not look away,
permit them, permit them –

they are telling their names to the Marines
in one hundred thousand variations,
but no one is counting,

do not turn away,

for God is counting
all of us who are silent
holding our newspapers up, hiding.

HELEN DUNMORE

Helen Dunmore (*b.* 1952) is an English poet, novelist, short story and children's writer. Her novels include *Zennor in Darkness* (1993), set in Cornwall during the First World War where D.H. Lawrence and his wife Frieda were suspected of being German spies, and two novels set in Leningrad, *The Siege* (2001) during the Second World War and *The Betrayal* (2010) in 1952-53, the final year of Stalin's life.

In the Desert Knowing Nothing

Here I am in the desert knowing nothing,
here I am knowing nothing
in the desert of knowing nothing,
here I am in this wide
desert long after midnight

here I am knowing nothing
hearing the noise of the rain
and the melt of fat in the pan

here is our man on the phone knowing something
and here's our man fresh from the briefing
in combat jeans and a clip microphone
testing for sound,
catching the desert rain, knowing something,

here's the general who's good with his men
storming the camera, knowing something
in the pit of his Americanness
here's the general taut in his battledress
and knowing something

here's the boy washing his kit in a tarpaulin
on a front-line he knows from his GCSE
coursework on Wilfred Owen
and knowing something

here is the plane banking,
the *go go go* of adrenalin
the child melting
and here's the grass that grows overnight
from the desert rain, feeling for him
and knowing everything

and here I am knowing nothing
in the desert of knowing nothing
dry from not speaking.

HELEN DUNMORE

Phrase Book

I'm standing here inside my skin,
which will do for a Human Remains Pouch
for the moment. Look down there (up here).
Quickly. Slowly. This is my own front room

where I'm lost in the action, live from a war,
on screen. I am an Englishwoman, I don't understand you.
What's the matter? You are right. You are wrong.
Things are going well (badly). Am I disturbing you?

TV is showing bliss as taught to pilots:
Blend, Low silhouette, Irregular shape, Small,
Secluded. (Please write it down. Please speak slowly.)
Bliss is how it was in this very room

when I raised my body to his mouth,
when he even balanced me in the air,
or at least I thought so and yes the pilots say
yes they have caught it through the Side-Looking

Airborne Radar, and through the J-Stars.
I am expecting a gentleman (a young gentleman,
two gentlemen, some gentlemen). Please send him
(them) up at once. This is really beautiful.

Yes they have seen us, the pilots, in the Kill Box
on their screens, and played the routine for
getting us Stealthed, that is, Cleansed, to you and me,
Taken Out. They know how to move into a single room

like that, to send in with Pinpoint Accuracy, a hundred Harms.
I have two cases and a cardboard box. There is another
bag there. I cannot open my case – look out,
the lock is broken. Have I done enough?

Bliss, the pilots say, is for evasion
and escape. What's love in all this debris?
Just one person pounding another into dust,
into dust. I do not know the word for it yet.

513

Where is the British Consulate? Please explain.
What does it mean? What must I do? Where
can I find? What have I done? I have done
nothing. Let me pass please. I am an Englishwoman.

JO SHAPCOTT

Jo Shapcott (*b.* 1953) is an English poet whose 2010 collection *Of Mutability* won the Costa Book of the Year Award. 'Phrase Book' was written in response to the Gulf War. In 2003, as Britain prepared in invade Iraq for a second time, she sent a copy of the poem to the cabinet office with a letter turning down a CBE.

White Hats, Black Hats

In war our guys are white as snow,
    The baddies, oil-slick black.
The monster with the big moustache
    Gets all the moral flak.

But things are otherwise in peace;
    It doesn't work like that.
Money's far more vital than
    The colour of the hat.

We have to weigh our interests up.
    Morality is grey.
Tomorrow's evil enemy
    May be a friend today.

We'll overlook his vicious side,
    That massacre of Kurds,
(Conventions guarding human rights
    Are merely forms of words),

And greet him with a chummy smile,
    And shake him by the hand,
And build him bomb-proof bunkers deep
    Beneath the desert sand.

But don't those million dollar sales,
   Those contracts in the sun,
Seem rather poor investments now
   The shooting has begun?

Our smiling erstwhile customer
   Is now the Prince of Lies,
Committing vile atrocities,
   Surprise, surprise, surprise...

[2 February 1991]

SIMON RAE

General Schwarzkopf, the Commander of Allied forces in the Gulf likened the war to a Western, with the Coalition forces the good guys in white hats ranged against baddies in black hats. It remained one of the war's ironies that the West had been largely responsible for supplying Saddam Hussein's vast arsenal, and, in the case of Britain, for advising on the construction of bunkers which sheltered Iraq's airforce from Allied attacks. [SR]

Simon Rae (*b*. 1952) is an English writer and broadcaster. From 1998 to 1991 he contributed a topical weekly poem to *The Guardian*, the best of which were collected in his book *Soft Targets* (1991).

Agamemnon

He came back
from the dusts of war
with a wounded heart, his
arms full with drums & gold
dreaming of Clytemnestra's
honeyed lips that at that very
moment Aegisthus was melting
with his own, as every night.
And as he opened the door
he sensed on her lips' grease
the thousands of corpses he'd

abandoned under the open sky
& recalled how he'd forgotten
to leave his own body there.

[Baghdad, 14 January 1993]

ADNAN AL-SAYEGH
translated from the Arabic by Stephen Watts & Marga Burgui-Artajo
➤ 498

Full Moon, 18 March 2003

The moon rises over Binn Mhór,
Clarifying the far
And wide world
In silver and black.
This moon is not crescent
Or fertile. It is a desert moon
Preparing to explode, a shell
About to fragment itself
Into craters, sockets, skulls.

This moon still hears gods
Commanding their own
Deaths and resurrections.

This moon is a new century
Howling at itself.

This moon knows its real colours
Full well: pitch-black,
Blood-red, gold.

This moon yearns
To gild minarets.

Now it trembles
Over the dark horizon
Like an unshed tear.

PADDY BUSHE

Retreat

The city abandoned; its citizens fled.
A paper chain hung on the wall left standing.
A single flip-flop graced the hardpacked floor.
The rest diminishes their loss: these were barracks,
and yesterday the men tried to blow a hole
through me as I squatted up the road
and took note of their grim frenzy,
like termites, no, more like tiny sailors
from a different time, when war came
over water and the battle arrived at a delay.
There was nothing to do but watch the enemy
grow from blot to galleon; colors nailed
to the mast. Like the bright orange flashing
we hung on our car's hood that said to the sky,
Don't bomb us, we are your friends.
These others, they had no friends in the sky.

[Kirkuk, northern Iraq, April 2003]

ELIZA GRISWOLD

Eliza Griswold (*b.* 1973) is an American poet and journalist who has reported from some of the world's most dangerous and unstable countries, in Africa, the Middle East and Asia. Her books include a first collection, *Wideawake Field* (2007); *The Tenth Parallel: Dispatches from the Fault Line Between Christianity and Islam* (2010), a study of people living north of the equator in Africa and Asia where the two faiths intersect and interact; and *I Am the Beggar of the World: Landays from Contemporary Afghanistan*, translated by her with photographs by Seamus Murphy (2014). ➢ 530, 551, 562, 564, 582.

Paddy Bushe (*b.* 1948) is one of the foremost poets writing in both Irish and English, publishing several books of poetry in both languages, most recently, *To Ring in Silence: New and Selected Poems* (2008), *My Lord Buddha of Carriag Éanna* (2012) and *Choill go Barr Ghearáin* (2013). He lives in Waterville, Co. Kerry. This poem was written on the eve of the invasion of Iraq. ➢ 516

Apache Video: December 1st 2003

Helicopter voices
checkpoint just outside Baghdad

I got a guy   running   and throwing a weapon
surgical cross-hairs follow

smoke him   smoke him
unidentified soldier voice

get the guy in the field
lieutenant voice from the ground

man in frame turns back
runs to a tractor

in an open field
at the end of a fresh-ploughed row

driver jumps off   runs away
machine-gun

shoots too low fires short
takes aim again

and the tractor driver's hit
got him   the voice in the sky

good   the voice below
now   get the second one   hit the other one

and the tractor
explodes with bone and flesh

camera finds
another man hiding behind a truck

hit him   the voice on the ground again
and the truck explodes

then nothing until the gray consuming eye
in the sky

detects a movement
someone crawling away from the burning truck

he's wounded   the helicopter voice
hit him   orders

officer voice from the ground
go   forward of it   and hit him

a fourth methodical time
machine-gun opens up and then

pulls back from the scene
four black smears on the countryside

burnt-out tractor and tractor-driver
burnt-out lorry and pick-up truck

what do you say?   three?   hey?
what do you say?

three killed   the officer voice
affirmative three   *mission complete*

Affirmative three repeat repeat
affirmative   three mission complete

Army code: '223 Gun Video, 01 Dec '03'
'PC CW2 Nager, CPG-CPT Alioto'

MACDARA WOODS

Macdara Woods (*b.* 1942) is an Irish poet and one of the founding editors of
the literary journal *Cyphers*. He has published several books of poetry, including
Artichoke Wine (2006), from which this poem and the extract from 'Driving to
Charleston' [➤ 529] are taken, and *Collected Poems* (2012). He lives in Dublin.

Here, Bullet

If a body is what you want,
then here is bone and gristle and flesh.
Here is the clavicle-snapped wish,
the aorta's opened valves, the leap
thought makes at the synaptic gap.
Here is the adrenaline rush you crave,
that inexorable flight, that insane puncture
into heat and blood. And I dare you to finish
what you've started. Because here, Bullet,
here is where I complete the word you bring
hissing through the air, here is where I moan
the barrel's cold esophagus, triggering
my tongue's explosives for the rifling I have
inside of me, each twist of the round
spun deeper, because here, Bullet,
here is where the world ends, every time.

BRIAN TURNER

Brian Turner (*b*. 1967) served for seven years in the US Army. He was an
infantry team leader for a year in Iraq from November 2003 with the 3rd
Stryker Brigade Combat Team, 2nd Infantry Division. In 1999-2000 he was
deployed to Bosnia-Herzegovina with the 10th Mountain Division. Born in
California, he studied at Fresco State and taught English in South Korea for
a year before joining the army. He has published two collections, *Here, Bullet*
(2005/2007), written while serving in Iraq, and *Phantom Noise* (2010), written
shortly afterwards, and a war memoir, *My Life as a Foreign Country* (2014).
➤ 522, 523, 524, 530, 535

Kevin Powers (*b*. 1980) grew up in Richmond, Virginia, the son of a factory
worker and a postman, and enlisted in the US Army at the age of 17, serving
a one-year tour in Iraq as a machine-gunner with an engineer unit in 2004-05
in Mosul and Tal Afar. His debut novel, *The Yellow Birds* (2012), is a fictional
account of a soldier trying to deal with the horrors of war in Iraq. His first
book of poems, *Letter Composed During a Lull in the Fighting* (2014), is a self-
portrait of a life shaped by the Iraq War, by his years in the army and by his
Virginia upbringing. ➤ 521, 523, 534

Great Plain

Here is where appreciation starts, the boy
in a dusty velour tracksuit almost getting shot.
When I say boy, I mean it. When I say almost
getting shot, I mean exactly that. For bringing
unexploded mortars right up to us
takes a special kind of courage I don't have.
A dollar for each one, I'm told,
on orders from brigade HQ
to let the children do the dirty work.

When I say, I'd say fuck that, let the bastards find them
with the heels of boots and who cares if I mean us
as bastards and who cares if heels of boots mean things
that once were, the way grass once was a green thing
and now is not, the way the muezzin call once was
five times today and now is not

and when I say heel of boot I hope you'll appreciate
that I really mean the gone foot, any one of us
timbered and inert and when I say green
I mean like fucking Nebraska, wagon wheels on the prairie
and other things that can't be appreciated
until you're really far away and they come up
as points of reference.

I don't know what Nebraska looks like.
I've never been. When I say Nebraska
I mean the idea of, the way an ex-girlfriend of mine
once talked about the idea of a gun. But guns are not ideas.
They are not things to which comparisons are made. They are

one weight in my hand when the little boy crests the green hill
and the possibilities of shooting him or not extend out from me
like the spokes of a wheel. The hills are not green anymore
and in my mind they never were, though when I say they were
I mean I'm talking about reality. I appreciate that too,

knowing
the hills were green,

521

knowing
someone else has paid him
for his scavenging, one less
exploding thing beneath our feet.
I appreciate the fact
that for at least one day I don't have to decide
between dying and shooting a little boy.

KEVIN POWERS

16 Iraqi Policemen

The explosion left a hole in the roadbed
large enough to fit a mid-sized car.
It shattered concrete, twisted metal,
busted storefront windows in sheets
and lifted a BMW chassis up onto a rooftop.

The shocking blood of the men
forms an obscene art: a moustache, alone
on a sidewalk, a blistered hand's gold ring
still shining, while a medic, Doc Lopez,
pauses to catch his breath, to blow it out
hard, so he might cup the left side of a girl's face
in one hand, gently, before bandaging
the half gone missing.

Allah must wander in the crowd
as I do, dazed by the pure concussion
of the blast, among sirens, voices
of the injured, the boots of running soldiers,
not knowing whom to touch first,
for the dead policemen cannot be found,
here a moment before, then vanished.

[Mosul, Iraq, 2004]

BRIAN TURNER

Death, Mother and Child

Mosul, Iraq, 2004

Kollwitz [1] was right. Death is an etching.
I remember the white Opel being
pulled through the traffic circle on the back of a wrecker,
the woman in the driver's seat
so brutalised by bullets it was hard to tell her sex.
Her left arm waved unceremoniously
in the stifling heat and I retched,
the hand seemingly saying, *I will see*
you there. We heard a rumor that a child
was riding in the car with her, had slipped
to the floorboard, but had been killed as well.
The truth has no spare mercy, see. It is this chisel
in the wood block. It is this black wisp
above the music of a twice-rung bell.

KEVIN POWERS

1. Käthe Kollwitz (1869-1945), German artist whose work included powerfully
expressive drawings, etchings, lithographs, woodcuts and sculptures showing
the victims of war, notably depictions of mother and child.

Eulogy

It happens on a Monday, at 11:20 A.M.,
as tower guards eat sandwiches
and seagulls drift by on the Tigris River.
Prisoners tilt their heads to the west
though burlap sacks and duct tape blind them.
The sound reverberates down concertina coils
the way piano wire thrums when given slack.
And it happens like this, on a blue day of sun,

when Private Miller pulls the trigger
to take brass and fire into his mouth:
the sound lifts the birds up off the water,
a mongoose pauses under the orange trees,
and nothing can stop it now, no matter what
blur of motion surrounds him, no matter what voices
crackle over the radio in static confusion,
because if only for this moment the earth is stilled,
and Private Miller has found what low hush there is
down in the eucalyptus shade, there by the river.

PFC B. Miller
(1980 – March 22, 2004)

BRIAN TURNER

Letter Composed During a Lull in the Fighting

I tell her I love her like not killing
or ten minutes of sleep
beneath the low rooftop wall
on which my rifle rests.

I tell her in a letter that will stink,
when she opens it,
of bolt oil and burned powder
and the things it says.

I tell her how Pvt Bartle says, offhand,
that war is just us
making little pieces of metal
pass through each other.

KEVIN POWERS

The Wretched of the Heavens

We will go to God
naked.
Our shroud is our blood,
our camphor:
the teeth of dogs
turned wolves.

The closed cell suddenly swung open
for the female soldier to come.
Our swollen eyes could not make her out,
perhaps because she comes from a mysterious world,
she did not say a thing;
she was dragging my brother's bloody body behind her,
like a worn-out mat.

We will walk to God
barefoot:
our feet lacerated,
our limbs wounded.

Are Americans Christians?
We have nothing in the cell to wipe the lying body,
only our blood
congealing in our blood
– and this smell coming from the continent of slaughterhouses
... Angels will not come here,
the air is perturbed,
these are the wings of hell's bats,
the air is motionless.

We have been waiting for you, O Lord.
Our cells were open yesterday.
We were lifeless on their floor,
and you did not come, O Lord.

But we are on the way to you.
We will remain on the way even if you let us down.

We are your dead sons and have declared our resurrection.
Tell your prophets to open the gates of cells and paradises!

Tell them that we are coming!
We have wiped our faces and hands with clean earth.
The angels know us one by one.

[London, 10 May 2004]

SAADI YOUSSEF
translated from the Arabic by Sinan Antoon & Peter Money

This poem was written following the Abu Ghraib scandal [➤ 495]. In 'We have wiped our faces and hands with clean earth', Youssef uses a particular verb (*tayammamna*) with important resonance. In the Islamic tradition, '*tayammum*' is using clean earth for ablutions and purifications if and when water is not available. The sentence appears in the Qur'an a few times, but as a form of a command: '[If]…you do not find water, then use some clean earth and wipe your faces and hands.' See *The Qur'an: A New Translation*, tr. Tarif Khalidi (Penguin Books, 2009), verses 4:43 and 5:6. [Tr.]

Saadi Youssef was born in 1934 near Basra, and was forced to leave Iraq in 1979 after Saddam Hussein's rise to power. One of the leading poets of the Arab world, he has published over 30 books, including two selections translated into English, *Without an Alphabet, Without a Face: Selected Poems* (2002) and *Nostalgia, My Enemy* (2012). He now lives in London. ➤ 501

from Driving to Charleston

The "Noise" You Hear
Is The Sound Of Freedom –

1

Chiselled letters
cut into the wall
of the Marine Base
in Beaufort South Carolina

the day we drove to Charleston –
I wanted to see Fort Sumter
and the US Army
was making for Baghdad –
the beautiful black girl
in the filling-station
a flower of the forest
in a bright yellow singlet
whose every cell was a hymn to life

Bomb em all she said
crossing the forecourt
Bomb em all
                    and bring
Our boys back home.

In the Low Country
                just to the north of the Gullah people
with palmettos
prayer houses
African fish-nets spread in the shade and indigo Batik
a sea-road back
to Sierra Leone

Terrible to see
the Stalinist slogans
blowing in on the wind like spores
from the edge of the mind
and finding root:

The night before
at the Junior Chamber of Commerce Awards
when Billy Bob gave thanks
in the name of Christ
and our boys who serve overseas
so that we may continue
to have meals like this

The man on my right
Marine Captain
in full Dress Uniform

He'd been there before
in Desert Storm...
for him it was *deja vue*
he said
And how do they feel in Europe
about the Action?
His own parents were Portuguese
and of course they supported the war

But I hear there's people
over there
who don't get to see American TV
and don't know what's going on...
and of course when...
when...those Lefts
                    get into it...
Well... there's a time and a place...
there's a time and a place:

And those guys now
will get twice as many medals as these:

Triumphal voice of Fox avant la lettre
and a year later
I'm looking at the sad pictures
of Lynndie England
holding a naked Iraqi on a leash[1]
and her grinning lover
in bright-green latex gloves
arms folded
behind a pyramid of naked prisoners

Specialist Charles Graner[2]
who had 'a history of troubles'

Looking at them and thinking
of that young woman on the way to Charleston
so beautiful
my breath stopped –
                    Bomb em all
                    Bomb em all
And bring our boys back home

528

And thinking of Jessica Lynch [3]
whose story was stolen
after she was saved   traduced
and taken away
to be turned into myth:

In fraud we trust
when truth is lost

2

Said Colleen Kesner [4]   from Fort Ashby:

To the country boys here
if you're
a different nationality   a different race
you're subhuman
that's the way girls   like Lynndie were raised

Tormenting Iraqis
would be no different from shooting a turkey

[May/August 2004]

MACDARA WOODS
➤ 519

1 & 2. Macdara Woods was in the US when torture and prisoner abuse carried
out by US Army military police and CIA personnel at the Abu Ghraib prison
in Baghdad in 2003-04 had just come to public attention. Some of the soldiers
responsible took photographs of themselves humiliating naked Iraqi prisoners
which were later published by press and media, including Lynndie England
and Charles Graner, two of eleven soldiers court-martialled, given prison
sentences and dishonourably discharged.

    3. Private Jessica Lynch, a supply clerk with the US Army during the 2003
invasion of Iraq, was seriously injured when the convoy she was travelling in
was ambushed. The media turned her into a combat heroine after her rescue
by US Special Operations Forces, despite her protestations: her M16 rifle
had jammed, and she'd been knocked unconscious when her Humvee had
crashed. Hers was the first successful rescue of an American prisoner of war
since Vietnam and the first ever of a woman.

    4. Colleen Kesner: a bar tender from Lynndie England's home town of
Fort Ashby, West Virginia, quoted in a widely syndicated article by Sharon
Churcher (*Daily Telegraph*, 7 May 2004).

Water Cure

Before drowning, after the gasp
when firefly lights pop and sputter
around the prisoner's eyes:
this is the line to recognise.
The manual recommends a pause
to let the man confess.
If there is no water and you must press on,
then strip him naked. After the shock,
watch him watch the fake-out clock and realise
the hours are yours to stretch against him.
Shock, or better, dunk again.
Try self-inflicted pain.

[*c.* 2005]

ELIZA GRISWOLD

➤ 517

The water cure is a form of torture, also known as the question, used by the French during the 17th and 18th centuries. During the 'ordinary question', an interrogator forced eight pints of water into the stomach; during the 'extraordinary question', sixteen pints. The United States currently employs a variant called waterboarding, first used during the Philippine-American War. [EG]

Al-A'imma Bridge

This will leave a scar in our souls...[1]
PRESIDENT JALAL TALABANI

They fall from the bridge into the Tigris –
    they fall from railings or tumble down, shoved by panic,
        by those in the crushing weight behind them,
    mothers with children, seventy-year-old men
        clawing at the blue and empty sky, which is too beautiful;

some focus on the bridgework as they fall, grasp
    the invisible rope which slips through their fingers,
some palm-heel the air beneath them, pressing down
    as their children swim in the oxygen beside them,
lives blurring with no time to make sense, some
    so close to shore they smash against the rocks;

the pregnant woman who twists
    in a corkscrew of air, flipping upside down,
the world upended, her black dress
    a funeral banner rippling in the wind,
her child never given a name;

they fall beside Shatha and Cantara and Sabeen,
    Hakim, Askari, and Gabir – unraveling years
        and memory, struggling to keep heads above water,
    the hard shock sweeping them downstream
        as Askari fights to gain the shoreline
where emerald flags furl in sunlight,
    and onlookers wave frantic arms
at Gabir, who holds the body of a dead child
    he doesn't know, and it is only 11:30 A.M.,
And this is how we die, he thinks
    on a day as beautiful as this;

and Shatha, who feels the river's cold hands
    pulling her under, remembers once loving
the orange flowers opening on the hillsides
    of Mosul, how she lay under slow clouds
drifting in history's bright catalogue;

they fall with 500 pound bombs and mortars,
    laser-guided munitions directing the German Luftwaffe
        from 1941, Iraqi jets and soldiers from the Six-Day War,
the Battle of Karbala, the one million who died fighting Iran;

and Alexander the Great falls, and King Faisal,
    and the Israeli F-16s that bombed the reactor in '81,
and the Stele of the Vultures comes crumbling,
    the Tower of Samarra, the walled ruins of Nineveh;

the Babylonians and Sumerians and Assyrians join them,
    falling from the bridge with Ibn Khaldun's torn pages,
        The Muqaddimah – that classic Islamic history of the world,
    and Sheherazade falls too, worn out, exhausted
        from her life-saving work, made speechless by the scale of war,
    and Ali Baba with an AK-47 beside her;

    whiskey and vodka, pirated Eastern European porn videos
        the kids hawk to soldiers – the *freaky freaky* they call it,[2]
    and foil-wrapped packages of *heroin, heroin*
        thrown to the river;

the year 1956 slides under, along with '49 and '31 and '17.
    the month of October, the months of June, July, and August,
        the many months to follow, each day's exquisite light,
    the snowfall in Mosul, the photographs a family took
        of children rolling snowballs, throwing them
    before licking the pink cold from their fingertips;

years unravel like filaments of straw, bleached gold
    and given to the water, 1967 and 1972, 2001 and 2002:
        What will we remember? What will we say of these?

it awakens the dead from the year 1258
    who cannot believe what is happening here, *Not a shot fired –*
        our internalised panic deeply set by years of warfare,
    the siege and adrenaline always at the surface, prepared;

the dead from the year 1258 read from ancient scrolls
        cast into the river from the House of Wisdom,
    the eulogies of nations given water's swift erasure;

and the dead watch as they are swept downstream –
    witness to the soft, tender lips of the river fish
        who kiss the calves and fingertips of these newly dead,
    curious to see how lifeless bodies stare hard
        into the dark envelopment, hands
    waving to the far shore;

the *djinn* awaken from their slumber
    to watch the dead pass by, one fixed

with an odd smile, the drawn-out vowel
of a word left unfinished, and they want to hold these dead
   close and tight, the lung's last reserve given
as a whisper of bubbles for the ear held up to it;

the *djinn* swim to reach the bony ankles of Sabeen,
   the muscled Askari, clasping to stop them
from this tragic undertaking;

and some are nearly saved by others diving in
   to rescue the terrified and the stunned,
      but drown beneath a woman's soaked abaya;

and the Tigris is filling with the dead, filling
   with bricks from Abu Ghraib, burning vehicles
      pushed from Highway 1 with rebar, stone, metal,
   with rubble from the Mosque bombed in Samarra,
      guard towers and razor wire imprisoning Tikrit,
   it fills with the pipelines of money;

      marketplace bombs, roadside bombs, vehicle-driven
         bombs, and the bombs people make of themselves;

Gilgamesh can do nothing, knows that each life is the world
   dying anew, each body the deep pull of currents below, lost,
      and lost within each – the subtle, the sublime, the horrific,
   the mundane, the tragic, the humorous and the erotic – lost,

      unstudied in text books, courses on mathematics,
         the equations quantifying fear,
      or the stoppage of time this eternal moment creates,
         unwritten history, forgotten in American hallways, but still –

give them flowers from the hills, flowers from the Shanidar cave,
   where mourning has a long history, where someone in the last Ice Age
      gathered a bouquet – give daisies and hyacinths
   to this impossible moment, flowers to stand for the lips
      unable to kiss them, each in their own bright beauty, flowers
   that may light the darkness, as they march deeper into the earth.

BRIAN TURNER

1. The epigraph is a quote from President Jalal Talabani, 31 August 2005, from a CNN reported story ('Iraq Mourns Stampede Victims'). It was reported that 965 died and that over 400 were injured. Not one shot was fired – someone in the crowd of worshippers was said to have claimed a suicide bomber was among them, and panic ensued. 2. *Freaky Freaky* is a slang term used to denote bootlegged porn videos, copied onto blank disks and sold, usually, for one US dollar. I personally had Iraqi children try to hawk all of the items mentioned in this poem as my unit would prepare to enter US bases in Iraq, to include having children offer foil-wrapped packages they hawked as 'Heroin'. [BT]

Field Manual

Think not of battles, but rather after,
when the tremor in your right leg
becomes a shake you cannot stop, when the burned man's
tendoned cheeks are locked into a scream that,
before you sank the bullet in his brain to end it,
had been quite loud. Think of how he still seems to scream.
Think of not caring. Call this 'relief'.

Think heat waves rising from the dust.
Think days of rest, how the sergeant lays
the .22 into your palm and says the dogs
outside the wire have become a threat
to good order and to discipline:
some boys have taken them as pets, they spread
disease, they bit a colonel preening for a TV crew.

Think of afternoons in T-shirt and shorts,
the unending sun, the bite of sweat in eyes.
Think of missing so often it becomes absurd.
Think quick *pop*, yelp, then puckered fur.
Think skinny ribs. Think smell.
Think almost reaching grief, but
not quite getting there.

KEVIN POWERS
➤ 520

At Lowe's Home Improvement Center

Standing in aisle 16, the hammer and anchor aisle,
I bust a 50 pound box of double-headed nails
open by accident, their oily bright shanks
and diamond points like firing pins
from M-4s and M-16s.
                              In a steady stream
they pour onto the tile floor, constant as shells
falling south of Baghdad last night, where Bosch
kneeled under the chain guns of helicopters
stationed above, their tracer-fire a synaptic geometry
of light.
          At dawn, when the shelling stops,
hundreds of bandages will not be enough.

                    ❧

Bosch is walking down aisle 16 now, in full combat gear,
improbable, worn out from fatigue, a rifle
slung at his side, his left hand guiding
a ten-year-old boy who sees what war is
and will never clear it from his head.

Here, Bosch says, *Take care of him.*
I'm going back in for more.

                    ❧

Sheets of plywood drop with the airy breath
of mortars the moment they crack open
in shrapnel. Mower blades are just mower blades
and the Troy-Bilt Self-Propelled Mower doesn't resemble
a Blackhawk or an Apache. In fact, no one seems to notice
the casualty collection center Doc High is marking out
in ceiling fans, aisle 15. Wounded Iraqis with IVs
sit propped against boxes as 92 sample Paradiso fans
hover over in a slow revolution of blades.

The forklift driver over-adjusts, swinging the tines
until they slice open gallons and gallons of paint,

535

Sienna Dust and Lemon Sorbet and Ship's Harbor Blue
pooling in the aisle where Sgt Rampley walks through –
carrying someone's blown-off arm cradled like an infant,
handing it to me, saying, *Hold this, Turner,*
we might find who it belongs to.

ಱ

Cash registers open and slide shut
with a sound of machine guns being charged.
Dead soldiers are laid out at the registers,
on the black conveyor belts,
and people in line still reach
for their wallets. Should I stand
at the magazine rack, reading
Landscaping with Stone or *The Complete*
Home Improvement Repair Book?
What difference does it make if I choose
tumbled travertine tile, Botticino marble,
or Black Absolute granite. Outside,
palm trees line the asphalt boulevards,
restaurants cool their patrons who will enjoy
fireworks exploding over Bass Lake in July.

ಱ

Aisle number 7 is a corridor of lights.
Each dead Iraqi walks amazed
by Tiffany posts and Bavarian pole lights.
Motion-activated incandescents switch on
as they pass by, reverent sentinels of light,
Fleur De Lis and Luminaire Mural Extérieur
welcoming them to Lowe's Home Improvement Center,
aisle number 7, where I stand in mute shock,
someone's arm cradled in my own.
                                    The Iraqi boy beside me
reaches down to slide his fingertip in Retro Colonial Blue,
an interior latex, before writing
T, for *Tourniquet*, on my forehead.

BRIAN TURNER
➤ 520

Remains

(for Rob, who fought in Basra)

On another occasion, we get sent out
to tackle looters raiding a bank.
And one of them legs it up the road,
probably armed, possibly not.

Well myself and somebody else and somebody else
are all of the same mind,
so all three of us open fire.
Three of a kind all letting fly, and I swear

I see every round as it rips through his life –
I see broad daylight on the other side.
So we've hit this looter a dozen times
and he's there on the ground, sort of inside out,

pain itself, the image of agony.
One of my mates goes by
and tosses his guts back into his body.
Then he's carted off in the back of a lorry.

End of story, except not really.
His blood-shadow stays on the street, and out on patrol
I walk right over it week after week.
Then I'm home on leave. But I blink

and he bursts again through the doors of the bank.
Sleep, and he's probably armed, possibly not.
Dream, and he's torn apart by a dozen rounds.
And the drink and the drugs won't flush him out –

he's here in my head when I close my eyes,
dug in behind enemy lines,
not left for dead in some distant, sun-stunned, sand-smothered land
or six-feet-under in desert sand,

but near to the knuckle, here and now,
his bloody life in my bloody hands.

SIMON ARMITAGE

Simon Armitage (*b.* 1963) is a well-known British poet who has worked on many radio and TV documentaries. This poem and 'The Black Swans' [➤ 488] are based on the testimonies of traumatised veterans of the Gulf War and the Balkan conflicts (as well as the Malaya Emergency) who appeared with him in *The Not Dead*, a film shown on Channel Four in 2007:

'For some of the men, being in the film meant re-living their worst night-mares; most of the poems I wrote revolved around a key "flashpoint" scene, requiring each soldier to re-visit the very incident he was desperately hoping to forget. [...] Like many servicemen, being a soldier had been Rob's dream from boyhood. [...] As he says in the film, he was fully prepared for battle, but not prepared at all for coming home. Since absconding, his life has followed an all too familiar pattern of insomnia, alcoholism, drug abuse, homelessness, violence and crime. He feels damaged and helpless, but most of all he feels forgotten, or worse, ignored.' [SA]

Situational Awareness

These past few weeks I'm more than just aware
of where he is – I'm hypersensitive,
stretched thin as a length of wire, a hair-
trigger mechanism. Nothing can live
near me. I twitch each time the telephone
rings through the dark, so like a warning bell
I want to run from it, escape the Green Zone
of this house. Who said that war is hell?
Well, waiting can be worse. Show me a guy
shipped overseas, and I'll show you a wife
who sees disaster dropping from the sky.
The ambush always comes, her husband's life
a road of booby traps and blind spots made
to hide the rock, the shell, the thrown grenade.

JEHANNE DUBROW

Jehanne Dubrow was born in 1975 in Vicenza, Italy, the daughter of two American diplomats, and grew up in Yugoslavia, Zaire, Poland, Belgium, Austria and the US. She is the Director of the Rose O'Neill Literary House and an Associate Professor of Creative Writing at Washington College, Mary-land. Her collections include *Red Army Red* (2012), and *Stateside* (2010), about her experiences as the wife of a serving officer in the US Navy often deployed overseas and in war zones for many months at a time.

Against War Movies

I see my husband shooting in *Platoon*,
and there he is again in *M*A*S*H* (how weird
to hear him talk like Hawkeye Pierce), and soon
I spot him everywhere, his body smeared
with mud, his face bloodied. He's now the star
of every ship blockade and battle scene—
The Fighting 69th, A Bridge Too Far,
Three Kings, Das Boot, and *Stalag 17.*
In *Stalingrad* he's killed, and then
he's killed in *Midway* and *A Few Good Men.*
He's burned or gassed, he's shot between the eyes,
or shoots himself when he comes home again.
Each movie is a training exercise,
a scenario for how my husband dies.

JEHANNE DUBROW

The War Works Hard

How magnificent the war is!
How eager
and efficient!
Early in the morning,
it wakes up the sirens
and dispatches ambulances
to various places,
swings corpses through the air,
rolls stretchers to the wounded,
summons rain
from the eyes of mothers,
digs into the earth
dislodging many things
from under the ruins...
Some are lifeless and glistening,
others are pale and still throbbing...

It produces the most questions
in the minds of children,
entertains the gods
by shooting fireworks and missiles
into the sky,
sows mines in the fields
and reaps punctures and blisters,
urges families to emigrate,
stands beside the clergymen
as they curse the devil
(poor devil, he remains
with one hand in the searing fire)...
The war continues working, day and night.
It inspires tyrants
to deliver long speeches,
awards medals to generals
and themes to poets.
It contributes to the industry
of artificial limbs,
provides food for flies,
adds pages to the history books,
achieves equality
between killer and killed,
teaches lovers to write letters,
accustoms young women to waiting,
fills the newspapers
with articles and pictures,
builds new houses
for the orphans,
invigorates the coffin makers,
gives grave diggers
a pat on the back
and paints a smile on the leader's face.
The war works with unparalleled diligence!
Yet no one gives it
a word of praise.

DUNYA MIKHAIL
translated from the Arabic by Elizabeth Winslow

Dunya Mikhail was born in Baghdad in 1965, studied at the University of Baghdad, and worked as a translator and journalist for the *Baghdad Observer*. She published two collections in Iraq including poems about the Iran-Iraq War and the first Gulf War. Facing increasing threats from the Iraqi authorities, she fled first to Jordan, then to the US, and now works as an Arabic instructor for Michigan State University. She has published three books of poems in English translation, *The War Works Hard* (2005), *Diary of a Wave Outside the Sea* (2009) and *The Iraqi Nights* (2014).

I Was in a Hurry

Yesterday I lost a country.
I was in a hurry,
and didn't notice when it fell from me
like a broken branch from a forgetful tree.
Please, if anyone passes by
and stumbles across it,
perhaps in a suitcase
open to the sky,
or engraved on a rock
like a gaping wound,
or wrapped
in the blankets of emigrants,
or canceled
like a losing lottery ticket,
or helplessly forgotten
in Purgatory,
or rushing forward without a goal
like the questions of children,
or rising with the smoke of war,
or rolling in a helmet on the sand,
or stolen in Ali Baba's jar,
or disguised in the uniform of a policeman
who stirred up the prisoners
and fled,
or squatting in the mind of a woman
who tries to smile,
or scattered

like the dreams
of new immigrants in America.
If anyone stumbles across it,
return it to me please.
Please return it, sir.
Please return it, madam.
It is my country...
I was in a hurry
when I lost it yesterday.

DUNYA MIKHAIL
translated from the Arabic by Elizabeth Winslow

On the Tenth Anniversary of Murdering My Country

My country disappeared without a funeral
Because it shunned the beauty of palm trees
It avoided its marshes
Thought that mountains were secrets
They looted the tablets of the first kingdom
with gigantic ships
Now they are covered with spiders
Its springs, fruit, and books
are scattered among hills of salt

SALAH FAIK
translated from the Arabic by Sinan Antoon

Salah Faik (*b.* 1945) is an Iraqi poet of Turkish descent. Born in Kirkuk, Iraq, he has published several collections and worked as a journalist in Iraq and later in exile. After living in London during the 1970s and 80s, he moved to the Philippines.

AFGHANISTAN WARS | 1980–present

Soviet War in Afghanistan: Iran-Iraq War: 24 December 1979 – 15 February 1989. Part of the Cold War: ➤ 334

In 1978 the People's Democratic Party of Afghanistan seized power in Afghanistan, leading to a civil war between a communist government helped by thousands of Soviet military advisors and guerrilla *mujahideen* trained by Pakistan and assisted by the US. In 1979, the assassination of Afghan president Nur Muhammad Taraki by political rivals was followed by the Soviet invasion, "commemorated" in Joseph Brodsky's poem with its witheringly understated title, 'Lines on the Winter Campaign, 1980' [➤ 544]. DEATHS: Soviet forces, 14,453; Afghan forces, 18,000; Egypt, Jordan and Syria, 4,000–15,000; mujahideen, 75,000–90,000; Afghan civilians, 850,000–1,500,000.

The eventual departure of Soviet troops from what became 'the Soviet Union's Vietnam War' was followed by the Afghan Civil War which brought about the fall of the Soviet-backed Afghan government in 1992 and the Taliban takeover on September 1996.

War in Afghanistan: 7 October 2001 – present.

US policy towards Afghanistan changed after the 1998 US embassy bombings in Dar es Salaam and Nairobi. Following the terrorist attacks on New York and Washington on 9 September 2001, President George W. Bush committed the US to a war in Afghanistan to capture Osama bin Laden, destroy al-Qaeda and overthrow the Taliban, supported on the ground by the Northern Alliance, the main resistance to the Taliban in the Afghan Civil War since 1996, and by the British Army. Kabul fell to coalition forces after the Taliban fled the city overnight on 12 November, followed by much of southern Afghanistan by early December, but few al-Qaeda or Taliban fighters were captured, most escaping to remote mountainous parts or to Pakistan. The country has since been largely ungovernable, with NATO, US and UK forces tied down in a protracted war of attrition with Taliban insurgents. DEATHS TO DATE: Coalition, 3,424 (including US, 2313, UK, 448); Afghan security forces, 11,000; Northern Alliance, 200; Taliban and allies, unknown; civilians, 16,725–19,013.

War in North-West Pakistan: 16 March 2004 – present.

After beginning with the Pakistan Army's hunt for al-Qaeda fighters in Waziristan, this conflict has escalated into a US-backed war, spilling over from Afghanistan, between the Pakistan government and militant groups including the Taliban and al-Qaeda, with over 3.44 million civilians displaced. Eliza Griswold's poem 'Arrest' [➤ 551] relates to her capture in this war zone in 2005. Imtiaz Dharker's poem 'A Century Later' [➤ 594] celebrates the example of Malala Yousafzai, the schoolgirl campaigner for women's right to education, who survived a Taliban attempt on her life near her home in the north-west Pakistani district of Swat in October 2012. DEATHS TO DATE: Pakistan Army, 5,000; US Special Forces, 15; militants, 27,946; civilians 18,494–48,782.

Lines on the Winter Campaign, 1980

The scorching noon, the vale in Dagestan...
MIKHAIL LERMONTOV

I

A bullet's velocity in low temperatures
greatly depends on its target's virtues,
on its urge to warm up in the plaited muscles
of the torso, in the neck's webbed sinews.
Stones lie flat like a second army.
The shade hugs the loam to itself willy-nilly.
The sky resembles peeling stucco.
An aircraft dissolves in it like a clothes moth,
and like a spring from a ripped-up mattress
an explosion sprouts up. Outside the crater,
the blood, like boiled milk, powerless to seep into
the ground, is seized by a film's hard ripples.

II

Shepherd and sower, the North is driving
herds to the sea, spreading cold to the South.
A bright, frosty noon in a Wogistan valley.
A mechanical elephant, trunk wildly waving
at the horrid sight of the small black rodent
of a snow-covered mine, spews out throat-clogging
lumps, possessed of that old desire
of Mahomet's, to move a mountain.
Summits loom white; the celestial warehouse
lends them at noontime its flaking surplus.
The mountains lack any motion, passing
their immobility to the scattered bodies.

III

The doleful, echoing Slavic singing
at evening in Asia. Dank and freezing,
sprawling piles of human pig meat
cover the caravansary's mud bottom.
The fuel dung smoulders, legs stiffen in numbness.
It smells of old socks, of forgotten bath days.
The dreams are identical, as are the greatcoats.

544

Plenty of cartridges, few recollections,
and the tang in the mouth of too many 'hurrahs'.
Glory to those who, their glances lowered,
marched in the sixties to abortion tables,
sparing the homeland its present stigma.

IV

What is contained in the drone's dull buzzing?
And what in the sound of the aero-engine?
Living is getting as complicated
as building a house with grapes' green marbles
or little lean-tos with spades and diamonds.
Nothing is stable (one puff and it's over):
families, private thoughts, clay shanties.
Night over ruins of a mountain village.
Armour, wetting its metal sheets with oil slick,
freezes in thorn scrub. Afraid of drowning
in a discarded jackboot, the moon
hides in a cloud as in Allah's turban.

V

Idle, inhaled now by no one, air.
Imported, carelessly piled-up silence.
Rising like dough that's leavened,
emptiness. If the stars had life-forms,
space would erupt with a brisk ovation;
a gunner, blinking, runs to the footlights.
Murder's a blatant way of dying,
a tautology, the art form of parrots,
a manual matter, the knack for catching
life's fly in the hairs of the gunsight
by youngsters acquainted with blood through either
hearsay or violating virgins.

VI

Pull up the blanket, dig a hole in the palliasse.
Flop down and give ear to the *oo* of the siren.
The Ice Age is coming – slavery's ice age is coming,
oozing over the atlas. Its moraines force under
nations, fond memories, muslin blouses.
Muttering, rolling our eyeballs upward,

we are becoming a new kind of bivalve,
our voice goes unheard, as though we were trilobites.
There's a draught from the corridor, draught from the square windows.
Turn off the light, wrap up in a bundle.
The vertebra craves eternity. Unlike a ringlet.
In the morning the limbs are past all uncoiling.

VII

Up in the stratosphere, thought of by no one,
the little bitch barks as she peers through the porthole:
'Beach Ball! Beach Ball! Over. It's Rover.'
The beach ball's below. With the equator on it
like a dog collar. Slopes, fields, and gullies
repeat in their whiteness cheekbones
(the colour of shame has all gone to the banners).
And the hens in their snowed-in hen coops,
also a-shake from the shock of reveille,
lay their eggs of immaculate colour.
If anything blackens, it's just the letters,
like the tracks of some rabbit, preserved by a wonder.

[1980]

JOSEPH BRODSKY
translated from the Russian by Alan Myers

Joseph Brodsky (1940-96) was one of the foremost Russian poets of the 20th century. Expelled from the Soviet Union in 1972, he was awarded the Nobel Prize in Literature in 1987.

Oh Warrior of My Sacred Land

Oh warrior of my sacred land
the gun you bear on your shoulder
has neither eyes nor feet.
It steals your eyes to watch my step
it steals your feet to track me,

to blast a hole through my chest,
to hear my dying cry with your ears.
Oh warrior of my sacred land
this gun you bear on your shoulder
is it crippled, deaf and blind?
Has it shed its eyes, ears and feet
to take yours in their place?

You may know nothing about this gun –
but I know that our mutual enemy
schemes in a land far away.
He schemes for us to destroy our brothers,
to smash each other's jaws with brutal force
while he is safely out of reach.
He wants to mix our blood with soil
while his blood stays unspilt.
He wants us to freeze each night on the front
while he stays warm by a fire.
This is how our enemy schemes:
leaving his body at home like a shirt
he comes to our land in the form of a gun.

Oh warrior of my sacred land
when this sinister, limbless enemy
comes to our land in the form of a gun
he doesn't come alone, but in hordes
exceeding the headcount of this land,
each gun roaming and shooting ceaselessly:
not one with a bone that could break,
not one with skin that could burn,
not one with veins that could rip,
not one with blood that could spill.
All its limbs are safe at home
and instead it uses our limbs here.
One gun pursues me with your feet,
another marks you with my eyes,
a third lies on another man's shoulder –
just as this gun lies on yours.
All of its limbs left at home,
it came with only its mouth.

The shoulder is yours but the mouth is his –
a toothless mouth that speaks in bullets.
But when a bullet pierces a man
he doesn't see that gun's toothless mouth;
instead it's your shoulder, your hand he sees,
he takes you for his enemy, not the gun:
and he seeks revenge from you.

Oh warrior of my sacred land
the gun you bear on your shoulder –
how much blood has it spilt on our land
and never been called to account?
You alone are blamed for this blood
and revenge is sought from you
as they hoist another gun to their shoulder
aiming the bullet from its mouth at your heart.

Oh you who crave the crown,
one day this bullet will piece your heart
you're edging closer to a coffin than a throne –
take care and think again
before the enemy hurls you in a grave.
To save yourself from this dark fate
you must know the enemy who plots your end.
I am your brother: our mutual enemy
lies on your shoulder, crippled, deaf and blind.
It watches my footsteps with your eyes,
it pursues me with your feet
to blast a hole through my chest
and to hear my dying screams with your ears.

[6 December 2001]

DARWESH DURRANI
translated from the Pashto by Dawood Azami
and The Poetry Translation Centre Workshop

Darwesh Durrani (*b.* 1953) is one of the most famous contemporary Pashto
poets. His family is originally from Kandahar in southern Afghanistan; they
later settled in Quetta, Pakistan. He has a Masters degree in English literature,
a subject he teaches to college students in Quetta.

The War Reporter Paul Watson
and the Boys with the Bomblet

A gang of shepherd boys minding their own
rib-caged cows. When a yellow can appears
in a dust cloud. Like soda or a sleeve
of tennis balls, clasped in a corona
of tabs known as The Spider. Casing scored
so as to better shatter in a blast
of stampeding shrapnel that will strip all
clothes and flay any naked skin, leaving
pulped, cauterised stumps. Tinkling like wind chimes
after the wetter thuds. *The tiny chute*
hangs limply from the lip. Designed to drift
silently, otherworldly, increasing
our scatter radius. Preset to detonate
at precise heights or times. Or with the thrum
of traffic, the plosives of speech. Tremors
of the lightest footfalls. Two boys running
off in search of a father. The one boy
holding the canister suggests, Maybe
we'll find some food inside? The other one
slips his knife beneath the tab to find out
what's inside The Spider.

DAN O'BRIEN
➤ 550

The War Reporter Paul Watson
and the Chief's Embrace

One in the afternoon, Pashtun police
are fondling bodies at the gate. Chieftains
with uprooted beards, turbans like nests, dust
on the tongues of their sneakers. Gossiping
on conference room couches, slurping mint tea,
collecting cell messages while casting

aspersive glances. The police chief laughs
as he embraces. Slings tobacco juice
towards his spittoon. Another hero
of the Soviet war. With cars exploding
down the road, the road itself exploding
en route to the airfield. Ambulances
exploding the dead. Says the Taliban
is almost finished. *Most murders are due
to squabbling families. They are all hoping
to join us now.* Two in the afternoon
and a man in uniform is waiting
for the chief to step into the courtyard
till they embrace. Cold cylinders pressing
into both their bellies. Wrestling settling
of ball bearings and nails. The man fiddling
with something like a camera trigger till
both men explode. Chunks of corpses rain down
like volcanic cinders. Wind sprints, senseless
shouts. The assassin has taken several
out with the chief, and everyone's wounded
who survives.

DAN O'BRIEN

Dan O'Brien is an American playwright and poet originally from New York
who now lives in Los Angeles. The following note introduces his collection
War Reporter (2013):

Paul Watson has been a war reporter for more than two decades. He is best
known, perhaps, for his 1994 Pulitzer Prize-winning photo of the body of an
American soldier dragged from the wreck of a Black Hawk through the streets
of Mogadishu. When Paul took this picture he heard the dead man speak to
him: 'If you do this, I will own you forever.'

These poems are derived from Paul's memoir *Where War Lives*, his jour-
nalism, recordings and transcripts and, most valuably to me, our emails and
conversations. Some of the poems take place in Ulukhak-tok in the Canadian
High Arctic, where I visited Paul in the winter of 2010 while he was enjoying
a hiatus from war reporting, covering the Arctic and Aboriginal Beat' for the
Toronto Star. He has since gone back to covering Kandahar and other, more
recent war zones.

Several years ago my birth family disintegrated for bewildering, mysterious reasons. That I discovered Paul's work around the same time wasn't a coincidence. Early in our correspondence Paul sent me something I'll paraphrase: 'Do you know that quote of Camus' where he says he's solved the mystery of where war lives? It lives in each of us. In the loneliness and humiliation we all feel. If we can solve that conflict within ourselves then maybe we'll be able to rid the world of war.' Paul's writing, and mine in response, are as much about our private, internal wars as they are about the constantly roving holocaust of modern warfare. [DO'B] ➤ 549, 572

Arrest

The joins in the highway rise below the tires
as if we are running over bodies.
The windows are covered in butcher paper
and night coming cools the car's frame.
My head hangs the way cows' do:
complete submission to being led.
The last thing I saw was the red cloth coming
before it was tied around my eyes.
My spirit thumps in the darkness.
I've seen the pictures on the internet.
Sometimes I fake a swoon or cry,
hoping it might free me.
Sometimes I refuse to answer
questions they already know.
They feed me water from a cup;
I swallow. How human we are,
the tender, puncturing skin,
the illusion we can save ourselves
if we find the right words
and try with all our might.

[North Waziristan, spring 2004]

ELIZA GRISWOLD
➤ 517

The Pomegranates of Kandahar

The bald heft of ordnance
A landmine
shrapnel cool in its shell

Red balls
pinioned in pyramids
rough deal tables stacked to the sky

A mirrored shawl
splits
and dozens tumble down –

careering through the marketplace
joyful fruit
caught by the shouts of barefoot children

Assembled, they are jewels –
jewels
of garnet, jewels of ruby

A promise deep as the deep red of poppies
of rouged lips (concealed)
Proud hearts

built of rubble
Come, let us light candles in the dust
and prise them apart –

thrust your knife through the globe
then twist
till the soft flesh cleaves open

to these small shards of sweetness
Tease each jellied cell
from its white fur of membrane

till a city explodes in your mouth
Harvest of goodness,
harvest of blood

SARAH MAGUIRE

Sarah Maguire (*b.* 1957) is the founder and director of The Poetry Translation Centre in London. Her poetry books include *The Pomegranates of Kandahar* (2007), her multilingual anthology, *My Voice: A Decade of Poems from the Poetry Translation Centre* (2014), and *Almost the Equinox: Selected Poems* (2015).

The Silenced

I have no desire for talking, my tongue is tied up.
Now that I am abhorred by my time, do I sing or not?
What could I say about honey, when my mouth is as bitter as poison.
Alas! The group of tyrants has muffled my mouth.
This corner of imprisonment, grief, failure and regrets –
I was born for nothing that my mouth should stay sealed.
I know O! my heart, It is springtime and the time for joy.
What could I, a bound bird, do without flight.
Although I have been silent for long, I have not forgotten to sing,
Because my songs whispered in the solitude of my heart.
Oh, I will love the day when I break out of this cage,
Escape this solitary exile and sing wildly.
I am not that weak willow twisted by every breeze.
I am an Afghan girl and known to the whole world.

NADIA ANJUMAN
translated from the Dari by Abdul Salam Shayek

Nadia Anjuman (1980-2005) was a young Persian poet and journalist from Afghanistan who risked execution under Taliban rule by studying books other than the Qu'ran in one of Herat's renowned "sewing circles" where women were educated in secret. In 2005 she was killed by a husband whose family felt shamed by her publication of a book of poems about love, beauty and the oppression of Afghan women.

from **Pink Mist**

The sound of boots on the ground, walking slowly

HADS

We called it Afghan roulette.
Every day, more or less.
Going out on the ground
to take our chances
with what was under it.

Low metal content. Infra-red switches. Trip wires.
Filled with nails, ball-bearings, human shit.
Or old Russian stuff. Anti-tank, pressure-plates.
Or just some bloke on a phone pressing 'dial'.
Any of it enough
to turn you or your mates
into dust.

It was me who was meant to stop all that.
Up front, slow-sweeping my Vallon left and right.
Listening for the tone
that would stop me in my tracks,
send up my hand to freeze the patrol at my back.

After Catterick I wanted to be a medic.
And after we deployed too,
I kept applying for the course.
But they reckoned I was good at this stuff,
so they kept me at it.
Eighteen, and the lives of the patrol depending on me.
I had dreams.
Missing a massive IED, turning round too late
to see them eaten up by the earth – Arthur, Taff,
the whole section, my mates.
Gone in the blink of a boom,
a cloud of grey ash.

ARTHUR

But you didn't, did you, Hads?
Never missed a thing. At least, not till…
They were right. You were good. Had some kind of sense.
You could smell when something was up.
When the atmospherics changed –
locals leaving, birds flying from a tree.
I don't know how you did it, but believe me,
an ant could have farted
and I swear you'd have caught it.
[…]

ARTHUR

I was there when it happened.
Routine patrol, showing the locals and Terry Taliban
we could still own the ground, take control.
Hads was up front, like he always was,
sweeping his Vallon like a metronome,
low and slow, reading the unseen earth.
And all of us behind him, trying to follow his route,
off the path, across a field.
Two kids just metres away, gathering crops,
and us in full kit; ospreys, packs, helmet and gats,
going firm at the slightest of sounds. It was hot, tense.
Just three hours from the gate,
and I'd already drained my CamelBak.

The ICOM chatter was high, so we were taking it steady.
Hads wasn't happy, so he changed the route again.
The Corp didn't question him, he knew he'd saved us before.
For three months now he'd always brought us home.
But we were jumpy. The Sarge told him to hurry.
The whole patrol was out in the open, in the kill zone.

HADS

I could feel it there, somewhere. Close.
There was a bridge up ahead.
I'd already seen two locals
take the long way to reach it,
avoid the patch we were in.

555

I was looking for a sign –
some crossed sticks, a pile of stones.
That would be there too, somewhere.
I swung the Vallon again.
Left, right. Left, right.
But nothing, just the midday sun
burning my neck, the boys going firm,
dotting the field,
the terp in the FOB, relaying the comm.
Then –

ARTHUR

The tree line opened up.
Muzzle flashes in the bushes,
the whine and whizz of Afghan wasps
as the rounds came in and our boys hit their buckles,
flat to the ground, faces in the dirt,
doing what they could so's not to get hurt.

HADS

I knew we had to get out, find cover.
I'd seen an irrigation ditch, fifty metres ahead,
if I could find a safe route over –
The boss ordered suppressing fire,
and as the boys laid down a volley of lead
I took a step back.

ARTHUR

I saw it go up.
A sudden tree of earth and smoke,
the ground dropping and rising,
like a heartbeat under the soil.
It threw Hads twenty metres at least.
I can still see him now, as clear as then.
Arching in the air, his arms flung wide,
as if he was back at school again,
high-jumping for top spot – a record-beating Fosbury flop
that left his legs behind.

The sounds of a hospital

At first, when they pulled back the curtain
I felt relief.
A wave of warm joy.
There'd been a mistake, a crossing of wires.
This wasn't my boy.
How could it be? There'd been a wrong call.
Whoever he was, he didn't look like Hayden at all.
Poor sod didn't have his face.
And yes, I did think of his poor mother too,
the woman who'd have to take my place.
But when I told them, the nurse asked me
to look at his shoulder.
'Is this,' she said, 'Hayden's tattoo?'
My stomach dropped. I wanted to be sick:
I traced it with my fingertip
then looked up at his face again.
It was swollen, bruised about the eyes,
four days' growth, singed dark along his chin.
'Yes,' I said. 'It's him.'
[…]
Some hope in that. That wasn't Hads.
But then, nor was this. A living lie –
This boy in the hospital bed,
dried blood below his ear,
the sheet going flat
a couple of feet too soon,
just nothing after his thighs.

What have they done to him? – That was all I could think.
What have they done to my lad, my boy, my Hads?

OWEN SHEERS

1. *Vallon:* mine detector. 2. *IED:* Improvised Explosive Device. 3. *CamelBak:* personal hydration system. 4: *ICOM:* integrated communications or unsecured walkie-talkie transmissions. 5. *terp:* Afghan interpreter. 6. *FOB:* Forward Operating Base.

Owen Sheers (*b.* 1974) is a Welsh poet, author, actor and scriptwriter who has played Wilfred Owen on stage. Drawing upon interviews with soldiers and their families, *Pink Mist* is a verse-drama (broadcast by BBC Radio 4 in 2012) about three young soldiers from Bristol who are deployed to Afghanistan. School friends still in their teens, Arthur, Hads and Taff each have their own reasons for enlisting. Within a short space of time they return to the women in their lives (a mother, a wife, a girlfriend), all of whom must now share the psychological and physical aftershocks of their service.

Sheers' other work includes *Resistance* (2007), a novel set in Wales in 1944, later made into a film, in which the D-Day landings fail and Germany occupies half of Britain, and *The Two Worlds of Charlie F.* (2012), a play staged by the Bravo 22 Company based on the experiences of wounded and injured service personnel who made up most of the cast.

The Next Thing

My heart stopped but my hands kept working away.
I had a job to do. I threw the mortar down the barrel

and waited for the splash to come up, just waited.
It was bang on. The next thing was to extract our own –

but lifting a dead body from the ground is not easy.
The first must have weighed fourteen stone; plus radio

he was half a ton. I could not get him off the ground,
not properly, not enough to put him over my shoulder.

I thought, Jesus Christ! But I managed. It is only right.
Later on we met some elders from the village to discuss

the bodies of the enemy; they were shot up very badly.
Two were dressed in black – obviously foreign fighters

with grenades on them and mobile phones and notebooks.
Their skin was strangely waxy and suspicious-looking.

A third was wearing traditional dress with a red sash
and a turban that was off at the time; his eyes were sunk

and had rolled backwards – there was no brain left in there.
I dug a bullet out of the wall behind him with my bayonet

for a keepsake, and could clearly see the swirl on the casing.
Then I went down the valley to a stream with the other men

and we stripped to wash our hands and faces in the water.
After that we stayed firm and finished our clearance patrols.

ANDREW MOTION

Several poems in Andrew Motion's collection *The Customs House* (2012) take the words of soldiers (from accounts in books, interviews and meetings) to create 'found poems' which he hopes can be read as collaborations between the author and his source. 'The Next Thing' is indebted to Cpt Dave Rigg, Cpt George Seal-Coon, Lance Corporal Daniel Power, Warrant Officer Class 2 Keith Knieves, Cpt Adam Chapman and Ranger David McKee, quoted in *Spoken from the Front*, edited by Andy McNab (2009). ➤ 128, 248.

Pamir[1]

I know the black, black mountains;
I know the desert and its problems.
My home is the mountain, my village is the mountain and I live
        in the mountains;
I know the black ditches.
I always carry a rocket-launcher on my shoulder;
I know the hot trenches.
I always ambush the enemy;
I know war, conflict and disputes.
I will tell the truth even if I am hung on the gallows;
I know the gallows and hanging.
I don't care about being hot or cold;
I know all kinds of trouble.
I am the eagle of Spin Ghar's high peaks;
I know Pamir's canyons.
I walk through it day and night;
I know the bends of Tor Ghar.
Bangles are joyful on the girls' hands;
I know swords.

Those who make sacrifices for religion;
Faizani, I am familiar with such young men.

[21 May 2008]

FAIZANI
translated from the Pashto by Mirwais Rahmany & Hamid Stanikzai

1. The Pamir mountain range extends over Afghanistan, China, Kyrgyztan, Pakistan and Tajikistan.

Faizani is a Taliban fighter.

Trenches

Hot, hot trenches are full of joy;
Attacks on the enemy are full of joy.
Guns in our hands and magazine belts over my shoulders;
Grenades on my chest are full of joy.
The enemy can't resist when he sees them;
Black hair and stiff moustaches are full of joy.
He who fights in the field is manly;
Houses full of black-haired women are full of joy.
We become eager two times after hearing it:
The clang, clang and rockets are full of joy.
Leave the lips and spring, O poet!
Poems full of feeling are full of joy.
Jawad, I say, on the true path of *jihad*,
All kinds of troubles are full of joy.

[21 May 2008]

JAWAD
translated from the Pashto by Mirwais Rahmany & Hamid Stanikzai

Jawad is a Taliban fighter.

Poem

Who am I? What am I doing?
How did I get here?
There is no house or love for me;
I am homeless, without a homeland.
I don't have a place in this world;
They don't let me rest.
There are shots fired, and gunpowder here,
A shower of bullets.
Where should I go, then?
There is no place for me in this world.
A small house
I had from father and grandfather,
In which I knew happiness,
My beloved and I would live there.
They were great beauteous times;
We would sacrifice ourselves for each other.
But suddenly a guest came;
I let him be for two days.
But after these two days passed,
The guest became the host.
He told me, 'You came today.
Be careful not to return tomorrow.'

[28 November 2008]

NAJIBULLAH AKRAMI
translated from the Pashto by Mirwais Rahmany & Hamid Stanikzai

Najibullah Akrami is a Taliban fighter.

These three poems by Taliban fighters are taken from the anthology *Poetry of the Taliban* (2012), edited by Alex Strick van Linschoten and Felix Kuehn, co-founders of the website and media monitoring service AfghanWire, for which many of the poems in their book were first transcribed and translated from oral sources. Drawing on the long tradition of Persian or Urdu verse as much as Afghan legend and recent history, Taliban poetry is an aesthetic oral form with love, beauty and warfare among its main themes. Poems are memorised and passed on, but latterly the mode of wider transmission has shifted from cassette tapes to mp3 files.

Eleven Landays

translated & presented by Eliza Griswold

In Afghan culture, poetry is revered, particularly the high literary forms that derive from Persian or Arabic. But the poems below are folk couplets – landays – an oral and often anonymous scrap of song created by and for mostly illiterate people: the more than 20 million Pashtun women who span the border between Aghanistan and Pakistan. Traditionally, landays are sung aloud, often to the beat of a hand drum, which, along with other kinds of music, was banned by the Taliban from 1996 to 2001, and in some places, still is.

A landay has only a few formal properties. Each has 22 syllables: nine in the first line, thirteen in the second. The poem ends with the sound *ma* or *na*. Sometimes landays rhyme, but more often not. In Pashto they lilt internally from word to word in a kind of two-line lullaby that belies the sharpness of their content, which is distinctive not only for its beauty, bawdiness, and wit, but also for its piercing ability to articulate a common truth about love, grief, separation, homeland, and war. [...]

Now people share landays virtually via the Internet, Facebook, text messages, and the radio. Landays are usually sung, and singing is linked to licentiousness in Afghan consciousness. Women singers are viewed as prostitutes. Women get around this by singing in secret – in front of only close family or, say, a harmless-looking foreign lady writer. Usually in a village or family one woman is more skilled than others at singing landays, yet men have no idea who she is. Much of an Afghan woman's life involves a cloak-and-dagger dance around honor – a gap between who she seems to be and who she is.

My love gave his life for our homeland.
I'll sew his shroud with one strand of my hair.

*

In battle there should be two brothers:
one to be martyred, one to wind the shroud of the other.

*

Be black with gunpowder or blood-red
but don't come home whole and disgrace my bed.

*

Who will you be but a brave warrior,
you who've drunk the milk of a Pashtun mother?

*

May God destroy the White House and kill the man
who sent U.S. cruise missiles to burn my homeland.

*

Bush, don't be so proud of your armored car.
My *remoti* bomb will blow it to bits from afar.

In 1998, after Osama bin Laden attacked the US embassies in Kenya and
Tanzania, President Clinton retaliated by launching cruise missiles on Tora
Bora and Khost. The first poem above grew popular at the time.

Remoti, which means 'remote control', applies to both remote-control bombs
and to unmanned aircraft, or drones. The second landay was posted on the
Pashto Landay Facebook page with a photograph of a metal scrap scrawled
with Pashto characters. This, the comment read, was the door of an American
MRAP, a Mine Resistant Ambush Protected vehicle, a modern-day tank.
According to the post, the Afghan Taliban left this landay for US forces to
find on the torn-off door of an MRAP that they'd blown up in Tangi Valley,
Maidan Wardak Province, in 2009.

May God destroy your tank and your drone,
you who've destroyed my village, my home.

*

The drones have come to the Afghan sky.
The mouths of our rockets will sound in reply.

*

My Nabi was shot down by a drone.
May God destroy your sons, America, you murdered my own.

In addition to landays, hymns and videos calling for death to America are
common all over Afghanistan. Many Afghans keep such recordings on their
smartphones as a security measure. (Smartphones are *de rigueur* for young
Afghans.) If militants stop an ordinary person at a checkpoint, they're likely to
smash his phone if he has Western movies or music stored on it. If the owner
has uploaded Taliban propaganda, he's more likely to survive with his phone
intact. Anti-American songs aren't solely of Taliban provenance. Rage at the
occupying forces, especially in the south-east of the country, which has borne
the brunt of war, is such that anti-American landays are fairly commonplace, as
they were during the wars against the British and the Russians. Drone attacks
make it worse. Because of their omnipresence in the skies above the border

between Afghanistan and Pakistan, drones have found their way into landays. Their seemingly indiscriminate strikes and relentless noise have taken a heavy psychologically toll on those who live under their flight path. The fear of drones also drives support for the Taliban; the militants are viewed as the only Afghans brave enough to resist the invaders.

The loathing is often intensely personal. A woman named Chadana sang the third of these landays. She is the mother of a Taliban fighter called Nabi who was killed, apparently, by a US drone strike in Zormat, in the south-eastern province of Paktia, in 2011. (Chadana had three sons: two became Taliban fighters and the third a policeman. Such divisions are common in families.) She sang this landay about Nabi at a wedding, where it was recorded on a cell phone and sent to her cousin, a businesswoman named Sharifa Ahmadzai, who repeated it to me in her home in Jalalabad over a plate of freshly quartered pomegranates.

May God destroy the Taliban and end their wars.
They've made Afghan women widows and whores.

*

God kill the Taliban's mothers and girls.
If they're not fighting jihad, why do their oil their curls?

There's a good deal of pride – and power – in being related to a high-ranking member of the Taliban. In the woman's sphere, Taliban wives and mothers have high status. The second poem pokes fun at the haughtiness of Taliban female relatives, asking why they are so arrogant, since it's their men who are risking their lives, not they.

Homeland

He detonates at 5 a.m.

The sound is unmistakable:
first flesh, then second thoughts.

The windows rattle as we two women do in aftershock.

Bolt upright from the floor, you mutter, *Bismillah*.
I shudder, *Shit*, and grab my swelling belly.

Usually, the head survives intact, a hand in a tree.

By 6 a.m. we quit Jalalabad.
I apologise and disregard

your cold, coal eyes when I reach for the backseat's only belt.

[Winter 2013]

ELIZA GRISWOLD
➤ 517

The Dirt on Afghanistan

I thought the US troops had come to bring
electric washers, Tide, and heat to us.
I watched my home and thought *goodbye to this*
big filth. But now, my neighbors are preparing
more guns, more bullets, RPGs. Toenail
to forehead. It'll be bloody. Larger than
the past. Let's holler, 'yes, hello to hell'.
The Afghan Army – it's a joke. Its men
steal and rape and drive the US Humvees.
The foreigners are getting out and hoping
that this large mess won't stick to them. Let's be
more honest, there's no soap, no water, there's
not one good toilet. The shit storm's coming.
It's awful what we'll face. There's no plan B.

AMIN ESMAIELPOUR

Amin Esmaielpour is a poet, literary translator and writer. Born in Tehran
in 1988, he moved to the US from Iran in 2011. He is an MFA in poetry
and also holds an MA in American and New England studies and a BA in
English translation. His English poems have been published in several American
journals.

WORLDWIDE WAR | 1970s–present

This final section covers poems relating to other wars and conflicts as well as to terrorist incidents in various parts of the world over the past four decades.

The most deadly of all the terrorist actions has been the attacks on 9 September 2001 (9/11) by al-Qaeda hijackers who crashed four passenger planes in the US, two of these into the World Trade Center in New York and one into the Pentagon: see poems by X.J. Kennedy, Wisława Szymborska, X.J. Kennedy and Deborah Garrison [➤ 573-74]. Nearly 3,000 people were killed in the attacks, including 227 passengers onboard the four planes, and a further 343 firefighters and 72 law enforcement officers died during or following the rescue operations. Alan Smith's 'Kidding Myself in Kuta, Bali: A Pantoum' [➤ 575-76] relates to Australia's worst terrorist incident, the nightclub bombing in Bali on 12 October 2002 which killed 202 people (including 88 Australians).

Poems by Gavin Ewart and Tony Conran [➤ 569-71] relate to the ten-week Falklands War of 1982 when Argentina invaded 'Las Malvinas' and Britain's Margaret Thatcher despatched a task force to recapture its overseas territory, the Falkland Islands, at a cost of 255 British lives and 649 Argentinians.

Started in 1991, the continuing Somali Civil War included a disastrous UN intervention during the mid 90s, the setting of Dan O'Brien's 'The War Reporter Paul Watson Hears the Voice' [➤ 572], written in response to Watson's famous photograph from 1994 of an American soldier dragged from the wreck of a Black Hawk through the streets of Mogadishu [➤ 550].

Two poems by Adrie Kusserow [➤ 577-80] relate to the Second Sudanese Civil War (1983-2005) between the central Sudanese government and the Sudan People's Liberation Army. One to two million people died during the war, mostly civilians, due to starvation and drought. Kevin Higgins's 'Firewood' [➤ 580] is a response to the humanitarian crisis and genocide in Darfur. Begun in 2003, the War in Darfur has involved ethnic cleansing of non-Arabs by the government of Sudan. Several hundred thousand people are thought to have died and millions have been displaced. The Sudanese dictatorship forced Al-Saddiq Al-Raddi [➤ 577] into exile in 2012.

'Ruins' by journalist and poet Eliza Griswold [➤ 582] is a poem of recovery, written in Rome, in which she recalls seeing a dead man during the war in Eastern Congo 'missing an ear, which had been removed, probably by whoever killed him – either to be worn as a totem or to be eaten. [...] Consuming human flesh became a means to consume an enemy's power' (*Poetry*, December 2012).

This is followed by five poems from the Arab Spring, the revolutionary wave of protests and civil wars that began in December 2010. Khaled Mattawa writes of Libya's liberation from Gadaffi's dictatorship [➤ 583]; 'the poet of Tahir Square', Mostafa Ibrahim, presents his manifesto for action [➤ 586]; and Fouad Mohammad Fouad and Golan Haji [➤ 589-93] give their accounts of the war in Syria. This is very much a provisional selection lacking the poetry of some writers, such as Syria's Noury al-Jarrah, whose key work has not yet been translated into English. But if the poetry of these continuing conflicts follows the pattern of others, much of the significant work is still to be written.

Casual Wear

Your average tourist: Fifty. 2.3
Times married. Dressed, this year, in Ferdi Plinthbower
Originals. Odds 1 to 9
Against her strolling past the Embassy

Today at noon. Your average terrorist:
Twenty-five. Celibate. No use for trends,
At least in clothing. Mark, though, where it ends.
People have come forth made of colored mist

Unsmiling on one hundred million screens
To tell of his prompt phone call to the station,
'Claiming responsibility' – devastation
Signed with a flourish, like the dead wife's jeans.

[1984]

JAMES MERRILL

James Merrill (1926-95) was an American poet known for his earlier lyric poetry and later apocalyptic epic *The Changing Light at Sandover* (1982). Drafted in 1944, he served eight months in the US Army during the Second World War.

The One Twenty Pub

The bomb is primed to go off at one twenty.
A time-check: one sixteen.
There's still a chance for some to join
the pub's ranks, for others to drop out.

The terrorist watches from across the street.
Distance will shield him
from the impact of what he sees:

A woman, turquoise jacket on her shoulder,
enters; a man with sunglasses departs.
Youths in tee-shirts loiter without intent.

One seventeen and four seconds.
The scrawny motorcyclist, revving up
to leave, won't believe his luck;
but the tall man steps straight in.

One seventeen and forty seconds.
That girl, over there with the walkman
– now the bus has cut her off.
One eighteen exactly.
Was she stupid enough to head inside?
Or wasn't she? We'll know before long,
when the dead are carried out.

It's one nineteen.
Nothing much to report
until a muddled barfly hesitates,
fumbles with his pockets, and, like
a blasted fool, stumbles back
at one nineteen and fifty seconds
to retrieve his goddamn cap.

One twenty
How time drags when...
Any moment now.
Not yet.
Yes.
   Yes,
      there
        it
           goes.

[*1976*]

WISŁAWA SZYMBORSKA
version from the Polish by Dennis O'Driscoll

Wisława Szymborska (1923-2012) was one of Poland's four great 20th-century poets. She won the Nobel Prize in Literature in 1996. Her poems are concerned with large existential issues, exploring the human condition with sceptical wit and ironic understatement. ➤ 314, 573.

The Falklands, 1982

This must have been more like the Boer War
than anything seen in our lifetime,
with the troopships and the cheering,
the happy homecoming, the sweetheart-and-wifetime,
everything looking over and solved,
and no civilians involved –

except a few stewardesses, Chinese in the galleys
almost by accident taken
willy-nilly on The Great Adventure,
where the Argentine fusing of the shells was often mistaken –
lucky for each floating sitting duck.
Oh yes, we had luck!

Luck that the slaughtered World War I soldiers
who died on the Somme and at Arras
would have welcomed, in their dismal trenches –
though that's not to belittle the victory of the Paras,
who lost, all in all, very few dead,
good men, well led.

At home, indeed, it was terribly like the World Cup,
though far less bright, commentated, stagey,
security making the war news nil, mostly,
but good value when they finally stopped being cagey.
Was the *General Belgrano* really offside?
A few hundred died.

And the outstanding achievements of the great Press,
particularly that section called 'yellow',
that wrote 'Up yours!' on missiles, went berserk
and shouted 'GOTCHA!' in a giant coward's bellow –
and circulation rises, like *The Sun*.
But was it well done?

Kipling's 'Recessional' told us to beware of Hubris,
and not give way to flag-waving
(they don't in the Lebanon, or Northern Ireland) –

569

if men's lives are worth giving, they're also worth saving.
Who let them start the bloody thing?
That's the question, there's the sting.

GAVIN EWART

➤ 289

Elegy for the Welsh Dead, in the Falkland Islands, 1982

> *Gŵyr a aeth Gatraeth oedd ffraeth eu llu.*
> *Glasfedd eu hancwyn, a gwenwyn fu.*
>   Y GODODDIN (6th century)
>
> *(Men went to Catraeth, keen was their company*
> *They were fed on fresh mead, and it proved poison.)*

Men went to Catraeth. The luxury liner
For three weeks feasted them.
They remembered easy ovations,
Our boys, splendid in courage.
For three weeks the albatross roads,
Passwords of dolphin and petrel,
Practised their obedience.
Where the killer whales gathered,
Where the monotonous seas yelped.
Though they went to church with their standards
Raw death has them garnished.

Men went to Catraeth. The Malvinas
Of their destiny greeted them strangely.
Instead of affection there was coldness,
Splintering iron and the icy sea,
Mud and the wind's malevolent satire.
They stood nonplussed in the bomb's indictment.

Malcolm Wigley of Gonnah's Quay. Did his helm
Ride high in the war-line?
Did he drink enough mead for that journey?
The desolated shores of Tegeingl,
Did they pig this steel that destroyed him?

570

The Dee runs silent beside empty foundries.
The way of the wind and the rain is adamant.

Clifford Elley of Pontypridd. Doubtless he feasted.
He went to Catraeth with a bold heart.
He was used to valleys. The shadows held him.
The staff and the fasces of tribunes betrayed him.
With the oil of our virtue we have anointed
His head, in the presence of foes.

Phillip Sweet of Cwmbach. Was he shy before girls?
He exposes himself now to the hags, the glance
Of the loose-fleshed whores, the deaths
That congregate like gulls on garbage.
His sword flashed in the wastes of nightmare.

Russell Carlisle of Rhuthun. Men of the North
Mourn Rheged's son in the castellated vale.
His nodding charger neighed for the battle.
Uplifted hooves pawed at the lightning.
Now he lies down. Under the air he is dead.

Men went to Catraeth. Of the forty-three
Certainly Tony Jones of Carmarthen was brave.
What did it matter, steel in the heart?
Shrapnel is faithful now. His shroud is frost.

With the dawn men went. Those forty-three,
Gentlemen all, from the streets and byways of Wales,
Dragons of Aberdare, Denbigh and Neath –
Figment of empire, whore's honour, held them.
Forty-three at Catraeth died for our dregs.

TONY CONRAN

Tony Conran (1931-2013) was a Welsh poet who became a distinguished translator of Welsh poetry, teaching for many years at UCW Bangor, despite being born with cerebral palsy. This was his most celebrated poem, combining remembrance of the sixth-century Welsh (or British) defeat at Catraeth with the deaths of soldiers at Bluff Cove during the Falklands War on 8 June 1982, many of these Welsh Guards killed aboard RFA *Sir Galahad*.

The War Reporter Paul Watson Hears the Voice

We ask them, Have you seen the American
soldier? Someone says he saw him tied up
in a wheelbarrow. I take a picture
of children bouncing on a rotor blade
in the smoldering wreckage of a Black Hawk.
Has anyone seen the dead American
soldier? The mob parts around me, I look
down in the street. And I meet the man. When
you take a picture the camera covers
your face, you shut the rest of the world out,
everything goes dim. And I hear a voice
both in my head and out. *If you do this,*
I will own you forever. I'm sorry
but I have to. *If you do this, I will*
own you. I'm sorry, I'm not trying to
desecrate your memory. If you do this
I will own you forever. I took his
picture. While they were beating his body
and cheering. Some spitting. Some kid wearing
a chopper crewman's goggles, face screwed up
in rapturous glee while giving the dead man
the finger. An old man's raising his cane
like a club and thudding it down against
the dead flesh. Men holding the ropes that bind
the dead man's wrists are stretching his arms out
over his head, rolling him back and forth
in the hammering morning light. I'm standing
outside myself. I'm watching someone else
take these pictures. Wondering, You poor man.
Who are you?

DAN O'BRIEN
➤ 550

572

Photograph from September 11

They jumped from the burning floors –
one, two, a few more,
higher, lower.

The photograph halted them in life,
and now keeps them
above the earth toward the earth.

Each is still complete,
with a particular face
and blood well hidden.

There's enough time
for hair to come loose,
for keys and coins
to fall from pockets.

They're still within the air's reach,
within the compass of places
that have just now opened.

I can do only two things for them –
describe this flight
and not add a last line.

WISŁAWA SZYMBORSKA
translated from the Polish by Stanislaw Baranczak & Clare Cavanagh
➤ 315

September Twelfth, 2001

Two caught on film who hurtle
from the eighty-second floor,
choosing between a fireball
and to jump holding hands,

aren't us. I wake beside you,
stretch, scratch, taste the air,
the incredible joy of coffee
and the morning light.

Alive, we open eyelids
on our pitiful share of time,
we bubbles rising and bursting
in a boiling pot.

X.J. KENNEDY

X.J. Kennedy (*b.* 1929) is an American poet and children's writer.

I Saw You Walking

I saw you walking in Newark Penn Station
in your shoes of white ash. At the corner
of my nervous glance your dazed passage
first forced me away, tracing the crescent
berth you'd give a drunk, a lurcher, nuzzling
all comers with ill will and his stench, but
not this one, not today: one shirt arm's sheared
clean from the shoulder, the whole bare limb
wet with muscle and shining dimly pink,
the other full-sheathed in cotton, Brooks Bros
type, the cuff yet buttoned at the wrist, a
parody of careful dress, preparedness –
so you had not rolled up your sleeves yet this
morning when your suit jacket (here are
the pants, dark gray, with subtle stripe, as worn
by men like you on ordinary days)
and briefcase (you've none, reverse commuter
come from the pit with nothing to carry
but your life) were torn from you, as your life
was not. Your face itself seemed to be walking,
leading your body north, though the age

of the face, blank and ashen, passing forth
and away from me, was unclear, the sandy
crown of hair powdered white like your feet, but
underneath not yet gray – forty-seven?
forty-eight? the age of someone's father –
and I trembled for your luck, for your broad
dusted back, half shirted, walking away;
I should have dropped to my knees to thank God
you were alive, O my God, in whom I don't believe.

DEBORAH GARRISON

Deborah Garrison (*b.* 1965) is an American poet and editor. This poem is
one of a number in her collection *The Second Child* (2007) concerned with her
experience of 9/11 and its aftermath; others relate to motherhood.

Kidding Myself in Kuta, Bali: A Pantoum

They've hired too many actors for the scene
The piles of bodies really are a laugh
The wounds are so extreme that they're obscene
With limbs ripped off and bodies cut in half

The piles of bodies really are a laugh
The blood however excellently done
With limbs ripped off and bodies cut in half
While all around the crimson rivers run

The blood however excellently done
Confused? Concussed? A little drunk perhaps
While all around the crimson rivers run
I am the one in shock who laughs and claps

Confused? Concussed? A little drunk perhaps
At last it dawns, there is no camera crew
I am the one in shock who laughs and claps
Hawaiian shirt with blood now streaming through

At last it dawns, there is no camera crew
A laugh chokes in my throat, I'm sobbing now
Hawaiian shirt with blood now streaming through
A man in white sticks something on my brow

A laugh chokes in my throat, I'm sobbing now
The frantic search for living victims starts
A man in white sticks something on my brow
He smiles and whispers sorry and departs

The frantic search for living victims starts
A second man comes close, and shakes his head
He smiles and whispers sorry and departs
I can't accept I'm very nearly dead

A second man comes close, and shakes his head
I do not want to face my life's conclusion
I can't accept I'm very nearly dead
It's just a film: my final self delusion

I do not want to face my life's conclusion
They've hired too many actors for the scene
It's just a film: my final self delusion
The wounds are so extreme that they're obscene

ALAN SMITH

Alan Smith (*b.* 1945) is an Australian poet who served in the Royal Australian
Navy for 25 years before retiring to teach business communication. A Parkin-
son's sufferer, he now lives in a Sydney nursing home. Les Murray has called
this 'one of Australia's great war poems'. It's a pantoum, a poetic form adopted
by English and French writers from the Malay *pantun* consisting of a series
of quatrains with lines repeated to a set pattern, here used to disconcert and
disturb with its subject being so shocking: the bombings in and near a nightclub
in Kuta on the Indonesian island of Bali on 12 October 2002, which killed
202 people (including 88 Australians) and injured another 240. According to
the Islamist group responsible, Jemaah Islamiyah, the attacks were carried out
in retaliation for support for the so-called US war on terror and Australia's
role in the liberation of East Timor. Two suicide bombers died in the attacks,
three other perpetrators were later executed, one was killed in a shootout with
police, and another is in prison; others are still sought.

Poem

I saw the angel
and the singing birds slaughtered.
I saw the horse,
the soldiers,
the grieving women,
the dead trees, and other women
inured to screams and wailing.
I saw the streets, the gusting wind,
the sports cars
racing by, the boats, the innocent kids.

I said, 'Master of the Water, this is
how things are: tell me about the clay,
the fire, the smoke, the shadows, the smell
of reality.' Deliberately, I did not ask
about our homes.

AL-SADDIQ AL-RADDI
translated from the Arabic by Mark Ford & Hafiz Kheir

Al-Saddiq Al-Raddi (*b.* 1969) is one of the leading African poets writing in
Arabic. Famous since a teenager, he is admired for the lyric intensity of his
poetry and for his principled opposition to Sudan's dictatorship. His *Collected
Poems* was published in 2010. A distinguished journalist, he was forced into
exile in 2012 and now lives in London.

Skull Trees, South Sudan
(for Atem Deng)

Arok, hiding from the Arabs in the branches of a tree,
two weeks surviving on leaves,
legs numb, mouth dry.
When the mosquitoes swarmed
and the bodies settled limp as petals under the trees,

he shinnied down, scooping out a mud pit with his hands
sliding into it like a snake,
his whole body covered except his mouth.
Perhaps others were near him,
lying in gloves of mud, sucking bits of air through the swamp holes,
mosquitoes biting their lips,
but he dared not look.

What did he know of the rest of South Sudan, pockmarked with
        bombs,
skull trees with their necklaces of bones,
packs of bony Lost Boys[1]
roving like hyenas towards Ethiopia,
tongues, big as toads, swelling in their mouths,

the sky pouring its relentless bombs of fire. Of course they were
tempted to lie down for a moment,

under the lone tree, with its barely shade,
to rest just a little while before moving on,

the days passing slyly, hallucinations
floating like kites above them

until the blanched bones lay scattered in a ring around the tree,
tiny ribs, skulls, hip bones – a tea set overturned,
as the hot winds whistled through them
as they would anything, really,

and the sky, finally exhausted,
moving on.

[*2007*]

ADRIE KUSSEROW

1. The Lost Boys (and Girls) refers to the 20,000 children who fled their
homes from the Second Sudanese Civil War. They walked 1,000 miles before
they finally found protection in refugee camps in Ethipia and Kenya. Half of
them died along the way. About 3800 have been resettled in America. There
is currently a second wave of Lost Boys and Girls now fleeing the bombings
in the Nuba Mountains of Sudan. [AK]

War Metaphysics for a Sudanese Girl

(for Aciek Arok Deng)

I leave the camp, unable to breathe,

me Freud girl, after her interior,
she 'Lost Girl', after my purse,

her face:
dark as eggplant,
her gaze:
unpinnable, untraceable,
floating, open, defying the gravity
I was told keeps pain in place.

Maybe trauma doesn't harden,
packed, tight as sediment at the bottom of her psyche,
dry and cracked as the desert she crossed,
maybe memory doesn't stalk her
with its bulging eyes.

Once inside the body does war move up or down?
Maybe the body pisses it out,
maybe it dissipates, like sweat and fog
under the heat of a colonial God?

In America, we say 'Tell us your story, Lost Girl
you'll feel lighter,
it's the memories you must expel,
the bumpy ones, the tortures, the rapes, the burnt huts.'

So Aciek brings forth all the war she can muster,
and the doctors lay it on the table, like a stillbirth,
and pick through the sharpest details
bombs, glass, machetes
and because she wants to please them
she coughs up more and more,
dutifully emptying the sticky war
like any dutiful Lost Girl in America should
when faced with a flock of white coats.

This is how it goes at the Trauma Center:
all day the hot poultice of talk therapy,
coaxing out the infection,
at night, her host family trying not to gawk,
their veins pumping neon fascination,
deep in the suburbs, her life flavoring dull *muzungu*[1] lives,
spicing up supper really,
each Lost Girl a bouillon cube of horror.

[*2007*]

ADRIE KUSSEROW

1. *muzungu* means 'white person' in many Bantu languages of east, central and South Africa.

Adrie Kusserow (*b.* 1966) is a cultural anthropologist who has worked with Sudanese refugees in trying to build schools in war-torn South Sudan. She is Professor of Cultural Anthology at St Michael's College, Vermont. Along with some of the Lost Boys of Sudan resettled in Vermont, she and her husband Robert Lair helped found ELI (www.africaeli.org), a non-profit organisation helping refugee girls attend schools in South Sudan. Her books include two poetry collections from BOA, *Hunting Down the Monk* (2002) and *Refuge* (2013).

Firewood

A bone field fifty metres by fifty.
It's problematic to describe this as genocide.
I gather firewood at eight o'clock in the morning.
My son clings to my dress. Men in uniforms
with military insignia stop their car
and throw him into a fire. Then five of them
one after the other. I am paralysed.
It's problematic to describe this as genocide.
The solution is not military intervention. We demand
the US keep its hands off Sudan.
Children start jumping out windows
when the Janjaweed come into the school.

The police begin firing. Everyone,
mainly babies and the elderly,
falls down. I am standing on bodies.
A military barracks.
No bathroom. People stay still,
suffering their wounds.
People stay still. No bathroom.
A military barracks. I am standing on bodies,
fall down. Mainly babies and the elderly.
Everyone. The police begin firing.
When the Janjaweed come into the school,
children start jumping out windows.
The solution not military intervention.
The US keep its hands off Sudan, we demand
It's problematic to describe this as genocide.
I am paralysed. One after the other,
five of them. They stop their car
and throw him into a fire. Men
in uniforms with military insignia.
My son clings to my dress.
At eight o'clock in the morning I gather firewood.
It's problematic to describe this as genocide.
A bone field fifty metres by fifty.

[2007]

KEVIN HIGGINS

The non-italicised lines in the poem are quotations from eye-witness accounts from Darfur. [KH]

Kevin Higgins (*b.* 1967) lives in Galway, Ireland. He has published four collections of poems, all with Salmon Poetry, as well as *Mentioning The War* (2012), a collection of essays and reviews.

Ruins

A spring day oozes through Trastevere.
A nun in turquoise sneakers contemplates the stairs.
Ragazzi everywhere, the pus in their pimples
pushing up like paperwhites in the midday sun.

Every hard bulb stirs.

The fossilised egg in my chest
cracks open against my will.

I was so proud not to feel my heart.
Waking means being angry.

The dead man on the Congo road
was missing an ear,
which had either been eaten
or someone was wearing it
around his neck.

The dead man looked like this. No, that.

Here's a flock of tourists
in matching canvas hats.
This year will take from me
the hardened person
who I longed to be.
I am healing by mistake.
Rome is also built on ruins.

[2010]

ELIZA GRISWOLD
➢ 517

After 42 Years

Five years old when the dictator took over in a coup –
curfew shut our city down
Bloodless coup, they said –
The many who thought this could be good.
The dictator, a young man, a shy recluse assumed the helm, bent
    in piety,
the dead sun of megalomania hidden in his eyes.
Could not go to the store to buy bread or newspaper,
could not leave home, visit friends,
the radio thundering hatred, retching blood-curdling song –
Signs that went unread
Factories built and filched, houses stolen, newspapers shut down,
decades of people killed, 42 years.

But that's all over now –
How can you say over when it took 42 years –
I was five when the dictator took my brother away
Over now, 42 years, must look ahead.
His face half blood-covered, half smirking
Like Batman's Joker,
hands raised, fingers pressed together upward
Saying wait, calm down, wait
Wait 42 years – five years old when my father was killed
standing in front of a hotel.
Bloodless coup,
the country like a helpless teenage girl
forced into marriage hoping her groom will be kind.

In between there was blankness
that burned like a million of suns into our eyes,
Death like air, everywhere.

What was it like to be held by his men?
Fingers pulled out, testicles fried,
To be hung from a clothesline rope, the dictator's mistress pulling
    at my legs?
How many killed by his men over the decades,
The cracked skulls, the mass graves, the uncounted dead?

What and who taught you O sons of my country to be so fearless cruel?
Him, they say, for 42 years, 42 years of him.

Who taught you to be reckless heroic?
The no-life we had to live, under him, the lives we were asked to live
    as dead.

Alive we want him alive, many kept shouting.
So that they could give him tastes of his own medicine?
Alive, alive!
And many others disbelieving they'd caught him.
Their shrill Allahu Akbars exclamations of astonishment –

What have I done O Lord to deserve the honor of capturing the rat?
Exclamations of disbelief –
The nightmare – GAME OVER – the night-game of breaking into
    houses, arresting sons;
the day game of civility – we'll bring him in a few hours –
we'll bring him back in 42 years –
Could it be so easy – GAME OVER – the capturing of a 69-year-old
    rat?
A clown in a rat-colored outfit, a wild mop of hair, a wig
Holding a golden pistol like a child playing hero, high-heeled boots.

Is that what our history amounted to?

No.
Because somewhere there were suns that would never light.
Somewhere, there were holes in the air that was full of death.
We managed to hold our breath and live our lives.

Could it be so simple O Lord to end an epoch? –
killing kidnapping murder massacre slit throats vaginal tests for
    women he wished to sex vaginal rapes anal rapes of dissidents he
    wished to humiliate – humiliation denigration outsourced
    whippings money changed on oil tankers boiling water poured on
    the entreating heads of maids hot iron pressed on servant flesh slit
    throats broken ribs feet whipped until swelled like cantaloupes
    bodies left hanging in public squares –
I was five when my brother disappeared,

I was thirteen, I was twenty, I was seventy-six, I was never allowed
    to reach birth.

What will be our aftermath?

One minute and all of that history is found hiding
like a rat, history like a rat,
hiding in a sewer drain.
History too hot to hold –
the magic was in seeing it come to end –
the pain too dark to bear, too light, too cold,
the astonishment unbearable, would kill you if it lasted too long.

He died of his wounds.
No, no, they just shot him dead.

Perhaps he was a magnet and he drew evil out of men's chests,
his hands, his hands saying wait, wait
reached into their lungs and wound and knotted their raw souls,
a magnet now siphoning cruelty to itself.

No, no, they just shot him dead.
But I heard he died of his wounds.

Too much for a young man who could not stop being a killer,
a young man who did what millions wished to do.
To tear him to bits, my mother's friend once said,
to tear him to bits, six millions hearts had prayed –
O God grant me the sight of him dead!

One bullet, or two, some say three,
despite the pleading fingers tainted with their own blood.
Surprised as if he'd never seen or heard of blood,
Surprised that he too would bleed if cut.
One bullet, two, or three and it's done with, our history, our epoch.
The book of misery read
The rabid beast captured, kicked about and shot in the head.

O Lord is that our history tossed into a freezer like a lump of
    rotting flesh?

O Lord how little our lives must be, when so much can be buried
  lost, dumped in a hole, forgotten
                                dust!

No, because
somewhere, an earthly sun is shining on us, with us, again.
There is air in the air again.

What will our aftermath be then?

We wash our hands,
put on spotless clothes.
There is no 'after' until we pray for all the dead.

[2011]

KHALED MATTAWA

Khaled Mattawa (*b*. 1964) is an Arab-American poet and translator who grew
up Benghazi, Libya, and moved to the US as a teenager in 1979. He has
published several collections, most recently *Tocqueville* (2010), and translated
numerous volumes of contemporary Arabic poetry, including Maram al-
Massri's *A Red Cherry on a White-tiled Floor* (2004), *Miracle Maker: Selected
Poems of Fadhil Al-Azzawi* (2004) and *Adonis: Selected Poems* (2010). He cur-
rently teaches at the University of Michigan.

Manif-sto

M

Maspero[1] is deadlier than the castle and guns.
Mire your eyes in blood before you go.
Maintain your lines united, no flags shall divide you.
Many may stand beside you but serve the foe.

A

Align yourself with the revolution's end.
A chant is born of its time and place.

Embrace the fire to lighten the smoke.
Allow retreat but don't turn back.
Attack with all your might.
All of history is on the line.

N

Name these names: lies, fear, treason.
Know that surprise is half the battle;
Run fast, return numerous.
Narrow the gap before you aim.

I

Is caution the way to safety?
Is a thief's word the way to honesty?
Is a chanter anything but the echo of a chanting voice?
Is bravery inspiration or the gift of its own enactment?

F

Fearlessness is not the fall of the fool.
Identify the self-serving and the faithful friend.
Fix your eyes on what others fail to see;
Shut them if your sight deceives.
Diffuse your pain in bread and blood not tears.

S

Seal the way behind you.
Seek cover in a burning tyre's smoke.
Spread a carpet of nails across the street.
Save their soldiers an escape route.
Surrender the dream to those of its youth.
Surrender the cross to those who will bear it.

T

Traitors deserting the battle condemned.
Turn to the eyes your friends have lost.
Tired? Pay a matching cost.
Fight while you can.
Time's on your side but not for long.
Take heart from the trail of followers behind you;
If you have no use for hope, they do.

O

Open the front when many; close it when on the low.
Glow the torches among you whenever the rhythm's slow.
Do right by the neighbours, overcome their confusion.
Provide for the injured before you take a bite.
Blow out every street light.
If you must bow down, stay looking up.
If lured to a long alley, stop.
Offer alternatives.
Accept truce, only if their dogs withdraw.
If all may drop, be the last to go.
One alone can make a difference.
So, when you're tired or caught by doubt,
Move for one behind to join your row.

MOSTAFA IBRAHIM
translated from the Arabic by Nariman Youssef

1. Maspero Building is the headquarters of the Egyptian Radio and Television Union, a symbol of state-run media. In October 2011, following an attack on a church, a protest against sectarianism was staged outside Maspero. The violent military crackdown that followed left at least 27 dead and over 200 injured. The incident has been since remembered as the Maspero Massacre.

Mostafa Ibrahim was born in 1986 in Giza, Egypt. He writes in Egyptian Arabic, and has been lauded by the country's two leading colloquial poets, Abdel-Rahman Al-Abnudi and the late Ahmed Fuad Negm. His first collection of poems, *Western Union, Haram* (Merit, 2011), came out in January, days before the first spark of revolution in Egypt. His second collection, *Manifesto* (2013), sold out in less than six months. The majority of poems in this last book, including the title poem, chronicle and meditate on the events of revolution in Egypt between 2011 and 2013, echoing the experiences of Ibrahim's generation in both content and spirit.

The Arabic title of the poem shares meaning and pronunciation with the word 'Manifesto', except that in Arabic the short vowel in place of the 'e' is pronounced but not written. I made a choice in favour of reproducing the structure of the poem – 8 stanzas, each emphasising one of the title's letters – and dropped the 'e', giving the poem in English its current title.

The first attempts at translating 'Manif-sto' took place during a workshop at the 4th Annual Translation Conference in Doha, Qatar, and while the translation has undergone several transformations since, I owe the initial spark of inspiration to the participants of that workshop. [Tr.]

Aleppo Diary

1

Writing is pain.

And the blood that drips down the screen pollutes the atmosphere
staining the couch with what looks like dried coffee, which we
touch with trembling fingers so we don't get infected.

We manage with broken backs as if going to hell seeing dark red,
no, brown as well, which deposits a residue like rust in the soul.

We stroke their old heads then turn aside to lick away the tears.

Those who crawl from street to screen leave green traces on the
asphalt that spring into bushes of basil; they toss us a flower and
die in haste to spare our shame.

Now you've entered the sacred valley, take off your shoes and
walk on broken glass.

2

The comrades in reading have fallen asleep.
You wander alone through the book stacks
with no sign of an exit.
From the third shelf on the right comes a groan
a whole chapter expelled from a novel.
Laughter the tragic title
for a book of philosophy.
Politics flows like phlegm from one shelf to another.
There is no time for epic
for *The Book of Delight and Intimacy*
as Machado eases open the book covers
gently, so as not to disturb the ornaments.

We are the proofs of books
full of paragraphs in need of revision.

3

I sit on the balcony. Aleppo spread before me black and deserted.
The clatter of crockery in the dark means life goes on. No sound
save sporadic gunfire from somewhere, then a single shell preceded
by a peculiar whistle. Someone is leaving this planet with a dry
throat. Aleppo before me black and still. These huge shadows might
be trees or childhood goblins or black vapours exhaled by women
waiting for children who are already numbers in a news report.

Aleppo. No oud plucked. No 'Swaying Silhouette'. No drinks in
The Nightingale. No drinkers. No song.[1]

One by one
they awaken
the beasts of darkness.

4

Marina Shihwaro[2]

I am Marina Constantine
widow of the priest George Shihwaro
companion of Marcel as we walk, late at night, to our home;
I am she, endowed with secrets of the holy church,
with cherries at the bottom of a glass of liqueur,
busy with laughter at the age of fifty,
hair braids forgotten in an old chest of drawers.
..
..

I am Marina
returning from the Carlton
where life clings to music
and thickens like frankincense
Freely
I scatter salt
even though I know that meat will not spoil
I dip a finger in wine to rejoice my heart.
..
..

I am Marina
who, at the wrong turn, smelled
the odour of fear exuding from sweating fists
piercing the air like lead
before the Citadel vanished in a magician's hat
..

..

I am Marina
who did not know she had died
until, alongside the thousands bearing roses wearing white,
she heard
the words of the priest in the church of Prophet Ilyas:
O dearly beloved,
in God's hands and with humble hearts
let us pray:
May the soul of our daughter
who ascends with the crown to our Lord in Heaven
rest in peace.
...

...

Al-Fatihah.[3]

FOUAD MOHAMMAD FOUAD
translated from the Arabic by Samuel Wilder
& the Poetry Translation Centre Workshop

1. 'Swaying Silhouette': a famous Syrian song. The bar, The Nightingale, was where all of Aleppo's artists and thinkers would congregate. 2. Marina Shihwaro was killed in Aleppo on 18 June 2012. 3. *Al-Fatihah:* opening Sura of the Quran.

Fouad Mohammed Fouad was born in Aleppo, Syria, in 1961. The author of four collections of poetry, he has taken part in readings and events across the Arab-speaking world and in France. A doctor and public health researcher, he has been forced into exile by recent events in Syria and is now living and working in Beirut.

A Soldier in a Madhouse

'Slow it!' when the raid came
And they gagged men with their leather belts,
My scream turned back in my throat
And wore away what was left of my luggage.
The numbness in my arm wakes up
Too much I had lain myself on it
And I see all those who were staring at me just now
And the sutures of the air are unpicked as if they
        are my mouth and I hear nothing,
I stare at the dot in the dirty white
As it turns out to be an eye staring back at me,
And wherever I looked I found myself multiplying.
There are stares devouring me leave nothing but
                        a crust
If I touch it with my fingertips I'd vanish.
I am the bread of the invisible :
How terrified I am by the eyes of the terrified,
Everyone who's terrified, terrifies.

GOLAN HAJI
translated from the Arabic by Golan Haji & Stephen Watts

Shooting Sportsmen

Passengers in minibuses paid for their death in the morning with
        ten liras.
The cupboard buried the sleepers,
Windowpanes tore off the curtains and severed necks like guillotines.
A speechless pond of blood on the asphalt
Where a clamour of noise hovers.
Then they came, cancelled their appointments,
Picked their teeth to throw the remains of our hearts to ants
And shouted: 'No one is accused. All are sentenced.'
They closed the pharmacies and bridges.
They blocked the entries of cities and the openings to the squares,

And lifted a wrong address on the end of a spear:
Either the chasm or the wall.
They left us insomnia and a list of names,
Dust which the hungry licked off their shoes,
Armour of trash bins,
Tigers drawn on shrouds in the night of vineyards,
Jugs of turbid water, a shoe on the road,
Cold and candles, the spit of merchants,
Bullets in the refrigerator door, the screen and the cistern's belly,
A barrack in a museum, the contusions of painters,
The monk's cloak, a ripped off nail, bulldozed cactus farms,
A bullet in the eye, the heart, and the warmth of testicles;
And they took the amateur actors, the physician, the passersby,
Musicians, bread-seekers, lottery vendors and goalkeepers.
They smashed the sky and coloured the tanks with its blood
To raise the piano, the coffin of music.
They murdered the madman of the quarter, the milk vendor and
       the parsley seller.
They killed the window and the sister who looked from it,
Neither the neighbours' cow survived
Nor the streetlamp.
They spat in the spring and ripped off the lens –
The tearful sanguine eye of life,
The eye of hope.
With knives they tore off the used couch,
The suitcase and the rope-bound blanket.
They crucified the carpenter, strangled the goldfinch and slaughtered
       the singer.
They burnt the barley spikes, the books and bicycles.
Then they lay down on playground grass and snoozed off.
These are not images.
These are the guardians of pictures.

GOLAN HAJI
translated from the Arabic by the author

Golan Haji is a Syrian poet and translator with a postgraduate degree in
pathology. Born in 1977 in Amouda, a Kurdish town in the north of Syria,
he studied medicine at the University of Damascus, and lived in Damascus
until he had to flee the country. He has now settled in France.

A century later

The school-bell is a call to battle,
every step to class, a step into the firing-line.
Here is the target, fine skin at the temple,
cheek still rounded from being fifteen.[1]

Surrendered, surrounded, she
takes the bullet in the head

and walks on. The missile cuts
a pathway in her mind, to an orchard
in full bloom, a field humming under the sun,
its lap open and full of poppies.

This girl has won
the right to be ordinary,

wear bangles to a wedding, paint her fingernails,
go to school. *Bullet*, she says, *you are stupid.*
You have failed. You cannot kill a book
or the buzzing in it.

A murmur, a swarm. Behind her, one by one,
the schoolgirls are standing up
to take their places on the front line.

[2012]

IMTIAZ DHARKER

1. Malala Yousafzai (*b.* 1997), who campaigned for women's right to education
from the age of 11 and survived a Taliban attempt on her life in October 2012.

Imtiaz Dharker is a poet and artist, the author of six collections illustrated
with her own drawings. Born 1954 in Pakistan, she grew up a Muslim Calvinist
in a Lahori household in Glasgow, was adopted by India, and married into
Wales. Her main themes are drawn from a life of transitions: childhood, exile,
journeying, home, displacement, religious strife and terror, and latterly, grief.

Drummer [1]

The pavement is a drum beneath your feet.

When you return as usual, crossing the square,
walking down the familiar street,
you need no signposts to take you home.
You feel the hum of buses, trains booming
underground, strong and close as your own
heartbeat.

Drummer, you know these thoroughfares,
you have played them. These roads
lay claim to you.

So when the blade meets skin,
the whole street stops, feels the sting.
Hack at you, and the city bleeds.

Even in broad daylight, the alleys
turn dark and glitter with long knives,
but the nightmare cannot hold you in.
You fall out of it. You fall back
into the city's sickened heart,
and it beats harder, begins to speak
in every language, deep down
where the blood thunders

Not in my name. Not in my name.
The city's heart becomes a drum,
dhak, dhak, dhak.
It speaks the name you understand,
the difficult name, the name of peace.

[2013]

IMTIAZ DHARKER

1. Drummer Lee Rigby, aged 25, was hacked to death by two Muslim fanatics
on a London street on 23 May 2013.

ACKNOWLEDGEMENTS

Edmond Adam: 'Gamecocks', tr. Ian Higgins, first published in *The Lost Voices of World War I*, ed. Tim Cross (Bloomsbury, 1988), by permission of the translator. **Valentine Ackland:** *Journey from Winter: Selected Poems*, ed. Frances Bingham (Carcanet Press, 2008). **Adonis:** *Selected Poems*, tr. Khaled Mattawa (Yale University Press, 2010), by permission of the publisher on behalf of the author. **Chris Agee:** 'Mass Grave, Padališta' from *First Light* (The Dedalus Press, Dublin, 2003), by permission of the author. **Anna Akhmatova:** *Selected Poems*, tr. Richard McKane (Bloodaxe Books, 1989/2006). **Najibullah Akrami:** 'Poem', tr. Mirwais Rahmany & Hamid Stanikzai, from *Poetry of the Taliban*, ed. Alex Strick van Linschoten & Felix Kuehn (Hurst & Company, 2012). **Al-Saddiq Al-Raddi:** 'Poem' tr. Mark Ford & Hafiz Kheir from *My Voice: A Decade of Poems from the Poetry Translation Centre*, ed. Sarah Maguire (Bloodaxe Books/The Poetry Translation Centre, 2014). **Adnan al-Sayegh:** 'Agamemnon' and 'The Sky in a Helmet', tr. Stephen Watts & Marga Burgui-Artajo, from *The Deleted Part* (Exiled Writers Ink, London, 2009), by permission of the translators. **Yehuda Amichai:** 'Jerusalem' and 'The Place Where We Are Right' from *The Selected Poetry of Yehuda Amichai*, tr. Chana Bloch & Stephen Mitchell (HarperCollins, 1986; rev. ed. University of California Press, 1996), by permission of the University of California Press; 'Patriotic Songs' and 'The Diameter of the Bomb' from *Selected Poems*, ed. Ted Hughes & Daniel Weissbort (Faber & Faber, 2000), by permission of the publisher. **Doug Anderson:** *The Moon Reflected Fire* (Alice James Books, 1994), by permission of the author. **Nadia Anjuman:** 'The Silenced', tr. Abdul Salam Shayek, from *Naweed Monthly*, issue 5 & 6, by permission of the translator. **Guillaume Apollinaire:** 'Desire' and 'War Marvel', tr. Michael Copp; 'The Bleeding-Heart Dove and the Fountain', tr. Ian Higgins; all first published here by permission of the translators. **Simon Armitage:** *The Not Dead* (Pomona Books, 2008), by permission of the author. **W.H. Auden:** *Collected Poems*, ed. Edward Mendelson (Faber & Faber, 2007), by permission of Curtis Brown Group Ltd. **Nobuo Ayukawa:** 'Saigon 1943' and 'Maritime Graves', tr. Hajime Kajima, from *Post-War Japanese Poetry*, ed. Harry Guest, Lynn Guest & Kajima Shôzô (Penguin Books, 1971).

    Ingeborg Bachmann: *Darkness Spoken: The Collected Poems*, tr. Peter Filkins (Zephyr Press, Brookline, MA, 2006), by permission of Zephyr Press c/o BOA Permissions. **Mourid Barghouti-Palestine:** *Midnight and Other Poems*, tr. Radwa Ashour (Arc, 2008), by permission of the publisher. **Tomica Bajsić:** poems from *Juzni Kriz / Southern Cross* (Croatia, 1998) tr. Damir Šodan by permission of the author and translator. **Adisa Basić:** 'People Talking', tr. Ulvija Tanović, from *The World Record: international voices from Southbank Centre's Poetry Parnassus*, ed. Neil Astley & Anna Selby (Bloodaxe Books, 2012), by permission of the author. **Peter Baum:** 'At the Beginning of the War', tr. Patrick Bridgwater from *The German Poets of the First World War* (Croom Helm, 1985), by permission of the translator. **Martin Bell:** *Collected Poems*, ed. Peter Porter (Bloodaxe Books, 1988). **Aleksandr Blok:** *Selected Poems*, tr. Jon Stallworthy & Peter France (Carcanet Press, 2000), by permission of the publisher. **Edmund Blunden:** *Selected Poems* (Carcanet Press, 1982), by permission of Carcanet Press. **Johannes Bobrowski:** *Shadow Lands: Selected Poems*, tr. Ruth & Matthew Mead (Anvil Press Poetry, 1984) by permission of the publisher. **Eavan Boland:** *New Collected Poems* (Carcanet Press, 2005) by permission of the publisher. **B.G. Bonallack:** 'Retreat from Dunkirk', extract from 'British Expeditionary Force', first published in *Lowdown*, the journal of the 92nd Field Artillery Regiment, Royal Artillery, Anzio beachhead, May 1944, by permission of the estate of B.G.

Bonallack. **Sargon Boulus:** 'News About No One' was translated by the author and published first in *Banipal* 12 (Autumn/Winter 2001), and then collected in *Knife Sharpener: Selected Poems* by Sargon Boulus, published by Banipal Books in 2009 as a posthumous celebration of the poet; it is republished here with the kind permission of *Banipal*. **Bertolt Brecht:** 'War Has Been Given a Bad Name', originally published in German in 1964 as 'Der Krieg ist geschandet worden', copyright © 2014 by David Constantine, copyright © 1964 by Bertolt-Brecht-Erben / Suhrkamp Verlag; extracts from '1940', originally published in German in 1961 as '1940', copyright © 2014 by David Constantine, copyright © 1961 by Bertolt-Brecht-Erben / Suhrkamp Verlag; extracts from 'Finland 1940', originally published in German in 1964 as 'Finnland 1940', copyright © 2014 by David Constantine, copyright © 1964 by Bertolt-Brecht-Erben / Suhrkamp Verlag; 'General, your tank is a powerful thing', originally published in German in 1938 as 'General, dein Tank ist ein starker Wagen', copyright © 2014 by Tom Kuhn, copyright © 1939, 1961 by Bertolt-Brecht-Erben / Suhrkamp Verlag; extracts from 'A German War Primer', originally published in German in 1938 as 'Deutsche Kriegsfibel', copyright © 2014 by Tom Kuhn, copyright © 1939, 1961 by Bertolt-Brecht-Erben / Suhrkamp Verlag; all from *Collected Poems of Bertolt Brecht* by Bertolt Brecht, tr. Tom Kuhn and David Constantine, used by permission of Liveright Publishing Corporation. **Clive Branson:** 'Death Sentence Commuted to Thirty Years', 'Sunset', and 'Spain. December 1936', from *The Penguin Book of Spanish Civil War Verse* (Penguin Books, 1980). **Vera Brittain:** 'The Lament of the Demobilised' from *Oxford Poetry 1920* (B.H. Blackwell Ltd, 1920), is included by permission of Mark Bostridge and T.J. Brittain-Catlin, Literary Executors for the Vera Brittain Estate 1970. **Joseph Brodsky:** 'Lines on the Winter Campaign, 1980' tr. Alan Myers, from *Collected Poems in English*, ed. Ann Kjellberg (Carcanet Press, 2001), by permission of the publisher. **Basil Bunting:** *Complete Poems* (Bloodaxe Books, 2000). **Paddy Bushe:** *To Ring in Silence: New and Selected Poems* (The Dedalus Press, 2008), by permission of the publisher.

Mary Wedderburn Cannan: 'Rouen: April 26–May 25, 1915' from *In War Time*, published by Blackwell and printed by Humphrey Milford at OUP, 1917, reproduced by permission of Mrs C.M. Abrahams on behalf of the May Wedderburn Cannan estate. **Ciaran Carson:** *Collected Poems* (The Gallery Press, 2008), by kind permission of The Gallery Press, Loughcrew, Oldcastle, Co. Meath, Ireland, www.gallerypress.com. **Michael Casey:** 'A Bummer' from *Obscenities* (Yale University Press, 1972), by permission of the author. **Jean Cayrol:** 'Return', tr. Ian Higgins, this translation is first published here by permission of the translator and Robert Laffont/Nil/Julliard/Seghers. **Paul Celan:** 'Deathfugue' and 'Aspen Tree' from *Selected Poems and Prose of Paul Celan*, tr. John Felstiner (W.W. Norton & Company, 2000), copyright © 2001 John Felstiner, by permission of W.W. Norton & Company, Inc. **William Childress:** 'Shellshock', first published in *Poetry* (September 1962), reprinted in *Burning the Years and Lobo: Poems 1962-1975* (Essai Seay Publications, East St Louis, 1986), by permission of the author. **Lois Clark:** *The Dance of Remembered Days* (Ver Poets, 1974). **Gillian Clarke:** *Collected Poems* (Carcanet Press, 1997), by permission of the publisher. **Jean Cocteau:** 'Then my guide in the blue overcoat...', tr. Michael Copp, this translation first published here by permission of the translator and Éditions Gallimard. **Margaret Postgate Cole:** 'The Falling Leaves' and 'Afterwards' from *Poems* (George Allen & Unwin Ltd, by permission of David Higham Associates. **David Connolly:** *Lost in America* (Vietnam Generation Inc & Burning Cities Press, Woodbridge, CT, 1994). **Tony Conran:** *The Shape of My Country: Selected Poems and Extracts* (Gwasg Carreg Gwalch, 2004). **David Constantine:** *Collected Poems* (Bloodaxe Books, 2004).

R.N. Currey: *The Other Planet* (Routledge, 1945).
József Choli Daróczki: 'They Took Away the Gypsies', tr. Jamie McKendrick
& Mari Gömöri, from *I lived on this Earth... Hungarian Poets of the Holocaust*, ed.
George & Mari Gömöri (Alba Press, 2012), by permission of the translators. **Mahmoud
Darwish**: 'In Jerusalem' and extracts from 'A State of Siege' from *The Butterfly's
Burden*, tr. Fady Joudah (Bloodaxe Books, 2007); 'He Embraces His Murderer', tr.
Sarah Maguire & Sabry Hafez, from *Being Alive*, ed. Neil Astley (Bloodaxe Books,
2004), by permission of the translators. **Bruce Dawe**: *Sometimes Gladness: Collected
Poems, 1954-2005*, 6th Edition (Longman Cheshire, Southbank, Victoria, Australia,
2006). **C. Day Lewis**: *The Complete Poems* (Sinclair-Stevenson, 1992), © 1992 in this
edition, and the estate of C. Day Lewis, reprinted by permission of the Random
House Group Ltd. **Lucie Delarue-Mardrus**: 'All Souls' Day', tr. Ian Higgins, this
translation first published here by permission of the translator. **Boris Dezulović**:
'Boraja', tr. Hamdija Demirović, from *Poezija* V. 1-2 (June 2009), and from *If We
Crash into a Cloud, It Won't Hurt: Croatian Poetry 1989-2009*, ed. Ervin Jahić, by
permission of Damir Šodan. **Imtiaz Dharker**: *Over the Moon* (Bloodaxe Books, 2014).
Patric Dickinson: *Stone in the Midst: A Play in Verse and Poems* (Methuen, 1948).
Eva Dobell: *A Bunch of Cotwold Grasses* (Arthur H. Stockwell Ltd, 1919). **Keith
Douglas**: *The Complete Poems*, ed. Desmond Graham (Faber & Faber, 2000). **Jehanne
Dubrow**: *Stateside* (Triquarterly Books/Northwestern University Press, 2010). **Helen
Dunmore**: *Out of the Blue: Poems 1975-2001* (Bloodaxe Books, 2001). **Paul Durcan**:
Life Is a Dream: 40 Years Reading Poems 1967-2007 (Harvill Secker, 2009), by per-
mission of the author and Rogers, Coleridge and White.

Richard Eberhart: *New and Selected Poems 1930-1990* (Blue Moon Books, 1990);
Blue Moon was an imprint of Avalon, now part of Persea Books Group. **W.D. Ehrhart**:
Unaccustomed Mercy: Soldier Poets of the Vietnam War, ed. W.D. Ehrhart (Texas Tech
University Press, 1989), by permission of Thunder Press. **Ivan Elagin**: 'The last foot
soldier has already fallen', tr. Vladimir Markov & Merrill Sparks, from *Modern Russian
Poetry: An anthology with verse translations*, ed. & tr. Vladimir Markov & Merrill Sparks
(MacGibbon & Kee, 1966). **Amin Esmaielpour**: 'The Dirt on Afghanistan', from
Prairie Schooner, 87.4 (Winter 2013), by permission of the author. **Gavin Ewart**:
Selected Poems 1933-1993 (Hutchinson, 1996), by permission of the Estate of Gavin
Ewart.

Salah Faik: 'On the Tenth Anniversary of Murdering My Country', tr. Sinan
Antoon, by permission of the translator. **Faizani**: 'Pamir', tr. Mirwais Rahmany &
Hamid Stanikzai, from *Poetry of the Taliban*, ed. Alex Strick van Linschoten & Felix
Kuehn (Hurst & Company, 2012). **Dahlia Falah**: *With an Iron Pen: Twenty Years of
Hebrew Protest Poetry*, ed. Tal Nitzan & Rachel Tzvia Back (State University of New
York Press, Albany, 2009), by permission of the publisher. **James Fenton**: *Yellow
Tulips: Poems 1968-2011* (Faber & Faber, 2012), by permission of United Agents. **Roy
Fisher**: *The Long and the Short of It: Poems 1955-2010* (Bloodaxe Books, 2012). **Bryan
Alec Floyd**: *The Long War Dead* (The Permanent Press, Sag Harbor, 1976). *Carolyn
Forché*: *The Country Between Us* (Jonathan Cape, 1983), by permission of the William
Morris Endeavour Entertainment Agency. **Fouad Mohammad Fouad**: 'Aleppo
Diary' tr. Samuel Wilder, by permission of the author and the Poetry Translation
Centre. **Gilbert Frankau**: *The Judgement of Valhalla* (Chatto & Windus, 1918). **Erich
Fried**: *100 Poems without a Country*, tr. Stuart Hood (Calder, 1978), copyright of
Stuart Hood and Alma Classics Ltd, 1991, 2011.

Deborah Garrison: *The Second Child* (Bloodaxe Books, 2008). **Alfonso Gatto**:
'For the Martyrs of Loreto Square', tr. Kendrick Smithyman, from *The FSG Book of
Twentieth-Century Italian Poetry*, ed. Geoffrey Brock (Farrar, Straus & Giroux, LLC,

2012). **Mordecai Gebirtig:** 'Our Town Is Burning', tr. Joseph Leftwich, from *The Golden Peacock: a worldwide library of Yiddish poetry*, ed. & tr. Joseph Leftwich (T. Yoseloff, 1961) by kind permission of Julien Yoseloff and Associated University Presses. **Zaqtan Ghassan:** *Like a Straw Bird It Follows Me, and Other Poems*, tr. Fady Joudah (Yale University Press, 2012), by permission of the publisher. **Pamela Gillilan:** *All-Steel Traveller: New & Selected Poems* (Bloodaxe Books, 1994). **Alan Gillis:** *Somebody, Somewhere* (The Gallery Press, 2004), by kind permission of the author and The Gallery Press, Loughcrew, Oldcastle, Co. Meath, Ireland, www.gallerypress. com. **Varda Ginossar:** 'And Today Is a Holiday', tr. Jean Nordhaus, from *After the First Rain: Israeli Poems on War and Peace*, ed. Moshe Dor & Barbara Goldberg (Syracuse University Press, 1998), by permission of the publisher. **Jon Forrest Glade:** *Photographs of the Jungle* (Chiron Review Press, St John, KS, 1990). **Yvan Goll:** 'Recitative', VII, from 'Requiem for the Dead of Europe', tr. Patrick Bridgwater, from *The Penguin Book of First World War Poetry*, ed. Jon Silkin (Penguin Books, 1979), by permission of the translator. **Albert-Paul Granier:** *Cockerels and Vultures: French Poems of the First World War* by Albert-Paul Granier, tr. Ian Higgins, by permission of the translator. **Eliza Griswold:** 'Ruins' from *Poetry* (December 2012) and 'Homeland' from *Prairie Schooner*, 87: 4 (Winter 2013) by permission of the author; 'Retreat', 'Water Cure', 'Arrest' from *Wideawake Field* (Farrar, Straus and Giroux, 2007); 'Eleven Landays' from *I Am the Beggar of the World: Landays from Contemporary Afghanistan*, with photographs by Seamus Murphy (Farrar, Straus and Giroux, 2014), first published in *Poetry* (June 2013). **Vona Groarke:** *Flight* (The Gallery Press, 2002), by kind permission of the author and The Gallery Press, Loughcrew, Oldcastle, Co. Meath, Ireland, www.gallerypress.com. **Ivor Gurney:** *Collected Poems*, ed. P.J. Kavanagh (Oxford University Press, 1982), by permission of Carcanet Press, on behalf of the Ivor Gurney Trust. **Bernard Gutteridge:** *Traveller's Eye* (Routledge & Kegan Paul, 1947).

  Golan Haji: 'Shooting Sportsmen', first published in *The Wolf*, 27, by permission of the author. **Tamiki Hara:** 'this is a Human Being' and 'Glittering Fragments', tr. Geoffrey Bownas & Anthony Thwaite, from *The Penguin Book of Japanese Verse*, tr. Geoffrey Bownas & Anthony Thwaite (Penguin Books, 1964) by permission of publisher. **Choman Hardi:** *Life for Us* (Bloodaxe Books, 2004). **Ra'aya Harnik:** *After the First Rain: Israeli Poems on War and Peace*, ed. Moshe Dor & Barbara Goldberg (Syracuse University Press, 1998). **Tony Harrison:** *Collected Poems* (Viking, 2007), by permission of the author. **Seamus Heaney:** *Opened Ground: Poems 1966-1996* (Faber & Faber, 1998), by permission of the publisher. **Anthony Hecht:** *Collected Earlier Poems* (Alfred A. Knopf, Inc, 1990). **Hamish Henderson:** *Elegies for the Dead in Cyrenaica* (1948; Birlinn, 2008). **Zbigniew Herbert:** *The Collected Poems 1956-1998* (Ecco/HarperCollins, 2007). **Miguel Hernández:** I Have Lots of Heart: Selected Poems (Bloodaxe Books, 1997). **John Hewitt:** *The Collected Poems of John Hewitt*, ed. Frank Ormsby (Blackstaff Press, 1991), by permission of Blackstaff Press Ltd on behalf of the Estate of John Hewitt. **Georg Heym:** 'War' tr. John Greening from *To the War Poets* (Carcanet Press/Oxford Poets, 2013). **Kevin Higgins:** *Time Gentlemen, Please* (Salmon Poetry, 2008) by permission of the author. **Geoffrey Hill:** *Broken Hierarchies: Collected Poems 1952-2012*, ed. Kenneth Haynes (Oxford University Press, 2013). **Roland Hinjosa:** *Klail City Death Trip* (Justa Publications, Berkeley, CA, 1978). **Vladimir Holan:** *Mirroring: Selected Poems of Vladimir Holan*, tr. C.G. Hanzlicek & Dana Hábová (Wesleyan University Press, 1985), by permission of the publisher. **Molly Holden:** *Air and Chill Earth* (Chatto & Windus, 1971), out of copyright. **Geoffrey Holloway:** *Rhine Jump* (London Magazine Editions, 1974), by permission of Patricia Pogson, widow of the late Geoffrey Holloway. **Miroslav Holub:** 'Five minutes after the air raid' and 'The Prague of Jan Palach', tr. George Theiner; 'The corporal who killed Archimedes' tr. Ian & Jarmila Milner; 'The end of the world' tr. Ewald Osers; from *Poems Before & After: Collected English Translations* (Bloodaxe Books, 1990). **A.D. Hope:** *Antechinus: Poems 1975-1980* (Sydney: Angus & Robertson, 1981), by arrangement with the Licensor, The AD Hope Estate, c/o Curtis Brown (Aust) Pty Ltd. **Peter Huchel:** 'Roads' tr. Michael Hamburger, from *East German Poetry: An Anthology*, ed. Michael Hamburger (Carcanet Press, 1972).

Mostafa Ibrahim: translation by Nariman Youssef, original poem from *Manifesto* (Dar El Shorouk Publishing, Cairo, 2014), first published in 2013 by Bloomsbury Qatar Foundation Publishing, Doha, by permission of the author and translator. **Gyula Illyés:** *What You Have Almost Forgotten: Selected Poems*, ed. & tr. William Jay Smith (Curbstone Press, CT, 1999). **Vera Inber:** extract from 'The Pulkovo Meridian', tr. Dorothea Prall Radin & Alexander Kaun, from *Soviet Poets and Society* by Alexander Kaun (University of California Press, 1943). *Elegies for the Dead in Cyrenaica* (1948; Birlinn, 2008).

Henry-Jacques: all poems tr. Michael Copp, from *Us Men of War* (The Hawthorn Press, 1996), by permission of the translator. **Randall Jarrell:** The Complete Poems (Farrar, Straus & Giroux, 1991). **Jawad:** 'Trenches' tr. Mirwais Rahmany & Hamid Stanikzai from *Poetry of the Taliban*, ed. Alex Strick van Linschoten & Felix Kuehn (Hurst & Company, 2012). **David Jones:** *In Parenthesis* (Faber & Faber, 1937), by permission of the publisher. **Denys L. Jones:** *Penguin New Writing* (1946).

Mitsuharu Kaneko: *The Penguin Book of Japanese Verse*, tr. Geoffrey Bownas & Anthony Thwaite (Penguin Books, 1964), by permission of Anthony Thwaite. **Dahlia Kaveh:** *With an Iron Pen: Twenty Years of Hebrew Protest Poetry*, ed. Tal Nitzan & Rachel Tzvia Back (State University of New York Press, Albany, 2009), by permission of SUNY Press. **X.J. Kennedy:** *The Lords of Misrule: Poems 1992-2001*, p.88, © 2002 X.J. Kennedy, by permission of The Johns Hopkins University Press. **Brendan Kennelly:** *Familiar Strangers: New & Selected Poems 1960-2004* (Bloodaxe Books, 2004). **Wilhelm Klemm:** tr. Patrick Bridgwater, from *The German Poets of the First World War* (Croom Helm, 1985), by permission of the translator. **Edvard Kocbek:** 'The Game', tr. Michael Scammell & Veno Taufer, from *The Poetry of Survival: Post-War Poets of Central and Eastern Europe*, ed. Daniel Weissbort (Anvil Press Poetry, 1991), by permission of the translators. **Yusef Komunyakaa:** *Neon Vernacular: New and Selected Poems* (Wesleyan University Press, 1993), by permission of the publisher. **Ko Un:** *Marinbo 2: Peace & War*, tr. Brother Anthony of Taizé & Lee Sang-Wha (Bloodaxe Books, 2015). **Ku Sang:** Even the Knots on *Quince Trees Tell Tales: Poems* by Ku Sang, tr. Brother Anthony of Taizé (DapGae Publishing, Seoul, 2004), by permission of the translator. **Günter Kunert:** *East German Poetry: An Anthology*, ed. Michael Hamburger (Carcanet Press, 1972). **Reiner Kunze:** 'The Bringers of Beethoven' tr. Gisela & Gordon Brotherston, from *East German Poetry: An Anthology*, ed. Michael Hamburger (Carcanet Press, 1972). **Adrie Kusserow:** 'Skull Trees, South Sudan' and 'War Metaphysics for a Sudanese Girl' from *Refuge* (BOA Editions, 2013), copyright © 2013 by Adrie Kusserow, reprinted by permission of The Permissions Company, Inc., on behalf of BOA Editions, Ltd, www.boaeditions.org.

Ilija Ladin: 'My Death in the Trenches', tr. Ken Smith & Igor Klikovać, from *Scar on the Stone: Contemporary Poetry from Bosnia*, ed. Chris Agee (Bloodaxe Books, 1998), by permission of the Estate of Ken Smith. **Ivan L. Lalić:** 'Requiem', tr. Francis R Jones, from *A Rusty Needle*, tr. Francis R. Jones (Anvil Press Poetry, 1996). **Lam Thi My Da:** *Green Rice*, tr. Martha Collins & Thuy Dinh (Curbstone, 2005), by permission of Martha Collins. **Philip Larkin:** *Collected Poems*, ed. Anthony Thwaite (Faber & Faber, 1990), by permission of the publisher. **Margery Lea:** *These Days: Poetry and Verse* (Wilding & Sons, Shrewsbury, 1969). **Winifred M. Letts:** 'The

Deserter' from *Hallowe'en and Poems of the War* (Smith, Elder & Co., 1916), by permission of John Murray (Publishers) Ltd. **Denise Levertov:** *The Collected Poems of Denise Levertov,* ed. Paul A. Lacey (New Directions Publishing Corporation, 2013), by permission of Pollinger Limited. **Primo Levi:** *Collected Poems,* tr. Ruth Feldman & Brian Swann (Faber & Faber, 1988/1992). **Alun Lewis:** *Raiders' Dawn and Other Poems* (George Allen & Unwin, 1942). **Alfred Lichtenstein:** all poems tr. Patrick Bridgwater, from *The German Poets of the First World War* (Croom Helm, 1985), by permission of the translator. **Michael Longley:** *Collected Poems* (Jonathan Cape, 2006), by permission of the Random House Group Ltd. **Robert Lowell:** *Col-lected Poems,* ed. Frank Bidart & David Gewanter (Faber & Faber, 2003), by permission of the publisher. **Tatjana Lukić:** *la, la, la* (Five Islands Press, Melbourne, 2009), by permission of the Estate of Tatjana Lukić.

Walter McDonald: 'Noon: Taking Aim', first published in *Phantasm,* vol. 3, no. 6, issue 18, 1978. **Gwendolyn MacEwen:** *The T.E. Lawrence Poems* (Mosaic Press/Valley Editions, Canada, 1982), by permission of the Estate of Gwendolyn MacEwen. **Thomas McGrath:** *The Movie at the End of the World* (Ohio University Press, 1973) by permission of Ohio University Press, www.ohioswallow.com. **Colin Mackay:** *Cold Night Lullaby* (Chapman Publishing, 1998). **Louis MacNeice:** *Collected Poems* (Faber & Faber, 2007), by permission of David Higham Associates.

Antonio Machado: 'The Crime Was in Granada' from *Border of a Dream: Selected Poems,* tr. Willis Barnstone. Copyright © 2004 by the Heirs of Antonio Machado, English translation copyright © 2004 by Willis Barnstone, reprinted by permission of The Permissions Company, Inc., on behalf of BOA Editions, Ltd, www.boaeditions.org. **Sarah Maguire:** *The Pomegranates of Kandahar* (Chatto, 2007), by permission of the Random House Group Ltd. **Derek Mahon:** *New Collected Poems* (The Gallery Press, 2011), by kind permission of the author and The Gallery Press, Loughcrew, Oldcastle, County Meath, Ireland, www.gallerypress.com. **André Martel:** 'Execution', tr. Ian Higgins, first published here by permission of the translator. **Assia Margoulis:** 'Corporal Rabinovitch's Corpse', tr. Elaine Magarrell, from *After the First Rain: Israeli Poems on War and Peace,* ed. Moshe Dor & Barbara Goldberg (Syracuse University Press, 1998). **Marcel Martinet:** 'The women say...' and 'Medals', tr. Michael Copp, first published here by permission of the translator. **Khaled Mattawa:** 'After 42 Years', first published in the *Los Angeles Times,* 25 October 2011, by permission of the author. **Semezdin Mehmedinović:** 'The Corpse', tr. Kathleen Jamie & Antonella Glavinić, from *Scar on the Stone: Contemporary Poetry from Bosnia,* ed. Chris Agee (Bloodaxe Books, 1998). **James Merrill:** *Collected Poems,* ed. J.D. McClatchy & Stephen Yenser, by permission of the Literary Estate of James Merrill at Washington University and the Random House Group Ltd. **András Mezei:** *Christmas in Auschwitz,* tr. Thomas Orszag-Land (Smokestack Books, 2010), by permission of the publisher. **Dunya Mikhail:** *The War Works Hard* (Carcanet Press, 2006), by permission of the publisher. **Agi Mishol:** 'Shaheeda', tr. Tsipi Keller, from *Poets on the Edge: An Anthology of Hebrew Poetry,* ed. & tr. Tsipi Keller (State University of New York Press, Albany, 2008), by permission of the publisher. **Eugenio Montale:** 'The Hitler Spring', tr. Jonathan Galassi, from *Collected Poems 1920-1944* (Farrar, Straus & Giroux, LLC, 1998). **Edwin Morgan:** *Collected Poems* (Carcanet Press, 1996), by permission of the publisher. **Andrew Motion:** *The Customs House* (Faber & Faber, 2012), by permission of the publisher. **Zvonimir Mrkonjić:** all poems tr. Ellen Elias-Bursac, from *Poezija V. 1-2* (June 2009) and later *If We Crash into a Cloud, It Won't Hurt: Croatian Poetry 1989-2009,* ed. Ervin Jahić, by permission of Damir Šodan. **Inge Müller:** 'Ordeal by Fire' ('Feuerprobe'), tr. Timothy Adès, from *Das Ich Nicht Ersticke am Leisesein* (Aufbau Verlag GmbH & Co, KG, Berlin, 2002), translation first published in *Agenda* 46/3 (April 2012), by permission of the publisher and the translator. **Taha Muhammad Ali:** *So What: New & Selected Poems 1971-2005*, tr. Peter Cole, Yahya Hijazi & Gabriel Levin (Bloodaxe Books, 2007). **Edwin Muir:** 'The Horses' from *Collected Poems* (Faber & Faber, 1963), by permission of the publisher. **Paul Muldoon:** 'Lunch with Pancho Villa' from *Mules* (Faber & Faber, 1977); 'The Boundary Commission' from *Why Brownlee Left* (Faber & Faber, 1980); 'Wire' from *Hay* (Faber & Faber 1998).

László Nagy: 'Squared by Walls' tr. Tony Connor & George Gömöri, from *Love of the Scorching Wind* (Oxford University Press, 1973), by permission of the translators. **Giam Nam:** *We Promise One Another: Poems from an Asian War*, ed. Don Luce, John Schafer & Jacqui Chagnon (Indochina Mobile Education Project, Washington, DC, 1971). **Howard Nemerov:** *The Selected Poems of Howard Nemerov*, ed. Daniel Anderson (Swallow Press,¢ Chicago, 2003), by permission of Alexander Nemerov. **Pablo Neruda:** *Selected Poems* (Penguin Books, 1975) by permission of Random House UK. **Naomi Shihab Nye:** *Tender Spot: Selected Poems* (Bloodaxe Books, 2008).

Dan O'Brien: *War Reporter* (CB Editions, 2013), by kind permission of the publisher. **Micheal O'Siadhail:** *Collected Poems* (Bloodaxe Books, 2013).

Dan Pagis: *The Selected Poetry of Dan Pagis*, tr. Stephen Mitchell (University of California Press, 1996). **Cécile Périn:** 'The north wind...', tr. Ian Higgins, first published here, by permission of the translator. **Görgi Petri:** 'To Imre Nagy' tr. Clive Wilmer & George Gömöri, from *Eternal Monday: Selected Poems* (Bloodaxe Books, 1999), by permission of the translators. **Mario Petrucci:** four extracts (near sonnets) from 'The Monk's Diary', in *Monte Cassino* (not yet published), by permission of the author. **Yisrael Pincas:** 'Yitzhak and Amalya', tr. Laura Fargas, from *After the First Rain: Israeli Poems on War and Peace*, ed. Moshe Dor & Barbara Goldberg (Syracuse University Press, 1998). **François Porché:** two extracts from 'Trench Poem', tr. Michael Copp, first published here by permission of the translator. **Peter Porter:** *The Rest on the Flight: Selected Poems* (Picador, 2010), by permission of Macmillan Publishers Ltd. **Kevin Powers:** *Letter Composed During a Lull in the Fighting* (Sceptre, 2014), by permission of the publisher.

Salvatore Quasimodo: *Complete Poems*, tr. Jack Bevan (Anvil Press Poetry, 1983), by permission of the publisher.

Miklós Radnóti: *Forced March*, tr. Clive Wilmer & George Gömöri (Enitharmon Press, 2003). **Simon Rae:** *Soft Targets: Poems from the Weekend Guardian* by Simon Rae, illus. Willie Rushton (Bloodaxe Books, 1991), by permission of the author. **Herbert Read:** *Collected Poems* (Faber & Faber, 1946), by permission of David Higham Associates. **Henry Reed:** *Collected Poems*, ed. Jon Stallworthy (Oxford University Press, 1991), by permission of Oxford University Press. **Elliot Richman:** *Walk On Trooper* (Vietnam Generation Inc & Burning Cities Press, Woodbridge, CT, 1994). **Alan Ross:** *Open Sea* (London Magazine Editions, 1975), by permission of Jane Ross. **Tadeusz Różewicz:** *They Came to See a Poet: Selected Poems*, tr. Adam Czerniawski (Anvil Press Poetry, 2011), by permission of the publisher. **Muriel Rukeyser:** *The Collected Poems of Muriel Rukeyser* (University of Pittsburgh Press, 2005), copyright © William L. Rukeyser, by permission of International Creative Management, Inc.

Nelly Sachs: 'If I only knew' tr. Ruth & Matthew Mead, from *O The Chimneys: Selected Poems* (Farrar, Straus & Giroux, LLC, 1967) [various translators]. **Nobuyuki Saga:** 'The Myth of Hiroshima', tr. Hajime Kajima, from *The Poetry of Post-War Japan*, ed. Hajime Kajima (University of Iowa Press, 1975). **Carl Sandburg:** *Cornhuskers*, copyright © 1918 by Holt, Rinehart and Winston, © renewed 1944 by Carl Sandburg, reprinted by permission of Harcourt, Inc. **Siegfried Sassoon:** 'In the

Pink', 'A Working Party', 'A Night Attack', 'Counter-Attack', 'The Hero', 'Base Details', 'The Rear-Guard', 'Attack', and 'The General' from *Collected Poems 1908–1956* (Faber & Faber, 1961/1984) and *The War Poems*, ed. Rupert Hart-Davis (Faber & Faber, 1983), copyright Siegfried Sassoon by kind permission of the Estate of George Sassoon. **Izet Sarajlić:** *Scar on the Stone: Contemporary Poetry from Bosnia*, ed. Chris Agee (Bloodaxe Books, 1998), by permission of the translator, Charles Simic. **Carole Satyamurti:** 'Striking Distance' from *Stitching the Dark: New & Selected Poems* (Bloodaxe Books, 2005); 'Memorial' from *Countdown* (Bloodaxe Books, 2011). **Anton Schnack:** 'Nocturnal Landscape', tr. Christopher Middleton, from *The Penguin Book of First World War Poetry*, ed. Jon Silkin (Penguin Books, 1979), by permission of the translator. **Pierre Seghers:** 'August 1941', tr. Ian Higgins, first published here by permission of the translator. **Jaroslav Seifert:** 'Never Again', tr. Ewald Osers, from *The Poetry of Jaroslav Seifert*, ed. George Gibian (Catbird Press, 1998). **Aharon Shabtai:** *J'Accuse*, tr. Peter Cole (New Directions Publishing Corporation, 2003). **Jo Shapcott:** *Her Book: Poems 1988-1998* (Faber & Faber, 2000), by permission of the publisher. **Owen Sheers:** *Pink Mist* (Faber & Faber, 2013), by permission of the publisher. **James Simmons:** 'Claudy' from *Poems 1956-1986* (Bloodaxe Books/The Gallery Press, 1986), by kind permission of Estate of James Simmons c/o The Gallery Press, Loughcrew, Oldcastle, County Meath, Ireland, www.gallerypress.com. **Louis Simpson:** *Voices in the Distance: Selected Poems* (Bloodaxe Books, 2010). **Kenneth Slessor:** *Collected Poems* (Angus & Robertson, Sydney, 1994). **Boris Slutsky:** 'How Did They Kill My Grandmother?', tr. Elaine Feinstein, from *The Poetry of Survival: Post-War Poets of Central and Eastern Europe*, ed. Daniel Weissbort (Anvil Press Poetry, 1991), by permission of the translator. **Alan Smith:** *The Poet of Oz* (Robyn Smith/Lulu, 2008), by permission of the author. **Ken Smith:** *Shed: Poems 1980-2001* (Bloodaxe Books, 2002). **Stevie Smith:** *Collected Poems*, ed. James MacGibbon (Penguin, 1985), by permission of Faber & Faber. **Bernard Spencer:** *Complete Poetry, Translations and Selected Prose*, ed. Peter Robinson (Bloodaxe Books, 2011), **Stephen Spender:** *New Collected Poems* (Faber & Faber, 2004), reprinted by kind permission of the Estate of Stephen Spender by Ed Victor Ltd. **Aleksandr Solzhenitsyn:** extract from *Prussian Nights*, tr. Robert Conquest (Collins/Harvill, 1977). **Leon Stroinski:** *Window: Collected Prose Poems*, tr. Adam Czerniawski, (Oasis Books, 1979), by permission of the translator. **Randall Swingler:** *Selected Poems*, ed. Andy Croft (Trent Editions, 2000) by kind permission of Judy Williams for the Estate of Randall Swingler. **Anna Swirszczynska:** 'He Was Lucky' and 'Building the Barricade', tr. Magnus Jan Krynski & Robert A. Maguire, from *Budowałam barykadę / Building the Barricade* (Wydanictwo Literakie, Kraków, 1979), by permission of Elizabeth Krynski and Robert Maguire. **Wisława Szymborska:** 'The One Twenty Pub' from *Quality Time* by Dennis O'Driscoll (Anvil Press Poetry, 1997); 'The End and the Beginning' from *View with a Grain of Sand: Selected Poems* by Wisława Szymborska, tr. Stanislaw Baranczak & Clare Cavanagh (Harcourt Brace & Company, 1993); 'Photograph from September 11' from *Monologue of a Dog: New Poems*, tr. Stanislaw Baranczak & Clare Cavanagh (Harcourt, Inc, 2006).

Jean Tardieu: 'Oradour', tr. Ian Higgins, the translation is first published here by permission of the translator and Éditions Gallimard. **Holger Teschke:** 'The Minutes of Hasiba' tr. Margitt Lehbert, from *Klaonica: poems for Bosnia*, ed. Ken Smith & Judi Benson (Bloodaxe Books, 1993), by permission of the translator. **Dylan Thomas:** *Collected Poems 1934-1953*, ed. Walford Davies & Ralph Maud (Phoenix House, 2003), by permission of David Higham Associates. **Edward Thomas:** *The Annotated Collected Poems*, ed. Edna Longley (Bloodaxe Books, 2008). **Ruthven Todd:** *The Acreage of the Heart* (William MacLellan, 1944). **Sankichi Toge:** 'At a First Aid Post' and 'To

Miss…' tr. James Kirkup, from *Modern Japanese Poetry*, ed. A.R. Davis (University of Queens-land Press, 1979); 'The Shadow' tr. Richard H. Minear, from *Poems of the Atomic Bomb, in Hiroshima: Three Witnesses* (Princeton University Press, 1990). **Miles Tomalin**: 'Wings Overhead', Volunteer for Liberty, I, No. 28 (Madrid, 27 December 1937), by permission of Stefany Tomalin. **Stevan Tontić**: 'Horror' tr. Mary Radosavljevic, from *Klaonica: Poems for Bosnia*, ed. Ken Smith & Judi Benson (Bloodaxe Books, 1993), by permission of the author. **Tran Da Tu**: 'Love Tokens', tr. Linh Dinh, from *Guernica: a magazine of art & politics* (2 August 2007). **Brian Turner**: 'Here, Bullet', '16 Iraqi Policemen' and 'Eulogy' from *Here, Bullet* (Bloodaxe Books, 2007) and 'Al-A'imma Bridge' and 'At Lowe's Home Improvement Center' from *Phantom Noise* (Bloodaxe Books, 2010).

Giuseppe Ungaretti: 'Vigil' and 'The Rivers' from *Selected Poems*, tr. Andrew Frisardi (Carcanet Press, 2003), by permission of Farrar, Straus and Giroux. **István Vas**: 'November', tr. George Szirtes, from *I lived on this Earth… Hungarian Poets of the Holocaust*, ed. George & Mari Gömöri (Alba Press, 2012), by permission of the translator. **Marko Vesović**: all poems tr. Chris Agee, from *Poljska Konjica* (Polish Cavalry, Sarajevo, 2002) by permission of the translator. **Evgeny Vinokurov**: 'I Don't Remember Him', tr. Anthony Rudolf & Daniel Weissbort, from *The War Is Over: Selected Poems* (Carcanet Press, 1976), by permission of the translators.

William Wantling: *San Quentin's Stranger* (Caveman Press, Dunedin, NZ). **Bruce Weigl**: *Archeology of the Circle: New and Selected Poems* (Grove Press, 1999). **Michael J. Whelan**: 'Grapes of Wrath' first published in *Galway Review* (February 2013); 'Search and Destroy' and 'Roadside Bomb', first published here by permission of the author. **David Widup**: *In Country* by Michael Andrews and David Widup (Bombshelter Press, Hermosa Beach, CA, 1994). **Meir Wieseltier**: 'You and We', tr. Rachel Tzvia Back, from *With an Iron Pen: Twenty Years of Hebrew Protest Poetry*, ed. Tal Nitzan & Rachel Tzvia Back (State University of New York Press, Albany, 2009) by permission of ACUM and the author. **Keith Wilson**: *Graves Registry* (Clark City Press, Livingston, Montana, 1992). **Tom Wintringham**: *The Collected Poems of Tom Wintringham*, ed. Hugh Purcell (Smokestack éBooks, 2006), by permission of the publisher. **Mac-dara Woods**: *Artichoke Wine* (Dedalus Press, 2006), by permission of the publisher.

Yevgeny Yevtushenko: *Selected Poems*, tr. Robin Milner-Gulland & Peter Levi (Penguin Books, 1962) by permission of the publisher. **Saadi Youssef**: 'Chemical Weapon' from *Without an Alphabet, Without a Face: Selected Poems*, tr. Khaled Mattawa, copyright © 2002 by Saadi Youssef. English translation copyright © 2002 by Khaled Mattawa; 'The Wretched of the Heavens' from *Nostalgia, My Enemy*, tr. Sinan Antoon and Peter Money, copyright © 2012 by Saadi Youssef, translation copyright © 2012 by Sinan Antoon and Peter Money, reprinted by permission of the Permissions Company, Inc., on behalf of Graywolf Press, www.graywolfpress.org.

Natan Zach: 'Befouled Language', tr. Rachel Tzvia Back, from *With an Iron Pen: Twenty Years of Hebrew Protest Poetry*, ed. Tal Nitzan & Rachel Tzvia Back (State University of New York Press, Albany, 2009) by permission of ACUM and the author. **ććFahrudin Zilkić**: 'Ricochet' tr. Francis R. Jones, from *Scar on the Stone: Contemporary Poetry from Bosnia*, ed. Chris Agee (Bloodaxe Books, 1998), by permission of the translator.

INDEX OF POETS & TRANSLATORS